# VIETNAM AIR WARS

£2.99
S (41)

# VIETNAM AIR WARS

René J Francillon

Temple Press/
Aerospace

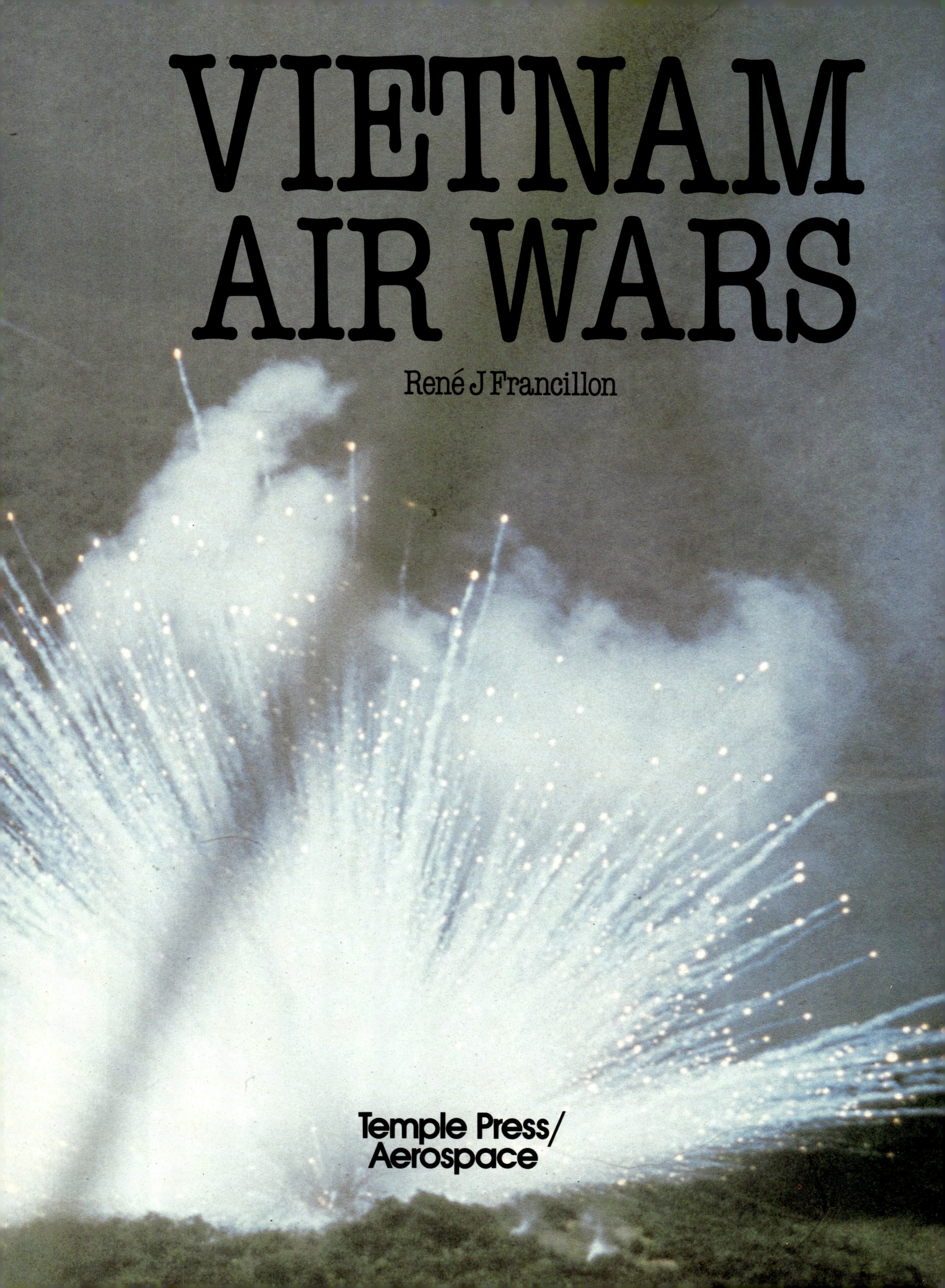

Published by Temple Press
an imprint of
The Hamlyn Publishing Group Limited
Bridge House, 69 London Road
Twickenham, Middlesex TW1 3SB, England
and distributed for them by
Octopus Distribution Services Limited
Rushden, Northamptonshire

Produced by David Donald
Aerospace Publishing Ltd
179 Dalling Road
London W6 0ES



First published 1987

ISBN: 0 600 55284 5



All correspondence concerning the content of this volume should be addressed to Aerospace Publishing Ltd. Trade enquiries should be addressed to Temple Press.

Printed in Hong Kong by
Mandarin Offset Marketing (HK) Ltd

# CONTENTS

A Boeing Vertol CH-46 cross-decks supplies from a support ship to US Navy forces sailing in the South China Sea. Throughout their involvement, the US forces poured much effort into the war, much of it to little effect due to political barriers.

# Preface and Acknowledgments

When, during the penultimate year of World War II, Tonkinese followed the siren call of Ho Chi Minh ('the one who enlightens') to begin guerilla operations against the Japanese occupiers and French colonizers they were prepared for a long and difficult struggle. Little did they know, however, that forty years later their children and grandchildren would still be dying in an effort to impose the political belief of 'the one who enlightens' on some of their brethren in the former French Indochina, specifically the unfortunate Kampucheans. Meanwhile, they achieved Ho Chi Minh's goal of uniting Vietnam under the Communist aegis and, in the process, inflicted political defeats to two of the world's major powers, France and the United States. The price was a staggering loss of human life and property paid by themselves and other inhabitants of the Indochinese peninsula, as well as by French, Americans and other nationals who came to help the South Vietnamese.

From 12 September 1945 (when C-47s brought French troops back to Indochina) until 30 April 1975, when the final evacuation of Saigon took place, military aviation played a significant role in the long series of conflicts which rocked this relatively small area of South East Asia. This book was planned to provide a comprehensive overview of air operations during that 30-year period. Clearly, size limitations did not enable the inclusion of details which can be found in volumes covering more limited segments of this vast subject (for example, the Office of Air Force History has devoted an 899-page volume to Tactical Airlift operations during the South East Asia War). Nevertheless, it is hoped that this book will give the readers a better appreciation of the devotion to duty shown by airmen, in spite of rising opposition to the war, first in France and then in the United States.

Obviously, to compile such a history one must obtain the cooperation of numerous agencies. No such help was forthcoming from the Socialist Republic of Vietnam but, indeed, I was most fortunate to receive much valuable assistance from various offices of the United States Department of Defense, and notably from the HQ USAF Historical Research Center; the Air Force Office of Public Affairs, Magazines and Books; the Air Force Museum; the Office of Air Force History; the Office of Air National Guard History; the Office of History, Pacific Air Forces; the Office of the Historian, HQ Strategic Air Command; the US Navy Public Information Division; the Navy Audiovisual Operations Branch; the Historian, Naval Air Systems Command; the Aviation History Unit and the Operational Archives Branch at the Naval Historical Center; the Division of Public Affairs, HQ US Marine Corps; the Marine Corps Historical Center; the US Army Library; the US Army Center of Military History; the US Army Military History Institute; and the Defense Audiovisual Agency.

Similarly, I could always count on Conrad M. Brown, Alain Crosnier, Patrick Facon, Mike Grove, Jean-Michel Guhl, R. Cargill Hall, Harold L. James, Peter B. Lewis, David W. Menard, Robert C. Mikesh, Jay Miller, Mark and Rick Morgan, George and Janine Olivereau, Marc Rostaing and Mick Roth for helpful leads, constructive criticism, photographs and illustrations, and editing of the book's typescript. Special thanks to my old friend Richard K. Smith for providing a roof, and much useful advice, while I was doing research in military archives.

To all, friends and staff of government agencies alike (who often became one and the same), a most sincere thank you for your generous assistance. I also thank my publisher, Stan Morse, for his unstinted support, even after the manuscript exceeded by 60 per cent its originally agreed-upon length! Last but not least, once again, it is to my wife that I am the most grateful. Not only did she spend long hours editing my mingled and mangled syntax and providing her usual encouragement, but this time her devotion went even further as she re-arranged her own work so that I could have access to our word processor long into the night.

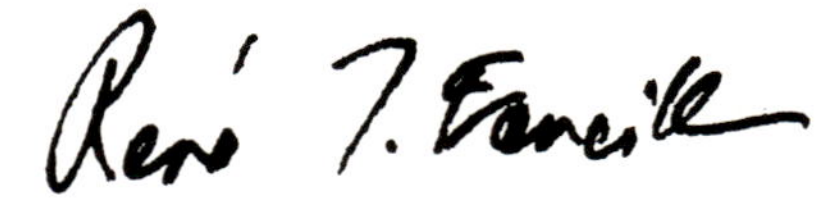

*René J Francillon*

# ABBREVIATIONS

## A

| | |
|---|---|
| AAA | Antiaircraft Artillery |
| AAAGV | Australian Army Assistance Group, Vietnam |
| AAFSS | Advanced Aerial Fire Support System |
| AAFV | Australian Army Force, Vietnam |
| AATTV | Australian Army Training Team, Vietnam |
| AB | Air Base |
| ABCCC | Airborne Battlefield Command and Control Centers |
| ACS | Air Commando Squadron |
| ACV | Air Cushion Vehicle |
| AEW | Airborne Early Warning |
| AFB | Air Force Base |
| ALARS | Air Launched Acoustical Reconnaissance Sensor |
| ANZAC | Australian-New Zealand Army Corps |
| APOE | Aerial Port of Embarkation |
| ARRSq | Aerospace Rescue and Recovery Squadron |
| ARefS | Air Refuelling Squadron |
| ARVN | Army of the Republic of Vietnam |
| ASW | Anti-Submarine Warfare |
| AWADS | Adverse Weather Aerial Delivery Systems |

## B

| | |
|---|---|
| BARCAP | Barrier Combat Air Patrol |

## C

| | |
|---|---|
| CBI | China-Burma-India Theatre of Operations |
| CBU | Cluster Bomb Units |
| CCTS | Combat Crew Training Squadron |
| CDS | Container Delivery System |
| CEFEO | Corps Expéditionnaire Français d'Extrême Orient |
| CIA | Central Intelligence Agency |
| CNAF | Chinese Nationalist Air Force |
| COD | Carrier Onboard Delivery |
| COMINT | Communications Intelligence |
| CONUS | Continental United States |
| CTF | Carrier Task Force |
| CVA | Attack Carrier |
| CVS | Antisubmarine Support Aircraft Carrier |
| CVSG | Antisubmarine Carrier Air Group |
| CVW | Carrier Air Wing |
| CW | Continuous Wave |

## D

| | |
|---|---|
| DIC | Division d'Infanterie Coloniale |
| DMZ | Demilitarized Zone |
| DOD | Department of Defense |

## E

| | |
|---|---|
| ECM | Electronic Countermeasures |
| ELINT | Electronic Intelligence |
| EMEO | Escadrille de Marche d'Extrême-Orient |
| EOGB | Electro-Optical Guided Bomb |
| EROM | Escadrille de Reconnaissance d'Outre-Mer |
| ERP | Escadrille de Reconnaissance Photographique |
| ESM | Electronic Support Measures |

## F

| | |
|---|---|
| FAC | Forward Air Controller |
| FAC(A) | Forward Air Controller (Airborne) |
| FCO | Fire Control Operator |
| FIS | Fighter Interceptor Squadron |
| FMF | Fleet Marine Force |
| FORCECAP | Task Force Combat Air Patrol |

## G

| | |
|---|---|
| GAOA | Groupe d'Aviation d'Observation d'Artillerie |
| GB | Groupe de Bombardement |
| GC | Groupe de Chasse |
| GCI | Ground-Controlled Intercept |
| GM | Groupe de Marche |
| GMTEO | Groupe de Marche de Transport d'Extrême-Orient |
| GPES | Ground Proximity Extraction System |
| GT | Groupe de Transport |

## H

| | |
|---|---|
| HC | Helicopter Combat Support Squadron |
| HE | High Explosive |
| HMA | Marine Helicopter Attack Squadron |
| HMH | Marine Heavy Helicopter Squadron |
| HML | Marine Light Helicopter Squadron |
| HMM | Marine Medium Helicopter Squadron |
| H&MS | Marine Headquarters & Maintenance Squadron |
| HU | Helicopter Utility Squadron |

## I

| | |
|---|---|
| IFF | Identification, Friend or Foe |

## J

| | |
|---|---|
| JATO | Jet-Assisted Take-Off |

## K

| | |
|---|---|
| KIA | Killed in Action |

## L

| | |
|---|---|
| LAPES | Low-Altitude Parachute Extraction System |
| LGB | Laser Guided Bomb |
| LLLTV | Low Light Level Television |
| LOC | Line of Communication |
| LORAN | Long Range Navigation |
| LS | Landing Site |
| LZ | Landing Zone |

## M

| | |
|---|---|
| MAAG | Military Assistance Advisory Group |
| MAC | Military Airlift Command |
| MAD | Mortar Air Delivery |
| MAG | Marine Aircraft Group |
| MARS | Mid-Air Retrieval System |
| MATS | Military Air Transport Service |
| MAW | Marine Aircraft Wing |
| MCAS | Marine Corps Air Station |
| MEB | Marine Expeditionary Brigade |
| MEF | Marine Expeditionary Force |
| MIA | Missing in Action |
| MIGCAP | Combat Air Patrol against MiG aircraft |

## N

| | |
|---|---|
| NAF | Naval Air Facility |
| NAS | Naval Air Station |
| NATO | North Atlantic Treaty Organization |
| NATRACOM | Naval Air Training Command |
| NMCB | Naval Mobile Construction Battalion |
| NVA | North Vietnamese Army |
| NVNAF | North Vietnamese Air Force |

## O

| | |
|---|---|
| OSS | Office of Strategic Services |

## P

| | |
|---|---|
| PACAF | Pacific Air Forces |
| PBR | Patrol Boat, River |
| PCI | Indochinese Communist Party |
| PJ | Parajumper |
| POL | Petroleum, Oil, and Lubricants |
| POW | Prisoner of War |
| PRC | People's Republic of China |

## Q

| | |
|---|---|
| QOR | Qualified Operational Requirement |

## R

| | |
|---|---|
| RAAF | Royal Australian Air Force |
| RC | Route Coloniale |
| RESCAP | Rescue Combat Air Patrol |
| RHAW | Radar Homing and Warning |
| RLAF | Royal Lao Air Force |
| RNZAF | Royal New Zealand Air Force |
| ROKAF | Republic of Korea Air Force |
| RPV | Remotely Piloted Vehicle |
| R&R | Rest and Relaxation |
| RTAB | Royal Thai Air Base |
| RTAF | Royal Thai Air Force |
| RTAFB | Royal Thai Air Force Base |
| RTNAF | Royal Thai Naval Air Facility |
| RVAH | Heavy Reconnaissance Attack Squadron |
| RVN | Republic of Vietnam |
| RVNAF | Republic of Vietnam Armed Forces |

## S

| | |
|---|---|
| SAC | Strategic Air Command |
| SACADVON | SAC Advanced Echelon |
| SAGETA | Société Auxiliaire de Gérance et de Transports Aériens |
| SAL | Sections Aérienne de Liaison |
| SAM | Surface-to-Air-Missile |
| SAR | Sea-Air Rescue |
| SAS | Special Air Service |
| SATS | Short Airfield for Tactical Support |
| SEATO | South East Asia Defense Treaty Organization |
| SIGINT | Signals Intelligence |
| SLF | Special Landing Forces |
| SOG | Special Operations Group |
| SOS | Special Operations Squadron |
| SRS | Strategic Reconnaissance Squadron |
| SRW | Strategic Reconnaissance Wing |
| STOL | Short Take Off and Landing |
| SW | Strategic Wing |

## T

| | |
|---|---|
| TAC | Tactical Air Command |
| TAC(A) | Tactical Air Controller (Airborne) |
| TACAN | Tactical Air Navigation |
| TACOS | Tanker and Countermeasures Strike Support |
| TAFDS | Tactical Airfield Fuel Dispensing System |
| TARCAP | Target Combat Air Patrol |
| TAS | Tactical Airlift Squadron |
| TASS | Tactical Air Support Squadron |
| TAW | Tactical Airlift Wing |
| TBS | Tactical Bombardment Squadron |
| TCS | Troop Carrier Squadron |
| TCW | Troop Carrier Wing |
| TDY | Temporary Duty |
| TF | Task Force |
| TFA | Task Force Alpha |
| TFS | Tactical Fighter Squadron |
| TFW | Tactical Fighter Wing |
| TK | Temporary Kit |
| TOW | Tube-launched Optical-tracked, Wire-guided |
| TRIM | Trail and Road Interdiction, Multisensor |
| TRS | Tactical Reconnaissance Squadron |
| TRW | Tactical Reconnaissance Wing |
| TUOC | Tactical Unit Operations Center |

## U

| | |
|---|---|
| USA | United States Army |
| USAAF | United States Army Air Force(s) |
| USAF | United States Air Force |
| USAFE | United States Air Forces in Europe |
| USAID | United States Agency for International Development |
| USIA | United States Information Agency |
| USS | United States Ship |

## V

| | |
|---|---|
| VA | Attack Squadron |
| VAH | Heavy Attack Squadron |
| VAL | Light Attack Squadron |
| VAP | Heavy Photographic Reconnaissance Squadron |
| VAQ | Carrier Tactical Electronics Warfare Squadron |
| VAW | Carrier Air Early Warning Squadron |
| VC | Viet Cong |
| VF | Fighter Squadron |
| VFP | Light Photographic Squadron |
| VMA | Marine Attack Squadron |
| VMA(AW) | Marine All-Weather Attack Squadron |
| VMCJ | Marine Composite Reconnaissance Squadron |
| VMFA | Marine Fighter Attack Squadron |
| VMF(AW) | Marine All-Weather Fighter Squadron |
| VMGR | Marine Aerial Refueler Transport Squadron |
| VMO | Marine Observation Squadron |
| VNAF | Vietnamese Air Force |
| VO | Observation Squadron |
| VP | Patrol Squadron |
| VQ | Fleet Air Reconnaissance Squadron |
| VR | Fleet Logistics Support Squadron |
| VRC | Fleet Tactical Support Squadron |
| VSF | Antisubmarine Fighter Squadron |
| VW | Fleet Early Warning Squadron |

## W

| | |
|---|---|
| WSO | Weapons Systems Officer |

# PROJECT AND OPERATION CODE NAMES

**Able Mable**
Reconnaissance operations over Laos by RF-101s deployed to Don Muang Airport, Thailand, beginning in the fall of 1961.

**Arc Light**
B-52 bombing operations during the South East Asia War.

**Banish Beach**
C-130 operations during which fuel drums were dropped to start fires in an effort to deprive forest sanctuaries to the Viet Cong.

**Barrel Roll**
Armed reconnaissance sorties flown over Laos beginning in December 1964.

**Belfry Express**
RPV reconnaissance operations from the USS *Ranger* beginning in November 1969.

**Bell Tone I & II**
Deployment of F-100s and F-102s to Don Muang Airport in 1960-61.

**Big Eye**
USAF EC-121 airborne early warning operations from April 1965 until March 1967.

**Blue Chip**
Call sign for 7 AF command center.

**Blue Springs**
RPV reconnaissance operations initiated in August 1974.

**Bolo**
Anti-MiG fighter sweep on 2 February 1967.

**Brave Bull**
C-97 fitted with infrared equipment for reconnaissance in South East Asia during 1963.

**Brown Cradle**
EB-66C equipped with ECM equipment for jamming enemy fire control radars.

**Bullet Shot**
Buildup of SAC B-52 forces in the Western Pacific beginning in February 1972.

**Candlestick**
Flare dropping operations.

**Candy Machine**
Intermittent deployments of F-102s to South Vietnam for air defence duty from Tan Son Nhut and Da Nang.

**Cheesebrick**
US code name for North Vietnamese passive tracking network.

**College Eye**
USAF EC-121 airborne early warning operations (replaced the previously used *Big Eye* code name).

**Combat Apple**
Electronic reconnaissance, MiG warning, and sea-air rescue support missions flown by RC-135Ms beginning in the fall of 1967.

**Combat Dawn**
Electronic data collection by RPVs operating from South Korea.

**Combat Lightning**
KC-135 radio relay missions to extend the range of ground communications in South East Asia.

**Combat Proof**
All-weather sorties controlled by ground-based MSQ-77 radars. Code name later changed to *Combat Skyspot*.

**Combat Skyspot**
New code name for all-weather sorties previously known as *Combat Proof* sorties.

**Combat Talon**
Support missions flown by C-130s during sea-air rescue operations in the North.

**Commando Hunt**
Interdiction campaign against enemy infiltration routes in Laos.

**Commando Sabre**
High-speed FAC sorties flown by F-100Fs beginning in June 1967.

**Commando Scarf**
Munition drop missions flown by C-130s in southern Laos.

**Commando Vault**
C-130 missions during which M-121 and BLU-82 heavy bombs were dropped to blast out helicopter landing zones in the jungle.

**Constant Guard**
Buildup of tactical aircraft forces in South East Asia starting in early 1972.

**Credible Chase**
Concept and plan to use Short Take-Off and Landing aircraft (Fairchild AU-23 and Helio AU-24) as mini gunships.

**Dragon Lady**
Clandestine U-2 reconnaissance operations begun from Bien Hoa in December 1963.

**Eagle Pull**
Final evacuation of US personnel and Cambodian VIPs from Phnom Penh in April 1975.

**Endsweep**
Mine sweeping operations in North Vietnam undertaken over a six-month period in 1973 by the US in accordance with the Paris Agreement.

**Enhance Plus**
Massive delivery of aircraft to the VNAF prior to the signing of the Paris Agreement.

**Fan Song**
Soviet-built fire-control radar for the SA-2 sol-air missile system.

**Farm Gate**
Detachment of USAF air commandos deployed to South Vietnam in November 1961.

**Field Goal**
RT-33 reconnaissance sorties over Laos in April-May 1961.

**Flaming Dart**
Initial air operations over North Vietnam in February 1965.

**Flycatcher**
Supply of aircraft to the Khmer Air Force in 1974.

**Fogbound**
ECM/ESM missions over North Vietnam by Marine EF-10Bs.

**Freedom Porch**
Initial B-52 operations over the Red River Valley in April 1972.

**Freedom Train**
Operations against North Vietnam, below the 20th parallel, in April 1972.

**Frequent Wind**
Final evacuation of US personnel and South Vietnamese VIPs from Saigon in April 1975.

**Game Warden**
Navy riverine operations in the Mekong Delta.

**Gunboat**
Modification of a C-130A to serve as prototype of a more advanced 'Gunship II.'

**Hawk Eye**
EC-47s fitted with radio direction finding equipment to locate Viet Cong radio transmissions.

**High Drink**
Refuelling of hovering rescue helicopters by US Navy vessels in the Gulf of Tonkin.

**Hilo Hattie**
C-54 fitted with infrared reconnaissance equipment which was operated in South Vietnam from March 1962 until February 1963.

**Homecoming**
Repatriation of POWs from North Vietnam in early 1973.

**Igloo White**
Surveillance system consisting of hand-implanted and air-delivered sensors, relay aircraft, and an infiltration surveillance centre. Previously known as *Muscle Shoals*.

**Iron Hand**
USN SAM suppression sorties.

**Junction City**
Large ground operation in South Vietnam's Tay Ninh Province from 28 February 1967 to 14 May 1967.

**Lam Song 719/Dewey Canyon II**
Large-scale offensive operations against Communist lines of communications in Laos from 30 January 1971 to 6 April 1971.

**Lima Site**
Primitive airstrips in Laos used for US covert operations and by rescue helicopters.

**Linebacker I & II**
Air operations over North Vietnam from April through October 1972, and in December 1972.

**Litterbug**
RPV operations during which propaganda leaflets were dropped over North Vietnam.

**Little Brother**
Projected use of Cessna 0-2s fitted with side-firing miniguns.

**Market Time**
Coastal and ASW operations by Navy Patrol Squadrons.

**Mud River/Muscle Shoals**
Initial code name for the *Igloo White* surveillance system along the Ho Chi Minh Trail.

**Mule Train**
Initial deployments of C-123 tactical transports to South Vietnam in January 1972.

**Niagara**
Air operations during the siege of Khe Sanh in early 1968.

**OPLAN 34-A**
Operation Plan for covert operations in North Vietnam in 1964.

**Patricia Lynn**
RB-57Es fitted with Reconofax VI infrared sensors to detect well-camouflaged Viet Cong targets.

**Pave Eagle**
Unmanned Beech QU-22s used as relay platforms for data collected by the *Igloo White* surveillance system.

**Pave Nail**
Night observation system fitted to some USAF OV-10As.

**Pave Spot**
Laser designator fitted to some USAF OV-10As.

**Pink Rose**
Three B-52 missions in 1967 to set the jungle afire by massive use of incendiary bombs.

**Pipe Stem**
Temporary deployment of RF-101Cs to Tan Son Nhut in the fall of 1961.

**Pocket Money**
Aerial mining campaign against North Vietnam beginning in May 1972.

**Prize Crew**
Operational evaluation of the Lockheed QT-2PC quiet observation aircraft.

**Proud Deep**
Navy protective reaction strikes flown again North Vietnam in December 1971.

**Ranch Hand**
C-123 detachment to South Vietnam for defoliation operations beginning in January 1962.

**Red Crown**
A radar-warning and aircraft control ship of the US Navy stationed in the Gulf of Tonkin on a rotational basis.

**Red Horse**
Air Force construction units.

**Rivet Top**
EC-121M early warning aircraft fitted with improved airborne radar.

**Rolling Thunder**
Air offensive against North Vietnam from February 1965 until November 1968.

**Shufly**
Initial deployment of Marine helicopters, with support fixed-wing aircraft, to South Vietnam beginning in April 1962.

**Skoshi Tiger**
Operational evaluation of the Northrop F-5A light fighter

**Steel Tiger**
Strike operations in southern Laos first undertaken in April 1965.

**Surprise Package**
Improved armament and systems first tested in a modified AC-130A.

**Tally Ho**
Marine strikes in the North Vietnamese panhandle beginning in July 1966.

**Task Force Alpha**
Infiltration surveillance center, first located at Tan Son Nhut AB and then moved to Nakhon Phanom RTAFB, to which was transmitted *Igloo White* data.

**Tiger Hound**
*Steel Tiger* operations in Laos undertaken south of the 17th parallel under FAC control.

**Topgun**
Navy training programme to improve air combat skills of fighter pilots.

**Tropic Moon**
A-1Es (*Tropic Moon I*), B-57Bs (*Tropic Moon II*), and B-57Gs (*Tropic Moon III*) fitted with LLLTV and other systems for night attacks along the Ho Chi Minh Trail.

**Water Glass**
F-102 and AD-5Q air defence operations in South Vietnam from March 1962 until May 1963.

**Water Pump**
Training of Laotian T-28 crews by 1st ACW in the spring of 1964.

**Wild Weasel**
Tactical aircraft (F-100Fs/F-105Fs/F-105Gs and some F-4Cs) fitted with RHAW and anti-radiation missiles for operations against North Vietnamese SAM sites.

# The Stage and the Actors

Airpower, which had made its appearance in South East Asia in 1884 when French colonial troops used balloons over Tonkin, is still very much an element in Vietnamese operations in Kampuchea and along the border with China. This book, however, is concerned only with air operations in South East Asia from 1945 to 1975, i.e. from France's attempt to regain control of its colonies in Indochina until the collapse of the Republic of Vietnam and the subsequent unification of the former French colonies of Annam, Cochinchina, and Tonkin under communist control.

The air wars over Indochina (1945-54) and South East Asia (1961-75) were fought over the Indochinese peninsula, a land mass extending between 5° 30′ and 23° north latitudes, from the Gulf of Siam to the southern Chinese province of Kwangsi, along the South China Sea. Bordered on the east by Thailand and Burma, the French colony of Indochina was divided into Cambodia, Laos and three Vietnamese regions (Tonkin in the north, Annam in the center, and Cochinchina in the South). From 1954 until 1975, Tonkin and the northern portion of Annam were part of the Democratic Republic of Vietnam, while the remainder of Annam and Cochinchina formed the State of Vietnam (renamed the Republic of Vietnam in 1955). Since the end of the South East Asia War in 1975, the two rival states of Vietnam have been unified as the Socialist Republic of Vietnam.

While the population of Cambodia and Vietnam are respectively made up of 85 to 90 percent Khmer and Vietnamese people, the population of Laos is more heterogenous and includes about 50 percent Lao people, 15 percent Thais, and various primitive mountain tribes. The present day Lao People's Democratic Republic was first settled in the 12th century A.D. by refugee Thai tribes from China, whereas the long-established Khmer Empire in Cambodia, the forebear of today's Democratic Kampuchea (a puppet state occupied by forces from the Socialist Republic of Vietnam), had earlier been saved from total dissolution at the hands of Thais and Vietnamese by becoming a French protectorate in 1867.

During the 2nd Century B.C., ancestors of the present-day Vietnamese, inhabiting part of what is now southern China and northern Vietnam, were conquered by forces of China's Han dynasty. Chinese rule lasted more than 1,000 years until the Vietnamese ousted their conquerors and began a southward expansion. Eventually settling along the entire seacoast of the Indochinese peninsula, they reached the Gulf of Siam by the mid-18th century.

### *Two centuries of struggle*

The Vietnamese, however, were rent by internal discords, and for nearly two centuries contending families in the north and the south struggled to control the powerless kings of the Le dynasty. (It is interesting to note that the feuding between Vietnamese from the north and south predated the South East Asia War by over 200 years. Contrary to what worshipers of Ho Chi Minh would want one to believe, there is nothing new under the Vietnamese sun!) It was during this period that French Catholic missionaries made their appearance in Annam. By 1787, French assistance to Prince Nguyen Anh, the future Emperor Gia-Long, had been rewarded by the granting of the small Poulo-Condore Archipelago as a base. For the next 72 years the French presence was benign. However, following the capture of Saigon in 1859 the colonial era began in Cochinchina and Annam. France, which had established a protectorate in Cambodia in 1867, gained control over Tonkin after its 1884-85 war against China and had its rule over Cochinchina and Laos recognized by Siam in 1893. Although Indochina then contributed its

**The Potez 25 was widely used by French forces throughout the world between the wars. It was still in use at the outbreak of World War II, used mainly as an observation platform. It could carry light bombs for a limited attack role. This example is seen in 1938.**

**This map shows the five nations making up French Indochina. Airfields and towns are also shown.**

two rice bowls, in the Red River Delta of Tonkin and the Mekong Delta of Cochinchina, its coal mines and its rubber plantations, from that point on France's outflow to its Indochinese colony exceeded its inflow.

Before the advent of World War II, Annam, Cambodia, Cochinchina, Laos and Tonkin were administered by France under the collective name of Indochine Française, with generally peaceful relations between the colonials and the local population. Until the late 1920's the only sources of trouble were traditional mandarin groups which sought, without success or much popular support, a return to the status quo of pre-colonial days. More serious and lasting difficulties were to come from European-educated Vietnamese, foremost among them was Ho Chi Minh. Born Nguen Tat Thanh, in the early 1890s Ho Chi Minh had become a member of the French Communist Party while studying in France. In 1930, after his return to Indochina as an official of the Komintern (*Kommunisticheskii Internatsional* – Communist International), this not-yet-infamous leader took the name of Nguyen Ai Quoc ('Nguyen the Patriot'); it was, however, under his later name of Ho Chi Minh ('the one who enlightens') that the world would come to know him best.

In 1930-31, in part as the result of the world's economic depression, great difficulties began to besiege the Indochinese economy and led to major protests. In the ensuing harsh repression by the French, the newly formed P.C.I. (Indochinese

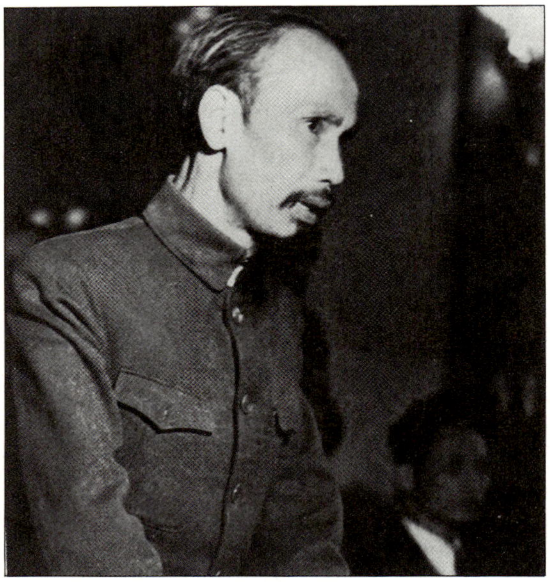

Communist Party) was nearly destroyed and Nguyen the Patriot was forced underground. Ten years later, by then known as Ho Chi Minh, he would resurface in Tsin-Si, China, to take the leadership of the Viet Nam Doc Lap Dong Minh (League for the Independence of Vietnam), better known as the Viet Minh.

As pre-World War II tensions rose in Europe, France began belated military preparations in anticipation of the war with Germany. In the process, even though Japan was an Axis Power, Indochina was neglected: the French considered Japan to present little threat to their Asian colony and they needed most of the limited military resources in Europe. Thus, the Armée de l'Air and the Aéronautique Navale maintained only token forces in Indochina and relied on obsolete aircraft to provide an illusory defence for the colony. To strengthen these meager forces and to provide them at last with some fighter aircraft, in 1939 the Ministère des Colonies (Colonial Ministry) had ordered 50 Dutch-built Koolhoven F.K.58As; however, only 18 of these single-engined fighters were delivered prior to the fall of France in June 1940 and all were retained in France. Consequently, in the summer of 1940 French aviation in Indochina had only some 100 aircraft, including mainly 1925-vintage Potez 25 observation and light bombing biplanes. The most modern aircraft in the inventory were 13 Morane-Saulnier M.S. 406 fighter monoplanes which, ordered by China in 1939, had been embargoed in transit and subsequently assembled in Haiphong for use by the Armée de l'Air. Used to equip two hastily organized fighter escadrilles, these aircraft lacked their standard engine-mounted cannon, which had already been shipped to China, and were armed with only a pair of light machine-guns.

## *French weakness*

In view of the wholly-insufficient forces available in Indochina, and the fact that its Vichy Government was under German control, France had no choice but to accede in September 1940 to Japanese demands for the right to use five French air bases in Tonkin and to station 30,000 troops in Indochina. Thereafter, while France remained in nominal control of its colony, effective power was transferred to the Japanese. France's weakness in Indochina also prompted Thailand to seek militarily to regain control of two French Cambodian provinces and, following sharp border incidents in November 1940, war broke out. Outnumbered three to one, the French aviators performed well (claiming the destruction of 20 Thai aircraft for the loss of two M.S. 406 fighters and one obsolete Farman F 221 four-engined bomber) but, with Japan forcing a settlement in favour of Thailand, the French had to give up some territory in Cambodia and Laos. These two consecutive French setbacks at the hands of Asians encouraged the Vietnamese Communists to prepare for the eventual overthrow of France in Indochina.

In southern China the various Vietnamese political refugees, foremost among whom were the Viet Minh cadre, initially had their fair share of problems with the Chinese authorities, and Ho Chi Minh was even jailed for some 18 months. Nevertheless, one of the Chinese warlords, Marshal Tchang Fa-kouei, encouraged the formation of a Vietnamese coalition government-in-exile close to the Tonkin border. Released from prison, Ho Chi Minh became a minister in this government and, in 1944, was given the responsibility for organizing guerrilla operations in Tonkin against the Japanese and the French. Due in part to French collaboration with the Japanese and in part to United States disapproval of a postwar return to colonial systems, Ho Chi Minh, after cunningly toning down his communist objectives, had little difficulty in obtaining the support of the OSS (Office of Strategic Services, the forebear of the Central Intelligence Agency). By the fall of 1944 Ho Chi Minh was leading a band of 700 guerrillas in the Viet-Bac, a mountainous area some 160 miles 257 km north of Hanoi, and was preparing to go on the offensive.

Aware of Ho Chi Minh's intents, French military forces prepared to take action against his guerrilla band while at the same time organizing their own resistance movement directed against the Japanese

**Above: The most potent aircraft available to France in Indochina in 1940 was the Morane Saulnier M.S.406, which featured two machine guns and a nose-mounted cannon buried in the engine. However, these cannon had already been delivered to the intended customer, China, when the aircraft were embargoed and impressed into French service.**

**Above left: Architect of the Vietnamese Communist state, Ho Chi Minh ('the one who enlightens') had been educated in France before becoming a Komintern member. During World War II he had the backing of the OSS for guerrilla operations against the French/Japanese.**

**Thailand's air force was fairly well-equipped, including the Martin 139 bomber. However, the Thai air force suffered from lack of training and suitable tactics, and suffered heavily at the hands of the well-trained French fighter pilots.**

occupants. However, these plans were upset when on 9 March 1945 the Japanese decided to nip in the bud the incipient French resistance. In four months of vicious fighting French forces in Indochina were decimated, leaving Ho Chi Minh's guerrillas (safely hiding in the impervious Viet-Bac) ready to take action to gain control of Indochina at the end of World War II. In the meantime, unwilling to let a communist takeover occur, France proposed on 24 March 1945 the regrouping of the five Indochinese entities (Annam, Cambodia, Cochinchina, Laos, and Tonkin) into a federation belonging to the Union Française, a loose commonwealth designed to link France and its colonies.

### *Bao-Dai joins Ho Chi Minh*

Ho Chi Minh and his colleagues of the government-in-exile were not alone in their desire to see the French relinquish their control of Indochina. In particular, in a message dated 20 August 1945, five days after the Japanese surrender, the Emperor of Annam, Bao-Dai, addressed an appeal to Général Charles de Gaulle in which he notably stated:

> I beg you to understand that the only way to preserve French interests and the spiritual influence of France in Indochina is to recognize, frankly, the independence of Vietnam and to renounce any idea of reestablishing here French sovereignty or administration of any type. We could so easily understand each other and become friends if only you were prepared to cease pretending to become again our masters.

Sadly, this wise advice went unheeded.

When the French were ousted by the Japanese in the spring of 1945, the Viet Minh began to move into the countryside from their base areas in the Viet-Bac. By the time Allied troops (Chinese to the north of the 16th parallel and British to the south) arrived in September 1945 to take the surrender of Japanese troops, the Viet Minh had already moved into Hanoi and most of Tonkin. More importantly, having obtained the abdication of Emperor Bao-Dai on 25 August 1945 and his subsequent participation in the coalition government, the Viet Minh announced the formation of a Democratic Republic of Vietnam and on 2 September 1945 boldly proclaimed its independence.

As detailed in Chapter 2, French forces returned to Saigon on 12 September 1945 and to Tonkin six months later. While the French immediately mounted operations in Cochinchina, Cambodia, and southern Annam to subdue Communist and other armed bands, they attempted to reach an agreement with the Viet Minh in the North. On 6 March 1946 France recognized Vietnam as an independent state within the Fédération Indochinoise (Indochinese Federation) and as a member of the Union Française and undertook to organize a popular referendum in Cochinchina in which it was to be decided whether or not Cochinchina was to become part of Vietnam. However, deep divisions between Communists and non-communist nationalists soon began to surface. Consequently, the French and Viet Minh never succeeded in implementing their March 1946 accord and the situation became progressively more tense. Finally, on 19 December 1946, the Viet Minh took the offensive in virtually all cities north of the 16th parallel. The limited fighting which had taken place in the south since September 1945 turned into the Indochina War.

From their modest début in the Viet-Bac in the fall of 1944, the Viet Minh forces had grown to some 60,000 troops by December 1946. Under the leadership of Vo Nguyen Giap, the brilliant Vietnamese strategist who was to lead military operations against the French, the Americans, and finally the South Vietnamese, these forces included the Tu-Vé guerrillas organized at the village level and forming the basis for regional forces, and the Chi-Doi, or regular troops. For several years these Viet Minh forces had to rely on locally-made primitive weapons and on armament captured from the French and the Japanese. However, after being recognized in January 1950 by the People's Republic of China and the Soviet Union, the Democratic Republic of Vietnam began receiving large amounts of Chinese and Soviet war armament. From then on, the limited character of the Indochina War gave place to heavy fighting and eventually led to the massive application of air power during the South East Asia War.

**Immediately after the war's end, the Royal Air Force provided a policing duty in Indochina. Seen here escorting the Allied Air Commander-in-Chief Sir Keith Park to Hong Kong is a Supermarine Spitfire Mk XIV of No 273 Sqn from Tan Son Nhut. This squadron was also employed on leaflet dropping sorties over Annam.**

# Air War over Indochina

For three and one half years, from September 1940 until March 1944, relations between the occupying Japanese forces and the French colonial authorities in Indochina remained relatively unstrained as the French, left without viable military strength and no source for reinforcements, had to bide their time. However, beginning in July 1944, after Allied forces had liberated France and Général Charles de Gaulle had installed his provisional government in Paris, Royal Air Force aircraft began bringing into Indochina liaison personnel, Free French personnel and some light armament and supplies, while the United States started inserting OSS agents to work with the insurgent forces of Ho Chi Minh. On 9 March 1945, after becoming aware of the covert operations and fearing Allied guerrilla operations behind their lines, the Japanese struck a preventive blow against French forces in Indochina. With minimal support from the last of the obsolete aircraft of the Armée de l'Air (18 Potez 25s, three Potez 542s, and one Loire 130) and limited air support by the US Fourteenth Air Force and the British South East Asia Command from 20 March, the French tried vainly to resist. In four months of scattered but often vicious fighting, they were defeated. Only a small number of troops succeeded in retreating into China to join up with the Allies.

As on all other fronts the Japanese were losing the war, the Allies had already prepared plans for disarming them in Indochina. In accordance with these plans, which were inspired to a large extent by US opposition to the prewar British, Dutch and French colonial systems, Japanese forces in Indochina were to be disarmed by the British, south of the 16th parallel, and by the Chinese north of the same parallel. In its own colony, France was not scheduled to participate in the disarming of the Japanese even though it was an ally which, during the summer of 1945, had sent airborne commandos with a detachment of C-47 transport aircraft to join the British in Bengal and had maintained liaison with US Forces in China. Nevertheless, the Potsdam Conference had established the eventual right of France to take over from the disarming British and Chinese forces. Faced with their own colonial problems and thus more understanding of the French desires, the British agreed from the onset to let French troops join them in the initial airlift to Indochina. Accordingly, on 12 September 1945, four weeks after the Japanese surrender, 150 French troops were airlifted to Saigon by C-47s of the E.M.E.O. (Escadrille de Marche d'Extrême-Orient) along with the first detachment

**The Douglas C-47 provided the backbone of the Armée de l'Air transport effort. Throughout the conflict, the ageless 'Gooney' paradropped, airlifted and medevaced, especially through the long siege at Dien Bien Phu. This aircraft demonstrates its low flying capabilities to an outpost in the swamps.**

Right: Close-up on the nose artwork of a Toucan of G.T. 2/62 'Franche-Comté' pictured at Bach Mai in late 1949. Personal markings like the one here depicting a female figure on a musical score with the word 'Souvenirs' were very seldom seen on French aircraft.

from Britain's 80th Brigade (20th Indian Division). Six months later, as the Nationalist Chinese which had disarmed the Japanese were worried by the Communist strength in Tonkin, the French were allowed to return to the northern half of the country. Although fighting broke out briefly between French and Chinese, the initial rapport between Général Philippe Leclerc and Ho Chi Minh was cordial.

On 24 March 1945, prior to the arrival of the first French troops and aircraft, which were greeted less than enthusiastically by some elements of the Vietnamese population, the French Government had announced a vague plan for the incorporation of Annam, Cambodia, Cochinchina, Laos and Tonkin, the five nations of Indochina, into a French-styled commonwealth (L'Union Française). However, as neither side was prepared to make significant concessions, there was little chance for the French to reach an agreement with the Government of the Republic of Vietnam, sponsored by the Viet Minh and incorporating Emperor Bao-Dai and other Vietnamese elements. On 2 September, ten days before the arrival of the first French forces, the independence of Vietnam was unilaterally proclaimed. Soon Viet Minh bands began murdering or incarcerating French settlers and officials and, accordingly, France decided to send more troops and aircraft, The '30-Year Air War' was about to start.

## *The Armée de l'Air in Indochina*

In the months immediately preceding the Japanese surrender, France had studied various plans to commit units of the Armée de l'Air to combat operations in South East Asia. To circumvent American reluctance to the return of French military forces in Indochina and the resultant feared

embargo of spares for US-made combat aircraft of the Armée de l'Air, the composition of the French aviation contingent scheduled to fight in the CBI (China-Burma-India) theatre of operations was to include British-made de Havilland Mosquito fighter-bombers and reconnaissance aircraft. US aircraft were limited to US-made Douglas C-47 transports. As the final collapse of Japan was accelerated by the nuclear bombing of Hiroshima and Nagasaki, this plan was never implemented. However, concern with the likely embargo of US aircraft parts became a key element in the subsequent planning of equipment for the Armée de l'Air in Indochina. This concern finally evaporated in 1949, after the take-over of mainland China by Mao Tse Tung.

With the arrival from France of additional C-47s to supplement its first six aircraft, the E.M.E.O. was re-organized in November 1945 as the Groupe de Marche de Transport d'Extrême-Orient

At Chartres air base, France, in July 1945, mechanics put the last touches to an ex-RAF Dakota of G.T. II/15 'Anjou' about to leave for Saigon and still sporting on the nose the emblem of G.T. I/61 'Touraine'. G.T. I/61 provided the back-up aircraft for all the transport squadrons of the Armée de l'Air assigned to the S/GMMTA in Indochina.

Above: A French-built Junkers Ju 52 trimotor of G.T. 1/64 'Béarn' pictured over the central plateau of Annam some time in the late forties.

Above right: Mishap on the wet and slippery Na San grass strip in the monsoon season of 1950. Toucan # 334 of G.T. 1/64 has ended in a side ditch after losing its starboard landing gear during touch-down.

(G.M.T.E.O.) and began operating regularly from Tan Son Nhut with 18 C.47s. In addition to making transport and liaison flights throughout most of Indochina, the unit (which became the Groupe de Transport Aérien II/15 [G.T. II/15] 'Anjou' in June 1946, and the G.T. 2/64 in July 1947) soon began to fly bombardment sorties with some of its aircraft modified in the field to carry HE bombs of up to 100 kg (220 lb) or bundles of incendiary bombs. Similar duties were performed by G.T. I/34 (renumbered G.T. 1/64 in July 1947) 'Béarn', which had arrived at Bien Hoa in February 1946 equipped with AAC.1 Toucans (French-built Junkers Ju 52/3m trimotors). Although most primitive, the C-47 and AAC.1 bombing missions provided much needed air support to the ground forces trying to regain control of the country.

## *First combat aircraft*

To equip its units in Indochina with their first genuine combat aircraft, the Armée de l'Air sent British-built Supermarine Spitfires, with aircraft for two Groupes de Chasse, G.C. I/7 'Provence' and G.C. II/7 'Nice', being shipped from France. In December 1945, pending arrival of their Spitfire Mk.IXs, pilots and ground crews of G.C. I/7, assisted by Japanese POWs, made valiant efforts to start operations with 12 of the 17 Nakajima Ki-43-II and Ki-43-III fighters (wartime Allied code 'Oscar') which the British had turned over to the French. The worn-out Japanese aircraft, for which spares were virtually unavailable, proved highly temperamental and the type was only used for a few familiarization flights. Thus, it was G.C. II/7 which on 13 December 1945, having received Spitfire Mk.VIIIs loaned locally by the Royal Air Force, flew the first fighter operations in Indochina.

Upon receiving their own aircraft, the two units stepped up operations from Nha Trang and Hanoi-Gia Lam. The Spitfires, however, were not well adapted to local conditions. With few suitable airfields, they lacked the range necessary to cover far-flung ground forces. Moreover, their limited armament (guns had only sufficient rounds for 15 seconds of firing, and the type could seldom carry more than two 250-lb/113-kg bombs) was not ideal for ground support sorties. The Spitfires, nevertheless, played an important part in early pacification operations if for no better reason than they were the only available combat aircraft. When the pilots and crews of G.C.s I/7 and II/7 were returned to France during the summer of 1946, their aircraft were transferred to two other Groupes, G.C. I/2 'Cigognes' and G.C. II/2 'Alsace'. The new units flew the British-made fighters from Saigon, Hanoi, Lang Son, Nha Trang, and Tourane until October 1947. Units and crew rotations then resulted in the Spitfires being passed on first to G.C. 1/4 'Dauphiné' and G.C. 2/4 'La Fayette', and then on to G.C. 1/3 'Navarre' and G.C. 2/3 'Champagne'. After one year in combat, it was the turn of these two Groupes to send their personnel back home.

Churning the thick moist air of the Delta with their three two-bladed propellers, a group of bomb-laden AAC.1 Toucans of G.T. 2/62 'Franche-Comté' taxi past their Bach Mai hangars on their way to a Viet Minh target of the Upper Region in the spring of 1950.

When personnel of Groupe de Chasse I/7 'Provence' arrived in Indochina without their Spitfire IXs, they attemped to become operational with twelve Nakajima Ki-43-IIs and Ki-43-IIIs. Commencing in December 1945, these war-weary Japanese fighters were used for training but not for combat. Aircraft 'A,' a Ki-43-III, was ground-looped on 2 January 1946 and the last 'Oscar' survived only until March 1946!

Supermarine Spitfire Mk. IXs of G.C. 1/3 'Navarre' and G.C. 2/3 'Champagne' lined-up at Nha Trang in 1950. The Spitfire proved only moderately successful in Indochina due to its limited range.

Looking suitably war-weary, a pair of bomb-carrying Spitfire Mk IXs make their way to a strike area. The pair are from G.C. I/4 'Dauphiné', one of a number of units to operate the type during the conflict, with only moderate successes.

By then few of these aircraft were still airworthy and, passed on to G.C. 1/6 'Corse' in April 1950, the last Spitfires were finally taken out of operation in November 1950.

In view of the limited range and armament of the Spitfire, it was with sanguine expectations that the Armée de l'Air had sent the de Havilland Mosquito Mk.VIs and XVIs of G.C. I/3 'Corse'. Unfortunately, the Mosquitoes of this unit were found ill-adapted to prevailing atmospheric conditions with their bonded-plywood structure quickly deteriorating. Furthermore, these twin-engined fighter-bombers could only be based in Saigon as they required longer airfields than the Spitfires. Consequently, after operating from January to July 1947, during which its aircraft averaged only two-thirds of the monthly utilization of the more flexible Spitfires, G.C. I/3 was sent back home.

The lack of suitable combat aircraft, such as a twin-engined light bomber of metal construction, carrying heavy armament and possessing a long endurance, was of limited consequence at this early stage of the war as the French had to contend only with antiaircraft fire from light weapons and had no air opposition. However, following the formation of the People's Republic of China in September 1949, the French situation in Indochina took a turn for the worse. The Viet Minh now had a sanctuary in China where its troops could be trained and a direct source of supplies and armament. To face this new threat, the Armée de l'Air was soon to need more and better aircraft.

In the late forties with the sophisticated US help still to come, the French used the old Junkers trimotors as bombers and suitably transformed tin drums filled with jellied gasoline as rudimentary fire-bombs to attack Viet Minh hide-outs in the deep jungle of Indochina. Crews of G.T. 1/64 are seen here about to drop a stick of gasoline drums from the hold of a Ju 52.

Jumping mainly from AAC.1 Toucans, French paratroops were used for rapid insertions into jungle areas to engage Viet Minh forces. These are seen jumping over Tonkin.

A single M.S.500 of Armée de l'Air's ELA 53 shares the grass flightline of an upper region airfield with others from the French Army 21st G.A.O.A. while a red-nosed C-47 of G.T. 1/64 is about to start its take off roll.

Above right: The first batch of Grumman F8F-1 Bearcats provided by the USA to the Armée de l'Air under MDAP funds arrived aboard the USS *Windham Bay* in January 1951. This later batch is seen being unloaded from the USS *Sitkoh Bay*.

Bell P-63 Kingcobras of Groupe de Marche (G.M.) 1/9 'Limousin' pictured at an unidentified airfield in Tonkin in February 1951. All three airplanes are fitted with belly and wing ferry tanks.

When the Communist takeover of China became likely, the American perception of French activities in Indochina changed markedly. France was no longer seen as a naughty colonial power but as a staunch anti-communist ally, and US aid was finally forthcoming. For the Armée de l'Air, this change of heart translated initially into the feasibility of sending US-made fighters. While its P-47Ds would have been ideal for operations in Indochina, they were needed in Europe where they still provided a large measure of France's first-line of defence. Accordingly, Bell P-63C Kingcobras were selected for overseas deployment, with the aircraft of G.C. 1/5 'Vendée' and G.C. 2/5 'Ile de France' being unloaded at Saigon in July 1949. These first two Kingcobra units were followed two months later by G.C. 2/6 'Normandie Niémen' based in Saigon and, in August 1950 at Hanoi, by G.C. 3/6 'Roussillon'. Thus, at the end of 1949, the Armée de l'Air had four Groupes de Chasse (three with P-63Cs and one, G.C. 2/3 'Champagne', with Spitfire IXs), three Groupes de Transport (G.T. 2/64 'Anjou' with C-47s, and G.T. 1/64 'Béarn' and G.T. 2/62 'Franche-Comté' with AAC.1s), one Escadrille de Reconnaissance d'Outre-Mer (E.R.O.M. 80 with Nord Centre NC 701 and NC 702 Martinet light twin-engined aircraft, French-built versions of the German Siebel Si 204D), two Sections Aériennes de Liaison (S.A.L. 52 and S.A.L. 53 with Martinets, Morane-Saulnier M.S. 500 Criquets [French-built Fieseler Fi 156s] and Nord 1001 and 1002 Pingouins [French-built Messerschmitt Bf 108s]), and the ler, 2ème, 3ème and 4ème Groupes d'Aviation d'Observation d'Artillerie (G.A.O.A.s with Morane Criquets). On the ground French forces then totalled some 130,000 troops, with North Africans, black Africans, Vietnamese and Foreign Legionnaires accounting for more than two-thirds of the strength.

## *Automatic weapons appear*

The progressive strengthening of French ground and air forces had come none too soon. The Viet Minh, thanks to Soviet and Chinese aid, was becoming a major power and was starting to field automatic antiaircraft weapons. (The first loss to these weapons was incurred on 19 January 1950 when a P-63C of G.C. 2/5 was shot down during a mission against Thai-nguyen. This was also the first time that French fighters used rockets in combat.) Close to the Chinese border in northern Tonkin, the French strongpoint at Dong-Khé had changed hands three times in the spring and summer of 1950, thus threatening the security of two other major outposts along the R.C. 4 (Route Coloniale 4). Accordingly, the French High Com-

**Right: Three Grumman F6F-5 Hellcats of G.C. 2/6 'Normandie-Niémen' on the alert ramp at Tan Son Nhut in early 1951. Of note is the single P-63 Kingcobra in the background.**

mand decided to withdraw its forces and ordered a retreat along R.C. 4. With Criquets flying as forward air controllers for the Kingcobras providing air support, C-47s resupplying the ground forces and AAC.1s flying transport and bombing missions, troops departed Cao Bang. The operation, however, had been ill-planned. On their way to Langson, and then on toward Hanoi, these troops and accompanying civilian refugees had to go through Viet Minh-held Don Khé. It was then that the notorious Vo Nguyen Giap took the offensive and, routing the French at Langson, gained the first of his major victories. In spite of the 844 combat sorties flown by the Armée de l'Air (391 by fighters, 326 by transports, 78 by reconnaissance aircraft, and 49 by AAC.1 'bombers'), the French forces took very heavy losses.

Better armed than the Spitfires, the Kingcobras (usually called Kings by their French crews) proved generally effective; however, they required fairly well prepared airfields and carried an insufficient weight of bombs. Moreover, the Armée de l'Air still did not possess the twin-engined bombers it deemed necessary for the types of operation it was called upon to perform. Fortunately, substantial help, not only with aircraft but also in terms of finance, weapons and supplies, was on its way as by then the start of the Korean War had warmed US support for the French undertaking in Indochina.

American assistance soon enabled the Armée de l'Air to modernize and strengthen its Indochina contingent. To re-equip the fighter units, Grumman F6F-5 Hellcats and F8F-1/F8F-1B Bearcats were supplied. Designed as carrier-based fighters and thus possessing relatively short take-off and landing characteristics, an asset of vital importance in Indochina where the lack of suitable airfields had been a major deterrent to the deployment of combat aircraft close to the battlefront, the

**French and Vietnamese mechanics servicing a Grumman F8F-1 Bearcat of G.M. 2/9 'Auvergne.' Note unit's insignia on the cowling panel on the ground. With its name being mispronounced by most French personnel, the F8F became known as the 'Beercat'; fuel, however, remained standard aviation petrol, beer being carefully conserved for the hard working personnel...**

Above: A camera equipped F8F-1B of E.R.O.M. 80 about to leave Bach Mai for a recce mission over the Tonkin Delta in 1952. Early Bearcats of E.R.O.M. 80 used for their reconnaissance missions specially field-modified US drop tanks fitted with two cameras!

Hellcats arrived in November 1950 and the Bearcats (known to the French as the 'Beercats') followed in January 1951.

The Hellcat was only an interim type in service with the Armée de l'Air and, until January 1953 when G.C. 2/21 'Auvergne' completed its conversion to Bearcats, was operated by three Groupes de Chasse (G.C. 1/6 'Corse', G.C. 2/6 'Normandie-Niémen' and G.C. 1/9 'Limousin'). A more important aircraft was the Bearcat which made its combat début in March 1951 with G.C. 3/6 'Roussillon' and remained in service until the final French withdrawal in April 1956. Ten Groupes, designated sequentially as Groupes de Chasse, Groupes de Marche (G.M.), and then again G.C.s (G.C.s 1/6 'Corse' and 3/6 'Roussillon', G.M.s 1/8 'Saintonge', 2/8 'Languedoc', 1/9 'Limousin', 2/9 'Auvergne' and 1/21 'Artois'; and G.C.s 2/21 'Auvergne', 1/22 'Saintonge' and 2/22 'Artois'), flew Bearcats at one time or another, but peak strength never exceeded four Groupes. These fighters were also operated by two reconnaissance units: Escadrille de Reconnaissance d'Outre-Mer 80 (EROM 80) flying Bearcats fitted with a locally-developed camera pod (from May 1951 until September 1955) and Escadrille de Reconnaissance Photographique 2/19 (E.R.P. 2/19) 'Armagnac', which supplemented its Douglas RB-26Cs with some photographic Bearcats.

## *Invader enters the fray*

Perhaps even more important to the French war effort was the Douglas B-26 Invader twin-engined attack aircraft. The staff of the Armée de l'Air had long advocated the use of light bombers in Indochina. However, with no locally-produced bombers, the Armée de l'Air was unable to implement this recommendation prior to the American change of heart. In comparison to the Hellcat and Bearcat, which were no longer needed by first-line units of the US Navy, the Invader was still much in demand with the USAF as the B-26 was proving itself in Korea as an effective night interdictor. Nevertheless, the United States yielded to the urgent need of the French and the first four Invaders arrived at Tan Son Nhut on 4 November 1950. Rapidly taken on charge by crews trained in France by the 126th Bombardment Wing, an ANG unit then on active duty, the B-26s first equipped Groupe de Bombardement 1/19 'Gascogne' at Tourane (later better known as Da Nang) in Annam, with combat operations commencing from this centrally-located base on 1 February 1951. The long endurance of the Invader, its bomb-

Grumman F8F-1 Bearcat of Groupe de Chasse 2/21 'Auvergne'. The number 780 appearing on the lower rear fuselage are the last three digits of the original USN BuNo 94780. The Bearcat was numerically the most important fighter operated by the Armée de l'Air in Indochina, with all Groupes de Chasse taking part in the fight for Dien Bien Phu being so equipped.

A mixed group of Douglas B-26B and B-26C Invaders fly over Annam near the town of Hue in 1953. They are from G.B. 1/19 'Gascogne' based at Tourane, during Operation 'Picardie'.

load of up to 6,000 pounds, (2722 kg), and its heavy forward-firing armament (up to fourteen 12.7-mm/0.5-in machine-guns) made the B-26 ideal for the task at hand. With the delivery of additional aircraft, the Armée de l'Air organized a second Groupe de Bombardement (G.B. 1/25 'Tunisie') in November 1951, and a third (G.B. 1/91 'Bourgogne') in June 1954. Furthermore, in its RB-26C version, the Invader was employed between November 1951 and the end of the war by the Escadrille de Reconnaissance B-26 (renamed E.R.P. 2/19, Escadrille de Reconnaissance Photographique 2/19 'Armagnac' in January 1954).

After the defeat at Cao Bang and Langson, Général Jean de Lattre de Tassigny took over as High Commissioner and Commander in Chief of French forces in Indochina, and ordered the construction of fortifications and strongpoints to help

Left: Bearcats from G.C. 1/21 drop 100 US gallon napalm tanks over a small Annam railway station beleaguered by Viet Minh troops in October 1952.

Right: The glazed bombardier nose identifies this as a B-26C Invader, of G.B. 1/25 'Tunisie', bombing Viet Minh positions over Tonkin on 24th May, 1952. The Invader represented the most potent form of airpower that the French could bring to bear during the conflict.

NO STEP
PUSH
AUVERGNE

## Grumman F8F-1 Bearcat

**Grumman F8F-1 Bearcats arrived in Indochina in January 1951, and rapidly adopted the position of being the premier fighter-bomber in the theatre. They were used almost exclusively for ground attack, a fate which befell other fighters during this and other conflicts in the region. High speed and manoeuvrability were good assets when faced with heavy ground fire, and, for its day, the Bearcat possessed both in abundance. It performed well throughout its combat career, notably during the abortive defence of Dien Bien Phu. This example is from G.C. 2/21 'Auvergne', complete with bomb shackles on the wings.**

hold the Tonkin Delta. Vo Nguyen Giap, meanwhile, to capitalize on his earlier success and not to have his forces bottled up by the French defensive network (which in the end proved far less impervious than had been hoped for by the new French commander) mounted an offensive against Vinh-Yen. Fortunately for the French, but unfortunately for Giap and his troops, the brilliant Viet Minh general had not counted on the newly found strength of the Armée de l'Air which, making its first use of napalm on 17 January 1951, succeeded in helping ground forces repulse the Viet Minh and inflicting over 6,000 casualties. Over the next months, rapidly increasing French air power inflicted new defeats on the Viet Minh (e.g., failure to take Haiphong and its port during the March 1951 offensive, battle of the River Day two months later, battle of Nghialo in October, etc.) but was unable to provide the decisive edge needed by the French Army during its inconclusive offensive along the Rivière Noire in the winter of 1951-52. As regards Giap and his forces, blocked in their attempts at conventional warfare, the future lay in increased guerrilla activities, a move which the French tried to counter by setting up heavily fortified strongholds (*camps retranchés*) to lure the Viet Minh into the open. Eventually, these tactics and counter-tactics culminated in the French defeat at Dien Bien Phu and in the partition of Vietnam, thus setting the stage for the second phase of the '30-Year Air War'.

By 1951, when French ground units began to rely increasingly on air support, the M.S. 500 Criquet (a French-built development of the German Fi 156 Storch) became paramount to the successful employment of the fighters and Invaders. This type of aircraft had been introduced in Indochina in late 1945 with the arrival of the Piper L-4Bs of the 9ème D.I.C. (Division d'Infanterie Coloniale). However, during the following year these US-built aircraft were replaced in units of the Aviation d'Artillerie de l'Armée de Terre (Artillery Aviation of the Army) by M.S. 500 Criquets and, in November 1949, the Criquets were transferred to the control of the Armée de l'Air. Soon their role was changed from limited use as artillery spotters to that of forward air controllers. Equipped with different sets of radios to communicate both with ground troops and tactical aircraft, the Criquets performed sterling services and were frequently credited with saving hard-pressed units by bringing in and directing air support. Other Criquets, progressively supplemented by Nord Pingouins, Nord Centre Martinets and Dassault Flamants, were operated throughout the war for liaison. Moreover, as the Germans had done during World War II with their Fi 156s, the French operated their Criquets for aeromedical evacuation of wounded personnel. In this role, helicopters (eventually to become almost synonymous with air operations in South East Asia) made their operational début in Indochina on 16 May 1950.

Well aware of their potential, the Armée de l'Air

**Above: A Morane-Saulnier M.S.500 Criquet of the Armée de l'Air ELA 53 sits on the Hanoi/Bach Mai flightline with NC.701 Martinets also belonging to the escadrille. Of all the aircraft used by the French in Indochina, the Criquet (né Fieseler Storch) was probably the best adapted to this difficult theatre of operations. Used principally by the Armée de l'Air for medical evacuations and for various liaison jobs, the Criquets were also used by the French Army, for artillery spotting and forward air control, and by the French Aéronavale for support and liaison tasks.**

**Above left: A Hiller Model 360 helicopter of the Armée de l'Air *Escadrille d'Hélicoptères Légers 1/65* overflies Camp Bernard de Lattre, Tan Son Nhut, in 1955. Named after the son of General de Lattre de Tassigny, heroically killed in action in Tonkin while resisting the Viet Minh at the head of his platoon, Camp Bernard de Lattre hosted the main heliport of the French Army light aviation (A.L.O.A.).**

**Lifting off from an improvised helipad in Hanoi some time in 1954, this Westland S-55 of Armée de l'Air's EHM 2/65 is seen during a downtown medevac.**

had been prevented by budgetary constraints from acquiring helicopters, and thus the first two Hiller 360-As to arrive in Indochina were acquired by the civilian Service de Santé d'Indochine (Indochina Health Service). Placed at the disposal of the Armée de l'Air and crewed by military personnel, these two light helicopters soon confirmed the extraordinary value of rotary-wing aircraft. Following this initial success, funds were made available for the acquisition in June 1952 of a first batch of four Westland S-51 Mk 1As. Later, additional S-51s as well as larger Westland S-55 Series 2s were procured in England, while Hiller H-23As and H-23Bs were supplied by the United States. These rotary-wing aircraft and their courageous crews (notably Capitaine Valérie André, a young woman combining the skills of helicopter pilot with those of a surgeon and qualified parachutist) flew countless missions to save the lives of their countrymen.

## *Viet Minh strengthens*

By the beginning of 1953 the war had taken a different character. The Viet Minh had become a major force of at least 139,000 men, including 125,000 regulars. True, France and its local allies held a theoretical 3 to 1 numerical advantage, but 90 percent of their strength was kept static in strongholds and in the major cities. Furthermore, at least in Tonkin and parts of Laos, the Viet Minh had taken the initiative and could concentrate its regular forces for attack on sites of its choosing, thus gaining local superiority. To counter this situation the new French Commander in Chief, Général Raoul Salan, relied on fortified centers called *hérissons* (hedgehogs) which, possessing airstrips, could be easily resupplied and reinforced by air, and on commando operations by paratroopers and other mobile forces to strike at Viet Minh dépots and troop concentrations. Both of these strategies depended on massive use of air power which was supplied by some 300 aircraft of the Armée de l'Air, including the Bearcats of four Groupes de Chasse and the Invaders of two Groupes de Bombardement. This tactical strength remained unchanged until after the fall of Dien Bien Phu, when a third and last Groupe de Bombardment, G.B. 1/91 'Bourgogne', was organized at Tourane.

After the withdrawal at the end of 1952 of its antiquated AAC.1 trimotors, the Armée de l'Air could field only three Groupes (G.T.s 2/62, 1/64 and 2/64) equipped with C-47s to provide the logistics required to support ground forces kept in *hérissons* and to mount commando operations. To beef up this insufficient transport force, the Armée de l'Air made increased use of impressed civil transport aircraft (including Douglas DC-3s and Bristol Freighters), added a fourth C-47 Groupe, G.T. 2/63 'Sénégal' in January 1954, and began supplementing the C-47s of G.T. 2/64 'Anjou' with Nord 2501 Noratlas five months later. Even more important was the assistance provided by the United States which, beginning in May 1953, lent six Fairchild C-119Cs. Initially flown by French crews of the Détachment C-119, this first batch of cargo transports was soon joined by additional C-119s flown by American mercenaries provided by the Formosa-based Civil Air Transport.

**Above: Douglas C-47 of G.T. 2/62 'Franche Comté' frames a Bristol Freighter, one of the more unusual types to be seen operating in Indochina. The Royal New Zealand Air Force would later use the type on SEATO exercises, and for low-key supply during the US involvement.**

**Above left: Nicknamed 'Joan' a Westland-built Sikorsky S-51 of an unidentified unit of the Armée de l'Air lifts off from Bien Hoa some time before the end of the war in Indochina.**

**A very famous picture. A Fairchild C-119 of the Armée de l'Air, forced down on the short 'Isabelle' dust strip at Dien Bien Phu after an engine failure, is about to return back to Haiphong at dawn.**

**Above: F8F-1 Bearcats of G.C. I/21 'Artois' move out of their makeshift airstrip for another mission to support the beleaguered troops at Dien Bien Phu. Each carries a pair of bombs under the wings.**

**Above right: G.C. I/21 aircrew in full flying kit take a last look at the map of the area surrounding Dien Bien Phu. Despite the attentions of many combat aircraft, and spirited fighting from within, the Viet Minh won a famous victory.**

Already controlling most of Annam and Tonkin, with the exception of a small triangle around Hanoi and Haiphong, as well as pockets in Cambodia and Cochinchina, the Viet Minh turned its attention toward Laos in December 1953. Anticipating this offensive, Général Henri Navarre, the French Commander in Chief since May 1953, decided to counter it. Lacking sufficient troops to mount a mobile counter-offensive, Général Navarre decided to revert once again to the use of a *hérisson* in the hope of immobilizing the bulk of the Viet Minh force in Laos and, by drawing it in the open, to inflict heavy losses through the massive use of aviation. The site selected for the new *hérisson* was Dien Bien Phu, a deep valley controlling one of the main access routes between Tonkin and Laos. Paratroopers were dropped on 14 November 1953 to secure the area for the construction of an airfield and a network of eight defensive bastions. An initial garrison of some 10,800 troops, which required 96 tonnes of supplies to be airlifted daily, was set up and confidently awaited the Viet Minh. Their wait was not long. Realizing his opportunity to strike a telling blow on the French, Vo Nguyen Giap massed four infantry divisions and one heavy division, with some 75,000 coolies building trails and transporting supplies and ammunition. Setting up a heavy concentration of artillery and ack-ack, the Viet Minh began the siege.

The fight for Dien Bien Phu began in earnest on 13 March 1954. Surprising the French defenders with the intensity of his artillery, Giap practically succeeded in five days to prevent the use of the airstrip. With aircraft being able to land only occasionally, the bulk of the supplies had to be air dropped. This task was made doubly difficult by heavy Viet Minh antiaircraft fire (by then including a fair number of Soviet-made 37 mm cannon) and the fact that, being spread out, the small bastions could easily be surrounded by the enemy. Bolstered by aircraft from the Aéronautique Navale, the Armée de l'Air mounted intensive efforts to break the Viet Minh offensive and supply the Dien Bien Phu garrison. In spite of the gallantry of the Armée de l'Air and Aéronautique Navale aircrews (many flying upward to 150 combat hours during the month of April), and the equal courage and determination of the troops under the command of Général de Castries, the situation worsened rapidly as the French did not have sufficient aircraft to throw into the battle. For a while it appeared that a request for direct American aid was going to succeed, as the United States seriously considered providing air support with B-29s of the Far East Air Forces Bomber Command and carrier-based aircraft of the Seventh Fleet. However, President Dwight Eisenhower, yielding to the advice of his Secretary of State, John Foster Dulles, rejected the French request and the defenders were left to fend for themselves. Finally, on 8 May 1954 the last of the over 15,000 troops committed to the defense of Dien Bien Phu were forced to surrender when the last bastion, 'Isabelle', was overrun by the Viet Minh. Losses were horrendous: 1,600 dead, 1,600 missing, 4,800 wounded and 8,000 prisoners on the French side; over 10,000 dead and nearly twice as many wounded for the Viet Minh.

In this last major operation of the war in Indochina, the role of aviation had been of vital importance. The failure to hold Dien Bien Phu could not be attributed either to the lack of dedication or valor of the aviators and ground troops; rather, it was due to the failure to appreciate the strength of the Viet Minh and the magnitude of the task

**On their Haiphong/Cat Bi pierced steel planks flightline in March or April 1954, a group of C-119B/C Box Cars of the Armée de l'Air *Détachement C-119* await dusk before starting their supply missions over Dien Bien Phu. Most of the C-119s leased to the French Air Force came from the 314th and 403rd Troop Carrier Groups in Japan and Korea.**

Above: During the evacuation of Na San in September 1953, a red-nosed Douglas C-47 of G.T. 1/64 'Béarn' shares a busy Tonkinese grass strip with Douglas DC-3s of three different civil companies: Air Viet-Nam, Air Outre-Mer and Aigle Azur. For such special flights the civilian pilots would earn sometimes up to five times the salary of their stablemates from the Armée de l'Air...

Right: A C-47 of G.T. 2/62 'Franche Comté' swings out on to a makeshift runway in the Dien Bien Phu area under heavy fire. The transport fleet was kept busy throughout the siege, flying in tons of supplies to the beleaguered post.

imposed on relatively meager air units. Over 10,000 sorties had been flown in support of Dien Bien Phu; 6,700 by transports and 2,650 by combat aircraft of the Armée de l'Air, plus 1,019 sorties by naval aircraft. Forty-eight aircraft had been shot down and a further 14 had been destroyed on the ground, while 85 percent of the aircraft committed to the battle were damaged.

## *Commercial assistance*

Throughout the war logistics had been weak, as the Armée de l'Air did not then possess a long-range transport element to airlift supplies and personnel from France to Indochina. Thus, to supplement sea transportation, the French forces had to rely on regular air service provided by Air France, first with Douglas DC-4s and then with Lockheed Constellations. In addition, private airlines operated a variety of transports including the four-engined Boeing SA-307B-1 Stratoliners of Aigle Azur. In 1953 a specialized company, SAGETA (Société Auxiliaire de Gérance et de Transports Aériens), was organized by Air France and independent carriers to operate seven SNCASE SE.2010 Armagnac heavy four-engined transports. However, even after the timely start of the SAGETA operations, insufficient aircraft were available to provide the emergency airlift of reinforcements made necessary by the deterioration of the situation at Dien Bien Phu. Accordingly, the United States agreed to come to the rescue. Flying Douglas C-124 Globemasters, then the world's largest military transport aircraft, the 62nd Troop Carrier Wing transported nearly 1,000 military passengers from Paris to Saigon in April-May 1954.

Viet Minh mortar crews have little respect for the red cross markings on this C-47. Following supply flights into Dien Bien Phu, transports were busy removing casualties.

**Above: After the end of the Korean War, the Americans started supplying the French Army with brand new observation light planes to replace the war weary Morane-Saulnier M.S.500. A Cessna L-19A Bird Dog of the 22nd G.A.O.A. (French Army) is pictured here overflying the Mekong River delta in 1955.**

**Above right: In May 1954, on a Laotian upper region grass strip, a wounded soldier is pictured arriving from the besieged Dien Bien Phu camp after a flight in a de Havilland L-20A Beaver of ELA 52. This aircraft, AF serial #52-61510, was one of a dozen supplied to the French for medevacs.**

**Right: Nord 2501 Noratlas #25 of G.T. 2/64 at Haiphong in November 1954. Thirty years after, the Noratlas is still in service with a few transport squadrons of the French Air Force!**

During the final phase of the war there was an acceleration of the already hefty American aid, which between 1952 and 1954 alone totalled 940,000 million Francs (43 percent of which was in the form of equipment). Among aircraft rushed from US stocks were 25 Douglas B-26 bombers, 25 Chance Vought AU-1 and 12 Grumman F8F-1 fighter-bombers, and 18 Douglas C-47 transports, as well as small numbers of Cessna L-19 observation aircraft, Beech C-45 and de Havilland Canada L-20 light transports, and Sikorsky H-19 helicopters. Arriving too late to influence the outcome of the war, many of these aircraft were quickly returned to the United States while others provided the initial equipment of the new Vietnamese Air Force.

**Below: The F4U-7 and AU-1 Corsairs of Flottille 14F on the ramp at Bach Mai in May 1954 at the peak of the battle for Dien Bien Phu. Very little importance was then given to the paint job and finish of the airplanes.**

After the fall of Dien Bien Phu fighting lasted for another two months, with the French suffering yet another defeat at the Mang Yang Pass in the central highlands while negotiations to end the war were taking place in Geneva. It was during this period that the Armée de l'Air organized its last bomber unit (G.B. 1/91) and introduced Noratlas transports into service. Finally, following the signing of the Geneva Agreement on 21 July 1954, the war in Indochina ended. The Armée de l'Air remained in Vietnam for another two years, with transport aircraft providing an air bridge between Hanoi and Saigon to bring refugees to the south, and with Bearcats and Invaders being retained to cater for contingencies. Then, one by one, the fighter and bomber Groupes were dissolved; their Bearcats were either scrapped or transferred to the fledgling Vietnamese Air Force (VNAF) along with C-47s, Criquets and other light transport and liaison aircraft, while all but one of the remaining Invaders were returned to the US. Peace then made a brief appearance, but fighting was again to engulf the former French colony and, at least as regards Western nations, would go on until 1975.

## *The Aéronautique Navale in Indochina*

As we have seen, aircrews of the small Aéronautique Navale (or Aéronavale) had joined their brethren of the Armée de l'Air in helping ground troops fight the onslaught of Viet Minh forces at Dien Bien Phu. This was not the first time that French naval aircrews had been used in combat over Indochina.

On 27 and 28 October 1945, less than seven weeks after C-47 transports of the Armée de l'Air had become the first French aircraft to return to Indochina, four Consolidated PBY-5A Catalinas of Flottille 8F (Naval Squadron 8F) joined the Corps

**Above: A Supermarine Sea Otter of Escadrille 9S is being hoisted afloat from the sea tender-ship *Robert Giraud* somewhere off the coast of Tonkin in 1951. Such amphibians searched for Viet Minh smugglers along the sea border with China.**

**Above right: Among the different types of aircraft supplied to the French by the US Government was the Grumman JRF-5 Goose amphibian flying-boat, all of which flew with Aéronavale units in a wide variety of rôles. This particular machine, BuAerNo. 37784, used for medical evacuations by Escadrille 8S during the fateful year of 1954 sports large conspicuous red cross markings over its overall dark blue paint scheme.**

Expéditionnaire Français d'Extrême-Orient at Tan Son Nhut. Significantly, these twin-engined amphibians, which were primarily intended for use on coastal patrols and anti-smuggling operations, were the first armed aircraft available to the French expeditionary corps. In fact, two days after their arrival, the Catalinas were called upon to use their gondola-mounted flexible 12.7-mm machine-guns to provide firepower while another PBY-5A was making an aeromedical evacuation. Flottille 8F soon expanded its operations when a few additional Catalinas were ferried from France and, from February 1946, began operating in Tonkin to provide coastal patrol missions, aeromedical evacuation, air support with machine-guns and bombs, paratroop transport, reconnaissance, and liaison. Finally at the end of 1950, with the availability of Consolidated PB4Y-2S Privateer four-engined bombers, the last weary Catalinas were transferred to Escadrille 8S to end their productive life in less demanding patrol operations.

## *Ex-Japanese equipment*

Escadrille 8S, organized in December 1945 at Cat Lai near Saigon, had initially operated ex-Japanese Aichi E13A1 (wartime Allied code name 'Jake') single-engined floatplanes and one, then two, Loire 130 prewar French single-engined flying-boats. In addition, unit personnel attempted to put back into service a Japanese single-engine Nakajima A6M-2N (code name 'Rufe') float fighter, but this aircraft crashed almost immediately after being overhauled. As the Aichi floatplanes had only a slightly longer career in French service, Escadrille 8S was re-equipped during the summer of 1947 with ex-British Supermarine Sea Otter single-engined flying-boats. Six more Sea Otters, acquired by the Douanes Françaises (French Customs Administration), were used in 1950 to equip Escadrille 9S, with this second unit taking over the Sea Otters of Escadrille 8S until its disbandment in March 1952. Upon losing its Sea Otters, Escadrille 8S began operating a dozen Grumman JRF-5 Goose flying-boats supplied by the United States in February 1952. In service with the Aéronavale, these light twin-engined seaplanes acquired the distinction of becoming the primitive precursors of the Vietnam War-era gunships, as several of them were fitted by the French with twin machine-guns mounted in the left side access door and firing sideways.

**The very first aircraft of the French Navy pictured shortly after its arrival at Tan Son Nhut, Indochina, on 27 October 1945. This Catalina from Flottille 8F attracted many curious Japanese P.O.W.s then still in large numbers all over Indochina.**

Above: The PB4Y-2s of Flottille 8F on their hard stand at Saigon/Tan Son Nhut. All airplanes now carry the French Navy 'hooked' roundel prominently on the wings and nose sides.

Significantly more effective than these make-shift gunships were the Consolidated PB4Y-2S Privateers, the heaviest aircraft operated by either French service during the war in Indochina. To re-equip Flottille 8F, the Aéronautique Navale had obtained an initial batch of ten four-engined Privateers, with the first of these aircraft arriving in Indochina in November 1950. Intended as a land-based patrol and anti-submarine aircraft, the PB4Y-2S carried 12 12.7-mm machine-guns and up to 12,000 pounds (5443 kg) of bombs. It was thus well suited to bombing operations in Indochina, a role in which it was quickly used following the military setbacks suffered by the French Army in Tonkin during the fall of 1950. Based at Tan Son Nhut, with a small detachment at Haiphong-Cat Bi being progressively enlarged, the Privateers of Flottille 8F (re-organized as Flottille 28F in July 1953) took part in all major operations from 1951 until the end of the war. During the battle for Dien Bien Phu, the PB4Y-2Ss of Flottille 28F and the Invaders of the Armée de l'Air made extensive use of the 500-lb (227-kg) Hail (Lazy Dog) antipersonnel cluster which, containing 11,200 finned missiles, proved effective in breaking open assaults by Viet Minh troops. Unfortunately for the defenders, there were not enough Lazy Dogs or aircraft to drop them around the clock. After the end of the war, during which four PB4Y-2Ss had been lost, six Privateers were returned to the US while 12 others were flown back to North Africa.

With the exception of occasional detachments of carrier aircraft, the only other combat aircraft operated from shore bases in Indochina were the Chance Vought AU-1 Corsairs of Flotille 14F. Equipped with the F4U-7 version of the famous bent-wing fighter, Flottille 14F had been based at Bizerte when it had been alerted in early April 1954 for immediate deployment to Indochina. Leaving behind its aircraft, the unit's personnel were airlifted to Saigon in SAGETA's Armagnacs and Globemasters of the USAF, while the US carrier *Saipan* rushed the delivery of ex-USMC AU-1s. With the gravity of the situation at Dien Bien Phu providing the incentive, Flottille 14F became combat-ready in record time and flew its first war mission on 25 April. Its contribution, however, was not enough to save the troops of Général de Castries.

### *Carrier operations*

In many parts of Indochina the lack of airfields capable of accommodating combat aircraft rendered the use of carriers natural as, operating in the Sea of China, they could provide air support in areas not accessible to land-based aircraft of the Armée de l'Air. However, in the immediate post-World War II period, the Marine Nationale had only the prewar *Béarn*, a rather primitive carrier

**Above: The dangers of through-deck carrier operations are evident in this photograph of a Curtiss SB2C-5 landing aboard *Arromanches*. As well as the arrester wires stretched across the rear deck, a barrier is stretched across the mid-deck to catch any aircraft that failed to trap safely.**

**Right: A Curtiss SB2C-5 of Flottille 3F crosses the *Arromanches*'s ramp on return from a strike mission. The Helldiver provided powerful and accurate support for ground forces, but was vulnerable to groundfire. Note the perforated flaps, which could double as dive-brakes.**

suitable exclusively for ferrying aircraft. This deficiency was initially remedied by the acquisition in England of the escort carrier HMS *Biter* which, refitted and renamed *Dixmude* in French service, embarked the nine Douglas SBD-5 Dauntless dive bombers of Flottille 3F. With these aircraft on board, the *Dixmude* arrived in the Sea of China in March 1947 and, after commencing combat operations from Tan Son Nhut on 11 March, the SBDs of the 3F made their first combat sorties from the carrier on 16 March. During the following weeks additional sorties were flown against targets in Annam and Tonkin. However, after its catapult became unoperable, the *Dixmude* and its SBDs had to return to France on 14 April. Repaired in Toulon, the escort carrier, this time embarking the

**Left: A Douglas SBD-5 Dauntless of Flottille 4F is catapulted from the deck of the *Arromanches*..**

**Following the Sikorsky S-51, Piasecki's HUP was employed in small numbers by Flottille 58S, flying from *Arromanches*. The French did much to further helicopter warfare during their use in Indochina.**

Dauntlesses of Flottille 4F, made one more combat deployment from 20 October 1947 until 29 March 1948. During its transit from France to Indochina the *Dixmude* had been used to ferry AAC.1s and Spitfires for the Armée de l'Air and, with the availability of the light carrier *Arromanches* (ex-HMS *Colossus*), the old escort carrier was re-assigned as an aircraft transport vessel.

Arriving off the Indochina coast for the first time at the end of November 1948, the *Arromanches* went on to make four combat deployments as follows: from 29 November 1948 to 5 January 1949 with the SBDs of Flottille 4F and two Supermarine Seafire XVs; from 24 September 1951 until 23 February 1952 with the Curtiss SB2C-5 Helldivers of Flottille 3F and Grumman F6F-5 Hellcats of Flottille 1F; from 29 September 1952 to 21 February 1953, when the carrier was sent back to France for much needed repairs and left behind the SB2C-5s of Flottille 9F and F6F-5s of Flottille 12F; and from 29 September 1953 until after the fall of Dien Bien Phu, with the SB2C-5s of Flottille 3F, the F6F-5s of Flottille 11F and the Sikorsky S-51s of Escadrille 58S. It should be noted, however, that during most of these deployments, and especially during the battle of Dien Bien Phu, the carrier-

**The French aircraft-carrier *Bois-Belleau* anchored among the scenic calcareous rocks of the Along Bay at the entrance of the Hanoi harbour at the beginning of 1954.**

**Operated by both the Armée de l'Air and Aéronautique Navale during the war in Indochina, the Grumman F6F-5 Hellcat was the first type of fighter aircraft supplied by the United States during that conflict. The aircraft illustrated belonged to Flottille 1F which took part in combat operations from September 1951 to February 1952.**

based aircraft frequently operated from land bases close to the battle lines. In addition, rather than using transit time for additional training of aircrews and deck crews, the Marine Nationale elected to use the deck and hangar space of the *Arromanches*, and later those of the light carriers *La Fayette* (ex-USS *Langley*) and *Bois Belleau* (ex-USS *Belleau Wood*), to ferry aircraft to Indochina.

The third carrier to be operated during the war in Indochina was the *La Fayette* which, arriving without aircraft on 9 April 1953, took over Flottilles 9F (SB2C-5s) and 12F (F6F-5s) from the *Arromanches* but remained in the war zone for only five weeks. Likewise, the only deployment of the *Bois Belleau* was of short duration. Sent to Indochina with replacement Helldivers and Hellcats for existing units and the Piasecki HUP-2s of Escadrille 23S, the *Bois Belleau* operated only briefly with the SB2C-5s of Flottille 3F between 30 April and 15 September 1954. By then, for the Aéronautique Navale the war in Indochina was over.

**The old French carrier *Dixmude* (ex-HMS *Biter*) pictured with a deck full of F6F-5 Hellcats on the Saigon River during 1950.**

## *The Geneva Conference and the Partition of Vietnam*

For France, whose economy had been ruined by World War II, the war in Indochina had represented a progressively more difficult burden to bear in spite of US financial and material help. With popular support for the war in the South East Asia colony decreasing over the years, and with foreign opposition to their military actions increasing, successive administrations began seeking diplomatic ways to extricate France from the war. This quest reached fruition in February 1954 when, during talks between the four major powers (France, the Soviet Union, the United Kingdom, and the United States), it was agreed to convene an international conference in Geneva to seek potential solutions for the conflicts in Indochina and Korea. Scheduled to start on 26 April 1954, but delayed by yet another government change in France, this conference did not start until 8 May. On that very day, the military fate of Dien Bien Phu had been sealed.

In Geneva, delegates from the four major powers as well as from the People's Republic of China and the four Indochinese Nations (the Democratic Republic of Vietnam, the State of Vietnam, the Kingdom of Cambodia, and the Kingdom of Laos) sought to end the war and provide ways for a long-term settlement. Finally, after French and Viet Minh representatives had haggled over the location of the line of demarcation between North and South Vietnam, the negotiations were concluded on 21 July 1954. The Geneva Agreement established two states separated along the Ben Hai River at the 17th parallel, a demilitarized zone (DMZ) on each side of the line, and the withdrawal of French troops from the North and of Viet Minh forces from the South. Introduction of fresh troops, arms, and munitions, as well as the building of new military bases in Vietnam were prohibited. Canadian, Indian, and Polish members of the International Control Commission were to supervise the implementation of the armistice and to report violations that might lead to resumed hostilities. Furthermore, the movement of population between the two Vietnams was to be free during a 300-day period (eventually some 880,000 people fled to the South while some 130,000 Viet Minh soldiers and civilians went North). Finally, prior to July 1955, representatives from the North and the South were to prepare for elections throughout Vietnam to unify the country, with the elections taking place no later than 20 July 1956.

The seeds for future trouble in South East Asia lay in the fact that the government of the State of Vietnam, fearing it would lose the 1956 elections as the greater population of the North was more cohesively held by its Communist rulers than were the looser population groups of the South, immediately contested the Geneva Agreement. Moreover, the United States had elected to remain an observer, not a signatory party.

In the State of Vietnam, where in June 1948 the former Emperor Bao-Dai had been restored to power by the French, South Vietnamese constituted about 90 per cent of the 16-million population with the balance being comprised of strong minority groups, Chinese, Cambodians, and Montagnards (aborigenes living in high plateaux). In terms of religion, the population of South Vietnam was 90 percent Buddhist, with Roman Catholics accounting for barely ten percent. Yet it was Ngo Dinh Diem, a Catholic from the North, who became

**The VIP Douglas C-47 specially assigned to the Chief of Staff of the French Army in Indochina. Général Ely, departs Hanoi after the truce following the Geneva Agreement in the summer of 1954.**

the country's first President after Bao-Dai was deposed and the October 1955 referendum created the Republic of Vietnam. Already in August 1955, while still Prime Minister, Diem had rejected elections for the unification of the two Vietnams 'as long as the Communist regime in the North refuses to grant democratic freedoms'. Meanwhile the Diem government was taking strong actions to counter the Viet Cong (the name Viet Cong identifying the Communist forces in South Vietnam, with the Hanoi-based Viet Minh providing the political leadership, cadres and weapons) and to repress rebellion by various other politico-religious groups.

### *Neutral Laos*

In accordance with the Geneva Agreement, the Kingdom of Laos, since 1949 a semi-autonomous state within the Union Française, became a neutral state. In 1957 negotiations between its Premier, Prince Souvanna Phouma, and the leader of the Communist Pathet Lao, Prince Souphanouvong, led to the formation of a coalition government. This coalition, however, was tenuous and soon fighting between pro-American forces and the Pathet Lao began anew. Similarly, the Kingdom of Cambodia, also a member of the Union Française since 1949, gained its full independence in 1954. Under Norodom Sihanouk, who after abdicating as King returned to power as Prime Minister and head of the Popular Social Communist Party, Cambodia increasingly aligned itself with Communist nations and soon provided a sanctuary for the Viet Cong.

While Ho Chi Minh was preparing the North Vietnamese for a 'long and arduous struggle' to unify the two Vietnams under unswerving Communist tutelage, and Ngo Dinh Diem was trying to gain full control of the South, the South East Asia Defense Treaty had been signed on 8 September 1954 by Australia, France, New Zealand, Pakistan, the Philippines, the United Kingdom, the United States, and Thailand. Intended to provide a shield against external aggression, with individual nations having primary responsibility for internal countersubversive activities, the SEATO agreement was soon to provide part of the rationale for US armed support to the Republic of Vietnam and the Kingdom of Laos.

**Above: Busy scene at Nam Dinh aerodrome during the evacuation of this large Christian populated town of the Tonkinese delta in July 1954. As the need for more aircraft was truly important, many civil airplanes were impressed into service such as Air Viet-Nam's Douglas DC-4s and Autrex's fleet of de Havilland Dragons Rapides.**

**Above left: Part of EHL 1/65's helicopter fleet at rest in a hangar at Bien Hoa during 1955. Hiller 360s and Westland S-55s provided the bulk of the 40 or so rotary wing aircraft.**

**Left: Commandant Crespin, Commanding Officer of the *Groupement des Formations d'Hélicoptères* of the French Army in Indochina.**

**Below: Nord 2501 Noratlases of G.T. 2/64 'Anjou' and Douglas C-47s of G.T. 2/63 'Sénégal' lined-up for a parade and farewell ceremony at Tan Son Nhut before the disbanding of G.T. 2/63 and the handing over of its aircraft to the fledgling Republic of Vietnam Air Force in June 1955.**

A Grumman F6F-5 Hellcat straddles the catapult on the starboard side of the carrier *Arromanches'* flight deck. Flown by Flottille 11F, such aircraft could still operate effectively, in the closing stages of the Indochina war, but what was needed was a political rather than a military answer.

# The USAF in South East Asia

The first combat aircraft bearing American military markings to appear over the Indochinese peninsula were four North American B-25s which on 9 August 1942, escorted by three Curtiss P-40s, bombed Japanese-held docks and warehouses in the port of Haiphong. No one then could have predicted that 30 years later the same port facilities, now under Communist hands, would again be rocked by US bombs, and that nearly three times the tonnage of air munitions used by the USAF in all World War II theatres would be expended by the USAF over that same peninsula in 13 years of costly and frustrating fighting.

Following the first operation by China-based aircraft of the Tenth Air Force during the summer of 1942, Indochina had remained for the United States a remote corner in a relatively minor theatre of operations. Likewise, early post-World War II French operations, frowned upon as colonialist activities by the US Government, had not drawn much attention on the part of the USAF. By February 1950, however, the United States finally became aware that the Viet Minh was not only an anti-colonialist movement but was also an arm of Communist activities threatening Western interests in South East Asia. With this awareness came a reappraisal of the French material needs and, soon, the USAF received a mandate to supply equipment to the Armée de l'Air. Accordingly, the first aviation aid furnished by the United States to the French in Indochina consisted of eight Douglas C-47 transports which were flown to Saigon by USAF crews at the end of June 1950. A few weeks later the initial elements of the US Military Assistance Advisory Group (MAAG) arrived in Saigon and by November 1950 MAAG-Indochina included an Air Force Section to handle air assistance duties.

### *Increasing involvement*

From this modest beginning until the signing on 21 July 1954 of the Geneva Agreement ending the war in Indochina, the USAF found itself increasingly drawn into the conflict. At first this assistance was limited to the supply of aircraft. Even though it needed these aircraft for operations in Korea, the USAF began transferring Douglas B-26 bombers and C-47 transports to the Armée de l'Air. Following the end of the Korean War, the USAF also loaned Fairchild C-119s and provided most of the necessary maintenance personnel to support these transports. However, by early 1954 material help (which also included large numbers of ex-US Navy aircraft) and the contribution of C-119 maintenance personnel proved insufficient as French air units remained undermanned. Accordingly, in

**A newly-arrived Fairchild C-119C of the US Air Force about to be turned over to the French Air Force after a ferry-flight from Clark Field in the Philippines in early 1954.**

**US troops march from Douglas C-124 Globemaster transports at Don Muang airport at Bangkok. These were taking part in the SEATO exercise 'Firm Link', involving the United States, Philippines and Thailand. Note the North American AJ Savage in the background.**

February 1954 the USAF was instructed to send some 300 maintenance and supply personnel to help maintain the French B-26s and C-47s. Beginning in April, the USAF also committed Douglas C-124 transports to airlift French reinforcements from France to Indochina. At the same time, serious consideration was given to using USAF B-29s, escorted by carrier-based aircraft of the Seventh Fleet, to bomb Viet Minh troops surrounding the French garrison at Dien Bien Phu. As it turned out, such direct American intervention was ruled out by President Eisenhower. Following the fall of Dien Bien Phu on 7 May 1954 and the end of French combat operations in Indochina two and one-half months later, all USAF personnel not assigned to MAAG or to the airlift of refugees out of North Vietnam quickly departed Indochina. Seven years later, however, US airmen came back. This time it was to engage in protracted combat operations.

## PACAF

As American airmen returned to the Indochina peninsula, first covertly and then openly, the major USAF command responsible for operations in this geographical area, PACAF (Pacific Air Forces), was ill-prepared for the task. Like most other USAF commands at the time, it had prepared only for a major war and was relying extensively on nuclear deterrence to accomplish its assigned missions. Thus, at the end of 1961, 28 PACAF squadrons operated some 600 aircraft (including 200 F-100D/F tactical fighters, 127 F/TF-102A interceptors, 49 B-57 tactical bombers, 44 RF-101C and RB-57A reconnaissance aircraft, 18 KB-50J tankers, 53 C-54 and C-130A transports, 45 support aircraft, and 38 Matador and Mace tactical missiles) from 12 bases in Hawaii, Japan, Korea, Okinawa, and the Philippines. None of its squadrons had been trained for counter-insurgency operations and none of its aircraft were adapted for the type of limited warfare first assigned to the USAF by President Kennedy. Consequently, the first USAF aircraft to deploy to Vietnam were provided by the Tactical Air Command. Later on, as the war expanded, PACAF assumed primary responsibility for operations in South East Asia, with the Military Air Transport Service (redesignated Military Airlift Command in January 1966), the Strategic Air Command, and the Tactical Air Command deploying additional aircraft as required by the level of activities.

## Five phases of war

From the standpoint of USAF operations, the South East Asia War can be divided into five

**As part of 'Firm Link', the United States sent jet combat aircraft to Thailand, such as these Republic F-84G Thunderjets fitted with refuelling probes on their tip tanks. Later, aircraft such as the North American F-100 would become regular sights during SEATO exercises.**

**A *Farm Gate* Douglas B-26 Invader during a strike against sampans smuggling supplies and arms to Viet Cong guerrillas on the east coast of the Republic of Vietnam in March 1962. At that time, South Vietnamese officers were required to ride in the right-hand seat to authorize dropping ordnance on approved targets.**

phases. The first was a period of covert activities which began in January 1961, when reconnaissance aircraft began flying regularly over Laos, and continued with the assignment of the *Farm Gate*, *Ranch Hand* and *Mule Train* detachments to train and assist the Vietnamese Air Force in the fight against the Viet Cong. Phase two began in June 1964, when tactical fighters were first employed over Laos and, following the Gulf of Tonkin Incident in August 1964, saw extensive air operations being conducted continuously over South Vietnam and off and on over North Vietnam and Laos. Phase three, lasting from the summer of 1969 until the spring of 1972, was a period of transition; numerous USAF units in South East Asia were then either inactivated or transferred out of the theatre, several air bases were handed over to the VNAF, and the number of sorties flown by the USAF dropped from a high of 1,034,839 in 1968 to 450,031 in 1971. Phase four, brought about by the North Vietnamese offensive of the spring of 1972 and sustained by the efforts of the Nixon Administration to force the Democratic Republic of Vietnam to conclude the Paris Peace Talks, saw a resumption of intense US air operations and culminated with *Linebacker II*. Finally, the fifth phase began for the USAF with the repatriation of POWs from North Vietnam in February/March 1973 and the concurrent withdrawal from South Vietnam; it continued with the progressive removal of USAF units from Thailand, and ended with the evacuation of Saigon at the end of April 1975 and the rescue from Cambodia of the crew of the steamship SS *Mayaguez* two weeks later.

## *The Covert War*

Shortly after his inauguration as the nation's 35th President, John F. Kennedy acted upon his concern with the US over-reliance on nuclear deterrence by instructing the Chiefs of Staff to prepare the Armed Forces for conventional wars and, especially, for countering guerrillas in friendly developing nations. The USAF responded to the presidential directive by establishing on 14 April 1961 the 4400th Combat Crew Training Squadron (nicknamed 'Jungle Jim' and manned by volunteers) at Eglin AFB, Florida, to develop tactics and select aircraft suitable for counter-insurgency operations. Thus, when on 11 October 1961 the

The 1st Air Commando Squadron received Douglas Skyraiders in 1964, and quickly put them to good use. The two-seat versions were required at first, so that a Vietnamese 'adviser' could accompany the US pilot. Most were A-1E (ex-AD-5), but this was an A-1G (ex-AD-5N).

Below left: The North American T-28 Trojan was the first US combat aircraft in the theatre. This example is seen after having received the tactical camouflage adopted by most aircraft in SEA. Note the underwing pylons and lack of national insignia.

A *Farm Gate* crew check over their B-26 Invader, which is armed with napalm canisters and rocket pods. VNAF Skyraiders are lined up in the background.

President authorized the deployment of a USAF detachment to Vietnam 'to serve under the Military Assistance Advisory Group as a training mission and not for combat at the present time', the Tactical Air Command was ready to provide the necessary aircraft and crews.

Departing its permanent station at Eglin AFB, Florida, on 5 November, Detachment 2A of the 4400th CCTS received the code name *Farm Gate* and became the first combat-ready unit to be stationed in Vietnam. However, for diplomatic and political reasons its aircraft could not be operated in US markings and a subterfuge had to be devised quickly. Thus it was that the original national markings applied to VNAF aircraft (yellow-orange roundels with three concentric red circles) gave place to an insignia derived from that applied to US aircraft (five pointed white star in blue circle, with one red and two orange-yellow horizontal bars on each side, the whole being outlined in red), with the new Vietnamese markings being immediately applied to the *Farm Gate* aircraft.

## *Farm Gate settles in*

While eight North American T-28s (Navy T-28Bs fitted with armament being selected in preference to USAF T-28As as they were powered by a more powerful engine) of the 4400th CCTS were airlifted to Clark AB and then flown on to Tan Son Nhut, four of its Douglas SC-47s (specially modified C-47s with strengthened landing gear and JATO rockets to facilitate operations from short dirt fields) were ferried from the United States, and four Douglas B-26Bs were drawn out of storage in the Far East for its use. Settling in at Bien Hoa, the *Farm Gate* aircrews were at first frustrated in their desire to commence combat operations as Secretary McNamara reconfirmed the presidential instruction. This provided that the USAF detachment was to be used for training VNAF personnel and was to participate in operational missions only if Vietnamese were riding rear seats and specifically authorized firing on targets. In spite of these instructions, on 26 December 1961 two US crews did manage to fly a strike on their own. For the USAF, the South East Asia War had begun.

Notwithstanding the necessity to abide strictly by the rules of engagement, with the need to carry Vietnamese crews on combat missions proving particularly frustrating, the *Farm Gate* detachment stepped up its operations. Inevitably this led to unwanted press coverage and in April 1962 General Curtis LeMay, the Air Force Chief of Staff, was forced to announce the existence of the detachment but insisted that *Farm Gate* was in Vietnam to instruct allied crews in all phases of air operations. In spite of this denial, the combat nature of the *Farm Gate* activities soon became well-known.

**The scene at Tan Son Nhut in February 1964 shows *Mule Train* Fairchild C-123 Providers awaiting their next mission. The Provider continued to perform sterling transport work throughout the conflict. In the background are a Douglas C-47 and a Cessna U-3 Blue Canoe.**

During 1962-63, the unit's inventory was progressively increased as two RB-26Cs were obtained in April 1962 to provide *Farm Gate* with limited reconnaissance capabilities; the first Helio U-10As were delivered in December 1962, 17 aircraft (ten B-26Bs, five T-28Bs, and two SC-47s) arrived in January 1963, and two RB-26Cs and two RB-26Ls were added two months later. Officially redesignated the 1st Air Commando Squadron on 8 July 1963, but remaining known for a while as the *Farm Gate* detachment, the unit was by then organized into a B-26 strike section with 12 aircraft, a T-28 strike section with 13 aircraft, and two support sections with four U-10s and six SC-47s, all based at Bien Hoa. In addition, the 1st ACS had two detachments operating a total of eight B-26s from Pleiku and Soc Trang. While the number of aircraft was sufficient for the limited role assigned to the unit, their age was becoming a major concern. In particular, the B-26s were showing signs of structural fatigue as they had been modified to carry eight 750 lb (340-kg) bombs on underwing racks, a load far exceeding the aircraft's design specifications. The inevitable finally happened and, after an aircraft had lost its wing during a combat sortie on 11 February 1964, all B-26s were grounded. Six weeks later the same fate befell a T-28B, practically forcing *Farm Gate* out of business.

### *Enter the Skyraider*

Fortunately, the situation had been anticipated and in May 1964 the 1st ACS received the first of its Navy-surplus Douglas A-1Es. Ideally suited to counter-insurgency operations, the A-1E version of the famous propeller-driven Skyraider had the added advantage of being a two-seater with room for the still mandatory Vietnamese observer. Moreover, as single-seat A-1Hs were already being

**The first jet bombers to deploy were the Martin B-57 Canberras of the 8th and 13th Tactical Bomber Squadrons, both moving in at Bien Hoa. This pair comprises a B-57B (left) and B-57C (right), sweeping over the Mekong delta.**

operated by the VNAF fighter squadrons, spare parts and support were already available in Vietnam. Commencing combat operations on 31 May 1964 with the 1st ACS, the A-1Es were also selected to equip the second *Farm Gate* squadron, the 602nd Air Commando Squadron, which was organized five months later at Bien Hoa. By then, however, the United States was fully involved in combat operations and the two special units were absorbed into the overall USAF activities in Vietnam. With this change, the long-standing requirement for Vietnamese observers was finally eliminated.

Typical *Farm Gate* missions undertaken from early 1962 until mid-1964 included air support of ARVN (Army of the Republic of Vietnam) units (with the required Vietnamese officers riding aboard the T-28s and B-26s), resupply of US Special Forces ('Green Berets') outposts, escort of VNAF, US Army and US Marine Corps helicopters, psychological warfare with the SC-47s, and escort for the *Ranch Hand* and *Mule Train* C-123s which had arrived in Vietnam in early 1962.

## *Ranch Hand* begins

Belonging to the USAF Special Aerial Spray Flight at Pope AFB, North Carolina, and fitted with underwing spray bars and chemical tanks in the fuselage, the first *Ranch Hand* C-123s were sent to Vietnam to determine if jungle foliage could be destroyed by chemical spraying. Flying their first operational mission from Tan Son Nhut on 10 January 1962, *Ranch Hand* crews took part in what was possibly the most controversial undertaking of the war. The special unit gained further notoriety when on 2 February 1962 one of its C-123s crashed and its crew of three became the first USAF casualties of the war. Initially assigned as a separate unit on TDY from TAC, *Ranch Hand* personnel and their UC-123Bs (later UC-123Ks) were successively attached to the 315th Troop Carrier Wing, the 315th Air Commando Wing, the 12th Air Commando Squadron, the 12th Special Operations Squadron, and the 310th Tactical Airlift Squadron, and remained in South East Asia until the end of January 1971. In nine years of operations over Vietnam and Laos, *Ranch Hand* aircraft had sprayed nearly 2.5 million hectares (6.2 million acres) with various herbicide mixtures, including the notorious Agent Orange. Results were far from satisfactory and side effects untold.

Far less controversial, the *Mule Train* C-123Bs were the first tactical transports deployed by the USAF to Vietnam, with four Providers of the 346th Troop Carrier Squadron arriving at Tan Son Nhut on 2 January 1962. Their achievements are de-

**When the USAF began using camouflage for its tactical aircraft in 1965, the size of the national markings remained unchanged, thus limiting the effectiveness of the camouflage. Photographed at Tan Son Nhut AB, the RF-101C in the foreground shows the original markings while that in the back has the reduced size insignia.**

**Clark-based Convair F-102s began deployments to Tan Son Nhut in March 1962 under the codename *Water Glass*. Later *Candy Machine* deployments became a regular feature, providing limited air defence for South Vietnam.**

Above: Peaceful looking in its shiny all-metal finish and US civil registration (N544Y), this de Havilland Canada Caribou was one of the 'Boos' flown by Air America as part of the covert activities undertaken throughout most of South East Asia by this 'airline' owned and operated by the Central Intelligence Agency.

Above right: A Fairchild-built Pilatus Turbo-Porter of Air America lands on the airstrip at the Bao Loc outpost during Operation *San Angelo* in January 1968. Army Cessna 0-1s are parked in revetments, built with dirt-filled 50-gallon drums, for protection against VC mortar attacks.

The Volpar Turboliner was a development of the Beech 18 which was used quite extensively by Air America for its operations in South East Asia. The building behind the aircraft is the Air America terminal at Tan Son Nhut where much activity took place on 29 April 1975 during the final evacuation from Saigon.

tailed further on in the story of the tactical airlifters.

While the propeller-driven *Farm Gate, Ranch Hand*, and *Mule Train* aircraft were the first USAF aircraft to fly combat missions in Vietnam, they had been preceded in operations over South Vietnam by jet-powered McDonnell RF-101Cs of the 15th Tactical Reconnaissance Squadron which flew 67 sorties between 20 October and 21 November 1961 during their *Pipe Stem* TDY deployment from Kadena AB, Okinawa, to Tan Son Nhut. Moreover, during the covert phase of the war preceding full US intervention, the USAF also deployed some interceptors after unidentified radar tracks along the border between South Vietnam and Cambodia had led the government of the Republic of Vietnam to request assistance in defending its airspace. Four F-102As of the 509th Fighter Interceptor Squadron went to Tan Son Nhut on 21 March 1962, but returned to their home base at Clark AB in the Philippines on 29 March without making any actual intercepts. Nonetheless, this *Water Glass* deployment inaugurated a year-long series of six-week rotations, with Douglas AD-5Qs of the US Navy alternating with TF-102As of the 509th FIS, which lasted until May 1963. For one year after the last *Water Glass* rotation had taken place, intermittent air defence continued to be provided for South Vietnam under the new code name of *Candy Machine*, as PACAF F-102As deployed frequently to Tan Son Nhut and Da Nang to take part in exercises.

## CIA connection

Albeit in no-way connected to the USAF (but indirectly receiving much of their equipment and support from it) a number of 'airlines' deserve mention in this story of the air wars in South East Asia, as they played an active military role and undertook operations in areas where the use of US military aircraft would have raised unacceptable diplomatic difficulties. The most notorious of these surrogate air forces was Air America, Inc. which was owned by the Central Intelligence Agency (CIA) and operated under contract from other government entities including the US Agency for International Development (USAID) and the US Information Agency (USIA). While some Air America activities, such as its work for USAID, were genuine charter airline undertakings, others were para-military operations. Notably, Air America resupplied and transported

**Right: Air America's Hueys were used widely throughout South East Asia, providing special forces and covert support, and search and rescue capability, often in the more remote areas of Laos. During the evacuation of Saigon, Air America pilots were the unsung heroes, performing hundreds of missions. This Huey is seen landing on a US Navy carrier during the final evacuation.**

**For many scheduled and non-scheduled airlines, notably Braniff, Continental, Pan American, TIA, and World Airways, the war in Southeast Asia was a source of additional revenues as substantial contracts were obtained from the Department of Defense to airlift personnel between the war zone and the United States. This Pan American 707-321C was photographed at Da Nang AB in 1966.**

Meo tribesmen operating in Laos against the Pathet Lao, and provided logistic support for the *Lima Sites* which the USAF had set up in Laos as temporary landing strips for its rescue helicopters and to house long range navigation aids. For its sundry activities Air America flew a great variety of transport aircraft including Beech 18s (and turbine-powered Volpar derivatives), Douglas C-47s, Curtiss C-46s, Fairchild C-123s, and Lockheed C-130s; as well as smaller STOLs such as the Helio U-10 and the Pilatus PC-6 Porter. It also operated Bell UH-1 and Sikorsky H-34 helicopters. Remaining in South East Asia until the bitter end, the Air America crews joined their Air Force, Navy, and Marine colleagues in the final evacuation of Saigon in April 1975.

## *Commercial participation*

Not to be confused with Air America or other pseudo airlines operating on behalf of US government agencies are the scheduled and supplemental air carriers which contributed significantly to the American war effort in South East Asia. Operating under public contracts, these airlines mainly flew charter flights between the United States and South East Asia. Furthermore, in the closing months of the war, after the US withdrawal from Vietnam, several of these airlines distinguished themselves during the so-called 'rice airlift' to Cambodia in early 1975 and during the evacuation of refugees in Vietnam. Particularly noteworthy is the last flight out of Da Nang on 29 March 1975, when a Boeing 727QC of World Airways took off with 330 persons, whereas the aircraft is certificated for a maximum of only 129 passengers!

**During the South East Asia War, Tan Son Nhut was one of the world's busiest airports. Photographed in December 1965, this is a typical scene at this congested base with two F-100Ds, a C-47, and a C-141A of the Air Force, as well as a 707 of Continental Airlines and a Navy C-1A, awaiting clearance.**

North American F-100 Super Sabres were among the initial influx of jets into the theatre, this squadron seen lined up at Tan Son Nhut in 1965. As yet, the aircraft have not received tactical camouflage. Anti-aircraft threats soon sent all aircraft scurrying to the paint shops.

## The Fast Movers Over the North

At the beginning of the sixties, although Osan AB in Korea was the only PACAF base on the Asian mainland from which 'fast movers' (jet fighters and light bombers) were operating regularly, tactical fighters were also occasionally taking part in joint exercises with friendly nations in Asia and throughout the Pacific basin. In addition, anticipating future requirements, the United States had begun funding major airfield construction projects at Ubon, Udorn, and Chiang Mai in Thailand, and new runways for the airfields at Vientiane and Saigon. While these projects were underway, Communist activities in Vietnam and Laos increased and the need was felt to boost the USAF presence on the continent with rotational deployments to Thailand being initiated in December 1960 when six F-100Ds of the 510th TFS were sent to Don Muang AB (Project *Bell Tone I*). Nine months later, *Bell Tone II* saw F-102As of the 509th FIS replacing the fighter-bombers at the Thai base. In South Vietnam, the first USAF fighters to be assigned on TDY were the four *Water Glass* F-102As of the 509th FIS sent to Tan Son Nhut AB in March 1962 to provide air defence against unidentified intruders along the Cambodian border. However, the role of these detachments was noncombatant until 9 June 1964 when eight F-100Ds, specially deployed from Clark AB to Da Nang and supported by RF-101C pathfinders and PACAF KB-50J tankers, flew a retaliatory strike against Communist antiaircraft sites to avenge the loss of two US Navy aircraft (an RF-8A and an F-8D) during reconnaissance operations over Laos.

Temporarily this strike remained an isolated incident but, less than two months later, the Gulf of Tonkin Incident cast the die for massive USAF air operations in South East Asia. Although the initial US response to North Vietnamese attacks against its destroyers operating in the Gulf of Tonkin was limited to 64 sorties by carrier-based aircraft on 5 August 1964, PACAF was soon ordered to send aircraft to the Indochina peninsula while TAC deployed a Composite Air Strike Force to Clark AB and Kadena AB, and SAC furnished KC-135A tankers. PACAF aircraft deployed at that time to South Vietnam and Thailand included 36 B-57 light bombers of the 8th and 13th TBS to Bien Hoa AB; eight F-100Ds of the 615th TFS and six F-102As of the 509th FIS to Da Nang AB; six RF-101Cs of the 15th and 45th TRS and six F-102As of the 16th FIS to Tan Son Nhut AB; ten F-100Ds of the 405th TFW to Takhli RTAFB; eight KB-50Js of the 421st ARefS to Tan Son Nhut AB and Takhli RTAFB; and eight F-105Ds of the 18th TFW to Korat RTAFB. However, no combat operations were then allowed as, on the one hand, the US Government still hoped to avoid going to war against North Vietnam and, on the other hand, the South Vietnamese government continued to require that VNAF personnel be on board US aircraft for operations in South Vietnam. Notwithstanding the fact that they were only providing a show of force, US aircraft were not immune to losses, as was dramatically shown on 1 November 1964 when five B-57s were destroyed in a Viet Cong mortar attack against Bien Hoa AB, forcing PACAF to remove most of its aircraft from Vietnam. Finally, the long-simmering tension burst into a raging war: on 14 December 1964, the first *Barrell Roll* armed reconnaissance mission was flown over Laos; on 8 February 1965, USAF aircraft struck North Vietnam; and, 11 days later, the first overt USAF mission in South Vietnam was undertaken at the request of the Republic of Vietnam.

Considered necessary by many military plan-

The 509th FIS was part of the 405th TFW based at Clark. Regular F-102A deployments were sent to both Tan Son Nhut and Da Nang. Resplendent in three-tone camouflage, this pair patrols the skies over northern Thailand.

A Douglas EB-66B Destroyer leads a flight of Republic F-105s on a blind bombing mission over North Vietnam. The EB-66 could not only navigate for the F-105s for strike accuracy, but supply ECM cover as well.

ners as early as mid-1962, air strikes against the North Vietnamese homeland had become part of contingency plans considered by the Joint Chiefs of Staff in the spring of 1964 but they were not then approved. Thus, the *Flaming Dart* strikes in which USAF aircraft took part in February 1965 were not part of a systematic air campaign against the North but were essentially reprisals for Viet Cong attacks against US Special Forces at Pleiku and Qui Nhon in the South. Adverse weather prevented USAF aircraft from joining US Navy aircraft in the 7 February strike but, on the following day, they made their first appearance north of the Demilitarized Zone when six *Farm Gate* A-1Es bombed barracks at Chap Le while F-100Ds struck antiaircraft sites and RF-101Cs provided pathfinding and damage assessment. On 11 February further USAF reprisal strikes were flown from South Vietnam

The flightline at Takhli RTAFB in Thailand bristles with F-105s eager to get at the North. The repainting schedule is getting under way, indicating a date of late 1965.

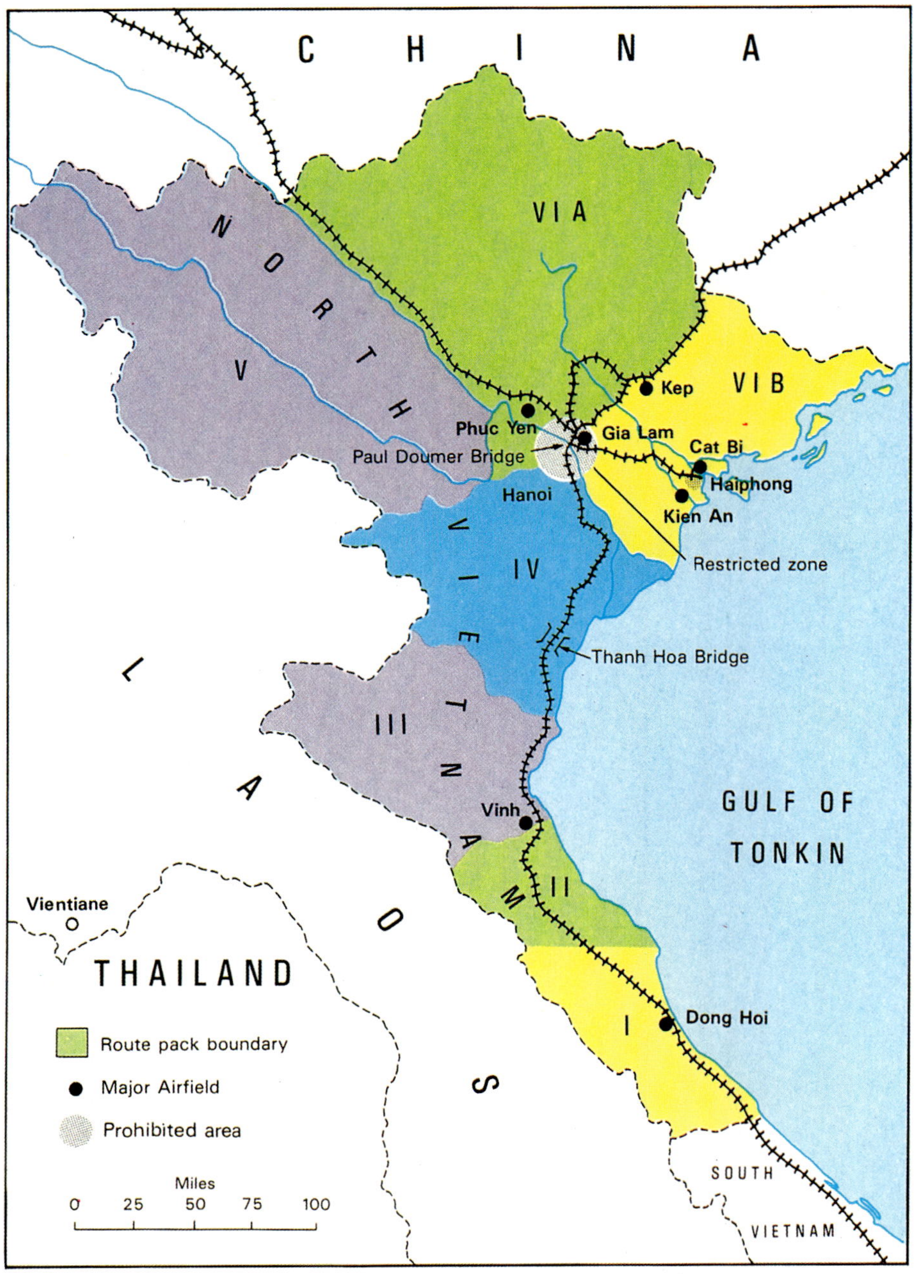


against NVA barracks at Chanh Hoa and Vit Thu Lu. Thereafter, operations against the North became part of *Rolling Thunder*, a sustained but politically constrained air campaign which lasted until the Paris Peace Talk Conference first convened in November 1968.

When it became likely that North Vietnam would have to be bombed in order to halt a losing situation in the South, the Joint Chiefs of Staff recommended a short, but unrestrained, series of operations aimed at forcing Hanoi out of the war. However, fearing the possible consequences of such an escalation, President Johnson rejected this plan and authorized instead more limited operations which were to be conducted within well-defined parameters. As *Rolling Thunder* began, objectives which could be attacked during a given week were selected in Washington from a pre-planned list of 94 targets, and local commanders received specific authorization concerning the number of sorties which could be flown. Thus deprived of the necessary flexibility to conduct an effective air campaign, the USAF and Navy aviators were sent to war with one hand, if not both, tied behind their backs. Later on, to coordinate Air Force, Navy and Marines operations when the offensive against North Vietnam was stepped up, the country was divided into seven sectors (officially designated "Route Packages", but commonly called "RPs" or "Packs".) The Air Force was assigned primary responsibility for operations in Route Package I (just north of the DMZ), Route Package V in the northwestern corner, and Route Package VIA, including Hanoi and the area northwest of the capital city. Operations in Route Packages II, III, and IV (three coastal sectors north of Route Package I) and Route Package VIB (the northernmost coastal sector, including Haiphong) were the responsibility of Task Force 77, the Navy carrier battle group operating in the Gulf of

**Left: This map shows the segmentation of North Vietnam into Route Packages. Also shown are the two bridges which caused so much trouble to the strike aircraft, both of the Navy and Air Force.**

**Below: Bearing the tail code JJ of the Korat-based 34th TFS/388th TFW, four F-105Ds drop six 750-lb bombs each during a medium-level *Rolling Thunder* sortie. During the first three years of operations against the North, Thuds were numerically the most important USAF aircraft.**

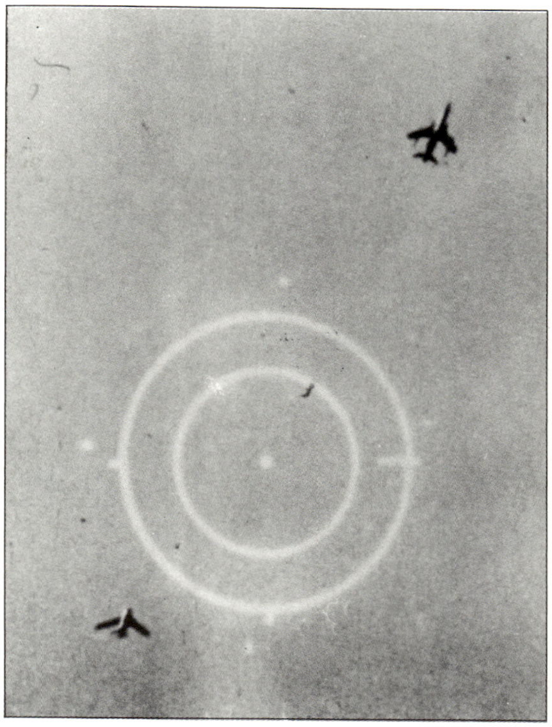

**Right: Dramatic action caught by the camera gun of an F-105 as a MiG-17 makes a firing pass at another Thunderchief. The camera-ship is trying to drive the MiG off his buddy's tail, following a strike on the notorious Paul Doumer Bridge.**

Tonkin. As could, and even should have been expected under the restrictive circumstances initially prevailing, *Rolling Thunder* never succeeded. In spite of the courage and dedication of its airmen and the heavy price paid by the nation in terms of lives, prestige and dollars, through mistakes made by its leadership the United States lost whatever chance it may have had to win the war.

Scheduled to start on 20 February 1965, Phase I of *Rolling Thunder*, a series of attacks against LOCs (Lines of Communications) in the panhandle of North Vietnam below the 20th parallel, did not get underway until 2 March as the first five missions were cancelled due to political disturbances in South Vietnam. On that date, no fewer than 111 USAF combat aircraft (44 F-105D/Fs, 40 F-100D/Fs, 20 B-57Bs and seven RF-101Cs), with KC-135As providing the necessary air refueling, attacked the Xom Bong ammunition dump some 35 miles (56 km) north of the DMZ. Only moderately successful results were obtained, five aircraft were lost and one of the pilots, Captain Hayden J. Lockhart, became the USAF's first POW of the war. The tempo of operations then increased rapidly, with USAF aircraft progressively ranging further north and strikes against preplanned targets being supplemented by armed reconnaissance sorties (flown by tactical fighters with the primary purpose of locating and attacking targets of opportunity). It was on 3 April, during this first escalation, that the USAF began its attacks against one of the most frustrating targets of the war, the Ham Rung (Dragon's Jaw) railroad and highway bridge over the Song Ma River at Thanh Hoa. Dropping 120 750-lb (340-kg) bombs and 32 Martin AGM-12 Bullpup guided missiles, the F-105Ds scored several hits but still the Chinese-engineered bridge stood up. A repeat strike the next day ended with equally disappointing results and unfortunately yielded the first USAF losses in air combat when two F-105Ds were shot down by MiG-17s south of Hanoi. For the duration of *Rolling Thunder*, the Ham Rung bridge at Thanh Hoa stubbornly refused

**Bomb-laden F-105Ds hit the tanker inbound to North Vietnam. The F-105 suffered somewhat from short range, and these refuellings were necessary to make it to Hanoi and back, especially if the fighters were going to tussle with MiGs.**

**Republic F-105D Thunderchief**

Carrying the brunt of strike operations against the North during *Rolling Thunder*, the 'Thud' had a poor reputation when first going into combat and was already scheduled to be replaced by F-4s. Reliability was progressively improved, but the F-105 required excessive runway length when operating with heavy loads in the high ambient temperature of South East Asia and was a poor performer at high altitudes. At lower altitudes, however, it was a superlative aircraft which could survive heavy battle damage. Weapons load in this view include eight 750-lb bombs, those on wing pylons being fitted with the 'daisy cutter' extended fuse.

USAF
91745
Keith Fretwell.

**Above left: Another type of Century fighter which did not fare well in South East Asia was the Lockheed Starfighter. The 435th TFS flew F-104Cs from Da Nang AB between April and December 1965. This squadron returned to South East Asia in July 1966 and operated its Starfighters from Udorn RTAFB (where this photograph was taken) until July 1967. During these two tours, the 435th lost two of its F-104s to SAMs, six to AAA, and six in operational accidents.**

**Most potent Weasel aircraft in the SEA war was the Republic F-105G, featuring the ALQ-105 integral ECM system in fuselage fairings. It also had the ability to carry the AGM-78B Standard anti-radiation missile, demonstrated here (with AGM-45 Shrike) by a 561st TFS, 388th TFW aircraft out of Korat.**

to collapse under repeated attacks by the USAF and US Navy, and it was only at the onset of *Linebacker I* in the spring of 1972 that spans of the bridge were finally brought down by laser-guided bombs dropped by F-4Ds of the 8th TFW.

## Further deployment

To support the increased scale of *Rolling Thunder* operations against the North, to undertake *Steel Tiger* interdiction strikes over Laos, and to provide air support for Allied forces in South Vietnam, the USAF began deploying additional F-100s and F-105s as well as other types of tactical fighters. McDonnell F-4C Phantoms made their appearance in South East Asia in April 1965, when the 45th TFS deployed to Ubon RTAFB; Lockheed F-104 Starfighters, which had been operating from Taiwan during the 1958 Quemoy Strait crisis, reappeared in the theatre when the 476th TFS arrived at Da Nang AB; and Northrop F-5As arrived in South Vietnam in October to conduct the *Skoshi Tiger* evaluation. However, both the B-57s and F-100s which were too slow, and the F-104s and F-5s which were too short-ranged and carried an insufficient warload, were found unsatisfactory for operations against the North. Consequently, the brunt of operations north of the DMZ was soon carried by F-105D/Fs, which became the primary strike aircraft, and by F-4Cs, which initially were used to provide MIGCAPs (combat air patrols to protect strike aircraft from the MiGs of the NVNAF), operating from Thailand and, to a much lesser extent, from South Vietnam.

In an effort to encourage North Vietnam to begin peace talks, *Rolling Thunder* operations were suspended for the first time between 12 and 17 May 1965. The lull was brief, and when US aircraft again undertook offensive operations as part of *Rolling Thunder* Phase II, new targets were authorized, including some north of the 20th parallel and along the rail line between Hanoi and the Chinese border. These raids were increasingly challenged by MiG-17s and, on 10 July 1965, two F-4C crews of the 45th TFS operating from Ubon RTAFB (Captain Thomas S. Roberts and Ronald C. Anderson, and Captains Kenneth E. Holcombe and Arthur C. Clark) shot down two enemy aircraft with Sidewinder missiles to obtain the first USAF confirmed victories of the war. No additional MiG encounters were reported for the rest of 1965, but US airmen now had to contend with a new threat as the North Vietnamese began firing Soviet-built SA-2 surface-to-air missiles.

The first SAM loss was recorded on 24 July 1965, when an F-4C was brought down. By the end of the year 180 recorded missile firings had resulted in the loss of five USAF aircraft and six USN aircraft. To counter this threat the USAF relied on four different methods: (1) in SAM-defended areas missions were flown at low altitude, thus bringing

**Northrop F-5As arrived in Vietnam for the *Skoshi Tiger* operational evaluation, but despite their astonishing agility, the type suffered from poor range and weapon load. It was not adopted by the USAF, but did form a substantial part of the VNAF strike force.**

Left: The first defence suppression aircraft were four North American F-100F *Wild Weasel I*, fitted with the APR-25/26 RHAW/launch warning receiver. Initially the F-100s were used to shepherd other strike aircraft to the radar site, but in time they gained offensive Shrike capability themselves.

Right: The 561st TFS, 388th TFW also carried the 'MD' tailcode on its F-105Gs. This bird is depicted carrying a Shrike missile. The F-105Gs were joined during the 1972 *Linebacker* raids by Weasel-configured F-4Cs.

Right: Boomer's eye view of a Republic F-105D nudging in for a post-strike refuelling. As well as carrying the war to the enemy in the form of bombing, the 'Thud' also fought many battles with the MiGs.

the aircraft below the SAMs' effective altitude but within the range of conventional antiaircraft defences; (2) violent evasive manoeuvers (jinking) were used to spoil radar tracking; (3) EB-66s were used to detect and jam enemy radars; and (4) *Wild Weasel* operations were initiated by Detachment 1 of the Tactical Warfare Center. Flying four North American F-100Fs specially fitted with RHAW (Radar Homing And Warning system), this detachment arrived at Korat RTAFB on 26 November 1965 to conduct a 90-day evaluation of SAM countermeasures. Using RHAW, the *Wild Weasel* F-100Fs were able to warn strike aircraft of impending SAM firings and, more importantly, to home in on the SAM's *Fan Song* radar guidance signals to direct strikes by F-105s assigned to *Iron Hand* SAM-suppression flights. Later on, the F-100Fs were armed with AGM-45 Shrike missiles to launch their own attacks against SAM sites but, beginning in May 1966, *Wild Weasel* operations were undertaken by specially modified EF-105Fs and, from September 1970, by the even more capable F-105Gs.

Below: An EF-105F two-seat 'Thud' hits afterburner as it departs Korat. The aircraft is from the 44th TFS, 388th TFW. The F-105F formed the basis for the most widely-used Weasel platform in South East Asia, the rear seat reconfigured to accommodate displays for the RHAWS gear.

Above: An F-4E on the tanker following a strike over North Vietnam.

Above left: The early Phantoms in South East Asia retained their peacetime colours of gull grey and white. This F-4C flies over South Vietnam in early 1966.

By the end of 1965 the USAF had 18 squadrons of fast movers in South East Asia. Five were equipped with F-105s (the 333rd, 334th and 354th TFS at Takhli RTAFB, and the 421st and 469th TFS at Korat RTAFB); six had F-4Cs (the 433rd and 497th TFS at Ubon RTAFB, the 390th TFS at Da Nang AB, and the 43rd, 557th and 558th TFS at Cam Ranh AB); four were flying F-100s (the 308th, 510th and 531st TFS at Bien Hoa AB, and the 416th TFS at Tan Son Nhut AB); the 4503rd TFS was equipped with F-5As at Bien Hoa AB, the 509th FIS was maintaining F-102A detachments at the Don Muang Airport and at Tan Son Nhut AB, and the 8th TBS was operating B-57B/Cs from Da Nang AB. Other USAF jet aircraft then stationed at air bases in South Vietnam and Thailand were the RF-101Cs of the 15th and 20th TRS, the KC-135As of the 4252nd Air Refueling Squadron at the Don Muang Airport, the RB-66s configured for Electronic Warfare of the 41st TRS, the F-100Fs configured for *Wild Weasel* operations with Detachment 1 of the Tactical Warfare Center at Korat RTAFB, and special detachments flying RB-57Es and U-2Cs.

## Phase II ends

Phase II of *Rolling Thunder* ended without achieving the hoped-for results when the United States unilaterally declared a 'Christmas Truce' in December 1965. However, as Hanoi still showed no sign of compromise, limited strikes were again flown over lower North Vietnam from 31 January until 31 March 1966 (*Rolling Thunder* Phase III), giving place in April to massive Phase IV air operations against all of North Vietnam, with the exception of a few sanctuaries around Hanoi and Haiphong, and along the Chinese border. New targets included petroleum-oil-lubricant (POL) storage areas, first bombed by the USAF on 29 June 1966.

Enemy aircraft, which in the meantime had increased in number and were now flown by better trained pilots, rose to the challenge, and losses quickly mounted on both sides. For the NVNAF, increased combat activities against USAF fast movers translated in the loss during 1966 of 13 MiG-17s and four MiG-21s (this new adversary was first encountered on 25 April and the first two MiG-21s were shot down by F-4Cs of the 480th TFS/35th TFW on 14 July). For the USAF, which failed to achieve air superiority over the North Vietnamese fighters effectively controlled by their GCI and favouring hit-and-run attacks, the most serious consequence was the loss of effectiveness of its operations as its heavily-laden strike aircraft were frequently forced to jettison their ordnance to fight off the interceptors. On the other hand, the increase in losses to enemy fighters was offset by better tactics and jamming techniques against SAMs, with 1,039 recorded missile firings result-

Although usually carrying bombs or napalm, the Phantom could also launch rockets, these carried in pods under the wings. Unlucky Vietnamese are about to receive a full salvo here.

**Above: Its pilot having failed to drop the external wing tanks, this MiG-17 burns fiercely after being hit by 20-mm shells. Shared by two pilots of the 388th TFW, Major Ralph L. Kuster, Jr. and Capt. Larry D. Wiggins, who respectively flew F-105Ds from the 13th and 469th TFS, this victory was gained on 3 June 1967.**

**Below: Douglas EB-66B ECM platform leads a flight of F-4C Phantoms on a medium level bombing mission.**

ing in only 34 US aircraft being lost to SA-2s during 1966.

Overall, USAF losses in South East Asia during the year totalled 379 aircraft, including no fewer than 126 F-105s (a whopping 15.1 percent of the 833 Thunderchiefs built by Republic). Of these, five were lost to SAMs, three to MiGs, 103 to ground fire and 15 to operational accidents. For comparison the F-4s, which by then were almost as numerous as the F-105s, suffered only 42 combat losses and 14 operational losses. Other aircraft lost in South East Asia during 1966 to all causes included 41 A-1s, 38 O-1s, 26 F-100s, 16 RF-101s, and 13 B-57s.

### *New Year: new fury*

Following Christmas and New Year interludes, the year 1967 began with a new fury as the USAF sought ways to reduce the MiG threat prior to stepping up its operations against the North. Hence on 2 January a force of F-4Cs from the 8th TFW, using new electronic jamming pods and simulating an F-105 strike, successfully engaged the NVNAF and destroyed seven MiG-21s without damage to USAF aircraft. Two more victories were obtained four days later when F-4Cs lured the MiGs by flying a mission profile similar to that used by unarmed reconnaissance aircraft.

A six-day truce in observance of the 1967 Tet (Lunar New Year) holiday marked the transition between Phases IV and V of *Rolling Thunder*, with the latter commencing on 14 February and ending on 24 December 1967. Once again, the United States increased its pressure on North Vietnam by authorizing attacks on a new series of targets: notably the key military airfields at Kep, Kien An and Hoa Lac, which were first struck in April; the all-important Phuc Yen Air Base, which was first attacked in October; and military facilities within the previously excluded areas around Hanoi and along the border with China. In the course of these operations an additional 52 enemy aircraft were shot down by USAF crews. On the other side of the ledger, the USAF ended its third year of operations over North Vietnam with the loss of 11 F-105s and 9 F-4s to MiGs, and 17 F-105s and 3 F-4s to SAMs. During 1967, other losses to hostile actions claimed 294 USAF aircraft, while 87 aircraft were lost to operational losses. As in prior years, it was the F-105 which bore the brunt of the fighting and 113 Thuds were lost to all causes during the year. Nonetheless, and even though they flew strike missions, the F-105s did fairly well in defending themselves against MiGs, with 22.5 of the 59 'kills' credited during 1967 to USAF fast movers being obtained by Thuds. On 10 March 1967 Captain Max C. Brestel of the 354th TFS/355th TFW became the first USAF pilot in South East Asia to destroy two enemy aircraft in the course of a sortie. New fast mover weapons introduced during 1967 by the USAF included the F-4D version of the Phantom, with which the 555th TFS/8th TFW at Ubon RTAFB was re-equipped at the end of May; the AGM-62A Walleye TV-guided missile, which was first used in combat on 24 August; and the AIM-4 Falcon air-to-air missile, which first scored a kill on 26 October when it was used by a 555th TFS crew to shoot down a MiG-17.

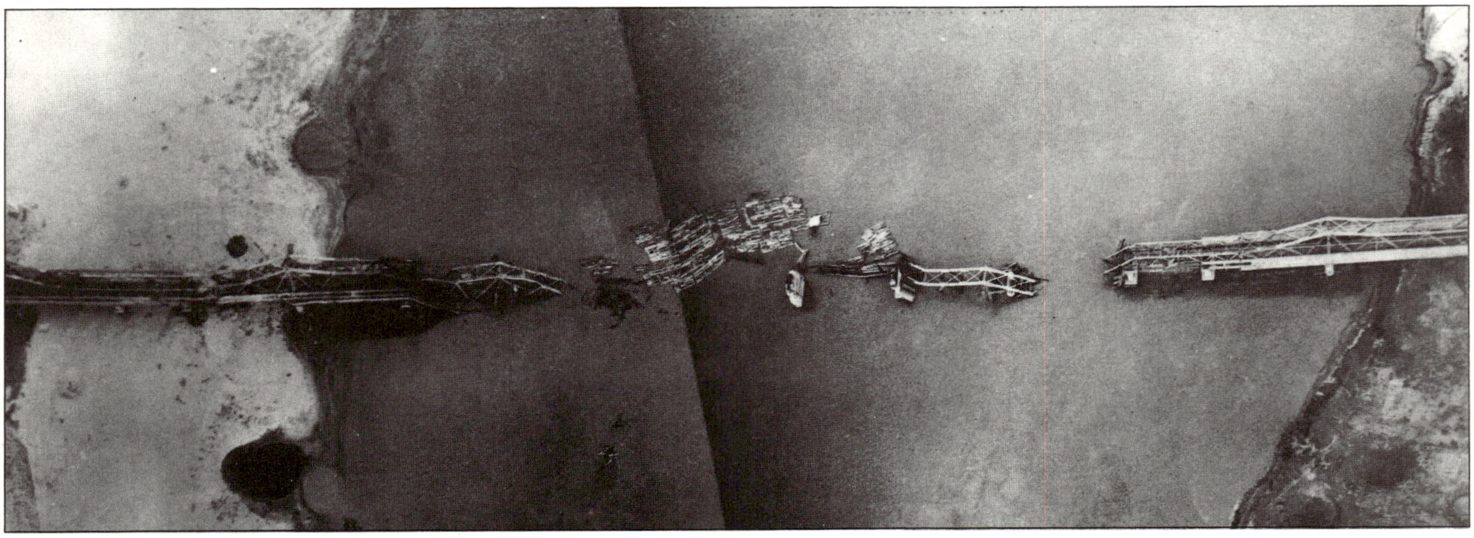

Top: The Paul Doumer Bridge was visited by F-105s on 18 December 1967, destroying several spans. These were not down long, the Vietnamese rapidly rebuilding this vital river crossing.

Loran-equipped 8th TFW F-4 releases a 3,000-lb laser-guided bomb. These weapons were used to finally drop the Thanh Hoa bridge.

Below: Aircraft from the 433rd and 435th TFS, 8th TFW inbound to North Vietnam. The nearest aircraft carries a pair of LGBs on the wing pylons. Two Sparrows are carried.

The sixth and last phase of *Rolling Thunder* was initiated at the beginning of 1968. However, three months later President Johnson imposed a halt to all attacks north of the 19th parallel while on 1 November 1968 he extended the halt of bombing operations to the whole of North Vietnam. Consequently, as USAF aircraft operated far south beyond the normal MiG operating areas for most of 1968, air combat was less frequent and the NVNAF only lost five MiG-17s and three MiG-21s to USAF fast movers. Likewise, USAF losses to SAMs and MiGs dropped from 50 in 1967 to 12 in 1968; an additional 379 USAF fixed-wing aircraft and helicopters were lost to all other causes, including 257 shot down by conventional ground fire and 35 aircraft destroyed in Viet Cong attacks on air bases in South Vietnam (most of them taking place during the 1968 Tet Offensive).

The bombing halt imposed by President Johnson in November 1968 was confirmed by President Nixon in January 1969 and remained in force for more than three years. During that period of relative calm, the fast movers did not take part in offensive operations over the North and only flew over North Vietnam to escort reconnaissance aircraft. Hence from 14 February 1968 until 21 February 1972, the USAF did not score a single aerial victory and lost only one fighter to MiGs.

## *Freedom Train*

The spring 1972 North Vietnamese offensive prompted President Nixon to authorize a resumption of the air war against the North. Initially, from 6 April 1972, *Freedom Train* operations were confined below the 20th parallel but, on 8 May, presidential authorization was received for the initiation of *Linebacker I*. Intended to stop the flow of supplies entering North Vietnam and thus curtail Hanoi's war-making capabilities, this operation was directed against the entire enemy transportation system, including rail lines in close proximity to the People's Republic of China. During *Linebacker I* the systematic aerial bombardment of major bridges in North Vietnam was characterized by the extensive use of precision guided weapons, the EOGB (Electro-Optical Guided Bomb) and the LGB (Laser Guided Bomb), the so-called 'smart bombs', and soon the expected results were obtained. On 27 April Phantoms from the 8th TFW badly damaged the notorious Ham Rung bridge at Thanh Hoa with 2,000-lb (907-kg) EOGBs and, 16 days later, finally dropped it with 3,000-lb (1361-kg) LGBs. A similar fate befell the Paul Doumer bridge on the outskirts of Hanoi when this durable target was put out of commission by smart bombs dropped on 10-11 May. By the end of May 20 other important bridges on the rail lines running northeast, northwest and south from Hanoi, and between that city and Haiphong, had also been rendered unusable. Moreover, as President Nixon had for the first time authorized the mining of the port of Haiphong and other important harbour facilities through which North Vietnam received most of its war supplies, the stated objectives of *Linebacker I* were achieved with conspicuous success.

While losses of strike aircraft were kept within acceptable limits through the employment of improved ECM pods, chaffs and *Wild Weasels*, the success achieved during *Linebacker I* was obtained at a fairly high cost, as between the end of 1967 and the spring of 1972 the NVNAF combat inventory had been quintupled (to over 200 interceptors) and as the North Vietnamese aircrews, GCI

operators and SAM crews had developed effective tactics. Thus, while the fast movers claimed the destruction of 34 MiG-21s and 8 MiG-19s between 16 April and 15 October 1972, the USAF lost 44 aircraft (27 to MiGs, 12 to SAMs and 5 to AAA) during *Linebacker I*. In spite of the disappointing 1.55 to 1 kill ratio, it was then that the USAF obtained all its three aces of the war. As by then Thuds were only used in the *Wild Weasel* anti-SAM role, top honours went to F-4 crews of the 432nd TRW (although designated a reconnaissance wing and assigned RF-4Cs, this unit also regrouped the F-4Ds and F-4Es of the 13th, 58th, 523rd, and 555th Tactical Fighter Squadrons which were given primary responsibility for MIGCAP). The aces from the 432nd TRW were Captain Charles B. DeBellevue, a 'backseater' Weapon Systems Officer (WSO) with the 555th TFS (four MiG-21s and two MiG-19s shot down between 10 May and 9 September 1972); Captain Jeffrey S. Feinstein, a WSO of the 13th TFS (five MiG-21s between 16 April and 13 October 1972); and Captain Richard S. Ritchie, a pilot of the 555th TFS (five MiG-21s between 10 May and 28 August 1972).

### Pressure mounts at home

Mounting public opposition to the war and perceived progress in the ongoing Paris peace negotiations led the US Government to refrain from exploiting the advantage gained during *Linebacker I* and instead to order on 23 October 1972 a halt of bombing operations north of the 20th parallel. However, hopes for a quick settlement were soon dashed as the North Vietnamese negotiators, seeking to capitalize on antiwar sentiment in the United States, stalled and raised new objections to previously agreed upon conditions for a cease fire. Once again President Nixon was forced to send American airmen over the North.

*Linebacker II*, conducted from 18 through 29 December 1972, was an intensive USAF and Navy day-and-night campaign against electrical power plants, lines of communications, rail yards, ports,

**Above: Captain Richard S. Ritchie, of the 555th TFS/432nd TRW, was the USAF's only fighter pilot ace of the South East Asia War. Teamed with Capt. Charles B. DeBellevue as his WSO, he shot down one MiG-21 on 10 May 1972, two on 8 July, and one on 28 August. His other victory, also against a MiG-21, was obtained on 31 May when Capt. Lawrence H. Pettit was his WSO.**

**Above left: Captain Jeffrey S. Feinstein, a WSO with the 13th TFS/432nd TRW, was credited with five MiG-21 kills between 16 April and 13 October 1972.**

**The F-4E Phantom introduced the internal gun, which proved useful for close-in work, with seven MiG-kills put down to the cannon. These sharkmouthed fighters are from the 469th TFS, 388th TFW out of Korat.**

## McDonnell F-4E Phantom II

Shown in the markings of the 469th TFS/388th TFW, which operated from Korat RTAFB, this F-4E-35-MC is typical of late model USAF Phantom IIs; it was assigned to Col. A. K. MacDonald, the C.O. of the 388th TFW. The aircraft is shown with typical armament for anti-MiG escort operations, i.e. nose-mounted 20 mm M61A cannon, four AIM-7 Sparrows beneath the fuselage, and four AIM-9 Sidewiders on wing pylons. The two external tanks each have a 600-gallon capacity. At first reluctant to comply with Secretary McNamara's mandate to acquire Navy-developed F-4s in lieu of additional F-105s, the Air Force went on to become the main user of Phantom IIs, with the type proving effective both in the air combat and strike roles.

JV
AF
70
308

**USAF MiG killers at Udorn RTAFB on 11 August 1972. From left to right are Lt. Col. Carl G. Baily, Capt. Charles B. DeBellevue, Capt. Jeffrey S. Feinstein and Capt. Richard S. Ritchie.**

**A most unusual and rather effective apron camouflage scheme was tested at Korat RTAFB in the last phase of the war. The aircraft on the ramp are Vought A-7Ds, with the tail code MB identifying the 355th TFS/354th TFW.**

POL storage, military depots and airfields in the Hanoi and Haiphong areas. Throwing all its reserves into the battle (no fewer than 1,293 SAM firings were reported during this 11-day period), North Vietnam attempted to blunt the decisive American offensive; however, some 3,800 sorties (729 B-52 sorties, 613 strike sorties by USAF tactical aircraft, 386 sorties by naval aircraft, and 2,066 sorties by various types of USAF aircraft) nearly overwhelmed enemy air defences. Still the most numerous among the fast movers the F-4D/F-4Es flew day and night sorties, providing MIGCAPS, long-range navigation and target acquisition for delivery of unguided bombs by strike aircraft; escorting strike aircraft and B-52s; laying down chaff corridors; and supplementing the F-105Gs in providing SAM suppression. A-7Ds and F-111As flew most of the tactical strike sorties, putting to good use their modern and highly accurate ordnance delivery systems, with the F-111As redeeming themselves from their earlier unsuccessful dêbut during low-level attacks in poor weather conditions.

## *Peace nears*

During *Linebacker II*, five air combat victories (three by F-4Ds of the 555th TFS and two by B-52 gunners) were scored and North Vietnam's transportation network and industries were devastated. More importantly, the primary political objective of this operation was achieved as Hanoi signaled its intent to conclude the peace negotiations without further delay. As a result, bombing north of the 20th parallel was halted on 30 December 1972; however, south of that parallel a further 716 tactical strike sorties and 535 bombing sorties were flown during the first two weeks of 1973. It was during this final phase of the war that the 137th and last USAF victory of the war was obtained on 8 January 1973, when Captain Paul D. Howman and First Lt. Lawrence K. Kullman shot down a MiG-21 while flying an F-4D from the 4th TFS/432nd TRW. One week later, as the peace negotiations were finally reaching their conclusion, all air strikes against North Vietnam were halted and, following the signing of the Paris Agreement on 23 January, all types of air operations ceased on 27 January. President Nixon could then proclaim that 'Peace with Honour' had been achieved. Virtually unrestrained use of air power during *Linebacker II*

had finally succeeded in forcing Hanoi to seek an end to the conflict with the United States. This was, however, a Pyrrhic victory foreboding a tragic ending for the wars in South East Asia.

Fast mover crews had accounted for 135 (66 MiG-21s, 61 MiG-17s, and eight MiG-19s) of the 137 USAF victories, with the other two victories being credited to B-52 gunners. The top scoring wing was the 8th TFW (38.5 kills), while the top scoring squadron was the 555th TFS (39 victories) which saw combat operations in South East Asia from February 1966 until January 1973 and was successively assigned to the 8th TFW and to the 432nd TRW. Of the 135 victories obtained by fighter crews, 107.5 were obtained while flying F-4C/F-4D/F-4Es, and 27.5 while flying F-105D/F-105Fs. More than two-thirds of these victories were obtained solely with air-to-air missiles (50 with Sparrows, 33 with Sidewinders, and five with Falcons), 38 solely with gunfire, and the balance resulted from combinations of weapons or manoeuvring tactics. Even the F-4E, which had been specially developed to provide a built-in gun for the Phantom, obtained only seven of its 21 victories with the nose mounted M61 Vulcan 20-mm cannon.

**ECM-equipped F-111As overfly Thailand. The F-111 had an inauspicious start to its combat record, losing several aircraft in a short space of time. After the initial evaluation deployment, the F-111s returned, and scored a series of successful raids, doing much to alleviate the disappointment.**

**An F-111A lands at Udorn AB in Thailand. The aircraft is from the 429th TFS, 474th TFW, detached from Nellis to the 432nd TRW for South East Asia operations.**

The Martin B-57G *Tropic Moon III* introduced low-light-level TV, FLIR and other sensors for interdiction work over the Trail. This 13th TBS aircraft exhibits the modified nose which contained much of the new equipment. Night attacks with laser-guided bombs were particularly successful.

## The Fast Movers over Over Laos and Cambodia

Combat operations over Laos, which had begun on 9 June 1964 and thus preceded those over North Vietnam, continued until 17 April 1973. Yet, they never attracted as much public attention as the air war against North Vietnam. Conducted from bases in South Vietnam and Thailand, the USAF air interdiction campaign in Laos fell into three broad categories: *Barrel Roll*, *Steel Tiger*, and *Tiger Hound*. *Barrel Roll* sorties were flown over northern Laos mainly by fast movers and A-1s, with B-52s entering the fray in February 1970, to provide support for the Royal Laotian Army and the CIA-trained Meo tribesmen led by Major General Vang Pao, and to defend US assets in Laos, notably *Lima Sites* and TACAN (TACtical Air Navigation) facilities. On the other hand, *Steel Tiger* and *Tiger Hound* operations were flown directly in support of the war in South Vietnam, as they were intended to interdict North Vietnamese traffic along the segments of the Ho Chi Minh Trail which ran south along the Laotian panhandle from the Mu Gia Pass to the border with Cambodia. North of the 17th parallel (i.e. west of the DMZ separating North and South Vietnam), *Steel Tiger* strikes could only be flown with the approval of the US Embassy in Vietnam, whereas southward *Tiger Hound* missions came under the responsibility of The Commander, US Military Assistance Command, Vietnam.

As the North Vietnamese favoured night movements along the Trail to avoid detection and air attack, for the most part USAF fast movers proved ineffective in the *Steel Tiger/Tiger Hound* areas. The B-57G, however, was the exception to the rule as this specially modified twinjet tactical bomber performed well in this difficult role. Night missions over the Ho Chi Minh Trail had been flown by the B-57s of the 8th and 13th Tactical Bomb Squadrons since 1965; however, while possessing the long loiter characteristics required for effective operations in the trail busting role, they lacked the necessary equipment to detect truck traffic at night and had to rely on FACs and flare-dropping aircraft to accomplish their tasks. To provide the Canberra with self-contained night interdiction capability, a few aircraft were fitted with a low light level television (LLLTV) camera in a wing pod and were used in combat from December 1967 until July 1968. Results of this *Tropic Moon II* programme were sufficiently promising to warrant the installation in 16 aircraft of a more sophisticated system comprising a forward-looking radar, an infra-red sensor, LLLTV and a laser marking device. Designated B-57Gs, the *Tropic Moon III* aircraft were operated by the 13th TBS from Ubon RTAFB between September 1970 and April 1972 and, when their complex systems operated reliably, were found highly effective in detecting traffic on the Trail and accurately attacking convoys with laser guided bombs.

### Tactical support

While the interdiction campaign along the Trail accounted for the bulk of its sorties over Laos, the USAF also flew tactical support sorties not only as part of the *Barrel Roll* operation but also to provide cover for ground troops operating across the Laos/South Vietnam border. In particular, fast movers and B-52s played an important role during Operation *Lam Son 719/Dewey Canyon III* in February-March 1971, and US tactical aircraft were credited with the destruction of nearly 100 Communist tanks and armoured fighting vehicles.

Whereas the Laotian Government had requested American military assistance as early as 1964, Cambodia, allegedly remaining neutral until 1970, effectively aligned itself with communist nations. Hence the Viet Cong and the NVA benefited from sanctuaries in Cambodia from which they mounted trans-border operations against Vietnam. Inevitably, this situation led to occasional violations of Cambodian neutrality by allied aircraft pursuing Communist forces as they retreated to safety across the border. The first of these intrusions was claimed to have taken place on 31 July 1966 when USAF aircraft were said to have bombed Cambodian villages: the United States, however, categorically denied the incident and stated that the villages which had been attacked were in South Vietnam. More incidents of this

This 432nd TRW F-4E lands back at Udorn following a strike over Cambodia. The date was 14th August 1973. On the following day, USAF strike aircraft flew their last combat mission in the theatre until the Koh Tang incident.

nature took place as time went by and as the Communists became more blatant in their use of sanctuaries. Nevertheless, the United States refrained from deliberately bombing enemy troops and facilities in Cambodia until 18 March 1969. Then, in retaliation for a new Communist offensive against Saigon which had been launched from sanctuaries in Cambodia, President Nixon at last authorized B-52 strikes against these bases. Thirteen months later the new Cambodian Premier, General Lon Nol, specifically requested direct American assistance in expelling Communist forces from his nation's territory. Jumping at the opportunity of finally being able to eliminate enemy troops and supplies in safe-havens across the border of South Vietnam, USAF and VNAF tactical aircraft struck at Communist targets in Cambodia beginning on 24 April 1970. Six days later fast movers and A-1s provided air support for US and RVN ground operations in Cambodia. Strongly opposed in the United States by the anti-war movement, this offensive was limited to areas within 20 miles (32 km) of the South Vietnamese-Cambodian border and lasted only two months. However, the withdrawal of Allied forces from Cambodia did not end USAF tactical operations in that country; fast movers and gunships went on to support Cambodian troops in their fight against the no longer wanted Viet Cong and NVA and to provide escort for convoys bringing food and supplies on the Mekong. In fact, American air operations in Cambodia went on even after the signing of the Paris Agreement and ended only on 15 August 1973, when an A-7D from the 354th Tactical Fighter Wing flew the last sortie over Cambodia to end USAF combat operations in South East Asia in compliance with a mandate from the US Congress.

**Many of the strikes in Cambodia and Laos were handled by the venerable A-1 Skyraider, its manoeuvrability and slow speed making it an accurate attack platform. Here an A-1E pulls hard away as a Communist hide-out receives a full dose of napalm, one of the favoured weapons for counter-insurgency work.**

The Martin B-57Bs of the 8th and 13th TBS were constantly involved with operations against Viet Cong in South Vietnam. Bombs were carried in a rotary bomb bay, which swivelled round to reveal the bombs before release.

## *The Fast Movers in the In-Country War*

In South Vietnam, where the role of the *Farm Gate* detachment had quickly progressed from its originally planned training nature to one of active involvement in counter insurgency operations (albeit in most instances with Vietnamese officers giving the authorization for releasing weapons), the fast movers initially were deployed only as a show of force as, flying without Vietnamese officers as crew members, they were forbidden from taking part in combat operations. However, on 18 February 1965 the South Vietnamese removed this constraint and specifically requested that the USAF commence flying in-country attack missions. The next day, B-57Bs of the 13th TBS flew the first combat sorties when they bombed Viet Cong concentrations near Bien Gia, east of Saigon. For the next eight years fast movers operated continuously in support of frustrating search-and-destroy ground operations and to blunt several Communist offensives.

By the end of 1965 the USAF had 11 squadrons of fast movers operating from Bien Hoa, Cam Ranh Bay, Da Nang, and Tan Son Nhut Air Bases in South Vietnam. Four of these squadrons were flying 72 F-100D/F-100Fs, four flew 72 F-4Cs, one had six F-102As for air defence, and one had 24 B-57B/B-57Cs; in addition, the 4503rd TFS (Provisional) had 12 F-5As to conduct the *Skoshi Tiger* combat evaluations of the small Northrop fighter.

Early success of VC mortar and satchel attacks forced the USAF to undertake an emergency construction programme to provide protection for aircraft at bases in South Vietnam. Sand bags quickly gave place to open steel revetments for two tactical fighters, with hardened shelters housing only one aircraft later becoming the standard.

**Above: Strike camera view as an F-100 lets fly with a full load of 2.75-in unguided rockets. The target was a Viet Cong position near Ban Me Thuot, South Vietnam.**

**Above right: Communist structures near Bac Lieu receive a pounding from a low-flying 'Hun'. Most 'dumb' ordnance was employed by the F-100s, including napalm.**

**With the afterburner of its Pratt & Whitney J57-P-21A turbojet glowing, an F-100D of the 615th TFS/35th TFW rolls down the runway at Phan Rang AB. During the war, the USAF lost 186 'Huns' to AAA, seven during enemy attack against its air bases, and 45 in operational accidents.**

The F-5A, however, was not retained for further use by the USAF (most *Skoshi Tiger* aircraft were ultimately transferred to the VNAF in April 1967), and the F-102A was found to be of limited value as it could not be used for ground support. On the other hand, even though well adapted to its mission, the B-57 was no longer available in sufficient number to equip additional squadrons, and soon F-100s and F-4s became numerically the most important fast movers in South Vietnam. In particular, the Super Sabre (affectionately known as the 'Hun', a contraction of its numerical designation) proved ideally suited as its performance was sufficient for in-country operations where there existed little or no risk of enemy air opposition. Accordingly, the number of F-100 squadrons grew rapidly and at the beginning of 1967 11 TFS were flying 198 of these aircraft from bases in South Vietnam; seven squadrons then flew 126 F-4Cs and one squadron was still equipped with F-5As.

## Construction work

To provide facilities for the additional fast movers and other types needed to support expanded operations in South Vietnam (between January 1965 and September 1967 USAF aircraft flew no fewer than 1,000,000 sorties), a massive construction programme had been approved which soon resulted in a first-class network of air bases throughout the Republic of Vietnam. Notably, operations began from Phan Rang AB in March 1966, from Tuy Hoa AB in November 1966, and from Phu Cat AB in May 1967, thus enabling the USAF to deploy more fast movers for in-

MY GAL
MY GAL
SAL III

### North American F-100D Super Sabre

Although Super Sabres flew sorties over Laos and North Vietnam in the early phases of American involvement in combat operations in South East Asia, 'Huns' were primarily used for in-country operations as their performance was not sufficient for missions over the heavily defended North. Peaking in 1968, when regular Air Force units were supplemented by four Air National Guard Squadrons, F-100s were finally withdrawn from South Vietnam in July 1971 after flying over 360,000 combat missions. Carrying four 750-lb bombs and two external tanks, this F-100D-75-NA bears the HE tail code of the 416th TFS/37th TFW at Phu Cat AB, Republic of Vietnam.

**Above:** The Martin B-57s flew many missions at night, when the good navigational aids carried by the Canberras came into play, and when ground defences were at a disadvantage. Bombs were also carried under the wings, as well as internally.

**Above right:** Agility, low-cost and good weapons-carrying ability were the main attributes of the Cessna A-37 Dragonfly, which was adopted during 1969 to replace some B-57 and F-100 outfits. This A-37A was used by the 14th SOW, out of Bien Hoa.

**One unusual job for the fast-movers was protection of *Ranch Hand* defoliation flights, which had suffered greatly at the hands of ground defences. These UC-123B spray-planes are closely guarded by an F-4C. During the conflict, some F-4Cs themselves were tested with spray gear to cut losses among the C-123s. The tests were dropped, and the Provider stayed on.**

country operations. On these new bases, as well as at older facilities, the USAF installed hardened aircraft shelters and steel revetments to provide effective protection against rocket and mortar attacks by the Viet Cong. The need for such protective measures can be gauged from the fact that during 1967 alone 47 US fixed-wing aircraft and helicopters, as well as 34 Vietnamese aircraft and helicopters, were destroyed or damaged in the course of enemy attacks against air bases.

## *The Guard joins in*

As the new bases became operational, Huns continued to bear the brunt of in-country operations (with the Air National Guard providing in 1968-69 four squadrons of F-100Cs and volunteer personnel to man a USAF F-100 unit) but newer aircraft were also on their way. Beginning in July 1967 an uprated version of the Cessna T-37 jet trainer, the A-37A, was tested under combat conditions by the 3rd TFW and its successful evaluation led to the adoption of the A-37B version as a standard light attack aircraft for operations in South Vietnam. Coming off the production line in 1968, A-37Bs were first used during the following year to replace the B-57s of the 8th TBS and the F-100s of the 90th TFS (respectively redesignated the 8th and 90th Attack Squadrons upon their conversion). Standard B-57s departed South Vietnam in October 1969, but F-100s soldiered on until July 1971, by which time they had flown 360,283 combat sorties for a loss of 243 (of which 45 were due to non-combat causes) of these aircraft.

Two-thirds of the fast mover sorties were flown on preplanned missions, with the balance being undertaken specifically to assist ground troops engaged by the enemy. Most of these sorties were day missions by flights of two to four aircraft. Typically, each aircraft in a flight was loaded with a different combination of weapons (general purpose bombs or rocket pods for use against fortifications, or CBUs or napalm cannisters for use against enemy troops in the open) to achieve maximum flexibility against any type of target. Daylight operations, however, were not sufficient to defeat an enemy which relied extensively on guerrilla tactics and made full use of inclement weather and darkness. Accordingly, using ground-based MSQ-77 radar, the USAF developed a system to direct fast movers and B-52s accurately on target regardless of the weather. A first MSQ-77 station was installed at Bien Hoa in April 1966 and, three months later, five units were in operation to cover each of the corps areas and enable the mounting of *Combat Skyspot*/*Combat Proof* sorties on a regular basis.

Albeit lacking the loiter capability of the venerable 'Spad' (the A-1 Skyraider), the fast movers

**Above: The *Skoshi Tiger* Northrop F-5As were found to be more suited to life over South Vietnam than they had over the North, but their load-carrying ability still left them short of the requirement. Most were handed over to the VNAF.**

generally proved effective in blunting VC and NVA attacks. Their success, however, was never more evident than in 1968 during the Tet offensive and the siege of Khe Sanh (during which as many as 350 fast movers were used daily to help the Marines beat off a major North Vietnamese offensive). After airpower had significantly helped to inflict these two costly defeats on the Viet Cong and its North Vietnamese backers, the United States felt confident enough to begin a phased withdrawal and implement a Vietnamization programme.

During 1970 this reduction in USAF activities resulted in the vacating of four air bases (Binh Thuy in March, Pleiku in June, Vung Tau in July, and Tuy Hoa in October) and the inactivation or return to the United States of three Tactical Fighter Wings. During the following year, Bien Hoa and Phu Cat Air Bases were handed over to the VNAF and one more TFW was transferred out of Vietnam. The transfer of bases from USAF to VNAF jurisdiction was scheduled to be completed during 1972 and, indeed, two more bases (Phan Rang and Cam Ranh Bay) were vacated by the USAF in March of that year. It was then, however, that North Vietnam mounted a major offensive against the Republic of Vietnam, thus quickly forcing the USAF to undertake the *Constant Guard* deploy-

**Above: A number of two-seat F-100F were used, including this 352nd TFS, 35th TFW aircraft out of Phan Rang. As well as accompanying strikes, these aircraft sometimes undertook fast-mover FAC missions.**

**'Bettie Boop' was an F-100D of the 615th TFS, 35th TFW. The 'Hun' bore the brunt of operations in the South, racking up more missions than any other type of aircraft in the inventory.**

Vought's A-7D Corsair II had flown many missions over the North from its Thai bases. During the *Mayaguez* incident during May 1975, the A-7s were called upon to provide tactical airpower against Khmer Rouge holding the island of Koh Tang. Illustrated is a 3rd TFS, 388th TFW aircraft which flew from Korat.

ments of air units to South East Asia.

Even though expected, the North Vietnamese offensive which began in the early morning hours of 30 March 1972 caught the USAF at the wrong time. On one hand, its strength in South Vietnam had been reduced to only some 83 fast movers (60 F-4Ds at Da Nang and 23 A-37Bs at Bien Hoa) in addition to 161 F-4s, 16 F-105s, and 10 B-57s at four Thai bases and, on the other hand, late monsoon weather curtailed its air operations. During the five weeks following the start of the enemy offensive, rapid trans-oceanic deployments brought an additional 174 fast movers to Thailand and South Vietnam, while improving weather conditions enabled the USAF simultaneously to step up its actitivies in the south (the number of fast mover sorties jumped from 247 in March 1972 to 7,516 in May) and to launch the *Linebacker I* operation against the North. Ten weeks after it had been launched, the North Vietnamese offensive was finally defeated, thanks in large part to the effectiveness of the air support by USAF tactical and strategic aircraft. Once again, the USAF could withdraw aircraft from the theatre while the last US ground combat troops left the Republic of Vietnam on 12 August 1972. Soon the war was also to end for American airmen.

F-100Fs (foreground) and F-100Ds (background) receive attention in their revetments. Individual bays for aircraft were common as the VC sapper activity reached epidemic levels. The base is Phan Rang and the aircraft from the 35th TFW.

In addition to their primary duty of providing air support for allied ground troops, the fast movers were also tasked for air defence. Initially, this mission had been assigned to specialized interceptor units, with the first *Water Glass* deployment taking place in March 1962 when four F-102As were sent to Tan Son Nhut AB. However, the threat of North Vietnamese operations over the South never materialized and the last F-102As were withdrawn from the Republic of Vietnam in September 1968. Just prior to that, however, F-4Ds of the 366th TFW were involved in a bizarre incident when on the night of 16/17 June 1968 they were sent to intercept enemy helicopters thought to be operating off the South Vietnamese coast near the DMZ. Getting poor return on their radar scope, the fighters believed they had made contact and fired AIM-7 Sparrow air-to-air missiles. Tragically, instead, three allied warships (the USS *Boston*, the HMAS *Hobart*, and the USS *Edson*) were struck by the missiles, killing two Australian sailors and wounding seven others.

After the spring 1972 offensive had been checked, fast mover operations in South Vietnam were rapidly reduced as the VNAF was by then quite capable of taking care of most of the ARVN needs for air support. Moreover, progress was finally being made at the Paris Peace Conference and the United States could at last prepare to complete the withdrawal of its forces from the Republic of Vietnam.

Following the signing of the armistice, the last in-country sorties were flown on 27 January 1973 and all USAF aircraft left the country by the end of the following month.

### *Final action*

The USAF retained a dwindling number of fast movers on Thai bases. In March 1975, however, the Thai government requested that all US forces be withdrawn within 12 months and plans were made to accede to this demand within the imparted timetable. Nevertheless, in May 1975 fast movers (A-7s, F-4s and F-111s) joined other USAF, USN, and USMC aircraft in the rescue of the SS *Mayaguez* and its crew at Koh Tang Island off the coast of Cambodia. This was the curtain call for USAF operations in South East Asia; on 31 October 1975 the final contingent of USAF personnel in Thailand departed Nakhon Phanom RTAFB, and on 20 June 1976 U Tapao RTNAF became the last wartime base to be returned to Thai control.

## *Spads and Gunships: Prop Forever*

In 1961 the selection of propeller-driven T-28s and B-26s as initial equipment for the combat element of the *Farm Gate* detachment had been a logical one as, on one hand, their use did not violate the clause of the Geneva Agreement prohibiting the introduction of jet aircraft in Vietnam and,

**In stark contrast to the sleek, clean fast-movers, the beloved Douglas Skyraider breathed oil, dirt and noise. This 22nd SOS A-1H, armed with cluster bombs, gun and rocket pods, demonstrates the lines of the type, which could only be described as rugged.**

The 'TT' tailcodes identify this as an A-1H of the 602nd SOS, 56th SOW, based at Nakhon Phanom. This unit flew interdiction missions over the Trail, and many 'Sandy' rescue missions, usually escorting rescue helicopters.

Above: A Skyraider rolls in towards a target in South Vietnam. The type proved an excellent dive-bomber, with accuracy that was unmatched by any of the fast-movers.

Below right: Dusk start-up for a 'Nimrod' B-26K at Nakhon Phanom. The role was night interdiction, and even the undersides of the napalm canisters were painted black in the interests of camouflage.

Below: The A-1E side-by-side two-seater was widely used by the Air Force. The second seat allowed an experienced pilot to ride with 'rookies' during their first few outings. Combat capability was only diminished by the lack of side airbrakes.

on the other hand, their performance was quite adequate for in country counter-insurgency operations. Moreover, both types provided accommodation for the Vietnamese observer required to ride with the US pilots during strikes. However, the use of propeller-driven combat aircraft, alongside Mach 2 jet fighters, might have appeared more surprising to the uninitiated but was equally logical as these apparently antiquated aircraft proved highly capable until the final stage of the war.

To replace its worn out *Farm Gate* T-28s and B-26s, the USAF had selected the Douglas A-1E, a heavily armed two-seat attack aircraft being phased out by the US Navy, and the type went into combat with Air Commando Squadrons beginning in May 1964. Flying all types of air support sorties, with and later without a VNAF observer on board, the A-1E Skyraider was greatly appreciated by the ground troops for its heavy load of ordnance, its long loiter capability, and its ability to operate under marginal weather when the jets were grounded. For their part, its pilots praised the aircraft's accurate weapons delivery capability and its strong structure which could absorb tremendous battle damage. It was while flying an A-1E in an air support sortie for the besieged Special Forces camp in the A Shau Valley on 10 March 1966 that Major Bernard Fisher earned the first Medal of Honor to be awarded to an Air Force officer during the South East Asia War. Seeing that one of his fellow A-1 pilots had crash-landed on the camp's airstrip and was in danger of being captured, Major Fisher landed his A-1E on the damaged airstrip and, in spite of intense enemy fire, safely picked up Major Wayne Myers. Eighteen months later another Skyraider pilot, Lieutenant Colonel William Jones, also earned the Medal of Honor for repeated attacks against enemy gun positions during the rescue of an F-4 pilot west of Dong Hoi in North Vietnam.

When the Air Force, satisfied with its initial use of A-1Es, requested the transfer of additional aircraft from US Navy surplus, this version of the Skyraider was no longer available in sufficient numbers. Fortunately by then Vietnamese officers were no longer required to authorize strikes, and USAF pilots were flying solo missions for which single-seat A-1Hs were ideally suited. Accordingly, release of a number of these aircraft was negotiated with the Navy to equip Air Commando Squadrons (later designated Special Operations Squadrons), providing air support for ground troops in South Vietnam and flying day and night interdiction missions over the Ho Chi Minh Trail. For the latter role the USAF even evaluated two A-1Es specially fitted with LLLTV, but it was determined that this mission could be better performed by the more sophisticated *Tropic Moon* B-57Gs.

### Helicopter escort

It was in escorting rescue helicopters that the Spad found its real calling. This nickname played on the original 'AD' designation given by the Navy to its Skyraiders prior to 1962, and on the gentle derision with which 'jet jockeys' compared the ageing propeller-driven A-1 to the World War I SPAD 7 and 13 biplane fighters. Combining long endurance with cruise performance compatible with those of the Jolly Green helicopters, and carrying a heavy load of ammunition and ordnance with which to suppress enemy fire during rescue attempts, A-1Hs were retained by the 1st Special Operations Squadron until December 1972.

Even older than its stablemate, the B-26, which had been withdrawn from the *Farm Gate* inventory in February 1964, made a second appearance in the theatre when aircraft rebuilt and modernized by On Mark Engineering were sent to Nakhom Phanom RTAFB in June 1966 for combat evaluation. Subsequently assigned to the 606th and 609th Air Commando Squadrons, these aircraft were flown on trail interdiction missions until November 1969. Although designated B-26Ks when they had been modernized, they were later redesignated A-26As when it was found more diplomatic to deploy 'attack' rather than 'bombing' aircraft to the Thai base.

Fixed-wing gunships, armed with guns mounted on one side of the fuselage and firing downward at a fixed angle, proved to be among the most innovative and effective means employed during the war for delivering concentrated firepower on a variety of targets. Following tests conducted by the Aeronautical Systems Division at Wright-Patterson AFB to develop proper weapon and sight

alignments, a Convair C-131B twin-engined transport was fitted with a 7.62-mm (0.3-in) General Electric SUU-11A Minigun on the left side to serve as a gunship test vehicle. Successful firing tests conducted at Eglin AFB with the experimental C-131B and a similarly altered C-47, led to the modification at Bien Hoa AB of two of the old Douglas transports for evaluation under operational conditions. These two aircraft, unofficially designated FC-47s, flew their first day mission on 15 December 1964, and their first night mission eight days later.

## 'Spooky'

Assigned the soon-to-be-famous 'Spooky' call sign, in November 1965 the 4th Air Commando Squadron became the first operational unit with fully modified AC-47s. Various gun installations were tried on these aircraft but, eventually, standard configuration called for three 7.62-mm MXU-470A Miniguns, each firing 6,000 rounds per minute, and up to 56 manually-dispensed flares. The mission of the 4th ACS was 'to respond with flares and firepower in support of hamlets under night attack, supplement strike aircraft in the defense of friendly forces, and provide long endurance escort for convoys'. The success achieved by the 4th and 14th Air Commando Squadrons (later respectively redesignated 4th and 3rd Special Operations Squadrons) in these demanding roles, as well as during armed reconnaissance sorties over the Ho Chi Minh Trail, soon led to the development of more potent gunships. Hence after four years of combat operations, 'Puff the Magic Dragon' was retired from USAF service. The 3rd SOS was inactivated in September 1969 and the 4th SOS two months later; most of their aircraft were transferred to the VNAF, eight went to the Royal Laotian Air Force, and three were tempor-

**The sun reflects off rice paddies as an A-1E returns to base following a strike in the Ca Mau peninsula.**

**Below and left: After earlier versions of the Douglas WWII vintage light bomber had had to be taken out of operations due to structural fatigue, the USAF reintroduced the type in the form of its modernized and strengthened B-26K version. Redesignated A-26As for political reasons, the newer Invaders were used by the 606th and 609th SOS.**

**Above: One of the AC-47's 7.62-mm Miniguns spews lead and fire during a night raid. Such devastating firepower soon led to 'Spooky' being a true friend of the 'grunts'.**

**Above right: The 4th SOS, 14th SOW AC-47Ds operated from several bases in Vietnam, deployed to FOLs from their main base at Nha Trang.**

**This spectacular demonstration of the awesome firepower of the Douglas AC-47 gunship was recorded on a time exposure during the VC infiltration into Saigon as part of the 1968 Tet Offensive.**

arily retained by the 432nd TRW, USAF, at Udorn RTAFB, for support of *Lima Sites*.

*Project Gunboat*, entailing the modification of a Lockheed C-130A as the prototype of a more advanced 'Gunship II', was undertaken by the Aeronautical Systems Division in January 1967. Armed with four 7.62-mm Miniguns and two M61 Vulcan cannons, and fitted with numerous sensors (side-looking and forward-looking radars, 'Starlight' scope, computerized fire-control system, etc.), this experimental aircraft entered flight trials in the United States in June 1967 and three months later was sent to South East Asia for combat evaluation. In spite of the unreliability of its sophisticated equipment, the Gunship II prototype proved particularly effective during sorties along the Ho Chi Minh Trail and, after being refurbished in the United States, was sent to Ubon RTAFB in February 1968 for additional evaluation. Meanwhile, conversion of additional aircraft to the AC-130A standard had commenced but only one had been obtained when on 31 October 1968 the 16th Special Operations Squadron (call sign 'Spectre') was activated to operate the type. Its primary mission was to undertake night interdiction and armed reconnaissance during *Barrell Roll* operations over Laos, a role in which the unit excelled (for example, during the first quarter of 1969 it destroyed an average of 2.7 trucks per sortie). The need to overhaul and refurbish the AC-130As led to their temporary withdrawal from Thailand during the summer of 1970, but they were returned to the war zone in January 1971.

## Ever larger guns

The enemy's buildup of antiaircraft guns along the Trail and later use of shoulder-fired SA-7 surface-to-air missiles, necessitated the installation of larger guns in the gunships to enable operations from safer altitudes. Once again the Gunship II prototype was modified to test the *Surprise Package* with two 40-mm M-1 Bofors cannon and two 20-mm M61 Vulcan cannons, as well as more advanced systems. Results from the *Surprise Package*'s combat evaluation exceeded expectations and additional AC-130As were returned to service with the heavier guns. Later on, a still more

**This close-up shows the three Minigun installations on the AC-47D. Each gun was a six-barrelled Gatling gun, capable of rates of fire up to 6,000 rounds per minute.**

**An AC-130 lets fly at a target with its 40-mm Bofors cannon. The gunship Hercs were packed with sensors to locate targets beneath the jungle canopy, and complicated night sights for aiming.**

potent armament (with a 105-mm howitzer replacing one of the 40-mm cannon) was fitted to the AC-130E version which made its combat debut in early 1972. Making good use of their heavier armament, the improved AC-130As and AC-130Es built up an impressive record of truck-killing and destroyed large numbers of antiaircraft batteries during interdiction missions. In addition, during the spring 1972 NVA offensive, these superb gunships proved highly effective in breaking up the enemy assaults and knocking off its tanks. At war's end all surviving AC-130s were retained by the USAF.

### *Shadow and Stinger*

The third type of transport aircraft modified as a gunship for use in South East Asia was the Fairchild C-119, with two versions seeing extensive combat use. The AC-119G, retaining the two reciprocating engines powering the standard transport models, was armed with four 7.62-mm Miniguns, whereas the AC-119K, which had two auxiliary J85 jet engines in underwing pods, was armed with four Miniguns and two 20-mm cannon. In addition, equipment fits differed in these two models as the AC-119K utilized a more sophisticated night detection and illumination system. Both the AC-119G and AC-119K versions were primarily used to replace the AC-47s in South Vietnam, but the AC-119K was also found to be a worthy complement to the AC-130 for night interdiction sorties along the Trail. AC-119Gs went into combat with the 71st SOS (call sign 'Shadow') in January 1969, but these aircraft began to be transferred to the VNAF in September 1971. Likewise, the AC-119Ks were first flown in combat by the 18th SOS (call sign 'Stinger') during the winter of 1969.

**16th SOS AC-130A at its Ubon base. The large radome on the port side of the nose housed the ASD-5 'Black Crow' sensor, which detected truck ignition motors. ECM pods carried under the wing are ALQ-87 units, directed against SA-2 missiles.**

### Lockheed AC-130A Hercules

The most capable USAF fixed-wing gunship was the AC-130 which packed a heavy punch. Aircraft 55-0046 was the 73rd production C-130A; after being used in its intended transport role it was loaned to the USMC for inflight refuelling tests prior to being modified as one of the initial batch of AC-130A 'Spectre' gunships. It was then armed with four 20-mm M61 cannon and four 7.62-mm Miniguns firing sideways and downward. For night operations against truck traffic on the Ho Chi Minh Trail, the aircraft was painted black, with the exception of the upper surfaces, and carried small national insignia and dull red tail code (FT identifying the 16th Special Operations Squadron at Ubon RTAFB). It is seen here after refit with two 40-mm Bofors cannon.

Left: A Fairchild AC-119K of the 18th Special Operations Squadron. More capable than the earlier AC-119G from which it differed in having two J85 turbojets in underwing pods, heavier armament, and more sophisticated sensors, the AC-119K was used both for in-country fire support and interdiction sorties in Laos.

Above: Fairchild's C-119 was the last of three major types to be modified for gunship purposes. Many were handed over to the VNAF, where they continued a sterling effort against the Viet Cong.

Under the *Credible Chase* programme, the Fairchild AU-23 Porter and Helio AU-24 Stallion were evaluated in the gunship role. Shown is the former, while undergoing tests in Thailand.

During the course of the South East Asia War, the USAF also considered the use of smaller aircraft as 'mini gunships' for use on close air support missions. Initially, the *Little Brother* concept called for the installation of a single side-firing Minigun in Cessna O-2As, but this was never implemented. Likewise, the more ambitious *Credible Chase* evaluation of the Fairchild AU-23 Peacemaker and Helio AU-24 Stallion did not result in the adoption of either model as a USAF operational type. In view of losses to antiaircraft fire sustained by the more potent gunships, this was undoubtedly a wise decision on the part of the USAF.

## *Arc Light and Tanker Ops*

The powerful Strategic Air Command made three main contributions to the air war over Southeast Asia: its Boeing B-52 Stratofortress heavy bombers flew the controversial *Arc Light* sorties; its Lockheed U-2s and SR-71s, Boeing RC-135s and RB-47s, and Ryan 147 RPVs provided vital, but little publicized, reconnaissance; and its Boeing KC-135As, the only USAF tanker aircraft employed in the theatre after the retirement in January 1965 of PACAF's last Boeing KB-50Js, made possible virtually all operations over North Vietnam while saving countless aircrews, aircraft and taxpayers' money.

During and immediately after the South East Asia War, the role of the Boeing heavy bomber (which was commonly nicknamed 'Buff' for Big Ugly Fat Fellow, with 'Fellow' more often than not being replaced by a less printable epithet) was a subject heatedly discussed. On one hand, the antiwar activists accusingly singled out the heavy bombing of suspected, but often already vacated, Viet Cong and NVA jungle hide-outs, and regarded the employment of B-52s as a wasteful and virtually ineffective case of using a sledgehammer to swat a fly. On the other hand, hardpressed Marines at Khe Sanh, who saw the siege broken up through heavy bombing, and POWs, whose freedom was

An early *Arc Light* strike is carried out against Viet Cong installations. The might of the B-52 came to be feared more than any other aircraft by the Communists, as the first thing they knew about the presence of the bombers was the whistling of the bombs.

Right: Somehow redolent of the dark days of airborne nuclear alert during the cold war, this B-52D chases the sun as it heads for North Vietnam during the *Linebacker II* raids. These missions were the longest bombing raids in history, challenged only by the Vulcan raids on the Falklands during 1982.

As the slogan of a well-known brand of salt claims 'when it rains it pours!' A Boeing B-52F-70-BW Stratofortress drops high explosives during an early *Arc Light* mission. Often coming unexpectedly due to the high altitude from which it was dropped, the rain of bombs had devastating physical and psychological effects on VC troop concentrations.

This 1966 photo shows a pair of B-52s releasing 750-lb bombs over South Vietnam, as part of a series of raids on troop concentrations, supply routes and base areas.

regained after B-52 operations during *Linebacker II* finally hastened the conclusion of peace negotiations, were prone to praise the SAC aircrews.

The use of B-52s had been first contemplated just prior to the start of *Rolling Thunder* when 30 Guam-based Stratofortresses had been armed for a night strike against the MiG base at Phuc Yen. However, as this planned strike against the North was not approved by Washington, it was over South Vietnam that the B-52's went to war on 17 June 1965 when they flew the first *Arc Light* mission to hit Viet Cong concentrations in Binh Duong Province. Later on, the heavy bombers were also employed against targets in Laos (the first missions against the Laotian side of the Mu Gia Pass near the border of North Vietnam being flown on 11 December 1965), in North Vietnam (the western approaches to the Mu Gia Pass being first bombed on 11 April 1966), and in Cambodia (the first B-52 strike taking place on 18 March 1969). In the process, the number of B-52 sorties flown annually twice reached over 20,000, with 20,568 sorties during 1968 and the all-time high being recorded during 1972 when 28,383 sorties were flown.

## Bombload increases

Initially, the B-52s operating against targets in South East Asia were unmodified strategic bombers whose internal bays, optimized for carrying nuclear weapons, could be used to carry 27 500- or 750-lb (227- or 340-kg) high-explosive bombs. Subsequently, as the weight of these bombs was substantially below the warload capability of the eight-engined aircraft, SAC authorized the modification of a number of B-52s to carry internally up to 84 500- or 750-lb bombs. Still later, B-52Ds were fitted with external racks to bring the total load to a staggering 108 bombs! Remaining under control of the Strategic Air Command, the B-52s operating in South East Asia were at first based at Andersen AFB in Guam. Typical sorties, which normally required inflight refueling on the outbound leg northeast of the Philippines and occasionally supplemental refueling on the inbound leg, lasted up to 12 hours. Hence the securing in March 1967 of Thai approval for the use of the new U Tapao RTNAF as a base for B-52s was welcome news as mission duration could then be reduced to a little over three hours without the use of inflight refueling and total duty hours for the crews went down to eight hours, instead of 18 hours when operating from Guam. Operations from U Tapao began in April 1967, and the 4528th Strategic Wing (inactivated in April 1970 and replaced by the 307th SW) operated from this base for the duration of the war. Nevertheless, Andersen AFB continued to be a major B-52 station as the 43rd Strategic Wing, the primary mission of which was to maintain aircraft and crews on strategic nuclear alert, was also assigned a conventional contingency plan in support of operations in South East Asia. Furthermore, both U Tapao RTNAF and Andersen AFB were used as bases for the large number of B-52s sent on temporary deployments during intensive air operations to stop the Communist offensive in the spring of 1972 and during *Linebacker II*.

In the south, B-52s were initially operated to bomb suspected Viet Cong concentrations and base areas hidden in the jungle. Direct results, in terms of casualties inflicted on the enemy per ton of bombs, were not spectacular considering the

cost of such missions, but there is no denying that these B-52 sorties had a tremendous psychological impact on the enemy, preventing it from building its forces. The limited effectiveness of the big bombers was not due to lack of accuracy; indeed, using only on board bombing radar, they proved highly accurate. Rather the problems stemmed from the selection of targets and the need to have such targets approved much in advance of the strikes, with Viet Cong intelligence being frequently able to learn the location of planned strikes and thus having time to disperse their forces. While sorties were flown during most of the war to deny safe areas to the Viet Cong, the B-52s were also flown to provide direct support to American ground troops during major search and destroy operations and to blunt major enemy offensives, with all-weather operations being made possible not only by the reliability of the aircraft bombing system but also by the use of MSQ-77 ground-based radars during *Combat Skyspot* sorties. Notably, during the siege of Khe Sanh in early 1968, B-52s were employed along the outer perimeter of the main defences and frequently dropped their bombs as close as 300 to 500 m (328 to 547 yards) from friendly troops. Similar missions were also flown in Cambodia in 1970 to support US and ARVN troops sweeping Communist sanctuaries along the border with South Vietnam. In addition, B-52s were used on at least three occasions to drop incendiary bombs in vain efforts to set the jungle afire; results were so poor that Operation *Pink Rose* was deemed ineffective and was abandoned.

## SAMs raise danger

Over North Vietnam, B-52 operations were long restricted to areas in the southern panhandle where they flew out of range of the MiGs based in the Hanoi-Haiphong area and where SAMs were not initially deployed. This relatively safe situation did not last forever as SAMs were first fired at B-52s on 17 September 1967 during a mission close to the DMZ. However, in this and many subsequent incidents, the heavy bombers foiled North Vietnamese attempts by making full use of their internal electronic countermeasures systems and relying on the effective support of EB-66 jammers and F-105 *Iron Hand* and *Wild Weasel* flights. This happy state was not encountered later when B-52s began flying missions over the Red River Delta on 15 April 1972 during *Linebacker I*. Furthermore, the risks taken by the bomber crews became very high during *Linebacker II*.

Operation *Bullet Shot*, a systematic buildup of B-52 and support forces to counteract the increased North Vietnamese infiltration in the south, was launched in early February 1972 and over the next several months the *Arc Light* force was increased until a peak strength of 206 B-52Ds and B-52Gs was reached in June 1972. (Including the aircraft sent on TDY from CONUS-based units, three-fourths of these aircraft were based at Andersen AFB and were assigned to the expanded 43rd Strategic Wing and to the 72nd Strategic Wing [Provisional] while the others were at U Tapao RTNAF with the 307th Strategic Wing and the 310th Strategic Wing [Provisional].) The number of heavy bombers at these two bases had been slightly reduced by 15 December 1972, when senior commanders received notification that President Nixon had authorized the use of B-52s as part of a major air offensive against North Vietnam. The striking power of these aircraft was nevertheless awesome and in the space of 11 days forced Hanoi to curtail its delaying tactics and agree to resume the peace talks in Paris.

## MiG kills

At long last employed in the role for which they had been designed, 129 B-52s (42-Ds from U Tapao, and 33-Ds and 54-Gs from Andersen) with 39 tactical aircraft providing escort and ECM support, struck airfields at Hoa Lac, Kep, and Phuc Yen, the Kinh No complex and the Yen Vien rail yard, all in the vicinity of Hanoi, during the night of 18 December 1972. Enemy air defences were alert and heavy (SAMs, heavy AAA, and MiGs); two B-52Gs and one B-52D were shot down, while Staff Sergeant Sam Turner, a B-52D Fire Control Operator (FCO or gunner), destroyed a MiG-21. Additional heavy raids were flown during the next six nights and again every night from 26 through

**Above: The devastating effects of an *Arc Light* strike 18 miles north of Saigon can be seen from the air on 19 December 1965. The B-52s had first bombed Viet Cong jungle hide-outs six months earlier and had immediately become one of the weapons most feared by VC guerrillas and NVA troops.**

**Above left: Base security was extremely important during the war in South East Asia, and much resources were expended in this direction. Even on Thai and Okinawa bases, the B-52s had to be protected from potential sapper attacks at all times.**

**The boys on the ground sustained the B-52s through the most concentrated and heaviest bombing campaigns in history, often working 24-hours or more on a shift. During *Linebacker II*, the maintenance men and armourers virtually worked until they dropped, keeping the massive effort going right through to the end.**

677

**Boeing B-52D Stratofortress**
For conventional bombing operations in South East Asia, SAC B-52Ds eventually acquired a coat of camouflage paint (in lieu of the original natural metal finish with radiation reflecting white paint on the lower surfaces) and were fitted with a modified bomb bay and external weapons pylons to carry up to 84 500-lb or 750-lb bombs. Flying their first *Arc Light* missions on 17 June 1965, BUFFs began operating against targets in the North Vietnamese panhandle six months later. Missions deep into the North were first flown during *Linebacker I* in the spring of 1972. Then in December 1952, B-52s distinguished themselves during 11 days of intensive operations, doing much to finally force North Vietnam to conclude the Paris Talks.

29 December, with the last bombs being dropped on the Trai Ca SAM storage area shortly before midnight on 29 December 1972. Thanks to improving tactics and fast dwindling supplies to North Vietnamese SAMs, losses were kept at a reasonable level (three B-52s were lost during the night of the 18th, six during that of the 20th, and two each during the nights of the 21st, 26th and 27th). The overall aircraft loss rate was an acceptable 2.06 percent and the loss of human lives was lower than had been feared (of the 92 B-52 aircrew members who went down, 14 were killed, 14 were reported missing in action, 31 were rescued, and 33 became POWs and were released in early 1973). Results exceeded the most sanguine expectations, with damage to civilian areas and civilian casualties (1,395 according to Hanoi) being kept to a remarkably low level even when targets were struck in the midst of heavily populated areas. The B-52s were credited with the destruction of one-fourth of North Vietnam's petroleum reserves, 80 percent of its electrical generating capacity, and virtually its entire supply of SAMs. As by then the mining of Haiphong and other harbours had brought shipping to a standstill, and as rail lines into the People's Republic of China were effectively interdicted, Hanoi's war making capability was at an end. Sadly, the ensuing Paris Agreement did not extract the necessary guarantees to safeguard the future of the Republic of Vietnam, and the sacrifices of Allied personnel soon became fruitless.

### *Final missions*

Although the last of the *Linebacker II* sorties against targets in the Hanoi-Haiphong area was flown by B-52s on 29 December 1972, the war was not yet quite over for their aircrews: missions against targets in the southern part of North Vietnam continued until 15 January 1973; those over South Vietnam until 27 January; those over Laos until 17 April: and those over Cambodia until 15 August 1973. In eight years of *Arc Light* operations, a total of 26 B-52s had been lost, including two which had collided in flight during the first sortie on 17 June 1965, and two others which had collided southeast of Saigon on 7 July 1967. (Among the casualties in this latter accident was Major General William J. Crumm, the commander of the 3rd Air Division at Andersen AFB).

### *Tanker operations*

When PACAF flew its first combat mission over Laos on 9 June 1964, the command had been forced to use four of its venerable KB-50J tankers to refuel the eight F-100Ds taking part in the strike. Converted from B-50 bombers and fitted with two auxiliary turbojets to supplement their four piston engines, and thus able to cruise at altitudes and speeds compatible with those of the fighters, the KB-50Js of the 421st Air Refueling Squadron had been scheduled to be phased out in early 1965 just as PACAF's needs for inflight refueling was about to explode. At that time the Strategic Air Command had already obtained exclusive control and management of the large fleet of KC-135A jet tankers. Unwilling to relinquish these valuable aircraft, but being ordered to provide tanker support for expanded PACAF's activities in Southeast Asia, SAC was forced to supplement the KC-135As of its 3960th Strategic Wing at Andersen AFB, Guam, by sending jet tankers on TDY to Kadena AB on Okinawa. Almost immediately this *Young Tiger* deployment was changed to a permanent change of station as SAC activated the 4252nd Strategic Wing at Kadena on 12 January 1965 and began its search for forward operating bases to support combat operations in South East Asia.

Four main tasks were assigned to these KC-135As: (1) refueling of tactical aircraft, mainly fighters and reconnaissance aircraft, during combat operations in South East Asia; (2) refueling of B-52s taking part in *Arc Light* operations; (3) refueling of tactical aircraft being ferried across the Western Pacific or to South East Asia bases; and (4) refueling of routine SAC reconnaissance and bomber operations in the Western Pacific. In addi-

**As part of Operation *Bullet Shot*, the strategic bomber force at Andersen AFB, Guam, and U Tapao RTNAF, Thailand, was increased by June 1972 to a peak of 206 B-52Ds and B-52Gs. Over 30 B-52Gs (foreground) and B-52Ds (background) can be seen at Andersen AFB occupying every available hardstand on this crowded base, which was nicknamed 'The Rock.'**

**Right: The B-52 bombing effort was ably supported by the KC-135 tanker fleet, which provided refueling support. Most refueling was accomplished during the ingress flight, with most aircraft being able to manage the rest of the flight without the need for further fuel. Emergency refueling was provided for aircraft short on fuel.**

Initial tanker coverage was provided by the ancient Boeing KB-50J, two of which are seen here over South Vietnam in 1964. The KB-50 had only the probe and drogue method available, and could therefore only refuel the aircraft of Tactical Air Command.

Above right: The refueling operator in the KB-50J sat at an observation blister in the side of the fuselage and monitored refueling from the wing-carried drogue pods. The receiver is a PACAF F-100D 'somewhere over South East Asia'.

tion, they were to be used to provide supplementary transport tasks, notably the ferrying of personnel between bases in the theatre. With such a busy schedule, it was not long before additional aircraft were added to the 4252nd SW, with a first group of 30 KC-135As arriving in February 1965 to support planned *Arc Light* operations.

## Search for bases

While the basing of KC-135As at Kadena AB was satisfactory to provide refueling for routine SAC operations or to support the deployment of aircraft to South East Asia, it entailed unduly long sorties when supporting combat operations in South East Asia. Accordingly, a search was rapidly undertaken for additional bases at which to station tankers. The more obvious option of stationing KC-135As on bases in South Vietnam was rejected as it would have placed these valuable aircraft in high threat areas due to probable Viet Cong attacks; moreover, these bases were already becoming too congested. Bases in Thailand offered a more logical alternative as they would place the tankers near or with the tactical aircraft they were to support (sortie duration was reduced significantly and the tankers could offload three to four times more fuel per sortie than when operating from Kadena AB). To do so, however, necessitated difficult diplomatic negotiations with the Royal Thai Government. Eventually, these negotiations bore fruit and four *Tiger Cub* tankers began operating from the Don Muang International Airport in Bangkok in March 1965. Later on, KC-135As were operated from Takhli RTAFB (*King Cobra* tankers from September 1965), from U Tapao RTNAF (*Giant Cobra* from August 1966), and from Korat RTAFB (*Tiger Claw* from June 1972). Furthermore, between February 1968 and January 1971, KC-135As were based at Ching Chuan Kang AB on Formosa specifically to support B-52 *Arc Light* operations and, in 1972-73, tankers were also based at Clark AB in the Philippines to support the *Constant Guard* deployments of tactical aircraft and to provide support for expanded B-52 operations during *Linebackers I and II*.

From its modest beginning in early 1965, when the first ten KC-135As were deployed, the tanker force rose and contracted along with the overall level of activity. By October 1967 there were 32 tankers at U Tapao, eight at Takhli, and 35 at Kadena; by July 1968 there were 40 tankers at U Tapao, 21 at Ching Chuan Kang, and 22 at Kadena; and by June 1972, after additional tankers were deployed along with the *Constant Guard* tactical aircraft and the *Bullet Shot* B-52s, the number of KC-135As had increased to 46 at U Tapao, 28 at Clark, 13 at Don Muang, 20 at Takhli, seven at Korat, and 58 at Kadena, for a peak tanker strength of 172 aircraft. As the KC-135A force increased, numerous refueling tracks were set up. For tactical aircraft operating against North Vietnam and Laos, 15 race track-shaped areas were provided in Thai airspace, four more were located over Laos, and five were over the Gulf of Tonkin; to support operations over South Vietnam, and to a lesser extent over Cambodia, four tracks were set up over the Republic of South Vietnam. Refueling of B-52s flying out of Andersen AB was undertaken outbound along five linear tracks north of the Philippines, while refueling of returning aircraft took place along two tracks across the central Philippines. Most refuelings took place at 27,000 to 30,000 ft (8230 to 9144 m) but refueling of heavily-laden F-105 fighter-bombers frequently had to take place as low as 15,000 ft (4572 m).

## Tanker exploits

All refueling sorties were not routine and there were numerous instances when tactical aircraft, critically low on fuel after air combat over North Vietnam, were saved only through the timely arrival of tankers. The most unusual sortie was probably that flown by a crew from the 902nd Air Refueling Squadron on TDY from Clinton-Sherman AFB in Oklahoma during joint USAF-Navy operations over North Vietnam on 31 May 1967. After first refueling two USAF F-104Cs, the KC-135A then came to the rescue of six Navy aircraft (two A-3Bs, two F-8Es, and two F-4Bs). So critical was the situation of some of these aircraft that a three-deep refueling became necessary, with

Fast-mover support added considerably to the KC-135's workload, and units were soon in place in Thailand to cope with the vast demand for refueling as the bombers moved North. Here F-105Ds take on gas, ready for the flight across the border into the North.

**Above: Early F-4Cs are grateful to see the KC-135 waiting for them at the rendezvous point, and quickly suckle up for their fuel. Once the refueling has been accomplished, their minds will turn to the impending bombing run, with its danger of MiGs, SAMs and AAA.**

**Right: 750-lb bomb-laden F-105s line-up for the tanker in December 1965. Most of Thailand and southern Laos was covered by tanker refueling racetracks, and during a large strike, many of these would be busy at any one time.**

one of the A-3Bs taking on fuel from the KC-135A while at the same time passing on fuel to an F-8E. All told, the KC-135A effected 14 refuelings, transferring 49,900 lb (22634 kg) of fuel, to save eight aircraft in a single sortie prior to making an emergency recovery at Da Nang AB, where it landed with less than 10,000 lb (4536 kg) of fuel!

After the signing of the ceasefire agreement in Paris, KC-135As continued to support operations in Laos and Cambodia until 15 August 1973. Thereafter, the number of tankers based in South East Asia decreased rapidly but some were still in the area to fly 40 sorties during the May 1975 *Mayaguez* incident. Finally, on 21 December 1975, the KC-135As flew their last war-related sorties when they escorted A-7Ds being redeployed from Korat RTAFB to Hill AFB, Utah.

From the first use of KB-50Js in June 1964 until the end of combat operations on 15 August 1973, tankers flew a total of 124,223 sorties in support of tactical aircraft, 40,882 sorties in support of B-52s, and 29,582 sorties in support of reconnaissance operations, deployments and redeployments, training, logistics and related activities. Average sortie length for the KC-135s had been 4.7 hours and had involved an average of 4.2 refuelings per sortie. All told, the tankers had flown 911,364 hours and had transferred 1,400 million US gallons (5300 million litres) of jet fuel in 813,878 refuelings. There were no tanker combat losses during this period and only one KC-135A was lost to operational causes (in addition, there were two fatal accidents on take-off and two on landing not directly related to operations in South East Asia).

**Below right: With refueling boom lowered, this KC-135A heads out to sea with its receiver following. This example is the second-to-last tanker supplied to the Air Force.**

**Below: Underview of the KC-135A reveals the two sets of 'traffic lights' under the forward fuselage. Controlled by the boomer, these signal to receiver pilots if they are too low or too high. A yellow-painted centreline on the tanker's belly helps with alignment.**

Fairchild C-123 Providers were widely used on Special Forces camp support. This aircraft begins its take-off role at Bu Dop camp in South Vietnam, after delivering vital supplies. It is a C-123K model, with the underwing jet engines augmenting the standard radials.

A Fairchild C-123K (54-0594) of the 311th Tactical Airlift Squadron, 315th Tactical Airlift Wing, which had been hit by a mortar shell while taking off from Khe Sanh on 7 March 1968. The aircraft was destroyed, but incredibly the only casualty was the loadmaster, who hurt his back.

## *Trash Haulers*

Often derided by the jet jockeys, who irreverently called them 'trash haulers', the TAC and PACAF transport aircrews flying intra-theatre missions were, with the forward air controllers and the helicopter crews, the almost forgotten heroes of the South East Asia War. Although in the eyes of the general public their work lacked appeal, it was of vital importance in a guerrilla war in which ground transportation was often undertaken at great risk and many outposts depended on air resupply for most of their needs. Likewise, the MAC aircrews, flying long and arduous trans-Pacific flights, effectively supported the whole war effort by providing logistic support and large-scale deployments of military forces to and from South Vietnam and Thailand.

USAF tactical airlift crews had first operated in the Indochinese peninsula during the last year of French operations against the Viet Minh when, from May 1953 until August 1954, volunteer personnel helped to man and maintain the Fairchild C-119Cs of the 314th and 403rd Troop Carrier Groups on temporary loan to the French. (Of note is the fact that these aircraft retained their USAF squadron markings but had their US insignia overpainted with tricolour roundels). Next came the *Farm Gate* and 'Dirty Thirty' aircrews which, beginning respectively in November 1961 and April 1962, flew USAF SC-47s and VNAF C-47s to provide logistical support for RVNAF and US Special Forces ('Green Berets') operations and to perform night flare missions, as well as occasional combat sorties as napalm bombers. The venerable Douglas piston-engined transport, however, was not to become a standard airlifter during the American involvement in the South East Asia War as this mission was performed for the USAF by more modern types: the Fairchild C-123 and de Havilland Canada C-7, which were both powered by a pair of radial engines, and the four-turbine Lockheed C-130.

As noted earlier, C-123s were initially flown in South Vietnam by *Mule Train* and *Ranch Hand* crews, with the first C-123Bs of the 346th TCS being deployed from Pope AFB, North Carolina, and arriving at Tan Son Nhut on 3 January 1962. Aircraft from this squadron, as well as the C-123Bs of the 777th TCS which had begun operations from Da Nang in May 1962, immediately supplemented *Farm Gate* and VNAF C-47s in a variety of tactical airlift missions. The C-123s were also used for combat drops of Vietnamese paratroopers, the first such operation taking place on 5 March 1962 when troops from the 5th Airborne Battalion, ARVN, jumped to relieve the garrison of the Bo Tuc outpost near the Cambodian border. For airlift operations in Vietnam and Thailand, two C-123 squadrons were added in 1963. However, it was only after the United States committed ground troops to combat operations that this force was substantially built up.

### *Jet augmentation*

Seeking to improve the take-off characteristics of its Fairchild transport, particularly when operating from short and primitive airstrips as found at isolated outposts, in January 1963 the USAF sent the sole YC-123H prototype (a standard C-123B fitted with two General Electric CJ610 turbojets in underwing pods) for combat evaluation in Vietnam. While initially this prototype was judged of limited interest, the idea was later revived and jet-augmented C-123Ks, first operated in

Above left: To supplement the insufficient capabilities of the Military Airlift Command, air crews of the Air Force Reserve and Air National Guard volunteered to fly missions not only within the United States but also across the Pacific to South East Asia. Photographed at Tan Son Nhut AB in September 1967, this Boeing C-97 belonged to the 191st Military Airlift Squadron, Utah Air National Guard.

Above: Introduced into Vietnam by the US Army, the Caribou was at first considered by the USAF to be inferior to its Fairchild Provider. However, after the C-7As had been transferred from the USA to the USAF, the 'blue suiters' found them ideal for resupply missions to primitive and muddy airstrips as used by this aircraft of the 459th TAS/483rd TAW.

South East Asia in May 1967, eventually supplanted the C-123Bs flown by the 315th Air Commando Wing (formerly designated 315th Troop Carrier Wing and finally becoming the 315th Tactical Airlift Wing). Peak C-123 monthly operations in Vietnam occurred in May 1969, when 9,707 sorties were flown, but the type began to be phased out in July 1970 when the 309th TAS and 12th SOS were inactivated. The last USAF C-123K missions were flown in June 1972; in all, C-123s had flown a total of 663,992 airlift sorties during the war.

### *Caribou goes to war*

Even though between January 1967, when the type was transferred from the US Army to the USAF, and the end of 1972, C-7s flew a greater average number of monthly sorties (773,342 sorties in 70 months, or an average of 11,049 sorties per month) than either the C-123s (6,651 sorties per month) or the in-country C-130s (8,597 sorties per month), this smaller Canadian-built aircraft remains the least known of the cargo aircraft operated by the USAF during the South East Asia War.

Largest aircraft operated by Army aviation units, the de Havilland CV-2 (redesignated C-7 in October 1962) was first deployed to South East Asia by the 1st Aviation Company in the spring of 1962. Initially based at Korat in Thailand, this unit had begun operating from bases in South Vietnam in July 1962, soon proving that the type could operate from airstrips too short for use by USAF C-123s and thus leading to the eventual deployment of five more C-7 Aviation Companies. The Air Force, however, was taking a dim view of the Army's independent air transport operation and actively campaigned to gain control of these aircraft. Finally, following a 6 April 1966 agreement between the two Chiefs of Staff, all C-7s were transferred to the USAF. Assigned to six squadrons of the newly established 483rd Troop Carrier Wing, the Caribou, once viewed by the Air Force as a rival of and inferior to the C-123, went on to be greatly appreciated by the USAF for its simplicity, sturdiness and short field characteristics. Flying mainly resupply missions to isolated outposts, the Air Force C-7s kept up a high operational rate in spite of the often primitve conditions under which they were operated. Force reduction, which began in June 1970 with the inactivation of the 459th TAS, was progressive and only three of the C-7 squadrons were still operational in early 1972. By then the USAF had decided to transfer 48 Caribous to the VNAF, and the 483rd TAW (ex 483rd TCW) was inactivated on 25 March 1972. Nevertheless the USAF still operated a few Caribous until the end of October 1972, when the last C-7s (some of

The de Havilland Canada C-7 Caribou proved extremely adept at getting in to the short, unprepared strips in the mountains of Vietnam.

Flying against an appropriately coloured sky, three Fairchild UC-123Ks spray Agent Orange. C-123 and UC-123 Providers were first sent to South Vietnam in early 1962 as part of the *Farm Gate* (for transport operations) and *Ranch Hand* (for chemical spraying) detachments.

Below right: The heaviest air-dropped ordnance used during the South East Asia War was the 15,000-lb BLU-82. The blast from this bomb instantly cleared out helicopter landing zones in jungle areas. A BLU-82 is seen here about to be loaded into a C-130 'bomber' at Cam Ranh Bay in March 1970.

Below: The Hercules was in many ways the workhorse of the USAF in South East Asia, supplying airlift capability wherever it was required, both in the warzone and behind the front in the huge logistic operation needed to continue the war effort.

which had been modified for tactical airborne communications relay work) were shipped back to the United States for duty with the Reserve and the Guard.

## *The labours of Hercules*

The method of bringing troops into the combat zone was initially also a source of argument between the Army and the Air Forcé, with the latter at first favouring traditional air drops of paratroopers while the Army and the Marine Corps soon adopted the air mobile concept with troops being brought into battle by helicopters. Eventually, however, the Air Force, realizing that in most instances the number of paratroopers that could be landed in a timely fashion was too small, reluctantly gave up the air-drop concept. From then on, airlift aircraft were used for airlanded operations (during which troops were transported to the landing strip nearest the combat zone to complement air mobile operations in which troops were carried in helicopters) and, primarily, to transport cargo, equipment and supplies. For these tasks, the four-turbine Lockheed C-130 proved ideally suited and, from July 1965 until November 1972, the type flew no fewer than 708,087 sorties in Vietnam, with peak monthly operations being recorded in May 1968 when in-country C-130s flew 14,392 sorties.

Whereas C-7 and C-123 units were based in south Vietnam, PACAF C-130 squadrons, as well as TAC rotational squadrons, remained for the most part offshore-based. For example, when the C-130 force reached peak strength in the spring of 1968, only four detachments were stationed in South Vietnam while the bulk of the C-130s were operated by four squadrons based at Naha AB, Okinawa; three squadrons each at Ching Chuan Kang AB on Formosa, Tachikawa AB in Japan, and Clark AB in the Philippines; and two squadrons at Mactan AB in the Philippines.

Prior to America's full involvement in combat operations, the C-130s were used mainly for logistic support between PACAF main stations and bases in Vietnam and Thailand as they had the required payload and range characteristics. However, after the spring of 1964, the Hercules became the most important intratheatre transport aircraft in terms of transported (maximum number of tons airlifted

This 345th TAS, 314th TAW C-130E was not so lucky, being hit by Communist mortars during an attack on Dak To airstrip. The large Hercules proved remarkably resilient in service, and could absorb a fair amount of punishment.

during one month respectively were 69,499 for the C-130s, 16,643 for the C-123s, and 10,264 for the C-7s), with this level of activity being made possible by the upgrading or construction of over 100 airstrips capable of accommodating C-130s.

Not all missions involved conventional or assault landings to unload the aircraft on the ground, as frequently C-130s parachuted their loads or made use of special delivery techniques. With the Low-Altitude Parachute Extraction System (LAPES) loads were extracted through the aft ramp by a parachute while the aircraft was flying a few feet from the ground, whereas with the Ground Proximity Extraction System (GPES) the loads were pulled out by means of a hook-and-cable arrangement. The C-130s also made use of the Container Delivery System (CDS), a highly accurate method by which loads could be parachuted from as low as 600 ft (183 m), and of two blind drop methods, the Adverse Weather Aerial Delivery System (AWADS) which relied on self-contained dual-frequency airborne radar and another method which relied on the guidance of ground-based radar.

Albeit most C-130 missions were undertaken to airlift personnel, equipment and supplies, transport versions of the Hercules were also used for intratheatre aeromedical evacuation, as Airborne Battlefield Command and Control Centers (ABCCCs) as noted later in this Chapter, and for *Banish Beach*, *Commando Scarf* and *Commando Vault* 'bombing' missions. *Banish Beach* missions were flown in 1965 in an attempt to deprive forest sanctuaries to the Viet Cong by starting forest fires with nearly simultaneous drops of fuel drums. Small XM-41 antipersonnel mines and CDU-10 noisemakers were dropped by C-130s during *Commando Scarf* sorties as part of the interdiction campaign in southern Laos. Finally, under Project *Commando Vault*, C-130s were used to drop five-ton M-121 and seven and one-half ton BLU-82 weapons to blast out helicopter landing zones in jungle areas or demolish enemy truck parks and caches. C-130s were also used twice in May 1966 to drop mines at night upstream of the infamous Thanh Hoa rail bridge. In the first mission, on 20 May, the drop was successful but reconnaissance did not show damage to the bridge. On the next night the aircraft failed to return and the scheme was abandoned.

A large fleet of Hercules waits for departure orders during the siege of Khe Sanh. C-130s and C-123s flew in virtually all the materiel that reached the Marines' base during the siege.

**Left: Ordered as an utility trainer, the T-39 was used in limited number in Southeast Asia as a staff transport. It was derived from the civil Sabreliner.**

**Below: Obsolete as a cargo transport due to the limited size of its cargo compartment, the Douglas C-118A Liftmaster was the primary aeromedical evacuation aircraft. In this role, it was used to carry wounded personnel not only in the Southeast Asia theatre but also within the United States.**

**Above: Long after airlines around the world had begun using jetliners, the Military Air Transport Service made its slow transition into the jet age. One of the early Boeing C-135Bs in MATS markings is seen here unloading supplies at Tan Son Nhut.**

After C-7s and C-123s had been phased out by the Air Force, C-130s remained the only USAF tactical transports in the theatre. Thailand-based during the final months of the war, in the spring of 1973 the Hercules switched their full attention to the airlift of supplies to Cambodia, with the last war-related sorties being undertaken in 1975 by an aircraft flown by civilian crews of Birdair, Inc., a contract-operator to which the Air Force provided equipment and technical assistance. A total of 126 tactical airlift aircraft (55 C-130s, 53 C-123s, and 20 C-7s) were lost by the USAF during the war.

Other transport aircraft operated by PACAF on intratheatre missions included a relatively small number of Douglas C-124s (the last of which was retired by the Command's 20th Operations Squadron in November 1971) and of Douglas C-118s. Both types were powered by four piston engines, with the C-124 being valued for its capacious fuse-

**Left: The wondrous, lumbering Douglas C-124 Globemaster continued on the air bridge until 1970, its huge fuselage and gaping clamshell mouth making up for the time it took to traverse the Pacific. This 'Globe' runs up prior to the start of another intrepid journey back to the States from Thailand.**

**Right: Blessed with a surfeit of power (only now rectified with the C-141B stretch programme), the Lockheed C-141A StarLifter could operate out of quite small airfields. It soon became the primary aircraft on the trans-Pacific route, its swift crossings shifting vital equipment in enormous quantities.**

lage while the C-118 (a military version of the DC-6B airliner) was well-suited for staff transport and for aeromedical evacuation. In this last capacity, the C-118s were supplemented by jet-powered Douglas C-9As beginning in February 1972.

***Air bridge***

To complement the intratheatre activities of PACAF and TAC tactical airlifters, the Military Air Transport Service (MATS), which was redesignated Military Airlift Command (MAC) in 1965, undertook a massive air bridge across the vast Pacific to bring in a steady flow of personnel and supplies from CONUS to the war zone. At first the Command had an obsolescent fleet (which in 1965 was comprised of 21 squadrons of piston-powered Douglas C-124s, 10 squadrons of turbine-powered aircraft [7 with Lockheed C-130s and 3 with Douglas C-133s], and three squadrons of jet-powered Boeing C-135s), to fulfill not only its obligations in support of the war but also to continue all of its normal peacetime activities within the United States and in support of US forces overseas. Moreover, only its oldest aircraft, the C-124s and C-133s, had sufficient internal volume and wide enough cargo-loading doors to transport large pieces of military and construction equipment. Fortunately, the long overdue modernization of the MAC fleet had already been initiated with the ordering of jet-powered Lockheed C-141A cargo transports in 1961 and of giant Lockheed C-5As in 1965.

Beginning in August 1965, less than four months after entering squadron service, C-141As began playing a major role in the airlift of personnel, equipment and supplies to, from, and within South East Asia. Initially most westbound flights departed from Travis AFB, California; however, as the volume of operations increased, new Aerial Ports of Embarkation (APOEs) were brought into use not only on the West Coast (Norton and McChord AFBs) but also in the Southwest (Tinker and Kelly AFBs) and the Eastern United States (Charleston, Dover and McGuire AFBs). On their return from South East Asia, the Lockheed StarLifters were frequently used for aeromedical evacuations (flying some 6,000 such missions between August 1965 and December 1972) and for the grimmer task of bringing home the bodies of US personnel killed in action. In the final stage of the

**Above:** Modern air warfare is not just shooting down enemy aircraft, dropping bombs, and ferrying troops and supplies. To support fighters, bombers and transports, specialized aircraft, such as this Lockheed C-140A of the 1867th Facility Checking Squadron taking off from Tan Son Nhut AB in December 1966, must ensure that communications and navigation facilities are kept in top shape.

**Above left:** Making its début on the long trans-Pacific cargo haul in August 1971 with the 475th Military Airlift Wing, the Lockheed C-5A Galaxy proved exceptionally valuable as it was capable of airlifting large pieces of equipment, such as this Vertol CH-47 helicopter, over the long overwater route from the US West Coast to Vietnam.

The McDonnell RF-101C Voodoos met most of the tactical reconnaissance requirements during the early years, and even after the advent of the RF-4C, the RF-101 continued to serve in the role, most pilots preferring the 'long bird' to the slower Phantom.

war, C-141As were selected as the principal transports for *Operation Homecoming*, the return of the 588 POWs released by North Vietnam between 12 February and 29 March 1973. Their final role in support of the South East Asia War was the evacuation of Vietnamese refugees in early 1975.

The much larger C-141A stablemate, the C-5A Galaxy, flew its first mission to the war zone in August 1971 and, as more became available, the type soon carried an increasing share of the trans-Pacific military traffic. Re-assigned to other MAC operations after the US pull-out from Vietnam in early 1973, C-5As returned to Saigon in April 1975 for the final evacuation of South Vietnamese refugees, It was then that one of these aircraft crashed near Saigon while carrying orphans and attendants, bringing the outstanding work of MAC aircrews to a tragic end.

## *To See, To Hear, To Talk*

During the course of the war in South East Asia the USAF, far from emulating the three proverbial monkeys, did much looking (reconnaissance), hearing (ELINT/COMINT/SIGINT) and talking (airborne warning and control/airborne command, control and communications/electronic countermeasures). In particular, its intelligence gathering activities covered the gamut of operations from visual observation to aerial photography, and from electronic reconnaissance to infrared detection. Continuing along already well established paths, but also pioneering new ways, these varied activities were undertaken with aircraft ranging from the 150-mph (241-km/h) Cessna O-1s of Forward Air Controllers to the 2,250-mph (3621-km/h) Lockheed SR-71s of the 9th SRW, and from small Remotely Piloted Vehicles (RPVs) to large aircraft such as Boeing RC-135s.

The first USAF reconnaissance activities in what was soon to become a war theatre were undertaken after the Douglas VC-47A of the US Air Attaché in Laos had obtained on 21 and 27 December 1960 photographs of Soviet aircraft dropping supplies to the Pathet Lao forces. Damaged by ground fire during the 27 December mission, the VC-47A was replaced by a camera-equipped SC-47D with which 38 reconnaissance missions were flown over Laos between 11 January and 24 March

The McDonnell RF-4C photo-Phantom introduced many important features to the tac recon role, notably infra-red linescan and side-looking airborne radar. This aircraft is undergoing a cartridge start in its revetment at Udorn.

**The RF-101C was the first jet aircraft in the combat zone, and the only version of the much-loved but tricky to fly Voodoo to see service in the war. Sensors were entirely optical, consisting of forward- and oblique-looking cameras, with panoramic cameras looking downwards.**

1961, on which date the aircraft was shot down by ground fire over the Plain of Jars. The damage suffered by the earlier aircraft and the loss of the SC-47D convinced the USAF of the need to use a higher performance aircraft and to establish Project *Field Goal* for monitoring Pathet Lao activities. For that purpose a Lockheed RT-33A, based at Udorn in Thailand, flew 33 sorties over Laos between 24 April and 10 May 1961, when *Field Goal* flights were temporarily suspended as the Laotian Government and the Pathet Lao had agreed to implement a cease-fire. On 4 October 1961 the RT-33A sorties over Laos resumed and, soon, growing Viet Cong activities in South Vietnam and the need to map that country and its neighbours led to stepped up reconnaissance activities in the region.

Still not officially involved in the anti-guerrilla operations mounted by the governments of South Vietnam and Laos, but desirous of fulfilling its SEATO obligations, the United States undertook Projects *Pipe Stem* and *Able Mable*. Under the former, four McDonnell RF-101Cs of the 15th Tactical Reconnaissance Squadron deployed to Tan Son Nhut AB in Vietnam on 20 October 1961, while under the latter four RF-101Cs of the 45th TRS were sent to the Don Muang Airport in Thailand on 6 November. *Pipe Stem* lasted only 45 days, during which 67 sorties were flown over South Vietnam and Laos, but *Able Mable* marked the beginning of long-term USAF reconnaissance activities in South East Asia. Flying most of their missions over South Vietnam, but remaining

based at Don Muang until December 1962, the *Able Mable* RF-101Cs flew their 500th sortie in May 1962 and their 1000th less than seven months later.

For reconnaissance operations within South Vietnam, the RF-101Cs were initially supplemented by four Douglas RB-26Cs of the *Farm Gate* detachment which had arrived at Bien Hoa in December 1961. Later, additional RB-26Cs (as well as two experimental RB-26Ls specially equipped for night photography and carrying Reconofax IV infrared sensors) were provided, but in early 1964 the type had to be withdrawn from use due to wing structural fatigue. Afterwards, most tactical reconnaissance in South East Asia was provided by jet aircraft (RF-101Cs, RF-4C and RB-57Es). Equipped with a variety of forward, vertical, oblique, split vertical and panoramic cameras in

**Photographed by his wingman, this RF-101C overflies the North Vietnamese airfield at Kep, with a complement of MiG-17s in their revetments. Such photo-runs were usually accomplished with a pop-up manoeuvre, the Voodoos approaching at low-level before pulling up to around 15,000 feet for their run. As they cleared the target, they dived back down to low-level for their egress.**

**Less glamorous than either RF-101 or RF-4, Martin's RB-57E *Patricia Lynn* was an important reconnaissance effort that lasted for many years, flying out of Tan Son Nhut. Reconofax VI infra red sensors provided much night-time intelligence.**

**Above: Early RF-4Cs in South East Asia carried the grey and white scheme, but tactical pressure soon changed this to the three-tone camouflage carried by other tactical aircraft. For some time, the RF-4 and RF-101 flew side by side on the tac recon mission, but eventually the RF-4 fully replaced the Voodoo in late 1970.**

**Above right: Close-up detail of SR-71A 64-17974 shows 'Habu' mission marks. The SR-71 gained its well-known nickname from a species of snake that inhabits the island of Okinawa, from where it flew on Far East missions.**

**Below right: Lockheed's U-2C began *Dragon Lady* operations from Bien Hoa with the 4080th SRW (later 100th SRW). Clandestine surveillance was undertaken, including Sigint missions. Occasional lower-level missions were also flown with optical sensors, and much co-operation with the same unit's drone operations existed.**

**Below: A Kadena-based SR-71A closes in on the KC-135Q tanker for a refuelling over the South China Sea. Missions over North Vietnam were by no means the sole responsibility for the Kadena 'Blackbirds': Korea and China were also receiving its unique attentions.**

the nose and the bomb bay, the Martin RB-57Es also carried Reconofax VI infrared sensors. First deployed to Tan Son Nhut in April 1963 as part of the *Patricia Lynn* project, the RB-57Es proved to be the most effective reconnaissance aircraft to detect well camouflaged Viet Cong targets such as base camps, arms factories and training areas through the use of infrared imagery. Thus, with only six RB-57Es having been modified to the special *Patricia Lynn* configuration, the crews of Detachment 1 of the 33rd Tactical Group (Det. 1 of the 460th TRW after the organization of this wing at Tan Son Nhut in February 1966) were kept busy until the last of these modified Canberras were taken out of operation in August 1971 when the 460th TRW was inactivated.

## *Voodoos fly North*

For nearly 18 months after their move from Don Muang to Tan Son Nhut on 14 December 1962, the *Able Mable* RF-101Cs operated exclusively over South Vietnam. However, at the request of Premier Souvana Pouma, *Yankee Team* reconnaissance sorties were resumed over southern and central Laos in mid-May 1964. Six months later, RF-101Cs also began flying as pathfinders for F-100Ds flying *Barrel Roll* strikes in the northern portion of Laos. Similarly, pathfinder and damage assessment sorties were flown by Voodoos as soon as the USAF began flying *Flaming Dart* strikes against North Vietnam in February 1965, and on 29 March 1965 the RF-101Cs also flew the first ECM sorties of the war in support of *Rolling Thunder*. For that purpose three aircraft were each fitted with four QRC-160 jammers, but these ECM pods proved unsatisfactory and were quickly withdrawn. As operations over northern Laos and North Vietnam were almost beyond the practical range of the Tan Son Nhut-based RF-101Cs, the Air Force again sent a Voodoo detachment to Thailand. Based at Udorn RTAFB, the RF-101Cs of the 15th TRS began flying regularly over the North, suffering their first loss on 3 April 1965, while the 20th TRS continued operating over the South from Tan Son Nhut. Most frequently operating in the 'alone and unafraid' tradition of reconnaissance crews, the pilots of the 15th TRS initially only had to fear the AAAs and SAMs, as their Voodoos enjoyed a substantial speed advantage over the MiG-17s then operated by the NVNAF. However, with the appearance of the first MiG-21s in late April 1966, the task of the USAF reconnaissance crews became significantly more dangerous and, after an RF-101C was shot down in September 1967 by one of the Soviet-made fighters, the USAF banned Voodoo operations over North Vietnam. In areas where enemy fighters were not a threat, the RF-101Cs continued to provide a substantial share of all tactical reconnaissance activities until 16 November 1970 when the last Voodoo of the 45th TRS/460th TRW departed from Tan Son Nhut.

To supplement its RF-101Cs, and eventually to supplant them, the USAF had acquired RF-4C all-weather, day-night reconnaissance aircraft which were equipped with side-looking radar and infrared sensors in addition to their cameras, and had the added capability for in-flight processing of films. First arriving in the theatre in October 1965, when the 16th TRS was transferred from Shaw AFB to Tan Son Nhut, the RF-4Cs soon equipped several squadrons and operated all over South East Asia. Faster and more manoeuverable than the RF-101C, the reconnaissance version of the Phantom nevertheless was not immune to the ever more sophisticated North Vietnamese defensive network and losses mounted rapidly (including the aircraft in which the Vice Commander of the 7th Air Force, Major General Robert F. Worley, was flying in the DMZ area; hit by enemy fire the aircraft crashed and General Worley and his pilot, Major Robert F. Brodman, were killed). Notwithstanding the risks, and even though much valuable

reconnaissance information was provided by other systems as described further on, RF-4Cs flew on for the duration of the hostilities. In South Vietnam, where the VNAF had acquired its own reconnaissance capabilities, RF-4Cs were withdrawn in August 1971 when the 460th TRW was inactivated, whereas RF-4C operations from Thailand were continued by the 432nd TRW until the fall of 1974.

## *View from the top*

Although the bulk of manned photographic reconnaissance activities was provided by tactical aircraft, the USAF also made extensive use of the high-flying Lockheed U-2s and SR-71s of the Strategic Air Command. Under the code name *Dragon Lady*, the 4028th SRS/4080th SRW had first sent U-2Cs and crews to Bien Hoa in December 1963 to provide clandestine surveillance of North Vietnam and to develop a contingency list of targets in the North. Redesignated 4025th SRS/4080th SRW on 1 July 1965, and then 349th SRS/100th SRW on 25 June 1966, this unit continued to fly U-2Cs and later U-2Rs during the South East Asia War, with its Bien Hoa detachment being transferred to U-Tapao RTAFB in July 1970. An idea of the intensity of the squadron's operations in this theatre, and of the covert nature of its activities, can be gathered by the fact that its U-2s exceeded the 500 flying hours per month mark in January 1973 and the 600-mark in December 1974, after the official ending of US operations over North Vietnam!

Possibly preceded by Lockheed A-12s of the Central Intelligence Agency, SR-71s of the 9th Strategic Reconnaissance Wing were also sent to overfly portions of China and North Vietnam soon after the type had entered service in January 1966. Virtually nothing has been released about SR-71 contributions to operations in South East Asia, but there is little doubt that their unique capabilities were put to good use.

Less glamourous than those of manned aircraft, and hidden under many security layers, the *Blue Springs* operations of Remotely Piloted Vehicles received little attention and few public plaudits. Yet, RPVs were used continuously in South East Asia from August 1976 until the spring of 1975 and their employment met with unqualified success. After an aborted start in 1960, the development of reconnaissance drones began in earnest in February 1962 when the USAF ordered prototypes derived from the Ryan Q-2C target vehicles. Successful evaluation of these prototypes led to pro-

**SR-71A 64-17972 taxis in at Kadena following a mission, passing RC-135s in their revetments. For years the USAF refused to admit the Mach 3 bird was operating from Japanese territory, yet two or three times a week, crowds gathered to witness the SR-71 roaring off on another mission, producing enough noise to wake up most of the island.**

**The U-2Cs and Fs of the 100th SRW gave way to the much larger U-2R as these became available. The U-2R went on to compile an excellent war record, with unrivalled flying hours achieved. The 100th SRW moved to U-Tapao in 1970, and the last U-2R flight was recorded in March 1976.**

Left: The DC-130E Hercules was the definitive drone carrier, this example seen carrying two AQM-34M models. Note the different sensor installations in the noses.

Above: At a predetermined point, the drone shut off its engine and deployed the main parachute. The helicopter moved in for the catch, aiming to snag the smaller 'chute with grapnels suspended from two rods beneath the rear fuselage.

duction contracts, with the first Ryan 147Cs and 147Ds becoming operational in July 1963 with the 4080th Strategic Reconnaissance Wing, Strategic Air Command, at Davis-Monthan AFB in Arizona. At the same time, the 4025th SRS was activated in the wing to operate the Lockheed DC-130As used to launch the drones. Less than 14 months later these units, and their RPVs and DC-130s, were ordered overseas in support of the war in South East Asia.

Over the next 11 years the 4080th SRW launched no fewer than 3,435 Ryan drones, including many electronic data collection flights from South Korea (Project *Combat Dawn*), to gather intelligence data over North Vietnam, mainland China and North Korea. In spite of great variations in wing span and area (lowest and highest values being 13 ft (3.96 m) and 32 ft (9.75 m) and 36 sq ft (3.34 $m^2$) and 114 sq ft (10.59 $m^2$), respectively, for the low-altitude and high-altitude versions), the operational versions of the Ryan 147 RPV were all of basically identical configuration, with swept wing and tail surfaces. They were powered by a single turbojet (Continental J69 for all models except for Models 147T, 147TE and 147TF, which had a more powerful Continental J100) mounted beneath their fuselage. They included 14 models fitted for photographic reconnaissance, four models for ELINT, the Model 147N used as a decoy, the 147NQ and NX for dual use as decoy and reconnaissance vehicles, the 147NC which was a leaflet dropping vehicle, and the 147SC/TV which was fitted for real-time TV reconnaissance.

Whatever their size or mission, the Ryan RPVs used by the 4080th/100th SRW were air launched from Lockheed DC-130As or DC-130Es, with standard practice calling for two drones to be taken up on any given sortie to provide a backup RPV in case of technical difficulties with the primary vehicle or to enable the launch of either two reconnaissance drones, or of a reconnaissance drone and a decoy vehicle. Recovery of the RPVs, and of the capsule containing the camera or electronic recorders, was effected by programming the guidance systems to bring the drones back to a preplanned point. At the designated location and time, a parachute was automatically extracted to bring the RPV down. At first, following parachute descent, the drones were retrieved on the ground or while floating in the sea. However, to expedite the recovery and minimize damage to the reuseable RPVs, the contractor and the USAF adapted the Mid-Air Retrieval System (MARS) developed earlier for the recovery of the camera capsule of SAMOS reconnaissance satellites. With this method, the RPVs were snatched in mid-air by Sikorsky CH-3C or CH-3E helicopters and nearly eight out of every ten used in South East Asia were so recovered (the reliability of the MARS was indeed spectacular as in 2,745 attempts the 4080th/100th SRW retrieved 2,655 drones for an operational success rate of 96.7 percent). An even faster means of obtaining the data without recovering the RPVs was achieved by converting the electronic signals gathered by Ryan 147Ds or 147Es to continuous wave signals and transmitting these CW

Two DC-130s and a collection of high-altitude AQM-34Ps are seen in revetments at Bien Hoa. The 100th's drone operations moved to U-Tapao in 1970, after several sapper attacks at Bien Hoa.

signals to Boeing RB-47Hs orbiting outside the range of North Vietnamese defences.

Following the Gulf of Tonkin Incident and initial air operations over North Vietnam, the United States feared a possible intervention by the People's Republic of China. Accordingly, to obtain data on Chinese troop concentration and movements and to assess the capability of the Air Force of the People's Liberation Army, the Joint Chiefs of Staff ordered the 4080th SRW to deploy its drones and launch aircraft to Kadena AB on Okinawa, and to begin preparations for RPV overflights of the southeast China coast from the border of Vietnam to the Strait of Quemoy. The first operational drone flight along this route was made on 20 August 1964 when a Ryan 147B was launched from a Lockheed DC-130A (serial 57-0496). Even though the drone was damaged beyond repair in the parachute recovery, the intelligence data was recovered and the value of the reconnaissance drone was proven. More flights over southeastern China were made during the following weeks but soon the focus of interest changed. Concentrating their efforts on gathering data on the North Vietnamese defences, the RPVs and launch aircraft moved to Bien Hoa AB to be closer to the new objectives, with recoveries being made at or near Da Nang AB. In July 1970, four years after the 4080th SRW had been renumbered 100th SRW, most of the RPV operations were transferred to Thailand, with the launch aircraft being based at U-Tapao RTNAF and the drones being recovered near Nakhom Phanom RTAFB, while another detachment of the 100th SRW continued operating from Osan AB in South Korea.

### *Recovery success*

Even the briefest summary of reconnaissance drone activities between 1964 and 1975 must point out that the 4080th/100th SRW averaged nearly 27 operational launches per month and that nearly 93 percent of the RPVs completed their mission successfully. In fact, the recovery rate surpassed the most sanguine expectations as each RPV flew an average of 7.3 missions whereas planning had been based on 2.5 missions per drone; one low-altitude photo-reconnaissance Ryan Model 147SC even flew 68 sorties before failing to return. Of the 578 losses incurred during wartime operations, 251 RPVs were confirmed as having been brought down by enemy defences, 80 were lost for unknown reasons, and the remainder were not recovered due to various failures.

Peaking during *Linebacker II*, when 91 drones were launched during a 30-day period, reconnaissance RPV activities brought back a wealth of information and, undoubtedly, saved the lives of countless aircrews by flying many of the missions over the most heavily defended targets. Among their many achievements, the RPVs were credited with obtaining the first photographic evidence of SAM deployment in North Vietnam, the first close-range photographs of SA-2 missile detonation, the first infrared record of an SA-2 night launch, the first inflight photographs of North Vietnamese MiG-21s, and the first photographs of the North Vietnamese *Cheesebrick* passive tracking network. However, their greatest ELINT success was achieved on 13 February 1966 when a Ryan 147E, prior to being destroyed by the nearby explosion of an SA-2, transmitted details on the missile's proximity fuse operation, radar guidance data, and detonation over-pressure. The wealth of data ob-

**The Sikorsky CH-3E was used as the catch helicopter, operating from either Da Nang or Nakhon Phanom. The job was extremely difficult, especially with the larger drones such as this AQM-34R, a high-altitude version. These *Combat Dawn* drones were also used over Korea and China.**

**Furnishing initial Sigint coverage in the theatre were the Boeing RB-47H Stratojets of the SAC's 55th SRW. These were involved with drone operations during the early days under the *United Effort* programme, where drones were used to decoy SAMs into the air, the RB-47 lapping up the fusing and guidance data. This was one of the most significant Elint feats ever.**

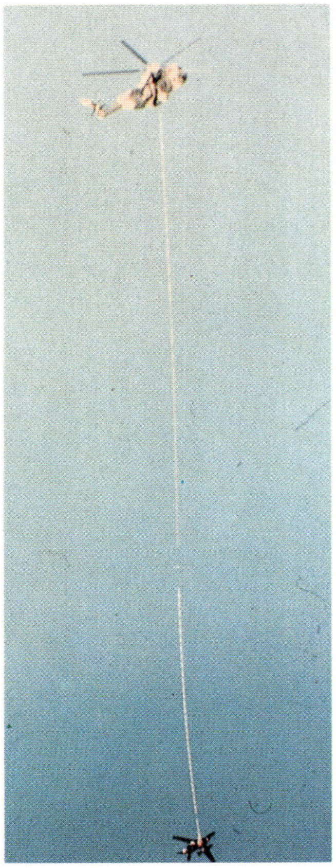

tained by this single flight enabled the development of the effective ECM systems which were soon fitted not only to aircraft operating in South East Asia, but also to most other tactical aircraft deployed by the United States and friendly nations around the world.

If the 4080th/100th SRW's use of RPVs for reconnaissance purposes was the most important, both in terms of number of launches and achievements, it was not the only application of drone technology as the unit also launched 22 chaff-dispensing decoy drones and 29 'Bullshit Bombers'. In typical military humour, this name was given to Ryan Model 147NCs which, fitted with underwing pods carrying propaganda leaflets, were sent over North Vietnam during the second half of 1972 as part of Project *Litterbug*. In addition, reconnaissance drones were evaluated under combat conditions by the US Navy.

### The Navy joins in

Following trials aboard the USS *Bennington* (CVS-20) off southern California, with a rocket booster being strapped beneath the fuselage for launch from the side of the flight deck, the Ryan Model 147SK was declared ready for combat use. Beginning on 23 November 1969, as part of Operation *Belfry Express*, 31 RPVs were launched from the USS *Ranger* (CVA-61) during operations in the Gulf of Tonkin, with recovery assistance being provided by CH-3 helicopters of the 100th SRW. Some spectacular photographs of North Vietnamese targets and defences were brought back by these Ryan 147SKs but, as the launch of the RPVs tied up the already over crowded carrier flight deck, the US Navy did not pursue this experiment.

Mention should also be made of the 4200th Test Wing's alleged use of Boeing B-52Hs to launch Lockheed D-21 drones over highly defended or sensitive targets in South East Asia. If, indeed, they took place, such operations remain highly classified.

The other unconventional method of intelligence gathering developed during the South East Asia War involved the use of seismic and acoustical sensors dropped from aircraft or helicopters. Developed under the direction of the Defense Communications Planning Group, beginning during the summer of 1966 to provide a means of monitoring traffic on the Ho Chi Minh Trail, these sensors had to be implanted with great accuracy. To do so the USAF first favoured using 'Helosid' sensors shot into the ground by CH-3C helicopters, while the US Navy modified 12 Lockheed SP-2E patrol aircraft into OP-2Es for use by Observation Squadron 67 (VO-67) to drop parachute-retarded sensors. Once implanted, the sensors broadcasted data to orbiting Lockheed EC-121Rs which relayed this to the 'Dutch Mill' Infiltration Surveillance Center at Nakhon Phanom RTAFB for interpretation by the *Task Force Alpha* of the USAF. At the 'Dutch Mill', computers compared incoming signals with previously stored data to determine what had caused the sensors to begin broadcasting. As other sensing devices successfuly reported the same sounds, the tactical analysis officers could determine the route followed by trucks or troops and could calculate their speed.

The initial deployment of the rudimentary sensors in Laos started in December 1967 as part of the *Mud River/Muscle Shoals* project. In practice, however, a number of technical problems with the

**Above: CH-3E seen about to reel in an AQM-34R.**

**Above left: AQM-34L (L229 Tom Cat) achieved the greatest number of missions, with 68. The L-model was the low-altitude photo-workhorse.**

**Below left: Officially 'neither denied nor confirmed,' the use of Lockheed D-21 supersonic reconnaissance drones for overflight of the People's Republic of China during the South East Asia War is likely to have taken place. Initially intended to be launched from specially modified Lockheed A-12s, the D-21s were launched operationally from beneath the wings of Boeing B-52Hs.**

**Below: A CH-3 sets down its precious cargo at the end of a mission.**

Above: Increased AAA defences along the Trail forced a switch to high speed delivery from McDonnell F-4Ds. This F-4D of the 25th TFS, photographed near Ubon RTAFB on 30 January 1969, carries a SUU-1 bomb dispenser, Mk-82 bombs, SAO-1 sensors, and AIM-7D Sparrows.

Right: This Beech YQU-22A (68-10532) was one of five relay aircraft deployed to Nakhon Phanom RTAFB in March 1969 as part of the *Pave Eagle I* programme.

Below right: Photographed from the starboard rear fuselage observation window (in which a flexible machine-gun has been mounted for flak suppression), parachute-retarded ALARS are seen being 'seeded' over the Ho Chi Minh Trail by an OP-2E of VO-67.

Below: Spikebuoy sensor canisters are shown about to be loaded on an USAF A-1E at Nakhon Phanom RTAFB.

sensors, delivery systems and interpretation soon surfaced, limiting the effectiveness of *Mud River/Muscle Shoals*. Frequently the helicopter-launched 'Helosids' did not survive impact with the ground, while the use of parachute-retarded sensors forced the Navy OP-2Es to fly low and slow over enemy defences, with losses soon becoming unacceptable. Likewise, as the North Vietnamese increased the number of antiaircraft guns along the Ho Chi Minh Trail, the risks for the slow orbiting EC-121R relay aircraft of the 553rd Reconnaissance Wing became prohibitive. To overcome the first set of problems, during the summer of 1968 the USAF adapted LORAN-equipped McDonnell F-4Ds to drop the sensors but, notwithstanding the use of sophisticated navigational equipment, accuracy was not as good as when slower aircraft or helicopters had been used. On the other hand, to reduce the vulnerability of its EC-121R relay aircraft, the USAF also experimented with *Pave Eagle*, the use of unmanned Beech QU-22Bs flying close to the sensors and relaying the data to the 'Dutch Mill', either directly or with intermediate rebroadcasting by EC-121Rs flying out of range of the enemy defences. Once some of the initial problems had been solved, *Igloo White* greatly increased the effectiveness of tactical aircraft on interdiction sorties along the Ho Chi Minh Trail by pinpointing enemy traffic. Moreover, the air-dropped sensors proved of exceptional value during the battle to break the siege of Khe Sanh during the spring of 1968, as they enabled artillery

**Above: Under the codename *Brown Cradles*, Douglas RB-66Bs (later EB-66Bs) moved to Tan Son Nhut to provide ECM escort for strike aircraft. They set up base at Takhli with the 6460th TRS, operating alongside EB-66C ESM platforms.**

**The USAF relied primarily on camouflaged Lockheed EC-121Rs of the 553rd Reconnaissance Wing to relay to the 'Dutch Mill' Infiltration Surveillance Center at Nakhon Phanom RTAFB data broadcasted by sensors 'seeded' by its helicopters and tactical fighters or by Navy OP-2Es. Also used in this role were the remotely-controlled Beech QU-22Bs.**

**Airborne early warning coverage was provided by the Lockheed EC-121D *Big Eye*. Occasionally aircraft operated without the large dorsal height-finding radar.**

fire and air bombardment to be concentrated in a timely manner against Viet Cong and North Vietnamese troops threatening the Marines' positions.

## *Electronic Warfare*

As soon as strikes north of the DMZ began to be flown on a regular basis, North Vietnam undertook with Soviet and Chinese help to beef up its defences, thus creating in turn a need for the United States to employ electronic countermeasures aircraft. Initially this function was fulfilled by six Douglas RB-66Cs (later redesignated EB-66Cs), deployed on a TDY basis from TAC to Tan Son Nhut in May 1965. These were equipped with four radar receiver positions to provide Electronic Support Measures (ESM, intended to locate and identify hostile electromagnetic signals) and nine jammers to furnish Electronic Countermeasures (ECM, the use of electronics to deceive, disrupt, jam, or negate the effectiveness of opposing electronics systems and techniques). Employed in a semi-escort role, these EB-66Cs penetrated North Vietnam with the strike aircraft and, orbiting in close proximity to the target areas, provided the strike forces with threat warnings and effectively disrupted the gun-laying radars with chaff and noise jammers.

Proving quite effective in the ESM role, the EB-66Cs detected the first evidence of *Fan Song* track-while-scan radar used by SA-2 surface-to-air missile batteries. However, six aircraft were not enough to provide both ESM and ECM and, to undertake the latter until most strike aircraft could be fitted with self-protection pods, in September 1965 USAFE sent five RB-66Bs (codenamed *Brown Cradles* and soon redesignated EB-66Bs) equipped with 23 jammers. Regrouped at Takhli RTAFB, the EB-66Bs of the 6460th TRS and the EB-66Cs of the 41st TRS (with all EB-66s being eventually assigned to the 42nd Tactical Electronic Warfare Squadron which moved from Takhli RTAFB to Korat RTAFB in September 1970) operated mostly over northern Laos and North Vietnam until SAMs began posing a serious threat to their employment as part of the strike force. As this threat materialized, with a first EB-66C being lost near Vinh on 24 February 1966, employment tactics were re-evaluated and the EB-66s were progressively forced to operate in a stand-off mode further and further away from the strike aircraft. The resultant loss in effectiveness was nonetheless partially made up by the use of improved detection devices and jammers (notably those fitted to the EB-66Es which began supplementing the EB-66Bs in September 1967), and EB-66s remained in service until January 1974 when the last 24 aircraft were ferried from Korat to Clark AB for reclamation.

Equally as important to the conduct of operations over North Vietnam were the *Big Eye*, *College Eye* and *Rivet Top* Lockheed EC-121 airborne early warning aircraft of the USAF, and their US Navy

**Accompanying most strikes north were the EB-66 Destroyers. Shown here is an EB-66B ECM platform, complete with a plethora of aerials, which grew and grew during the course of the war. The 'RH' tailcode belonged to the 42nd TEWS, 355th TFW, which operated all the EB-66s during the middle and late years of the conflict.**

counterparts. As recounted in Chapter 4, the first land-based AEW aircraft to deploy to South East Asia had been the Lockheed EC-121Ks of Airborne Early Warning Squadron One, which were sent to Vietnam in August 1964 to support initial strikes against North Vietnam by carrier-based aircraft and to provide coverage against potential North Vietnamese retaliatory air raids. In April 1965, as by then the USAF had been drawn into combat operations, the Air Defense Command first sent a five-aircraft detachment of its 552nd Aircraft Early Warning & Control Wing. Equipped with EC-121Ds, the *Big Eye* detachment was initially based at Tainan, Taiwan, but flew its first mission in support of *Rolling Thunder* from Tan Son Nhut on 17 April 1965. Subsequently, the detachment moved its operating base to Ubon RTAFB in February 1967, to Udorn RTAFB in July, and finally settled down at Korat RTAFB in October 1967.

## Radar coverage

At the onset of their deployment, the *Big Eye* aircraft had an important role in providing defensive radar coverage over South Vietnam. Fortunately, as the threat of offensive air operations by Ilyushin Il-28 jet bombers of the NVNAF never materialized and as ground-based radars were installed to provide adequate coverage over the Republic of Vietnam, the EC-121 air defence function was phased out in early 1967. On the other hand, the EC-121s continued to prove effective in controlling strikes against the North and in providing warning of MiG operations until the last *Linebacker II* sorties had been flown.

Operating over their own territory, the NVNAF interceptors enjoyed the distinct advantage of being GCI-controlled and of knowing with a fair degree of certainty the ingress and egress routes which the US strike aircraft had to follow. However, the assignment of EC-121s orbiting over the Gulf of Tonkin and over Laos, as well the use of carrier-based AEW aircraft and *Red Crown* radar warning and control vessels of the US Navy, went a long way in countering the first of these enemy advantages. Monitoring North Vietnamese activities and providing MiG warnings, EC-121Ds ensured that US aircraft did not stray into Chinese airspace.

As the USAF initially found that its *Big Eye* (renamed *College Eye* in March 1967) EC-121Ds lacked the necessary equipment to provide more than generalized warnings, new systems were quickly developed and led to the combat evaluation from 23 July to 15 December 1967 of a prototype EC-121M. Nicknamed *Rivet Top* and fitted with advanced airborne radar and IFF, this aircraft was able to transmit much more precise information quickly and directly to the strike aircraft. In addition, the EC-121M could locate active SAM

**Rapidly strengthened North Vietnamese defences, and the massive use of radar-directed AAA and SAMs by the enemy, rendered mandatory the deployment of electronic reconnaissance and jamming aircraft. This role saved the Douglas B-66/RB-66 series from an otherwise undistinguished career. Illustrated here is an RB-66C taking off from Takhli RTAFB in 1966.**

**A *College Eye* EC-121D over Thailand. Developed during the early fifties to extend the defensive radar network for the United States, the AEW versions of the Super Constellation were used by both the Air Force and Navy to provide control and MiG warning for tactical aircraft operating over the North.**

**Above right: Boeing RC-135D of the 6th SW in a revetment at Kadena. These aircraft flew *Combat Apple* missions when the RC-135M force was reduced due to aircraft away on maintenance. Used to operating in the cold of Alaska, the D-models proved troublesome in the South East Asia hothouse.**

sites and vector *Iron Hand* flights to attack them. Initial success with *Rivet Top*, with numerous 'kills' resulting from timely warnings and directions provided by this aircraft, led to extending its TDY deployment in stages until 31 January 1969. Later on, some of the systems tested with *Rivet Top* were retrofitted to the *College Eye* EC-121Ds. Nonetheless, the radar of these aircraft did not have the required 'look-down' capability to provide adequate warning against low-flying MiGs which, maintaining low level within radar ground clutter, trailed the US strike aircraft prior to making a quick zooming firing pass. In spite of this limitation, the EC-121Ds served with distinction until the end of May 1974, when the last eight *College Eye* aircraft departed Korat RTAFB to return to their home stations at McClellan AFB in California.

## Signals intelligence

The principal signals intelligence-gatherer during the war was the Boeing RC-135. For over four years, the six RC-135M aircraft of the 82nd SRS, 4252nd SW (376th SW after 1971) at Kadena maintained a 24-hour relay, MiG warning and surveillance effort. These *Combat Apple* missions involved a 19-hour flight with 12 hours on station over the Gulf of Tonkin or Laos. This monumental effort played havoc with the airframes, and aircraft had to return to the States periodically for maintenance. While one was away, an RC-135D from the 6th SW in Alaska filled the gap. KC-135R, RC-135C and RC-135U aircraft of the 55th SRW performed many special missions in the theatre. From their introduction, the RC-135 family kept the United States abreast of the North's military developments, particularly in the field of SAMs and radar.

Other types of Electronic Warfare aircraft operated during the South East Asia War included the EC-47D, EC-47N, EC-47P, and EC-47Q versions of the venerable Douglas C-47 transport, which were used primarily to locate Viet Cong radio transmissions under the code name of *Hawk Eye*; the Douglas C-54 specially fitted with infrared reconnaissance equipment for Project *Hilo Hattie* from March 1962 until February 1963; the *Brave Bull* Boeing C-97, which replaced the *Hilo Hattie* C-54; and special mission versions of the Boeing KC-135 and Lockheed C-130. Notably, SAC modified a few KC-135As to serve as *Combat Lightning* airborne relay platforms, with the first of these aircraft deploying to U-Tapao RTNAF in September 1966, and later also used the more capable EC-135Ls. For operations primarily outside of North Vietnam, but occasionally to support operations in the North (such as during major air rescue operations or to direct strikes along the Ho Chi Minh Trail), a number of C-130s were modified as Airborne Battlefield Command and Control Centers. ABCCC sorties were initially flown from Da Nang AB in Spetember 1965 but were later undertaken from Udorn RTAFB, first by a special detachment of the 314th TCW and then by the specially-constituted 7th Airborne Command and Control Squadron. Although several C-130 ABCCC configurations existed, the most frequent involved the installation of air-conditioned capsules containing electronic gear and data processing equipment to enable a crew of specialists to direct air strikes, relay friendly radio signals and record enemy transmissions.

## The FACs

Even though extensive use of high-resolution cameras, electronic sensors and other sophisticated systems appeared to dominate reconnaissance activities during the South East Asia War, these devices never fully replaced the old 'Mark

**Below right: During the last years of the war the highly-capable RC-135U *Combat Sent* flew missions in the war zone. The U-bird was not deployed specifically to Vietnam, but fitted it in to its global schedule. It was a prime vehicle for testing the latest in Sigint equipment.**

**Below: Sigint workhorse was the RC-135M *Combat Apple*, which provided non-stop MiG-warning, SAM-location, Comint, Elint and SAR-support for several years, flying 12-hour orbits over the Gulf of Tonkin and Laos. This heavy schedule played havoc with the aircraft, and they were covered in patches.**

One Eyeball', the eyes and common sense of forward air controllers. The FAC saga almost had an accidental beginning as it was due in large part to the personal initiative of two USAF officers. Sent on TDY assignment in early 1962 to fly with the VNAF Liaison Squadrons, Major Douglas Evans and Captain Thomas Cairney quickly became aware of the near impossibility of coordinating air-ground operations due to great variations in communications equipment installed in aircraft and helicopters of the VNAF or operated by ARVN troops. Moreover, they realized that the language barrier and the requirement of having Vietnamese observers direct strikes by *Farm Gate* aircraft also pointed out the need for well-established air control procedures and standardization of communications equipment. These findings promptly led to the assignment of USAF forward air controllers to advise and assist Vietnamese ground commanders and to develop procedures tailored to the theatre's requirements. From then on, almost forgotten by the media, the FACs performed their vital mission with great skill and dedication. The fact that two of the 12 Medals of Honor awarded to Air Force personnel went posthumously to forward air controllers (Captain Hillard A. Wilbanks, an O-1 pilot, and Captain Steven L. Bennett, an OV-10 pilot) is proof enough that this mission was indeed a demanding and dangerous one.

The first dedicated USAF forward air control unit to be assigned to Vietnam was the 19th Tactical Air Support Squadron which was activated at Bien Hoa AB in July 1963. Equipped with Cessna O-1Fs fitted with four underwing hardpoints for target marking rockets, the 19th TASS initially was

**Above**: The FAC had only his flying skill and his knowledge of the local geography to protect him from enemy guns. This Bird Dog pilot demonstrates the 'between the trees' method as he takes a closer look at the target.

**Above left**: A Cessna O-1F rolls in towards the jungle canopy. Carried under the wings are white phosphorus ('Willie Pete') rockets, which the FAC fires to mark the target.

The Cessna O-2A arrived in SEA to supplement and gradually replace the Bird Dog. O-2s were used as FACs over the North, their greater performance making them less vulnerable.

**Third-generation FAC aircraft in South East Asia was the North American OV-10A Bronco. The twin-turboprop aircraft introduced internal machine-guns for suppressive fire, and greater offensive capability with bomb and rocket racks.**

**Cessna O-2As at Nakhon Phanom RTAFB in 1970. Relatively few of this military version of the Cessna 337 light twin were painted glossy black for night FAC duty over the Ho Chi Minh Trail. Twenty-two O-2s were lost in operational accidents and 82 in combat (including three shot down by SA-7 shoulder-fired light SAMs).**

scheduled to remain in Vietnam no more than a year while Vietnamese pilots were trained to take over responsibility for forward air control duties. Meanwhile, the US pilots were to fly the aircraft with Vietnamese observers directing air strikes. In the end, however, American FACs were required even after the training of VNAF personnel as by then the tempo of operations was such that the need for forward air controllers had increased several fold. By the end of 1965, the USAF had assigned to Vietnam four Tactical Air Support Squadrons (the 19th, 20th, 21st, and 22nd) equipped with Cessna O-1Es and O-1Fs.

Most USAF forward air controllers were experienced jet pilots who required refresher training to fly light aircraft with tailwheel landing gear, as well as specialized in-country training provided in Hue at the grandiosely nicknamed FAC University (the name being irreverently abbreviated 'FAC U' by its high-spirited personnel). Once their training was completed, the FACs became the ground forces' favourite blue-suiters as, flying in close contact with the troops, they were able to spot and mark targets for the fast movers. Progressively, their O-1s, which lacked armour or self-sealing tanks and were too slow and too short-ranged, were supplemented by Cessna O-2As and North American OV-10As. Nevertheless, the older single-engined aircraft was never fully supplanted by O-2s and, in fact, the last Bird Dog departed

**Despite its higher speed and introduction of offensive weapons, the OV-10A was much louder, so that enemy gunners would be warned of its approach much earlier than with the O-2 it had superceded. This Bronco was involved in the rescue of the *Mayaguez* and its crew during the Koh Tang incident.**

**Right and below: Sent to South Vietnam to serve in the air defence role when North Vietnamese intrusion was feared, Convair F-102 Delta Daggers saw limited use over the South and flew only a few sorties over the North. The two- seat TF-102A was occasionally used in the fast-mover FAC role, and for flying chase on B-52 *Arc Light* raids.**

from Vietnam in June 1971, one month after the withdrawal of the 22nd TASS, the last of the O-2 FAC units. During their South East Asia service, the O-1s had flown 471,186 combat sorties, and had suffered 122 combat losses.

Preceded in Vietnam by a few O-2Bs, a version of the push-pull Cessna equipped with air-to-ground broadcasting equipment and a leaflet dispenser for psychological warfare missions, the O-2As began replacing O-1E/O-1Fs at Binh Thuy in June 1967. Still lacking adequate protection, the O-2As were faster than the O-1s and had four wing pylons to carry either double the number of target marking rockets or 7.62-mm Minigun packs. Specially developed as a counter-insurgency aircraft, the more capable OV-10A Bronco was substantially faster than either the O-1 or the O-2, was fitted with armour plating and self-sealing tanks, and carried a substantial armament (four 0.30-caliber machine guns and 3,600 lb/1633 kg of external load). Making its appearance in the theatre in July 1968, the twin-turbine Bronco proved well adapated to the FAC mission and remained in South East Asia until June 1974 when the last 12 were ferried from Nakhon Phanom RTAFB to Osan AB in Korea.

In addition to its large scale employment of propeller-driven FAC aircraft, the USAF also experimented with the use of two-seat jet fighters as high-speed airborne FACs in high threat areas, with the first *Commando Sabre* sortie being made on 28 June by an F-100F.

## *That Others May Live*

Rescue of downed aircrews was normally the responsibility of USAF fixed-wing aircraft and helicopters (the first pilot to be rescued by a helicopter was Captain E. C. Meek, a *Farm Gate* T-28B pilot, who had been shot down in South Vietnam on 10 September 1963), and during the war crews of the Aerospace Rescue and Recovery Service were credited with saving 3,833 persons from death or captivity, thus making good their motto: 'That Others May Live'. In the process, two helicopter pilots, Captain Gerald O. Young and First Lt. James P. Fleming, and the pilot of an escorting A-1H, Lieutenant Colonel William A. Jones, III, were awarded the Medal of Honor for their gallantry during rescue operations.

Prior to the arrival of its rescue helicopters, the USAF had deployed four Douglas SC-47 twin-engined rescue aircraft as part of the *Farm Gate* complement, which had arrived at Bien Hoa AB in

**Psychological warfare was a little-known aspect of the USAF involvement. This 9th SOS Cessna O-2B is fitted with a loudspeaker for broadcasting propaganda.**

**Principal psy-war type was the Douglas C-47. This speaker-equipped example is seen showering leaflets on to the jungle, offering rewards and safe conduct guarantees to defectors.**

Above: Standard USAF base rescue helicopter, the Kaman HH-43B Huskie was first deployed to South East Asia in June 1964. One of these early rescue helicopters is seen here hovering over a crash site. Later on, Huskies used for combat rescue were fitted with armour, additional fuel and a flexible gun.

Above right: The Sikorsky H-3 family were amphibious, and although this was not regularly practised, it did come in handy during rescues of airmen down in the swampy delta of the Mekong river.

November 1961. Two months later the USAF had organized Detachment 3, Pacific Air Rescue Center, to control air rescue operations from Tan Son Nhut AB. These fixed-wing rescue aircraft were later joined by additional SC-47s, by Grumman HU-16Bs (from June 1964), and by Douglas SC-54s (from June to December 1965). Of particular value were the HU-16Bs as these amphibians could pick up aircrews bailing out at sea. Accordingly, the first two HU-16Bs of the 33rd Air Rescue Squadron operating from Korat RTAFB were the precursors of a sizeable force of amphibians, with the number of available HU-16Bs being progressively increased, especially after USAF aircraft started operations against targets in North Vietnam. The HU-16B continued in operation until September 1967 when the type was finally replaced by helicopters, Lockheed HC-130H rescue communications aircraft and Lockheed HC-130P air tankers. In five years of service the Grumman amphibians had rescued 47 American aircrew members, but at a cost: enemy gunfire and weather had claimed the lives of nine HU-16 crew members.

The first USAF combat rescue helicopters to reach the war zone were two Kaman HH-43Bs of the 33rd Air Rescue Squadron, which in June 1964 were diverted to Nakhon Phanom RTAFB while they were on their way from Naha AB, Okinawa, to Bien Hoa AB. Soon, the USAF deployed additional detachments of HH-43Bs to Korat and Takhli Royal Thai Air Bases, and to Bien Hoa, Da Nang and Tan Son Nhut Air Bases in Vietnam. From this modest début, the use of combat rescue helicopters grew by leaps and bounds, reaching its apex with the attempted rescue of POWs from the Song Tay camp in November 1970.

While the HH-43Bs were well-suited for retrieving aircrews from burning aircraft, with their coaxial rotors clearing a swath in the flames and smoke, they lacked armour plating, self-sealing fuel tanks and armament to be regarded as effective combat rescue helicopters. Accordingly, the USAF requested that these features be incorporated in HH-43Fs modified from existing HH-43Bs. Fitted with 800 lb (363 kg) of titanium armour, a 350-US gallon (1325-litre) self-sealing fuel tank, a more powerful engine, and armed with a flexible M-60 0.30-caliber machine-gun, HH-43Fs arriving in Thailand in November 1964 were immediately given the responsibility of aircrew recovery throughout South East Asia. This, however, was only a temporary solution. The USAF was already planning to use the Sikorsky HH-3E Jolly Green Giant (this nickname being derived from a then-popular television advertisement for frozen food) and, later, the HH-53C Super Jolly Green for rescue of downed aircrews in enemy territory. Even in their base rescue role, HH-43s were progressively supplemented by Bell UH-1Fs which were also

Until the arrival in sufficient number of air-refuelable HH-3 and HH-53 helicopters, the Grumman HU-16B amphibian was the primary rescue aircraft for air crews forced to bail out over the Gulf of Tonkin. Often landing right next to the North Vietnamese coast, HU-16B crews took considerable risk to save their fellow air crews. Fortunately, only two HU-16Bs were lost in combat.

The Lockheed HC-130 *Crown* operated as overall command centre for rescue attempts. An equally important role was inflight refueling of the HH-3/HH-53 helicopters, one of the latter seen here demonstrating the technique.

flown on in-country rescue missions, as well as for other combat purposes, by Special Operations Squadrons.

The Jolly Green and Super Jolly Green helicopters (often simply known as the Jollies and Super Jollies) were among the great successes of the war and saved more Allied aircrews than any other type of aircraft. Development of the Sikorsky HH-3E, the first air-refuelable helicopter, had been undertaken in August 1964 in answer to a QOR (Qualified Operation Requirement) issued by the Air Rescue Service, Military Air Transport Service. Derived from the Sikorsky CH-3C twin-turbine transport helicopter, it incorporated most of the features (e.g., shatter-proof canopy, 1,000 lb/454 kg of titanium armour, powered winch with 240-ft/73-m cable and jungle penetrator, defensive armament, etc.) then deemed necessary for an effective rescue helicopter. Moreover, to provide it with the range and endurance required for SAR missions deep into enemy territory, the HH-3E had internal tanks of increased capacity, carried two 200-US gallon (757-litre) external tanks and could be air-refueled. For this latter purpose, the HH-3E was fitted with refueling probe on the right side of the forward fuselage and fuel was transferred by The British-developed probe-and-drogue system from external pods mounted beneath the wings of Lockheed HC-130P air tankers.

Preceded in South East Asia by two CH-3Cs on loan from the Tactical Air Warfare Center and operated from Nakhon Phanom RTAFB by Detachment 1 of the 38th Air Rescue Squadron, two HH-3Es were airlifted to Bien Hoa AB in November 1965 to initiate Jolly Green combat operations. In turn, the still more capable Sikorsky HH-53B and HH-53C Super Jolly Greens made their début in the theatre 22 months later with Detachment 2 of the 37th ARRSq and soon proved to be the ultimate rescue helicopter. Nearly twice as large as the HH-3E, faster, and carrying more armour and armament (three GAU-2B/A 7.62-mm Miniguns versus two M-60 0.30-caliber machine-guns), the HH-53C was more than three times as powerful as the Jolly Green. Consequently, it could hover longer and at higher elevation, a capability of great value in the tropical mountains where aircrews from the Aerospace Rescue and Recovery Squadrons were frequently operating.

## Parajumpers

The Jolly Green's aircrew was normally comprised of two pilots, a crew chief/gunner, and a parajumper, whereas the Super Jolly Green's aircrew included a second parajumper. The parajumpers (para-rescue jumpers or, simply, PJs), the unsung heroes of the Vietnam War, were trained scuba divers (for water rescue of downed aircrews), qualified parachutists, experts with small arms and in hand-to-hand combat, and fully

The mighty 'Super Jolly' introduced much greater flexibility to the rescue helicopter role, being able to hover at higher altitudes while being more heavily-armed and armoured. This Sikorsky HH-53C taxis in at Nakhon Phanom.

## Sikorsky HH-53C Super Jolly Green Giant

**Unsung heroes of the South East Asia War, the crews of the Aerospace Rescue and Recovery Service were credited with saving 3,833 lives during combat operations. Although it initially operated a number of fixed-wing aircraft, for combat rescues the AR&RS relied essentially on helicopters: HH-43, HH-3 and HH-53. The twin-turbined HH-53C was by far the best type for this role as it had good performance, adequate armour protection and armament, and long-range capability. For deep penetration in North Vietnam and Laos, HH-53Cs were refueled by Lockheed HC-130Ps, a retractable refueling probe being provided on the starboard side of the Super Jolly Green Giant.**

JET INTAKE
RESCUE

Above: Suppressive fire could be provided from the helicopter itself, using door-mounted Miniguns. The pararescue jumpers (PJs) operated these during the rescue attempt.

Above right: The HH-43 'Pedro' was quickly supplanted in the rescue role by the larger Sikorsky helicopters, but was used on other duties. Here a 38th ARRS machine moves fire suppression equipment at the base of Udorn.

trained medical corpsmen. Like the other rescue helicopter crewmen, they faced the array of dangers inherent in flying low and slow under often intense enemy fire, but in addition they regularly jumped, or were winched down, to assist downed aircrews requiring special assistance.

To refuel its Jolly Greens and Super Jolly Greens, the Aerospace Rescue and Recovery Service operated HC-130Ps commencing with the arrival of the first of these air tankers in South East Asia in September 1967. Obtained by installing fuselage fuel tanks and underwing refueling pods to existing Lockheed HC-130H airframes, the HC-130Ps were also fitted with the ARD-17 Cook Aerial Tracker system to locate downed airmen. Other methods used to increase the range of rescue helicopters included staging through temporary landing strips (*Lima Sites*) in Laos or, as first done in the spring of 1967, taking on fuel while hovering over US Navy ships operating in the Gulf of Tonkin (Operation *High Drink*).

With Jollies and Super Jollies, the deployed units of the Aerospace Rescue and Recovery Service (designated Air Rescue Service prior to 8 January 1966) were able to step up their activities and to begin flying missions deep into North Viet-

Although primarily used for cargo and troop transport and to recover RPVs, the CH-3E version of the large single-rotor Sikorsky helicopter was also operated in the rescue role. One is seen here hovering over dense jungle foliage, a difficult terrain in which to locate downed aircrews.

Below left: A CH-3 moves in to an F-5 crash site to rescue the pilot. A helo may come later to retrieve the aircraft.

Right: A Sikorsky HH-53 hovers while PJs winch up a downed airman.

Below: Helicopter escort was usually provided by a pair of Douglas A-1 Skyraiders.

**Operating from Nakhon Phanom RTAFB, the 1st SOS was one of the Air Force Skyraider squadrons providing escort and fire suppression for rescue helicopters. Even when carrying three external tanks, to have the necessary endurance for long rescue missions, the trusty 'Spad' still had 12 external store points to supplement the punch of its four 20-mm cannon.**

nam. As a rule, these deep-penetration rescue operations involved a large number of aircraft in addition to the air-refueled HH-3Es (HH-53Bs, or HH-53Cs) and their HC-130P tankers/airborne rescue command posts. For close-in protection of the helicopters, and to provide fire-suppression during rescue operations, the USAF relied mainly on Douglas A-1E and/or A-1H Skyraiders (the propeller-driven Spads, with their famous call-sign 'Sandy') of the Udorn-based 602nd Air Commando Squadron/Special Operations Squadron, and of the Nakhon Phanom-based 1st Special Operations Squadron. As the war went on the venerable A-1s were supplemented by Cessna A-37Bs and, later, by its intended replacement in the helicopter-escort role, the LTV A-7Ds of the 3rd TFS. Protection against potential interference by NVNAF MiGs was provided by tactical jet fighters, which also furnished fire-suppression. When conditions so dictated, more fire power could be provided for the rescuers by gunships such as Douglas AC-47s, Fairchild AC-119s, or Lockheed AC-130s. To direct the fire of the fighters and gunships and to provide other forward air control duties during search and rescue operations, North American OV-10s were extensively used. Equipped with the *Pave Nail* night observation system and the *Pave Spot* laser range designator, and thus capable of directing operations at night, the OV-10s proved to be a most useful addition to the integrated search and rescue task force.

## Rescue exploits

While many of these complex rescue operations were performed relatively smoothly and quickly, numerous other missions were protracted affairs lasting several days and involving large numbers of helicopter and fixed-wing aircraft sorties. The most famous of these arduous missions, but certainly not an atypical one, was the rescue of Lieutenant Colonel Iceal E. Hambleton, the sole survivor of the crew of an EB-66C of the 42nd TEWS/388th TFW which had been shot down near the DMZ on 2 April 1972. During the next 12 days jet fighters, A-1s, OV-10s, UH-1s, and HH-53s repeatedly made sorties, with the USAF crews of an OV-10 and an HH-53C, as well as that of an Army Huey, being lost prior to the safe recovery of Lieutenant Colonel Hambleton.

In addition to their usual , but far from routine, rescue operations, one HH-3E from the 37th ARRSq and five HH-53Cs from the 40th ARRSq, supported by USAF aircraft (C-130E *Combat Talon* and RC-135M *Combat Apple* aircraft, A-1Hs, F-4Ds, F-105Gs, EC-121Ds, HC-130Ps, and KC-135As), carrier-based aircraft, and Air America's C-123s, were used for a daring attempt at freeing allied personnel believed to be held captive in a POW camp at Son Tay, only 23 miles (37 km) from Hanoi. The raid was brilliantly planned and executed. However, faulty intelligence had failed to detect the prior transfer of the POWs to other North Vietnamese facilities and the disappointed rescuers returned empty handed. The crew of an F-105G, which had been forced to eject over Laos after being hit by a SAM during the operation, was rescued by one of the HH-53Cs.

After the US withdrawal from Vietnam in February 1973, the Air Force retained in Thailand its HH-43 base rescue helicopters, as well as the HH-53Cs of the 40th ARRSq and the HC-130P tankers of the 56th ARRSq, to support operations in Cambodia until 15 August 1973. Subsequently,

**'Sandy' Skyraiders suffered terribly from the attentions of enemy gunners. One of the bravest parts of the 'Sandy' mission was trolling for fire, deliberately flying over the rescue site to draw enemy guns into use, so that they could be located and attacked before the vulnerable and valuable helo came in for the rescue.**

'Sandy' flights often worked with FACs, whose local knowledge often proved invaluable. This OV-10A 'Nail' FAC machine is accompanied by two 1st SOS Skyraiders on their way to a rescue.

the Thailand-based helicopters and supporting aircraft, augmented by CH-53 transport helicopters, took part in two important operations: the evacuation of US and allied personnel from Saigon in April 1975, and the May 1975 recovery of the American-registered cargo ship *Mayaguez* and the rescue of its crew from their Cambodian captors on Koh Tang Island. With the inactivation of the 40th ARRSq at Korat RTAFB on 31 January 1976, all Aerospace Rescue and Recovery activities in South East Asia ended.

During the South East Asia War, the 37th, 38th, and 40th Air Rescue Squadrons (redesignated Aerospace Rescue and Recovery Squadrons on 8 January 1966) were wholly or partially equipped with HH-43/HH-3/HH-53 rescue helicopters. Fixed-wing rescue aircraft (SC-47s, SC-54s, HC-130Hs, HC-130Ps and HU-16s) were assigned to the 31st, 33rd, 36th, 37th, 38th, 39th, 56th, and 79th squadrons, or detachments thereof.

## *Frequent Wind: The Final Evacuation*

A little over one and a half years following the US withdrawal from the Republic of Vietnam, the situation in the South had deteriorated to such an extent that American plans for the inevitable had to be made. Sensitive equipment and materials (such as nuclear fuel for the 250-kv atomic reactor at Da Lat, Tuyen Duc Province) and, more importantly, large numbers of people, would have to be evacuated prior to the final overrun of the country by the NVA. To that effect, Operation *Talon Vise* was planned to evacuate some 8,000 Ameri-

With canopy slid back, an A-1H pilot relaxes during the flight back to Nakhon Phanom. Only in the later part of the war was the trusty 'Spad' replaced by Cessna A-37s and Vought A-7s in the rescue support role, and neither could hope to achieve as much as this much-loved anachronism.

cans and Third Country Nationals and up to one million Vietnamese through commercial and military airlifts from Tan Son Nhut AB, sealift from Saigon and Vung Tau, and helicopter transport to ships of the US Navy standing offshore. *Talon Vise* contingency plans were ready by the beginning of 1975 but, for two months, lacked a sense of urgency. However, the unexpected strength and rapidity with which the NVA offensive succeeded in March 1975 lead to the abandonment of *Talon Vise* in favour of an accelerated evacuation, *Frequent Wind*.

## Massive transport force

To undertake this massive evacuation, the United States disposed of Military Sealift Command ships and merchantmen flying friendly foreign flags, C-141As and C-5As of the Military Airlift Command, C-130s of the Tactical Command, and, initially, civil transport aircraft operating under MAC contracts. Transport helicopters were to be provided by the Seventh Air Force out of Thailand (CH/HH-53s), ship-based Marine units (CH-46s and CH-53s), and Air America (UH-1s). To provide the necessary communications and fire suppression support, the Air Force was to employ Thailand-based C-130s as Airborne Command Posts, KC-135s for radio relay and air refueling, AC-130 gunships and tactical aircraft (A-7s, F-4s, F-111s, and OV-10s), while the Navy was to deploy the USS *Enterprise*, *Kitty Hawk*, and *Midway* (the latter to act primarily as a helicopter platform) and the Marines were to supply ship-based AH-1J Cobra helicopter gunships.

The evacuation of US dependents and non-essential personnel, as well as the so-called 'baby-lift' (the airlift of Vietnamese orphans), got underway on 1 April 1975 using all available military aircraft and some commercial airliners. In spite of the discontinuation of C-5A operations following the tragic crash of a Galaxy on 4 April (with the loss of 155 persons, most of them children), the pace accelerated during the next two weeks, with C-141As and C-130s operating under peacetime load limitations of 94 and 75 passengers per flight respectively. After 20 April, as the situation became even more critical, massive efforts were made and load limitations were lifted, thus enabling both C-141s and C-130s to airlift loads of 180 evacuees. Even these limits soon went unheeded; for USAF aircraft records of 316 people on board C-141s and 260 on board C-130s were reported while a VNAF C-130A was said to have been flown out of Vietnam with 452 people on board! The rapid surrounding of Saigon by NVA troops, with their light and heavy AAA (including 85-mm radar-directed guns) and their SA-7 *Strella* ('Grail') shoulder-fired and SA-2 ('Guideline') ground-to-air missiles, finally forced the suspension of C-141 operations on 27 April. Flying day and night, the C-130s remained active until the early hours of the 29th when heavy and accurate Communist rocket fire at Tan Son Nhut forced an end to all fixed-wing US airlift operations. All together, from the 1st to the 29th of April, 50,493 persons had been airlifted in the course of 375 C-141 and C-130 sorties (plus a small number of C-5 sorties and numerous contract civil flights).

In anticipation of the last minute helicopter evacuation of personnel scattered in various locations throughout downtown Saigon, a Special Planning Group had identified and prepared 13 rooftop helicopter landing sites suitable for use by UH-1s of Air America and had set aside a fleet of 30 buses to pick up personnel in other areas. Buses and UH-1s were to bring the evacuees to the main evacuation center at the Defense Attaché Office complex at Tan Son Nhut for transfer by the larger Air Force and Marine helicopters to Thailand or to Navy ships in the South China Sea. In addition, the CH-46s and CH-53s were to evacuate personnel directly out of the US Embassy. In accordance with these plans, both air and surface shuttles between downtown Saigon and Tan Son Nhut began after daybreak on 29 April with Air America utilizing 20 UH-1s.

## Panic anticipated

Difficulties were soon encountered; in sometimes violent attempts to seek refuge, panick-stricken South Vietnamese interfered with the movements of helicopters and buses. This situation, however, had been anticipated by the planners who had provided for a show of force by low-flying US tactical aircraft, and for the use of an 840-man Ground Security Force from the 3rd Marine Amphibious Brigade to provide security at the main evacuation center at Tan Son Nhut. The Ground Security Force began arriving at 15:12 hours on 29 April aboard the first Marine CH-53s sent in for the final airlift from Tan Son Nhut. Under this Force's control the evacuation went on for nine hours, with the last helicopter departing the air base at 00:12 hours on 30 April.

Meanwhile, the evacuation at the US Embassy was threatened by an ugly mob as desperate Vietnamese sought to flee the approaching Communists. Accordingly, 130 Marines were brought in from Tan Son Nhut to assure the safety of American personnel and key Vietnamese officials who were scheduled to be evacuated. During the final hours CH-53s operated from a landing site in the Embassy's parking lot, while the lighter and smaller CH-46s flew from its rooftop. Finally, at 04:45 hours on 30 April, Marines from the Ground Security Force became the last Americans to de-

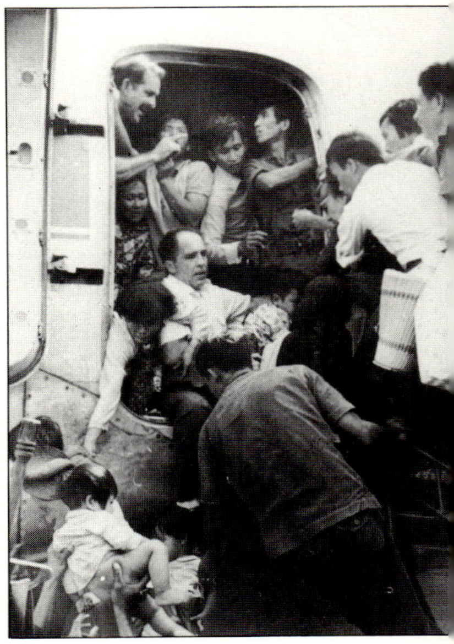

**A civilian pilot tries to keep back a surge of Vietnamese trying to board his aircraft at Nha Trang, hoping to escape south, away from the rapidly advancing armies from the North, not that going south would help. The evacuation south had thrown up some of the more amazing aviation stories, with 290 people cramming on to a World Airways Boeing 727 out of Da Nang, which completed its flight south with wheels down after being fouled by a body. Others hung on grimly in the wheel wells.**

**The Lockheed C-5A Galaxy was employed during initial stages of the airlift, but was withdrawn following a tragic crash after take-off from Tan Son Nhut. The passengers had been orphans flying to new homes in the US. 155 people died in the crash, mostly children.**

part the Embassy. Over the previous 24 hours, Air Force and Marine helicopters had flown 638 sorties under the cover of 173 Navy fixed-wing tactical aircraft sorties, 24 Marine helicopter combat sorties, and 212 Air Force tactical support sorties. Together with some 250 sorties by Air America UH-1s (many of which took their charges straight out to the Navy ships), the military helicopters had succeeded in extracting 7,815 evacuees (less than 18 percent of which were Americans) and 989 personnel of the Marine security forces. Remarkably, this was achieved with only minimal losses: two CH-46 crewmen and two Marine guards were killed, and one Navy A-7E and two Marine helicopters (an AH-1J and a CH-46) were lost. All told, some 130,000 people (44 percent of which left by air, the balance by sea) had been evacuated during the month-long *Frequent Wind* in the face of difficult and, finally, sickening conditions. Revolting as was the sight of forlorn and abandoned Vietnamese, *Frequent Wind* marked an end to America's most unpopular war and did save tens of thousands of Vietnamese who later relocated to the United States.

**USS *Enterprise* was one of the carriers covering the evacuation, seen here with a full load of CH/RH-53s to be used for airlift duties. On the rear are the Grumman F-14s of VF-1 and VF-2, on the type's first operational cruise.**

## *Long-term restrictions*

For the Air Force 'blue suiters', as for their fellow aviators of the US Navy and the US Marine Corps, the South East Asia War had been a long period of frustration and sacrifice in the face of growing opposition to the war and political restrictions on their operations. These ranged from the initially imposed requirement for the *Farm Gate* aircrews to take part in combat operations only if a qualified South Vietnamese officer was on board and authorized a strike, to the long standing restrictions concerning the types of targets that could be attacked in North Vietnam. Nevertheless, they performed their duty with dedication and pride in the flag, and showed conspicuous gallantry in the face of adversity. Their sacrifices, even though not yet fully appreciated by many of their countrymen, were finally vindicated by the successes achieved during *Linebacker I*, and more so during *Linebacker II*, when they were finally free to use the full might of American airpower. The war ended soon thereafter but the price paid had been high: 2,118 airmen had been killed between February 1962 and August 1973, and 3,460 others had been wounded. In addition, although 368 prisoners of war were returned by North Vietnam and its allies, 586 airmen remain unaccounted for, either missing in action or still prisoners. A total of 2,250 aircraft (including 442 F-4s, 397 F-105s, 243 F-100s, and 26 B-52s) had been lost to combat and/or operational causes in 5,226,701 sorties during which 6.16 million tons of munitions had been expended (compared to 2.15 million tons in all of World War II and 0.45 million tons in the Korean War).

**In the US Embassy compound, the Marines of the Ground Security Force supervise loading of a CH-53. while the large helicopters used the compound, smaller CH-46s and UH-1s used the roof.**

# US Navy Aviation in South East Asia

Among the many tragedies of the Vietnam War, none was to have greater consequences than the infamous Gulf of Tonkin Incident. Coming about as a result of a combination of human errors, faulty intelligence, and poor communications on both sides, this event and the ensuing Congressional Resolution of 10 August 1964 officialized the United States' participation in the conflict. In part, the resolution read:

> Consonant with the Constitution of the United States and the Charter of the United Nations and in accordance with its obligations under the Southeast Asia Collective Defense Treaty, the United States is . . . prepared, as the President determines, to take all necessary steps, including the use of armed forces, to assist any member or protocol state . . . requesting assistance in defense of its freedom.

By then, of course, US forces (including elements of naval aviation, which had lost their first aircraft on 6 June 1964 when a Vought RF-8A flown from the USS *Kitty Hawk* by Lt. Charles F. Klusmann of VFP-63 had been shot down over Laos) had already been fighting in South East Asia for over two years. Moreover, ever since the end of April 1961, when President John F. Kennedy had approved a plan for covert operations against North Vietnam in the hope of conveying American determination to help prevent a Communist takeover of South Vietnam, the United States had been masterminding clandestine operations in the North. At first unsystematic and poorly coordinated, these operations were expanded after *OPLAN 34-A* was approved in January 1964 by President Lyndon B. Johnson. Calling for a 12-month programme of covert actions, *OPLAN 34-A* notably included the use of US Navy destroyers to perform coastal reconnaissance in the Gulf of Tonkin, with one or more carriers of the Seventh Fleet steaming close by to provide assistance if needed, while South Vietnamese gunboats were to shell targets in the North Vietnamese panhandle.

## *The Tonkin Gulf Yacht Club*

During the afternoon of 2 August 1964 North Vietnamese motor torpedo boats attacked the USS

**Following the hectic activity of a day's air strike, crew get the chance to relax under a spectacular South China Sea sky. The carrier effort was maintained throughout the war, ably assisting the Air Force strikes in both North and South Vietnam.**

**Above: Unguided rockets remained a favourite weapon of all US pilots throughout the conflict, being extremely effective against 'soft' installations and vehicles. An A-4 of VA-23 looses off a pod at Viet Cong forces while cruising at 'Dixie Station'.**

**Above right: Full 'burner and steam clouds mark the launch of a VF-211 Vought F-8 Crusader from USS *Bon Homme Richard*.**

**The cat officer points to the wooden deck of the USS *Oriskany* as an F-8F of VF-111 is about to be launched from the No. 2 catapult for yet another sortie over the North. The squadron's nickname 'Sundowners' is painted on the raised fuselage decking.**

*Maddox* (DD-731), after possibly confusing it with one of the South Vietnamese gunboats. At that time the only carrier within close proximity was the USS *Ticonderoga* with Air Wing Five (CVW-5) comprised of two squadrons of F-8Es (VF-51 and VF-53), two squadrons of A-4Es (VA-55 and VA-56), and one squadron of A-1H/Js (VA-52), as well as detachments from VAH-4 (A-3Bs), VFP-63 (RF-8As), VAW-11 (E-1Bs), and HU-1 (UH-2As). Reacting swiftly, four VF-53 Crusaders came to the rescue of the US destroyer, sinking one of the North Vietnamese patrol boats with gunfire and Zuni rockets.

A tense situation prevailed for the next two days. The USS *Turner Joy (DD-951)* joined the *Maddox* close to the North Vietnamese shore, and the USS *Constellation* (CVA-64), and CVW-14 comprised of two squadrons of F-4Bs, two squadrons of A-4Cs, one squadron of A-1H/Js, one squadron of A-3Bs, and detachments of RF-8As and UH-2As) was sent into the Gulf of Tonkin. Taking the Navy show of force as a provocation, Hanoi attempted a new torpedo boat attack against the US destroyers during the night of 4 August. President Johnson, wishing to preserve the US right to operate in international waters, approved a retaliatory strike against five of the torpedo boats' support facilities. As ordered, the two Air Wings flew 64 attack sorties against North Vietnam on 5 August, destroying more than half of the North Vietnamese PT boat force and setting afire POL and supplies but losing one of their A-4Cs, while its pilot, Lt. (jg) Everett Alvarez became the first POW in North Vietnam. As another attack carrier, the USS *Ranger*, and an antisubmarine carrier, the USS *Kearsage*, were then added to CTF77 (Carrier Task Force 77), and as on 10 August Congress passed its Gulf of Tonkin Resolution, it appeared that the naval war was on. Reason, however, prevailed for a few months and no further strikes were flown against North Vietnam until February 1965.

Three attack carriers, the USS *Coral Sea*, *Hancock*, and *Ranger*, were 'on-the-line' in the Gulf of Tonkin when their Air Wings were ordered on 7

**With its tailhook partially retracted but still holding the arresting wire, this Douglas A-3B of VAH-4 Det 62 has just 'trapped' aboard the USS *Independence* (CVA-62). In April 1965, when this photograph was taken, CVA-62 was on the line in the Gulf of Tonkin. Bearing the tail code AG and the BuNo 151178, the Skyhawk parked to the side is an A-4E of VA-86.**

February 1965 to launch a 100-aircraft 'Alpha Strike' in retaliation for Viet Cong attacks against US facilities in South Vietnam. Impeded by heavy monsoon weather, this first *Flaming Dart* mission against the Chanh Hoa barracks in the North Vietnamese panhandle proved disappointing and resulted in the loss of three carrier-based aircraft to AAA fire; two of the pilots were rescued, but the pilot of an F-8D from VF-154 became the second naval officer to be taken prisoner.

In March 1965 the policy of attacking North Vietnam only on a retaliatory basis gave place to a sustained programme of bombing, *Rolling Thunder*. The first Navy *Rolling Thunder* strikes were flown on 18 March by Air Wings Fifteen and Twenty-One, respectively embarked aboard the *Coral Sea* and *Hancock*; from then on CTF77 played a major role, with two to three carriers being kept on-the-line throughout the duration of *Rolling Thunder*. Bombing mission by A-3Bs were initiated by VAH-2 on 29 March and the first nocturnal armed reconnaissance missions was undertaken by CVW-2 (*Midway*) and CVW-15 (*Coral Sea*) during the night of 15 April. On that date, naval aviators also flew their first in-country missions when enemy positions near Black Virgin Mountain were struck. Subsequently, carriers operating in support of the ground battle steamed on 'Dixie Station' in the South China Sea off the coast of South Vietnam, whereas those taking part in the war against the North operated from 'Yankee Station' in the Gulf of Tonkin.

## New types

Other noteworthy events affecting Air Wing operations during 1965 were the combat début of the Grumman A-6A Intruder all-weather attack aircraft (in July with VA-75 aboard the USS *Independence*) and of the Grumman E-2A airborne early warning aircraft (in November with Detachment C of VAW-11 aboard the USS *Kitty Hawk*); and the first combat cruise by the nuclear-powered USS *Enterprise*, which went on-the-line at Dixie Station on 2 December and moved to Yankee

**USS *Hancock* was among the first carriers 'on the line' following the 1964 Tonkin incident. It is seen here later in the war, complete with an air group of Vought F-8 Crusader fighters, Douglas A-4 Skyhawk attack aircraft, Grumman E-1 Tracer AEW platform and RF-8 photo-reconnaissance aircraft.**

**Left: Rivalry between F-8 and F-4 fighter units continued throughout the war. The Crusader proved itself an excellent dogfighter, and the carriage of cannon gave its pilots an added dimension, although in practise the 20-mm Colt-Brownings were prone to jamming, and only three MiG kills involved the use of the guns.**

**Right: Grumman Hawkeyes brought a dramatic increase in radar coverage with them when they joined the larger carriers in the South China Sea. Shown here is an E-2B of VAW-116, launching from USS *Constellation*.**

Station 15 days later. Also during that year the Navy suffered its first loss to a SAM (an A-4E of VA-23 being brought down on 12 August) and began using air-to-ground guided missiles; these were AGM-45 Shrikes for use during *Iron Hand* strikes against North Vietnamese radar sites and AGM-12 Bullpups for precision attacks against certain types of targets.

The carrier fighters got their first taste of air combat on 9 April 1965 when F-4Bs of VF-96, flying BARCAP from the USS *Ranger*, strayed too close to China and were engaged near the island of Hainan by MiG-17s of the Air Force of the People's Liberation Army; VF-96 claimed a probable but one of its Phantoms failed to return. More successful was the 17 June engagement when two NVNAF MiG-17s became the first confirmed 'kills' of the war, the victors being two crew of VF-21 (Cdr. Lou Page and Lt. John C. Smith, Jr., and Lt. Jack 'Dave' Batson and LCdr. Robert Doremus). Three days later a greater feat was achieved by Lts. Charlie Hartman and Clint Johnson who, flying piston-powered A-1H Skyraiders with VA-25, shared a victory over a MiG-17 when NVNAF pilots made the mistake of trying to tangle with the Skyraiders at low speed. During the remainder of the year only one more probable (by a VF-151 crew) was scored by naval aviators.

After the start of *Rolling Thunder*, carrier after carrier deployed to the Gulf of Tonkin, and the

**One can feel the awesome power shaking the deck as bomb- and rocket-laden Douglas Skyraiders prepare for a strike launch. Looking somewhat out of place on the carrier decks alongside the sleek jets, the 'Spads' enjoyed several years of intense combat with the Navy, before continuing their illustrious career with USAF and VNAF units.**

## Douglas A-1H Skyraider

**Looking somewhat antiquated in the midst of jet fighters and attack aircraft crowding the deck of carriers operating in the Gulf of Tonkin, the venerable Skyraider still played an important role in operations over the North and over the South. Bearing the attractive CAG markings during CVW-21 deployment aboard the USS *Ticonderoga* (CVA-14) between May and December 1964, this A-1H of VA-52 carries two 2,000-lb bombs, two 500-lb bombs and a 300-gallon Aero 1A ventral drop tank. In addition to the more common A-1H and A-1J single-seat versions, the Navy also made more limited use of four-seat EA-1Fs to provide ECM support.**

COM ATK CAR AIR WING NINETEEN
USS TICONDEROGA
NAVY
VA-52
NM
34569
A-1H
134569
Keith Fretwell

**Above: The North American RA-5C Vigilante provided tactical intelligence from the larger carriers. Armed with infra-red linescan, SLAR and a battery of cameras, the RA-5C was a Mach 2-capable aircraft, although it was often accompanied by Phantoms on operational missions. This RVAH-11 example is wearing an experimental scheme on USS *Kitty Hawk*.**

**Above right: The Douglas A-3 Skywarrior, known as the 'Whale', was used in many variants. Shown here is a KA-3B, used as a pure tanker. The hose and drogue deployed from the fairing under the rear fuselage.**

Navy implemented routine procedures to prepare the Air Wings and rotate ships and personnel. Typically, after working up independently, the squadrons of an Air Wing were brought together for a period of intensive training at NAS Fallon, in Nevada, prior to embarking aboard their carrier. Joint training continued while the carrier was underway and, unless the situation demanded that it immediately take up station in the Gulf of Tonkin, the carrier was first assigned to Dixie Station. There its new aircrews first gained combat experience during less demanding in-country sorties in support of allied ground forces. Following this first on-the-line period, the carrier and its Air Wing were sent to Cubi Point in the Philippines for a few days of rest and to take on supplies prior to reaching Yankee Station in the Gulf of Tonkin for operations against the North. For the next few months on-the-line periods on Yankee Station, usually lasting two to three weeks, alternated with spells spent at Cubi Point or for R&R (Rest and Relaxation) at such peaceful ports of call as Hong Kong. On occasion, carriers returned to Dixie Station for additional training if losses in the North had been made up by an influx of inexperienced aircrews, or to provide additional air support for ground troops during Communist offensives in the South. Every few days while on-the-line the carriers were refuelled at sea by fleet oilers and took on aircraft ordnance from ammunition ships. Delivery of urgent supplies, spares and mail, as well as personnel transfers and aeromedical evacuations, were accomplished by the Carrier's own Grumman C-1A Trader COD (Carrier Onboard Delivery) aircraft, by Traders and Grumman C-2A Greyhounds of Fleet Tactical Support Squadron Fifty (VRC-50), and by helicopters.

## *Mission variety*

While operating on Yankee Station the Air Wings flew a great variety of missions, BARCAPs and FORCECAPs were standing fighter patrols over or near the task force to provide cover against potential enemy air attacks. During offensive operations (which included armed reconnaissance sorties by small flights and Alpha Strikes by large formations of fighters, attack aircraft, tanker and ECM support aircraft in Route Packages IV and VIB along the northern coast of North Vietnam and Route Packages II and III in central North Vietnam), the fighters flew MIGCAPs, like their Air Force counterparts, and TARCAP escort sorties for strike and reconnaissance aircraft. RESCAP sorties were combat air patrols flown in support of aircrew rescue operations.

## *Carrier complements*

To undertake these missions, Air Wings aboard most carriers were typically composed of two VF (fighter) squadrons with McDonnell F-4 Phantoms or Vought F-8 Crusaders, two VA (light attack) squadrons with Douglas A-4 Skyhawks or Vought A-7 Corsair IIs, and one VA (medium attack) squadron initially with Douglas A-1 Skyraiders and later with Grumman A-6 Intruders. Other missions were performed by detachments, in less than squadron strength, of tankers, ECM aircraft, reconnaissance aircraft, AEW aircraft, and helicopters. Douglas A-3 Skywarriors of VAH (heavy attack) detachments initially flew a number of bombing missions but were soon almost exclusively used as tankers: in this latter role they were first replaced by KA-3Bs and/or EKA-3Bs of VAQ (tactical electronics warfare) detachments, and then supplemented by Grumman KA-6Ds assigned to the Air Wing's VA squadron flying A-6 medium attack aircraft. Additional air refuelling capability was provided by A-4s and A-7s of the Light Attack Squadrons, which could be fitted with refuelling pods on their weapons hardpoint. ECM support was at first provided by detachments of VAW-13 (Carrier Air Early Warning Squadron Thirteen)

**Left: Seen refuelling from a pod-equipped VA-55 A-4 Skyhawk, this Vought RF-8G is from the VFP-63. RF-8s were used from the smaller carriers for tactical reconnaissance, carrying only cameras. As with the RA-5s, these often needed an escort from F-8 fighters when heading North.**

**Right: An Attack Carrier Air Wing 15 Douglas EA-1F Skyraider prepares for launch from the USS *Coral Sea* (CV-43). VAW-13 flew electronic countermeasures in support of strike aircraft.**

777
JACK
POT
RESCUE
35028
135028

**Above: Douglas EA-3B Skywarrior of VQ-1 crosses the ramp. This specialised variant of the 'Whale' was occasionally deployed on board carriers to provide electronic intelligence and other special missions, a role it still performs today.**

flying Douglas EA-1Fs, but for most of the war this role was undertaken by EKA-3Bs and Grumman EA-6Bs of VAQs. Reconnaissance capability was provided aboard the smaller carriers by a detachment of Vought RF-8A/RF-8Gs from VFP-63 (Light Photographic Reconnaissance Squadron 63) and aboard larger carriers by a detachment of North American RA-5C Vigilantes from RVAHs (Reconnaissance Attack Squadrons). Airborne early warning was the task of VAW detachments flying Grumman E-1B Tracers or E-2 Hawkeyes. On occasion, Douglas EA-3Bs of VQ-1 (Fleet Air Reconnaissance One) and RA-3Bs of VAP-61 (Photographic Reconnaissance Squadron 61) also made short deployments aboard carriers operating on Yankee Station to provide special skills. Plane guard duty, aircrew combat rescue, and limited ASW capability were provided by detachments of Kaman UH-2 Seasprites and Sikorsky SH-3 Sea Kings from HU (Helicopter Utility) and after 1965 HC (Helicopter Combat Support) squadrons. Total aircraft complement reached up to 90 aircraft aboard the larger carriers (USS *America*, *Constellation*, *Enterprise*, *Forrestal*, *Independence*, *Kitty Hawk*, *Ranger*, and *Saratoga*), 75 aircraft aboard the *Midway*-class carriers (USS *Coral Sea*, *Midway*, and *F. D. Roosevelt*), and 70 aircraft in the very crowded smaller carriers (USS *Bon Homme Richard*, *Hancock*, *Intrepid*, *Oriskany*, *Shangri-La* and *Ticonderoga*).

## Combat shortages

Budgetary restrictions in existence prior to America's involvement in the South East Asia War resulted in serious shortages of aircrews, aircraft, ordnance, and carriers as soon as combat operations over the North were undertaken. While stepped up aircrew training at the various NATRACOM (Naval Air Training Command) bases and a massive increase in aircraft and munition production could be expected to remedy fairly quickly two of these shortages, the carrier situation was more serious. Construction of new carriers was a long drawn out affair (the only new carriers commissioned during the South East Asia War were the USS *America* in January 1965, and the USS *John F. Kennedy* in September 1968) and,

**Douglas A-1H Skyraider of VA-25, CVW-2, about to 'trap' aboard the USS *Midway* (CVA-41). With the rest of the Air Wing, VA-25 departed Alameda, then the *Midway*'s homeport, on 6 March 1965 and returned on 23 November 1965. During this combat cruise, two VA-25 pilots, Lt. Charlie Hartman and Lt. Clint Johnson, shared the destruction of a MiG-17 on 20 June 1965.**

**Left: Although *Ranger* embarked Grumman E-2A Hawkeyes for four of its five previous combat cruises, CVA-61 again had Grumman E-1B Tracers aboard for its last two wartime deployments, belonging to VAW-111.**

**Right: *Constellation*'s starboard catapult prepares to take the strain of an RA-5C Vigilante, embarking on a reconnaissance mission over the North. Cameras and other sensors were housed in the canoe fairing which ran under the belly.**

furthermore, several of the carriers then in service were reaching the end of their useful life or were due to undergo major refit. This was notably the case of the Pacific Fleet's USS *Midway* which, after making a deployment to Vietnam in 1965, went to the San Francisco Bay Naval Shipyard and was not recommissioned until January 1970. Consequently, to make up the shortage of carriers experienced by the Pacific Fleet (the command responsible for operations in the Western Pacific and the Indian Ocean) it became necessary for the Atlantic Fleet to divert some of its carriers for operations in the Gulf of Tonkin.

The first Atlantic Fleet carrier to make a deployment to Vietnam was the USS *Independence* which arrived on-the-line in June 1965 and returned to its homeport in December of that year. Later, five other Atlantic Fleet attack carriers, the USS *America*, *Forrestal*, *F. D. Roosevelt*, *Saratoga* and *Shangri-La*, made a total of seven deployments to the war zone. A more permanent contribution was made by the Atlantic Fleet in 1965 as its USS *Enterprise* left Norfolk, Virginia, in October and, after seven months on-the-line, returned to Alameda, California, for permanent assignment to the Pacific Fleet. Although unable to deplete

**Recognizing the value of camouflage during low-altitude operations over land, in 1965-66 the Navy evaluated drab colours for carrier-based aircraft. spotting during night operations was found more difficult and Navy aircraft retained their light colouring. Displaying the experimental camouflage are two A-4Cs from VA-113 aboard the USS *Kitty Hawk*.**

## Douglas A-4F Skyhawk

**Bearing the markings of Attack Squadron Two-Twelve, Carrier Air Wing Twenty-One, this Skyhawk displays the side number ending in '00' as traditionally given to aircraft assigned to the CAG (Air Wing Commander). While equipped with A-4Fs, VA-212 deployed four times to the Gulf of Tonkin aboard the USS *Hancock* (CVA-19). External stores include six 500-lb Mk 82 bombs, two AGM-12 Bullpup A air-to-ground missiles, and two 300-gallon drop tanks. The insignia of VA-212 was inspired by the lion appearing on cans of Coors beer, a favourite drink of aircrews!**

NP
300
ANCOCK
00
NP
NAVY
A-4F
154213

**Above: Zuni-armed F-8E Crusader streams wing-tip vortices as it dives towards a target in South Vietnam. Air Wings usually spent time on 'Dixie Station' in the South to work up proficiency. The 'Gunfighter' here is from VF-111 'Sundowners', carried aboard *Midway* in 1965.**

**Left: Not to be confused with the current *Wild Weasel* aircraft, the F-4G was similar to an F-4B, but had a smaller fuel cell in the fuselage, with extra datalink equipment. VF-114 'Aardvarks' flew this aircraft from *Kitty Hawk*'s decks.**

**Below: This voracious looking Vought F-8E Crusader of VF-111 was embarked aboard the USS *Oriskany* (CVA-34) in September 1966. On its cockpit sill, the Crusader bears the name of LCdr. Foster S. 'Tooter' Teague who on 11 June 1972, shot down a MiG-17.**

further its complement of attack carriers, the Atlantic Fleet contributed one of its antisubmarine carriers, the USS *Intrepid*, which made three deployments from Norfolk to the Gulf of Tonkin. Leaving its antisubmarine Air Group (CVSG) behind, the *Intrepid* went to war in May 1966 with CVW-10 comprised of two Skyhawk and two Skyraider attack squadrons and a detachment of Seasprite helicopters. For its May-December 1967 deployment, CVW-10 replaced one of its Skyraider squadrons with VSF-3 (one of the two Navy fighter squadrons equipped with A-4Bs, and carrying Sidewinder air-to-air missiles for limited air defence duty from the unreinforced deck of a CVS carrier) and added detachments of RF-8Gs and E-1Bs. Finally, during the July 1968-January 1969 deployment, the *Intrepid*'s CVW-10 included three squadrons of A-4/A-4Es and detachments of F-8Cs, RF-8Gs, EA-1Fs, E-1Bs, and helicopters.

## Bombing restarts

When *Rolling Thunder* operations south of the 20th parallel were again authorized by President Johnson in late January 1966, after the 'Christmas Truce', CVW-9 (USS *Enterprise*), CVW-11 (USS *Kitty Hawk*), and CVW-21 (USS *Hancock*) were on-the-line with Task Force 77 and immediately went to work against line of communications targets in the panhandle. While little enemy aircraft or SAM opposition was encountered in that area, losses to AAA were fairly heavy, notably during attacks against well-defended bridges. MiGs and SAMs became major threats when operations were enlarged in April to include targets in Route Packages IV and VIB (with the exception of 10-nautical mile prohibited zones around Hanoi and Haiphong). In an attempt to reduce the MiG threat, several of the aircraft from CVW-11 aboard the *Kitty Hawk* and from CVW-15 aboard *Constellation* were then painted in dark camouflage schemes to reduce their visibility while flying low.

**F-4 Phantoms were used for a number of duties. Having scored the first MiG-kills of the war, VF-21 found itself here dive-bombing with 500-lb (227-kg) Snakeye retarded bombs.**

Some improvements resulted, but as the darker colours made 'spotting the deck' (moving aircraft to their desired location) less safe during night operations, the darker schemes remained experimental and therafter Navy aircraft, unlike Air Force aircraft, retained their prewar colours (light gull grey above and glossy white underneath).

### *Fighters busy*

June 1966 was a particularly busy month for the fighters as VF-211, flying F-8Es from the USS *Hancock*, shot down three MiG-17s and claimed one probable, but lost one of its aircraft in air combat. Four more enemy aircraft, including two An-2 ('Colt') single-engine biplane transports which were caught at night by F-4Bs of VF-114 and VF-213, were claimed by the fighters during the second half of 1966, while a Skyraider pilot of VA-176, Lt. (jg) William Patton, shot down a MiG-17. Throughout the year the Air Wings divided their offensive activities between sustained operations against truck traffic along the Ho Chi Minh Trail and a systematic campaign to destroy the petroleum system in the North. Carrier-based aircraft also flew their first mining missions on 26 March when A-6As of VA-35 planted mines in the mouths of the Song Ca and Song Giang rivers to interdict barge traffic. In addition, in an action reminiscent of the Gulf of Tonkin Incident, on 1 July 1966 aircraft from the *Constellation* and *Hancock* sank three North Vietnamese torpedo boats which had attempted to attack two Navy destroyers. Albeit of a totally different nature, the good and bad fortunes of the USS *Oriskany* count among the most significant events of that year. On 16 September, after three periods on-the-line, the *Oriskany* found time during a break in operations to put her helicopters to good use by rescuing 44 British sailors from a merchant ship which was breaking up in heavy seas southeast of Hong Kong. This good deed, however, did not bring luck to this carrier as 40 days later she lost an equal number of sailors when fire broke out in a flare locker. *Oriskany* was pulled off the line and, after temporary repairs at Subic Bay in the Philippines, she sailed back to her homeport. Seven months later she again departed from San Diego for her third wartime deployment to the Gulf of Tonkin

For the men of the 'Tonkin Gulf Yacht Club', 1967 was for the most part a repeat of the previous year. On 29 July, the fifth day of her first on-line period, however, the USS *Forrestal* was less fortunate than the *Oriskany* and she was taken out of the war. As the *Forrestal*'s aircraft were being readied for the second launch of the day, a Zuni rocket was accidentally fired and hit an A-4's fuel

**Below left: The Navy's efforts over Vietnam kept armourers and maintenance men more than busy during a combat cruise. Here AIM-9 Sidewinders are loaded on to an F-8 Crusader.**

**Below: This VF-154 pilot was lucky to make it 'feet wet' before having to depart from his AAA-damaged Crusader, enabling naval rescue forces to pick him up. Note the Zuni/Sidewinder mix carried by the F-8s.**

## Vought F-8E Crusader

The last of the gunslingers! Still relying on four 20 mm cannon as its primary armament, the highly manoeuvrable single-seat Crusader was initially preferred by naval pilots over the missile-armed, two-seat Phantom II. When on 5 January 1967 Carrier Air Wing Five departed Alameda, California, aboard the USS *Hancock* (CVA-19), its two fighter squadrons, VF-51 and VF-53, were equipped with F-8Es. Armed with a pair of Sidewinder missiles, this VF-53 aircraft is shown on the side view with its wing raised in the take-off and landing position. During the war, Crusaders were credited with the destruction of 18 MiGs.

206
06
USS HANCOCK
USS HANCOCK
06
NF
06
149158
USS HANCOCK
NAVY
VF-53
F-8E
149158
Keith Fretwell

**Above: Grumman A-6As of VA-196 releasing Mk 82 bombs during this squadron's second combat cruise (May 1968 to January 1969) aboard the USS *Constellation* (CVA-64). During this cruise, VA-196 and the other squadrons of Carrier Air Wing Fourteen spent a total of 129 days on the line.**

**Left: Believed to be aboard the USS *Coral Sea*, this camouflaged Grumman A-6A carries a buddy refuelling store beneath its fuselage. During their first combat deployment, from June through November 1965, with VA-75 aboard the USS *Independence*, Intruders suffered relatively heavy losses as four were lost in combat (three of them as the result of premature detonation of their bombs).**

tank. Flames engulfed the carrier's fantail and spread below decks, touching off bombs and ammunition. In the ensuing inferno 134 officers and enlisted men were killed, 21 aircraft were destroyed and 43 others damaged, but the ship's armoured deck limited below-deck damage. Nevertheless, having lost more than half of her CVW-17's complement, the *Forrestal* was out of action. She went back to Norfolk and did not return to the West Pacific. For the other carriers operating in the Gulf of Tonkin, operational highlights during 1967 included strikes against North Vietnamese airfields (the first of which was flown on 24 April by aircraft from the *Kitty Hawk*'s CVW-11), the winning by Cdr. Michael J. Estocin of the only Medal of Honor awarded to a carrier pilot for combat during the South East Asia War (another aviator, Captain James B. Stockdale, earned his award for action on behalf of fellow POWs), the combat début of the Vought A-7A Corsair II (in December with VA-147, CVW-2, aboard the *Ranger*), and 16 victories against NVNAF fighters (one of which was obtained by LCdr. Ted Swartz who shot down a MiG-17 with a Zuni rocket while flying an A-4C of VA-76). CTF77, however, had suffered heavy combat losses during the year, with five of its aircraft being shot down by MiGs, 30 being brought down by SAMs, and 99 falling to AAA and small arms fire.

## *Crusader v. Phantom*

In the naval fighter community the kills scored by LCdr. Swartz and, earlier, by two other attack pilots flying Skyraiders, were a mere diversion. It was the long simmering rivalry between pilots flying the 'old' F-8 Crusader (with its primary armament of four 20-mm cannon being supplemented by two to four infrared-guided Sidewinder missiles) and the 'new' F-4 Phantom (with its armament consisting of a mix of Sidewinders and radar-guided Sparrow missiles) which occupied most minds. Long festering, this rivalry rose to fever

**Left: VA-165 flew Grumman A-6A Intruders from USS *Constellation* over North Vietnam. The accuracy of the A-6 enabled it to be used in all weathers, and it came to be known as the 'mini-B-52'. This aircraft is carrying 500-lb (227-kg) slick bombs.**

**Right: 750-lb bomb-laden VA-65 Intruder leaps into the air from the waist catapult while VA-147 Vought A-7 Corsair II awaits launch from the port catapult. The scene is aboard USS *Ranger*.**

pitch after 9 September 1966 when Cdr. Richard Bellinger, flying an F-8E of VF-162, had tied the victory tally of the two carrier fighters by shooting down the first MiG-21 claimed by naval aviators. Although F-8s operated only from the smaller carriers (with the exception of one deployment by VF-154 aboard the *Coral Sea* in 1965 and one deployment by VF-111 aboard the *Midway* during the same year) and spent only three-fourths the number of days on-the-line as did the F-4s which operated from the large carriers, the older Crusaders then steadily pulled ahead of the Phantoms in the race for air victories. Thus, by the summer of 1968, F-8 pilots led the F-4 crews by a score of 17 to 12. The odds in favour of the F-8 improved further on 19 September 1966, when Lt. Tony Nargi of VF-111 (the only fighter squadron then operating aboard the *Intrepid*) bagged a MiG-21. Unbeknown to the proud Crusader pilots, this was the last victory of the F-8. No victories were scored by either F-8s or F-4s between September 1968 and March 1970 (when an F-4J crew downed a MiG-21) and, when in the spring of 1972 the air war again heated up, the F-4s went on to score all the victories, ending up the war with a score of 38 kills versus the 18 of the F-8s. Interestingly enough, in view of the fact that F-8 pilots boasted that the built-in guns of their aircraft made them the 'last of the gunfighters' in the Old West tradition, 15 of their victories over NVNAF fighters were scored solely with Sidewinders, two resulted from a combination of hits with Sidewiders and guns, and one was obtained with guns and Zuni unguided rockets; none resulted from gunfire alone!

**Above: Cdr. Richard M. Bellinger, CO of VF-162, stands ready to alight from the cockpit of his F-8E after a combat sortie in September 1966. During this combat cruise aboard the USS *Oriskany* (CVA-34), Cdr. Bellinger was shot down by a MiG-17. He got his revenge on 9 October when he shot down a MiG-21 with a Sidewinder air-to-air missile.**

Equipped with Douglas EA-1Fs and embarked aboard the USS *Ticonderoga*, Det 14 of VAW-33 gained the distinction of making the last Skyraider deployment when it spent 66 days on-the-line from January to July 1968 during the last phases of *Rolling Thunder*. For the first three months of 1968, *Rolling Thunder* operations over the North continued to be the primary activity of carrier aviators; however, in April President Johnson once

**Vought A-7s were among the Navy attack types to carry APS-107 RHAW gear for anti-radiation attacks. This VA-146 A-7E carries an AGM-45 Shrike missile in addition to iron bombs.**

**Right: Vought A-7 Corsair II returns post-strike to its 'homeplate'. Bombs were usually carried on triple-ejector racks on the wing pylons, while fuselage rails often mounted Sidewinders for self-defence.**

**Below: USS *Enterprise* burns after the horrific accident while *en route* to the combat zone, 28 fatalities resulted from the Zuni rocket accident.**

again limited offensive operations against North Vietnam to missions below the 19th parallel. Consequently, during 1968 CTF77 lost fewer aircraft than in 1967: three to MiGs, seven to SAMs, and 51 to AAA. Only five confirmed victories were scored during the year by naval fighters, while a USAF pilot on exchange duty with VF-96 aboard the *Enterprise* claimed a probable. Completing her third war deployment in July 1968, the Navy's first nuclear carrier then spent less than six months on the West Coast prior to departing once again for the Gulf of Tonkin. It was while she was sailing west that the *Enterprise* became the third carrier to suffer a major accident when, during an ORI (Operational Readiness Inspection) on 14 January 1969, Zuni rockets under the wing of a Phantom overheated due to the close proximity of a jet starting unit. Fire quickly spread across the aft end of the flight deck and before it could be controlled 28 men were killed and 343 injured. Fifteen aircraft were destroyed and total damage was estimated at 56 million dollars. Repaired in six weeks at the Pearl Harbor shipyard, the *Enterprise* finally reached Yankee Station on 30 March.

At that time, as no bombing operations against the North were allowed and as US participation in ground operations in the South was being decreased, carrier-based aircraft mainly took part in the extensive *Commando Hunt* interdiction campaign against enemy infiltration routes in Laos. In April and May 1969 they also operated on 'Defender Station' in the Sea of Japan, as three attack carriers (the USS *Enterprise*, *Ranger*, and *Ticonderoga*) were temporarily transferred to TF71 to take part in a show of force after North Korea shot down an EC-121 reconnaissance aircraft. Following this interlude, carriers on Yankee Station again concentrated their activities on interdiction missions over Laos and on unarmed reconnaissance sorties over the North, with protective reaction strikes occasionally being flown in retaliation for North Vietnamese interference with the recce activities. The heaviest retaliatory operations took place between 26 and 29 December 1971 when aircraft

**Below: Another Zuni was responsible for this tragedy aboard USS *Forrestal* on 29 July 1967, when 134 men lost their lives and 21 aircraft were written off.**

NE

**Above: Not since World War One, when some of the aircraft of German *Schlachtstas* wore bright markings, had aircraft gone to war with such colourful schemes as used by some Navy squadrons in South East Asia. Belonging to VF-51, and bearing the markings of CVW-15's CAG, this F-4B was photographed at NAS Miramar on 9 April 1971, between the *Coral Sea*'s fifth and sixth war deployments.**

**Above right: Flying as a pilot-RIO team with VF-96 aboard the USS *Constellation* (CVA-64), Lt. Randall H. 'Duke' Cunningham and Lt (jg) William P. 'Irish' Driscoll shot down one MiG-21 and four MiG-17s between 19 January and 10 May 1972. After scoring their last three victories during a hectic sortie, the only Navy aces were shot down by a SAM while returning to their carrier. Fortunately, both were recovered unharmed.**

from the *Constellation* and *Coral Sea* flew 423 sorties as part of Operation *Proud Deep*. From Dixie Station carrier-based aircraft continued to provide air support to allied ground forces in the South but, as more US troops were pulled out of South Vietnam, even these activities slowly decreased after the summer of 1969 (with a single carrier operating on Yankee Station for the first time during January 1971); they reached a low in January 1972 when only eight sorties were flown over South Vietnam. No all-new aircraft made their combat début during these years, but improved models of existing types were first deployed aboard the USS *America* in April 1970 when she sailed from Norfolk. These were the A-7Es (Corsair IIs powered by a TF41 engine and fitted with a Head-Up Display) of VA-146 and VA-147, and the KA-6Ds (tanker versions of the Intruder) and A-6Cs (Intruders fitted with electro-optical sensors for night interdiction operations) of VA-165. Meanwhile, improved tactics were developed and stepped-up training was taking place at home to correct the deficiencies noted during the 1965-68 campaign against the North.

Although in fighter-versus-fighter combat naval aircrews had gained the upper hand over the NVNAF, and had achieved a kill-to-loss ratio of 5-to-1, the overall kill-to-loss ratio (less than 3-to-1) was unsatisfactory as the fighters were too frequently unable to prevent MiGs from shooting down attack aircraft. Accordingly, having determined that the training of its fighter pilots lacked sufficient emphasis on air combat manoeuvering, the Navy established *Topgun*, a specialized advanced course for fighter pilots. Lack of air combat during the mid-war period, from late 1969 to early 1972, did not permit seeing immediate results from this programme but renewed offensive operations in 1972 conclusively demonstrated the value of *Topgun*. During the last year of the war, Navy pilots achieved an impressive 12.5-to-1 kill ratio against enemy fighters and succeeded in preventing all but one loss of attack aircraft to MiGs.

Carrier aviation's many achievements during *Rolling Thunder*, the sustained interdiction campaign in Laos, and to a lesser extent during in-country operations, had already gone a long way to disarm many of its congressional and press critics. It was, however, the success it achieved during the all-important last year of the war (when its aircraft conducted more than 60 percent of the tactical air attack sorties flown over the North and claimed 25 of the 76 NVNAF aircraft shot down), that finally convinced all but its most stubborn opponents that carrier aviation was still a vital component of the United States' military might.

## *Freedom Train and Freedom Porch*

With the exception of two victories obtained during protective reaction strikes in January and March, the first Navy kills since March 1970, no pithy events marked the first three months of 1972. However, following the launching of the North Vietnamese spring offensive on 30 March, carrier-based aircraft stepped up operations in the South (with 680 sorties being flown during the first week of April as opposed to an average of 66 weekly sorties during the previous three months) and then

**Left: A VF-96 F-4J enters the landing pattern of USS *Constellation* with arrester hook deployed. Along with the Battle 'E', the aircraft displays the squadron's eight MiG-kills.**

**Right: While A-6 and A-7 aircraft flew *Iron Hand* anti-radiation missions from the larger carriers, the task was left to A-4Fs on board the smaller ships. Characterised by the undernose fairing for the APS-107 RHAW gear, this *Iron Hand* A-4 carries two Shrike missiles in addition to iron bombs.**

**One of the most famous colour schemes of the war was that worn by the F-4 Phantoms of VF-111 'Sundowners', aboard USS *Coral Sea*.**

supplemented Air Force aircraft in *Freedom Train* missions over the North. First undertaken on 5 April when the *Coral Sea*, *Hancock* and *Kitty Hawk* were on-the-line, these heavy raids had the following objectives (1) destruction of North Vietnamese aggression-supporting resources; (2) harassment and disruption of enemy military operations and; (3) reduction and impediment of movements of men and materials in the panhandle. Initially, strikes were limited to targets below the 19th parallel but by the end of April the northern limit had been moved to 20° 25′ N. In addition, special strikes were authorized on various occasions (notably on 16 April when, as part of *Freedom Porch*, 57 sorties were flown by carrier-based aircraft in support of B-52 raids in the Haiphong area). NVNAF opposition was intense and four MiGs were destroyed on 6 May by aircrews of VF-51, VF-111, and FV-114.

## *Haiphong mined*

Even more significant than strikes against land targets, militarily as well as diplomatically, was Operation *Pocket Money*, the mining campaign against the principal North Vietnamese ports which was announced by President Nixon on 9 May. Simultaneously with this announcement, in which three days were given for foreign vessels to leave North Vietnamese waters, aircraft from the *Coral Sea*'s CVW-15 seeded 36 mines (with 72-hour arming delays) in the outer approaches of Haiphong. Over the next eight months more than 11,000 mines were planted, effectively blockading maritime transport to and from North Vietnam.

On 10 May *Freedom Train* gave place to *Linebacker I* as restrictions on sustained operations above the 20th parallel were lifted. Air combat reached peak intensity on that day and Navy aircrews claimed eight confirmed victories, including the only triple-kill of the war scored by Lt. Randall H. Cunningham and his RIO, Lt. (jg) William P. Driscoll. Unfortunately the two jubilant men of VF-96, who had just become the only Navy aces of the war, had their F-4J damaged by a nearby SAM explosion while returning to the *Constellation*; both ejected 'feet wet' (i.e. after reaching the relative safety of the Gulf of Tonkin) and were quickly rescued by Marine helicopters. Carrier-based fighters scored nine more confirmed victories during *Linebacker I*.

Carrier operations reached their peak during May 1972 when 3,949 and 3,290 sorties were flown respectively against the North and over the South and, not surprisingly, the largest number of carriers on-the-line was recorded between 23 and 31 May when the USS *Constellation*, *Coral Sea*, *Hancock*, *Kitty Hawk*, *Midway*, and *Saratoga* operated in the Gulf of Tonkin. After the NVA spring offensive was halted, the number of sorties over the South decreased significantly, while sorties over the North dropped only slightly in June and July prior to reaching a new high of 4,819 sorties in August. Altogether, during *Linebacker I* the Navy flew 23,652 tactical sorties against North Vietnam, with nearly one-third of the armed reconnaissance sorties being flown at night.

Tactical air sorties above the 20th parallel were once more ended on 23 October 1972 and the level of operations fell sharply as peace was thought to be 'around the corner'. When this hope did not materialize, *Linebacker II* was initiated on 18 December with the Navy contributing the Air

**Above; Det.4 VAQ-130 operated Douglas KA-3Bs from USS *Ranger* for refuelling and ECM support of the carrier's Air Wing. Here a Skywarrior refuels a VA-113 'Stingers' A-7E while another stands watch.**

**Below: An instant from launch: a VF-92 pilot applies full afterburner and tenses himself for the full force of the catapult to hurl the aircraft off the deck. Behind the aircraft is a blast deflector, which is raised to protect parked aircraft and deck crew behind the launch.**

## McDonnell Douglas F-4B Phantom II

Whereas the Air Force made extensive use of its Phantom IIs in the strike role, the Navy primarily flew them to provide BARCAPs, FORCECAPS, and MIGCAPs. As a result, Navy F-4s had a better kill-to-loss ratio than their Air Force brethren. Fighter Squadron One Forty-Two (VF-142) deployed seven times to the Gulf of Tonkin, four times aboard the USS *Constellation* (thrice with F-4Bs and once with F-4Js), twice with F-4Js on the USS *Enterprise*, and once with F-4Bs aboard the USS *Ranger*. In the course of these deployments, VF-142 was credited with the destruction of one MiG-17 and four MiG-21s.

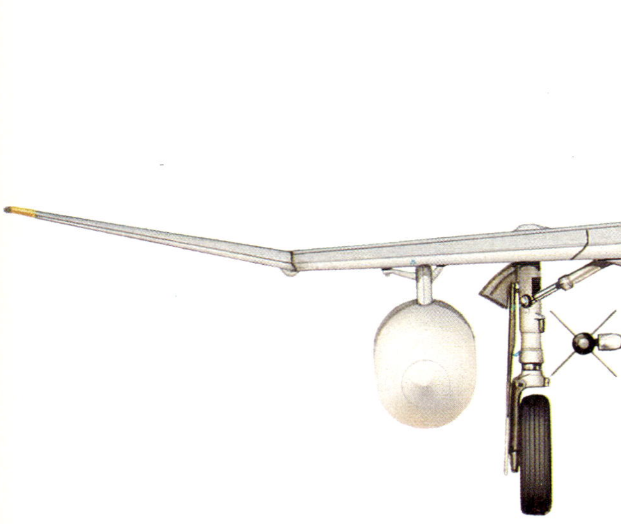

TELLATION
2244
VF-142
10
NK
NSTELLATION
2244
VF-142
NAVY
Keith Fretwell

**Above: This Kaman UH-2A of HC-1 Det 1 Unit M was photographed as it was on plane guard duty off the port side of the USS *Enterprise* (CVAN-65) in April 1966.**

**Above right: This Sikorsky SH-3A of HS-6 is preparing to land on the USS *Bennington*. The scheme was an experimental one, most SH-3s carrying high-visibility national insignia and codes.**

Wings of the USS *America*, *Enterprise*, *Midway*, *Oriskany*, *Ranger*, and *Saratoga* to the war's final effort. As mentioned in Chapter 3, *Linebacker II* forced Hanoi finally to adopt a more pliable attitude at the Paris Talks. Full-scale operations ended on 29 December, but skirmishes continued for four more weeks (Navy flyers claimed the last MiG of the war on 12 January) until the Vietnam cease-fire came into effect on 27 January 1973.

For the men of the Tonkin Yacht Club the war was not quite over. CVW-2 (*Ranger*), CVW-5 (*Midway*), CVW-8 (*America*) CVW-14 (*Enterprise*), and CVW-19 (*Oriskany*), operating from a position off the coast of South Vietnam, flew strikes against targets in southern Laos until 11 February and combat support missions over Cambodia until 27 February. Moreover, during various on-the-line periods between 27 February and 27 July 1973, the USS *America*, *Constellation*, *Coral Sea*, *Enterprise*, *Oriskany*, and *Ranger* provided logistical support during *Endsweep*, the clearing of mines from North Vietnamese harbours which was undertaken as part of the Paris Agreement, and provided air cover for these operations. At last, on 15 August 1973, all war-related activities stopped in accordance with the Congress-mandated end of US combat operations in South East Asia.

Nevertheless, carriers were to be involved three more times in the area before the long and unpopular war could finally be left behind. On 12 April 1975 they provided air cover and served as bases for Marine helicopters taking part in *Eagle Pull*, the evacuation of US personnel and some foreign nationals from Phnom Penh. One week later they provided similar services during *Frequent Wind*, the evacuation of Saigon. Finally, from 12 to 14 May 1975, the USS *Coral Sea* provided air support during the rescue operations to free the SS *Mayaguez* and its crew.

Albeit conducted on a smaller scale than those of the Air Force, Navy helicopter rescue operations were of great value to US aircrews flying over North Vietnam, particularly to those who sought safety by flying their crippled aircraft toward or over the Gulf of Tonkin. To rescue these aircrew the Navy initially relied on destroyers operating close to the North Vietnamese coast, on carrier-based plane-guard helicopters from HC-1 and HC-2, and on those from Helicopter Antisubmarine

**Left: Action during an attack on the port of Haiphong, through which much material was delivered to the North. It was only near the war's end that the US air arms were allowed to attack vital targets in the Hanoi/Haiphong region.**

**Right: To ferry personnel, mail, and urgently needed parts, the carriers of Task Force 77 relied principally on their own Grumman C-1A Traders and on the C-1As and C-2As of VR-21 and VRC-50. One of these COD (Carrier Onboard Delivery) C-1As is seen here deploying its wing prior to being launched from the USS *Bon Homme Richard* (CVA-31) on 16 August 1968.**

Squadrons operating from various ships of TF77. However, as operations over North Vietnam increased in intensity, the Navy began supplementing its standartd plane-guard helicopters with specialized small detachments from HC-7. Operating armed versions of the Kaman UH-2C and Sikorsky SH-3A/SH-3G until the final withdrawal of American forces, the Navy rescue helicopters flew sorties not only over the Gulf of Tonkin but also into North Vietnam under the protective cover of carrier-based combat aircraft; Lt. (jg) Clyde E. Lassen was awarded the Medal of Honor for recovering two downed aviators at night on 19 June 1968. The effectiveness of these operations can be gauged by the fact that HC-7 Detachment 110 alone conducted 48 rescues during 1972, while during that year HC-1 rescued a total of 36 people (including some sailors who had fallen overboard.).

## *Final tally*

Altogether 17 attack carriers (ten from the Pacific Fleet and seven from the Atlantic Fleet) made a total of 73 combat cruises and spent 8,248 days on-the-line during the nine years between the Gulf of Tonkin Incident and the Congress-mandated end of US combat involvement in South East Asia. With a total of eight, the USS *Hancock* (CVA-19) set the record for the number of combat cruises. The USS *Coral Sea* (CVA-43) spent the most days on-the-line (873 in seven cruises) and also held the record for the longest cruise (331 days between December 1964 and November 1965). Most days on-the-line during a single cruise was achieved by the USS *Midway* (CVA-41), which spent 208 days on-the-line between April 1972 and February 1973. Attack carrier fighters had scored 56 confirmed and four probable kills, while their attack aircraft added three victories to the total tally. Top honors went to squadrons embarked aboard the USS *Constellation* (CVA-64) with 15 kills.

On the debit side, in 12 years the Navy lost 530 fixed-wing aircraft (most of them carrier-based) and 13 helicopters to hostile action. Navy operational losses during the war totalled 299 fixed-wing aircraft and 35 helicopters. Human losses were even more grievous; 317 aircrews were lost in action, while death from all causes took the lives of 2,430 naval personnel. In early 1973, 144 naval aviators who had been taken POW were released by North Vietnam and the Viet Cong; however, 77 others remained unaccounted for.

**Above: Sikorsky SH-3As of HS-2 were used for combat search and rescue duties, both over the Gulf of Tonkin and into North Vietnam itself. This example, seen tied down on the destroyer *Mahan*, was lost soon after this photograph was taken, with no trace.**

**Above: Rare visitor to the combat zone is this NC-121J Constellation of VX-8, a development squadron.**

**Above right: In-theatre transport was provided by Douglas C-117Ds, this example is seen after it had run off the end of Vung Tau's runway.**

**For night sorties over the Ho Chi Minh Trail, a handful of Douglas RA-3Bs were finished in glossy black. Operated by VAP-61 and to a lesser extent by VAP-62, these Skywarriors primarily flew out of Da Nang AB but occasionally deployed to carriers in the Gulf of Tonkin as demonstrated by this photograph taken aboard the USS *Constellation*.**

## *Sailors Ashore*

While, both numerically and strategically, carrier operations represented by far the most important role of Naval Aviation during the war, naval aviators also flew combat missions from shore bases and seaplane tenders, and flew transport aircraft on lone trans-Pacific missions in support of operations in South East Asia.

In the early phase of active American involvement in the war, the Navy Transport Squadrons assigned to the Military Air Transport Service (notably VR-22 which in January 1966 was moved from NAS Norfolk, Virginia, to NAS Moffett Field, California, for operations over the Pacific) joined Air Force units in flying gruelling missions from CONUS bases to Vietnam and Thailand. In addition, beginning in May 1965, Naval Air Reserve volunteers supported the war's effort by providing trans-Pacific airlift with their old Douglas C-54s and C-118s. However, as airlifting was the primary responsibility of the USAF, the Navy squadrons assigned to the Military Airlift Command (formerly MATS) were not re-equipped with jet or turboprop transports and the Naval Air Transport Wing, Pacific, was decommissioned in June 1967. Thereafter, MAC's Lockheed C-141As and C-5As bore the brunt of the trans-Pacific airlift effort, while the smaller Navy Douglas C-118Bs and Lockheed C-130Fs provided specialized logistics support until January 1973.

Throughout the war, Da Nang was the main aviation facility in Vietnam. Not only was it the operating station for numerous squadrons of the US Marine Corps, but it also housed several special detachments of Navy aircraft and served as the primary recovery base for carrier-based aircraft forced to divert due to weather or battle damage. Among the first Navy squadrons to send detachments to operate from the Asian mainland, Airborne Early Warning One (VW-1) is noteworthy as in August 1964, right after the Gulf of Tonkin Incident, it deployed Lockheed EC-121Ks from NAS Agana, Guam, to support combat operations in Vietnam. First operating over the Gulf of Tonkin from Sangley Point in the Philippines, VW-1

**Right: This VAP-62 Douglas RA-3B Skywarrior is depicted in the three-tone grey scheme adopted by certain aircraft from this and its sister squadron, VAP-61. For camouflage detection the RA-3B cameras were loaded with infrared film.**

**Based at NAS Agana, on the island of Guam, Fleet Air Reconnaissance Squadron One (VQ-1) sent detachments of EC-121Ks to fly weather reconnaissance and Elint sorties from Da Nang AB, where this aircraft was photographed in April 1970. With its tail code PR, VQ-1 was already known as 'Peter Rabbit.'**

quickly moved to Da Nang. Its contribution, however, was of relatively short duration as Air Wings primarily relied on their own carrier-based Grumman E-1Bs and E-2A/Bs. Conversely, VQ-1 regularly deployed its EC-121Ks and EC-121Ms from NAS Atsugi, Japan, and after June 1971 from NAS Agana to Da Nang, to fly weather reconnaissance and ELINT missions. Moreover, in the latter role VQ-1 made extensive use of Douglas EA-3Bs, which flew missions over the North and over Laos from Da Nang, as well as from carriers.

Other versions of the multi-mission Douglas Skywarrior which were operated from Da Nang included the RA-3Bs of VAP-61 and VAP-62, and the KA-3Bs and EKA-3Bs from detachments provided by Heavy Attack Squadrons and Tactical Electronics Warfare Squadrons. The KA-3B tankers and EKA-3B TACOS (Tanker and Countermeasures Strike Support aircraft) provided air refueling for USMC aircraft operating over the North and for carrier-based aircraft which were forced to divert to South Vietnam or were flying in-country support missions, while the RA-3Bs of the two Reconnaissance Squadrons were primarily used for missions over the Ho Chi Minh Trail. Largest of the US tactical reconnaissance aircraft, the RA-3B could easily be fitted with a variety of cameras, including oversized items which could

**Below: Douglas EA-3B Skywarrior of VQ-1 uses its parachute to slow down its landing run at Da Nang. EA-3s augmented EC-121s and EP-3s on the Elint and Comint effort.**

Left: AP-2H Neptune of VAH-21. These gunship Neptunes carried specialised sensors for night interdiction, with engine exhaust silencers to reduce detectability during low-altitude missions.

Above: VO-67 used OP-2E Neptunes for delivering air-dropped sensors over the Trail for the *Igloo White* programme. Note the depressed Minigun pod on the wing pylon.

Below: A Lockheed P-3A Orion (BuNo 152185) flies low over the water during a routine *Market Time* patrol over the South China Sea on 4 September 1968. Its tail code SG identifies this aircraft as belonging to VP-50. During the war, the Navy lost one Orion to small arms fire and one in an operational accident.

not be carried by the RF-4, RF-8, or RA-5. Accordingly, the type was initially deployed from NAS Agana by VAP-61 to undertake a cartographic survey of the theatre. Later, supplemented after October 1966 by detachments from VAP-62, its sister squadron in the Atlantic Fleet, VAP-61 was mainly used for night and special reconnaissance sorties over the Trail from Da Nang AB and Don Muang Airport, as well as from carriers of Task Force 77. For these missions the RA-3Bs employed infrared films to 'see' through camouflage and locate enemy trucks; an on-board real-time display was used to direct strike aircraft against these targets. This combination of equipment proved most satisfactory but, to be fully effective required that the aircraft fly at a relatively low altitude, thereby making them easy targets for AAA and even small-arms fire. Hence, to reduce detectability during missions when the moon was shining, VAP-61 experimented with all-black and sea grey/medium grey/light gull grey camouflages. Nevertheless, losses were heavy (even though VAP-61 never deployed more than a handful of aircraft, it lost seven RA-3Bs between June 1966 and August 1969) and resulted in the squadron being decommissioned in June 1971.

Although less glamorous than carrier operations, maritime surveillance and antisubmarine patrol have always been important roles for naval aviation. Hence it is not surprising that among the

Below: *Market Time* sorties were flown by Martin's elderly SP-5B Marlin flying-boat, often using seaplane tenders as a forward 'base'. The advent of Lockheed's Orion sent the Marlins home.

first Navy aircraft to join the fray were the Lockheed SP-2Hs of Patrol Squadrons which were deployed to South East Asia to undertake *Market Time* patrols. Assigned to Fleet Air Wings Eight and Ten, these elderly aircraft operated from NAF Cam Ranh Bay in South Vietnam to seek Communist trawlers and junks infiltrating men and supplies into the Republic of Vietnam, and to provide aerial reconnaissance and ASW patrols for Carrier Task Force 77. Early in the war, the Navy had feared that submarines of the People's Republic of China might interfere with its operations in the Gulf of Tonkin; however, like expected enemy air strikes, this threat never materialized. In these roles the SP-2Hs were initially supplemented by even more obsolescent SP-5B Marlin amphibians flown from seaplane tenders in the South China Sea (VP-50 and its tender, the USS *Currituck*, being the last to complete a combat tour in May 1967), and were finally supplanted by Lockheed P-3A/P-3B Orions. After NAF Can Ranh Bay was vacated in December 1971 and until well after the end of the hostilities, Orions continued to fly patrols over the Gulf of Tonkin and the South China Sea from NAS Cubi Point in the Philippines.

In addition to using SP-2Hs for *Market Time* patrols, the Navy operated two special versions of the Neptune. Flying specially modified OP-2Es, in which all ASW equipment had been replaced by chaff dispensers and special radio and navigation devices, VO-67 was deployed to Nakhon Phanom RTAFB in November 1967 to seed parachute-retarded ALARS (Air Launched Acoustical Reconnaissance Sensors) along the Ho Chi Minh Trail as part of the *Mud River/Muscle Shoals* project. Even though they were fitted with two SUU-11 7.62-mm Minigun pods beneath each wing to suppress enemy fire, the low and slow flying OP-2Es became easy prey for Communist gunners. Three were lost

**Looking more like a travel poster than a combat setting photograph, this photograph shows a Lockheed SP-2H of Patrol Squadron One (VP-1, the 'Fleet's Finest') during a *Market Time* patrol over the South China Sea.**

**Photographed at NAF Cam Ranh Bay on 7 September 1968, are AP-2Hs of VAH-21, a Navy unit which flew night interdiction sorties over the Mekong Delta.**

**VAL-4 'Ponies' flew the North American OV-10A Bronco on missions over the Mekong Delta. Light attack could be undertaken, as well as FAC missions for carrier wings sailing at 'Dixie Station'.**

**Above: VAL-4 OV-10A keeps watch on riverine traffic in South Vietnam, OV-10s supported UH-1s on riverine patrol duties.**

during the first three months of operations, forcing the transfer of the sensor-seeding mission to the less vulnerable F-4Ds of the 25th TFS, USAF, and the disestablishment of VO-67 in July 1968. The combat tour of VAH-21 was only slightly longer as it began in September 1968 and ended in June 1969. Based at NAF Cam Ranh Bay and equipped with AP-2Hs which had been fitted with a special TRIM (Trail and Road Interdiction, Multisensor) package, this squadron flew night interdiction sorties over the Mekong Delta and helped develop equipment and tactics for this difficult mission.

Of all combat missions undertaken by Navy aircraft during the South East Asia War, those flown by Helicopter Attack Squadron Light Three (HAL-3) and Light Attack Squadron (VAL-4) remain the least known. Following combat evaluation of armed helicopters by HC-1 in 1966, the Navy obtained from the Army a number of armed Bell UH-1Bs and organized HAL-3 to provide reconnaissance and fire support for PBRs (Patrol Boats, River) and ACVs (Air Cushion Vehicles) operating in the Mekong Delta, and to complement the fixed-wing patrol aircraft in interdicting waterborne invasion routes to South Vietnam. For two years, beginning in March 1969, the helicopter gunships were supplemented by the North American OV-10A from VAL-4. The *Game Warden* riverine operations of these two unique squadrons finally ended in March 1971 and VAL-4 became the last Navy unit to leave the Republic of Vietnam.

**Left: Rocket-armed UH-1B escorts a PBR patrol boat up one of the numerous creeks of southern Vietnam. Under operation *Game Warden*, the Navy was responsible for cutting enemy supply routes through the delta.**

**Right: HAL-3 UH-1B skims over PBRs in the delta. The UH-1s watched ahead for ambushes, and then used their guns and rockets to attack the VC forces.**

**Below: An armed UH-1B of HAL-3 is about to touch down on the deck of the USS *Harnett County* (LST-821) during *Game Warden* riverine operations in the Mekong Delta. The Army UH-1B is on the forward section of the amidship deck belongs to the 197th Aviation Helicopter Company, the Army unit which provided combat training for HAL-3.**

# US Marine Aviation in South East Asia

Marine Corps policy having always emphasized the close integration of air and ground operations, the primary mission of its aviators has consistently been to support Fleet Marine Forces (FMFs) in the seizure and defence of advanced naval bases and in the conduct of land operations. Hence, after Marines were committed to ground operations in South Vietnam in 1965, it could only be expected that Marine aviators would carry on the tradition by providing effective air support to the 'grunts' slugging it out with the Viet Cong and the NVA in the jungle of Vietnam. By 1965, however, the Marines were no longer novices in the theatre as they had been flying helicopters in Vietnam since 1962 to assist local forces, and as detachments from VMCJ-1 had operated from carriers in the Gulf of Tonkin in 1964.

The Sikorsky UH-34D was the first type of helicopter deployed to Vietnam by the US Marine Corps. As interim gunships, a number of Marine UH-34s were fitted with TK-1 kits comprised of two M60 machine-guns and two 18-rocket pods. Obsolescent at the time of their combat début, the UH-34s were withdrawn from Vietnam in August 1969.

## *Marine Helicopters: From Shu Fly to Frequent Wind*

Marine Corps employment of helicopters during the South East Asia War closely paralleled that of the US Army, with the first Marine helicopters in Vietnam and Thailand respectively being the Sikorsky UH-34Ds of Marine Medium Helicopter Squadron Three Sixty-Two (HMM-362) at Soc Trang and the UH-34Ds of HMM-261 at Udorn. Supported by three Cessna OE-1 fixed-wing observation aircraft and one Douglas C-117 transport, the 24 helicopters of HMM-362 arrived at Soc Trang on 15 April 1962 as part of Operation *Shufly* and immediately began taking Vietnamese troops into combat. Until the completion of Operation *Shufly* on 8 March 1965, the brunt of Marine aviation combat in Vietnam was borne by one helicopter squadron at a time, with individual units (HMMs 162, 163, 261, 361, 362, 364 and 365) being rotated on a frequent basis.

As one of the *Shufly* helicopters had received combat damage within eight days from the start of operations in Vietnam, the Marine Corps soon became conscious of the urgent need to mount armament on its transport helicopters and to pro-

Sikorsky UH-34Ds were the main assault transport type until the CH-46 came into service. Here a group depart after dropping Marines into a typical LZ.

**Above left: The Marines employed gunships on a large scale, beginning with the UH-1E shown here. As well as fixed guns and rockets, this Huey also carried door-mounted M60s. The AH-1 Cobra replaced UH-1s in the gunship role.**

**Above: A Douglas C-117D of H&MS-16 at Marble Mountain Air Facility, near Da Nang, on 1 January 1971. After World War II, Douglas proposed to the world's airlines the Super DC-3, a modernized version of its ubiquitous DC-3. The type did not attract much civil interest but 100 Navy and Marine R4D-5/-6/-7 transports were converted into R4D-8s (C-117Ds after September 1962).**

vide either fixed-wing aircraft or armed helicopters to escort the rotary-wing aircraft transporting troops. Thus, as early as the fall of 1962, after HMM-163 had relieved HMM-362, UH-34D transport helicopters were armed with a door-mounted flexible M60 machine-gun. Six months later, after helicopter crews had been authorized to 'engage clearly defined VC elements considered to be a threat to the safety of the helicopters and their passengers', without waiting for the VC to shoot first, the rotating Marine helicopter units began using three UH-34Ds as their first gunships. Based on experience gained with these interim gunships, armed with an M60 flexible machine-gun on both sides as well as hand-held weapons, and with armed UH-1As provided by a detachment of the Army's Utility Tactical Transport Company, UH-34Ds armed with the TK-1 kit (two externally-mounted, forward-firing M60 machine-guns and two pods each containing 18 2.75-in rockets) were deployed in December 1964.

On 8 March 1965, when Battalion Landing Team 3/9 of the 9th MEB (Marine Expeditionary Brigade) came ashore northwest of Da Nang, the Marine Corps became the first of the US Armed Services to deploy large ground combat units to South Vietnam. To support their troops, the Marines began sending rapidly increasing numbers of fixed- and rotary-wing aircraft. The initial assignment of the UH-34-equipped HMM-162 and HMM-163 was soon supplemented by that of Marine Observation Squadron Two with the first Bell UH-1E gunships. Generally similar to the Army's UH-1Cs, the Marines' UH-1Es were at first armed with the TK-2 armament kit (four forward-firing M60C machine-guns and two rocket pods). Beginning in April 1967, these gunships were fitted with a pilot-controlled TAT-101 chin turret housing twin M60 machine-guns. Already quite effective, the single-engined UH-1Es were progressively supplemented by AH-1G Cobras beginning in April 1969, and by twin-engined AH-1J Sea Cobras in June 1971, when Marine Light Helicopter Squadron 167 (HML-167) became the first unit in Vietnam to be equipped with the new 'Super Huey'. Notwithstanding the deployment of these specialized

**A UH-34 delivers supplies to a hill outpost (Hill 861) near Khe Sanh. Supply of such installations relied almost totally on the helicopter, with few sizeable vehicles able to traverse the jungled hills and mountains.**

**Above: Heavy lift duties in the early days were handled by the venerable Sikorsky CH-37C Mojave. Rapid assault could be undertaken, using the clamshell doors in the nose to disgorge the load quickly. This pair is from HMR-461.**

**Above right: Marine CH-46 burns after being hit just south of the DMZ. The 13 crewmen and troops aboard lost their lives in the following crash.**

gunships, the UH-1Es of various Marine observation squadrons continued to fly as armed helicopters until the final withdrawal of the Marines. In addition, they were used to provide liaison, forward air control (alongside fixed-wing OV-10s of the same units), 'medevac' casualty evacuation (as a result of the fight for Khe Sanh and of the Communist Tet Offensive, peak medevac activity was recorded during 1968 when some 42,000 sorties were flown and 67,000 people were evacuated), reconnaissance, and search and rescue. It was while taking part in this last type of mission that two Marines, Captain Stephen W. Pless and PFC. Raymond M. Clausen, earned the Medal of Honor for actions taking place in South Vietnam on 19 August 1967 and 30 January 1970.

Losses during combat operations and from other operational causes had already placed a severe strain on the limited helicopter resources of the Marine Corps when, during the night of 27-28 October 1965, the Viet Cong destroyed 13 UH-1Es and six UH-34Ds in a daring attack against the Marine's facilities at Marble Mountain. Fortunately this setback was without long-term impact on operations in Vietnam as additional UH-34s and UH-1s were rushed to the theatre, and as deployment of the new twin-rotor, turbine-powered Boeing-Vertol CH-46A Sea Knight was accelerated. The first of these transport helicopters, capable of airlifting up to 17 combat-equipped troops versus 12 for the UH-34, were brought by HMM-364 to Marble Mountain on 8 March 1966. Although initially plagued by slow deliveries and transmission failures the Sea Knight, in its CH-46A and improved CH-46D versions, became the primary Marine transport helicopter, with the UH-34D being withdrawn from Vietnam in August 1969.

Larger and heavier helicopters were also employed in Vietnam by the Marine Corps. A few Sikorsky CH-37Cs were operated by Marine Aircraft Group Sixteen (MAG-16), with one of these heavy-lift helicopters being used on 12 September 1965 to make what is claimed to be the first lift of a

**Left: Like the Air Force, Army, and Navy, the Marine Corps made much use of the 'Huey,' first deploying the type with Marine Observation Squadron Two (VMO-2). During the war the Marines lost 270 helicopters (including 69 UH-1s) in combat and 154 in operational accidents (32 of which were UH-1s).**

**Below: During Operation *Lancaster II*, Marines of the 2nd Battalion, 3rd Marines board CH-46 helicopters to start the initial phase of a sweep north of Dong Ha Mountain, near the DMZ.**

Above: HMM-262 CH-46s prepare for lift-off from a Marine camp near the DMZ. The CH-46 was the Marine workhorse throughout most of the conflict, being used for both combat assault and heavylift duties.

Below: For heavy resupply duties, the CH-37 was replaced by the very capable Sikorsky CH-53. This example is seen slinging in an 81-mm mortar to a hilltop firebase during Operation *Cochise*.

Above: CH-53D Sea Stallions of HMH-463 joined Navy helicopters for Operation *Endsweep*, the mine-clearing of Vietnamese harbours. This giant is seen with mine-clearing gear in tow in the harbour at Hon Gay.

Above right: An army marches on its stomach, and even if it is stuck in a firebase for weeks on end, the well-fed troop fights better. Here a CH-53 airlifts in C-rations to Con Thion.

VMFA-542 F-4 Phantoms take their loads of 500-lb (227-kg) Snakeye retarded bombs and unguided rockets to northern I Corps, to help Marines involved in ground actions there.

downed aircraft under tactical conditions. In this role, and for the transportation of other heavy and bulky items, the obsolescent and temperamental CH-37 was replaced by the substantially more capable Sikorsky CH-53 Sea Stallion. In its CH-53B version, powered by two 3,985-shp (2972-kW) turboshaft engines, the Sea Stallion could carry up to 9,300 lb (4218 kg) under tropical conditions, and was thus able to lift a Sea Knight after its rotor and some of its equipment had been removed. In January 1967 the first CH-53As were taken to Vietnam by a detachment of Marine Heavy Helicopter Squadron Four Sixty-Three. The type soon proved its great value by enabling the recovery and subsequent repair of damaged helicopters, and by carrying heavy artillery pieces to forward zones, notably during the siege of Khe Sanh in 1968.

The progressive withdrawal of Marines from Vietnam began in August 1969; in May 1971, 97 months after the first *Shufly* helicopters had commenced operations, HML-167 became the last USMC helicopter squadron to leave the country. However, to fight off the North Vietnamese offensive in the spring of 1972, two Special Landing Forces (SLFs) with two squadrons of CH-46Ds and detachments of CH-53Ds, AH-1G/Js, and UH-1Es, returned to operations in Vietnam from April to December 1972. In addition to providing air mobility and fire support for South Vietnamese forces recapturing the territory conquered by the enemy at the onset of the spring offensive, Marine helicopters undertook a new role after the arrival of HMA-369 in August 1972. Equipped with AH-1J gunships, this Marine Attack Helicopter Squadron operated from the USS *Denver* against water traffic during day and night attacks. After the cease-fire, Marine helicopters from HMH-463 and HMH-165 were specially configured for mine sweeping and joined Navy helicopters from HM-12 in clearing North Vietnamese harbours and inlets of mines dropped during the war (Operation *Endsweep*). Finally, in April 1975 Sea Stallions from HMH-462 and HMH-463 provided the main transport for the final evacuation of Phnom Penh (*Eagle Pull*) and Saigon (*Frequent Wind*).

## *Marines at Sea*

Chronologically, operations from Navy carriers were the second contribution made by Marine aviators during the South East Asia War; in 1964 small RF-8A detachments form Marine Composite Reconnaissance Squadron One (VMCJ-1) operated from carriers as the Navy's VFP-63 then had an insufficient number of aircraft to satisfy the requirements of the Fleet. This small scale assistance was followed by the deployment in squadron strength of Marine All-Weather Fighter Squadron Two-Twelve (VMF(AW)-212) which, fulfilling the Marines' collateral mission as an integral component of Naval Aviation, went aboard the USS

*Oriskany* as the second fighter squadron in CVW-16. Equipped with Vought F-8Es, VMF(AW)-212 flew in-country missions beginning on 8 May 1965 and then moved to Yankee Station from which sorties over the North commenced on 10 May. With the *Oriskany* moving back and forth between the two stations, VMF(AW)-212 performed air support sorties from Dixie Station as its fighters had been modified to carry bombs beneath their wings. From Yankee Station it undertook mainly BARCAPs, MIGCAPs, and TARCAPs, and also flew armed reconnaissance sorties. During 141 days on-the-line, the Marine squadron flew 1,588 sorties and lost one aircraft (the pilot was taken prisoner after ejecting near Hanoi). Although both the Navy and Marine Corps were satisfied with the VMF(AW)-212 deployment, no other Marine squadrons went aboard carriers until 1971, as the limited number of USMC aircraft units made it necessary to give priority to their in-country operations from land bases close to the battle. However, after the Marines were withdrawn from South Vietnam, the practice of including Marine squadrons in Navy Air Wings was renewed.

## *Intruders go to sea*

The next squadron to deploy aboard a carrier bound for Vietnam was Marine All-Weather Attack Squadron Two Twenty-Four which, equipped with Grumman A-6As and KA-6Ds, departed Alameda on 8 December 1971 as part of the *Coral Sea*'s Air Wing Fifteen. Combat operations commenced from Yankee Station on 14 December and lasted until 30 June 1972, and VMA(AW)-224 lost three aircraft during the 148 days it spent on-the-line. The last three months proved to be the period of most intense activity as, after the Communists launched their spring offensive, VMA(AW)-224 and the other squadrons of CVW-15 first concentrated their efforts on in-country sorties in support of ARVN and US forces. On 16 April they renewed operations against the North as part of *Freedom Train* and soon the Marines had numerous opportunities to put to good use their A-6Bs; these had supplemented their initial complement of Intruders and were armed with AGM-78 anti-radiation missiles for use against SAM sites. VMA(AW)-224 gained further notoriety on 9 May when it became one of the three *Coral Sea* squadrons to initiate *Pocket Money* mining operations.

**A thoroughbred fighter used almost exclusively for shifting mud by the Marines was the Vought F-8 Crusader. Wing pylons were seldom seen on Navy F-8s, but Marines aircraft were rarely without them. This Crusader totes bombs fitted with 'daisy-cutter' fuse extenders for maximum above-ground blast effect.**

Two weeks after VMA(AW)-224 and the *Coral Sea* left the line, Marine Fighter Attack Squadron Three Thirty-Three (VMFA-333) and its McDonnell F-4Js arrived aboard the USS *America*. During 158 days on the line this squadron took part in *Linebacker I* and *Linebacker II* operations against the North and one of its crews, Major Lee T. Lasseter and his RIO, Captain John D. Cummings, shot down a MiG-21 on 11 September 1972. Both the victorious crew and the crew of the aircraft which had been flying in the wing position were brought down by SAMs while returning to the carrier; fortunately, all four Marine aviators were rescued by a helicopter. Combat operations over the North ended on 27 January 1973 and VMFA-333 and the other squadrons of CVW-8 arrived back at Norfolk on 24 March.

While the victory scored by Major Lasseter and Captain Cummings was the only all-Marine kill, it should be noted that two other Marine pilots had earlier obtained confirmed victories while flying from Thailand on exchange duty with the Air Force. Captain Doyle Baker, with USAF First Lt. John D. Ryan, Jr. in the back seat, had downed a MiG-17 on 17 December 1967 while flying an F-4D of the 13th TFS/432nd TRW; on 12 August 1972 it had been the turn of Captain Lawrence G. Richard,

**Heavily-laden A-6A Intruder rolls at Da Nang on a mission in support of ground forces in 1968. Intruders represented the heaviest attack platform available to the Marine Corps.**

**The Douglas A-4 Skyhawk provided the majority of ground-support missions for the Marines. This pair is from VMA-311, based at Chu Lai. Each aircraft carries its bombs on a multiple-ejector rack on two wing pylons with a fuel tank carried on centreline.**

and his Navy backseater LCdr. Michael Ettel, to come out victorious against a MiG-21 while flying an F-4E of the 58th TFS/432nd TRW. No victories were scored by Marine units operating over the North from South Vietnam.

## *Semper Fidelis: Air Support for the Grunts*

On 8 March 1965 when elements of the 9th MEB came ashore at Red Beach 2 northwest of Da Nang, 30 of the 54 squadrons of the Fleet Marine Forces were equipped with jets (18 others were flying helicopters, three were transport units, and three had observation aircraft). Of the 30 jet units, no fewer than 25 went on to fly one or more combat tours from Vietnamese and Thai bases. They included seven VMAs equipped with Douglas A-4s, three VMF(AW)s with Vought F-8s, two VMCJs with a variety of aircraft, five VMA(AW)s with Grumman A-6s (including two squadrons which had made earlier tours with A-4s), and 11 VMFAs with McDonnell F-4s, one of which was earlier deployed with F-8s. In addition, Marine Headquarters & Maintenance Squadrons (H&MS) flew Grumman TF-9Js and Douglas TA-4Fs in the Tactical Air Control (Airborne) role, as well as transport and liaison aircraft.

The first Marine combat aircraft to reach Da Nang were 15 F-4Bs of VMFA-531 which arrived on 10 April and flew their first in-country air-to-ground sorties three days later. They were followed on 17 April 1965 by a detachment of six Douglas EF-10B electronic warfare aircraft from VMCJ-1. Reporting to the 1st Marine Aircraft Wing (1st MAW), VMCJ-1 and VMFA-531 were the advanc-

**Da Nang was one of the busiest airfields in South East Asia, its proximity to the North making it a regular diversion for Air Force and Navy strike aircraft. As well as Navy units, the Marines had a large force based here, including the Phantoms of VMFA-115 and VMFA-323 shown here.**

**Marine Phantom squadrons regularly deployed to Vietnam in rotation. Trans-Pacific flights were accompanied by Lockheed KC-130s, which provided refuelling, navigation and airlift support.**

ed echelons of Marine Aviation assigned to support the 9th MEB, (deactivated in May 1965 when the larger Third Marine Expeditionary Force – III MEF – was organized) and to be in position for possible operations against the North.

Two squadrons were not enough to undertake the missions assigned to the Marine aviators in Vietnam, but in-country air base facilities were at a premium in 1965. Fortunately, over many years the Marines had planned austere Short Airfield for Tactical Support (SATS) facilities which could be quickly set up overseas. Thus in May 1965, after a suitable site had been identified at Chu Lai, about 50 miles (80 km) south of Da Nang, Naval Mobile Construction Battalion Ten (NMCB-10) was given the task of constructing the first SATS airfield ever installed in a combat environment. In less than four weeks 4,000 ft (1219 m) of AM-12 solid aluminium planks (each measuring 2 by 12 ft/0.61 by 3.7 m and weighing 140 lb/64 kg) were interlocked to obtain a runway capable of coping with the impact and static loads of aircraft operations and the temperature of jet exhaust. Other items built or installed during this period included the Tactical Airfield Fuel Dispensing System (TAFDS), comprised of 10,000-US gal (37854-litre) collapsible tanks and refueling nozzles, the M-21 arresting gear, taxiways and revetments. So efficient were the personnel of NMCB-10 that A-4Cs of VMA-225 arrived at Chu Lai on 1 June and were able to fly their first combat mission later in the day. Obviously, conditions were initially less than ideal, with aircrews and maintenance personnel living as true Marines in the midst of sand and mud, and with the short length of the runway imposing reductions in aircraft take-off weight and ordnance loads. At first this latter deficiency was overcome by frequent use of JATO and by having the A-4s take-off with limited fuel loads, to be air refueled by KC-130Fs from Marine Aerial Refueler Transport Squadrons One Fifty-Two and Three Fifty-Three (VMGR-152 and VMGR-353). Longer term solutions were provided by the extension of the AM-12 planking runway, the construction of a parallel 10,000-ft (3048-m) concrete runway in 1966, and finally by the addition of a cross-wing aluminium planking runway.

With two jet airfields, as well as a number of fields suitable for transports and helicopters, the Marine Corps was then able to quickly increase the number of air units assigned to Vietnam. From this point on, tactical squadrons were frequently rotated to Chu Lai and Da Nang. First of the Marine combat aircraft to operate in Vietnam, the F-4 remained the most numerous aircraft throughout

**The Vought F-8 was in the twilight of its Marine career during the war, with most units turning to the F-4 Phantom. This aircraft is from VMF(AW)-235, complete with Zuni rocket dispensers on the fuselage Y-racks. Despite the 'all-weather fighter' squadron designation, Marine F-8s had little chance to emulate their carrierborne cousins and tangle with the MiGs.**

Douglas A-4 Skyhawks and Grumman A-6 Intruders line up at Chu Lai in their makeshift revetments. Oil drums strapped together provided a considerable amount of protection, and would hopefully prevent damage spreading in the case of a successful VC sapper attack.

the duration of in-country operations, with 11 squadrons (VMFA-115, -122, -212, -232, -314, -323, -324, -334, -513, -531, and -542) flying Phantoms and relaying each other at the two bases. Equipped almost exclusively with the F-4B version of the Phantom (although some squadrons operated F-4Js during the last phase of the war), the Marine Fighter Attack Squadrons mainly flew air support sorties for the benefit of Marines, but also in support of ARVN and USA troops. (Noteworthy among missions flown for Army units were those undertaken during the evacuation of Green Berets from the A Shau Valley in March 1966. Three F-4s and two A-4s were severely damaged, and 21 of the 24 helicopters of HMM-163 had to be replaced as a result of battle damage.) Albeit designed with air combat as its primary mission, the F-4 proved to be an effective ground attack aircraft and, normally carrying an average ordnance load of 5,000 lb (2268 kg) as opposed to only 3,000 lb (1361 kg) for the A-4, performed well for the Marines. Marine Phantoms also were kept on runway alert to bolster air defence, for which role they substituted Sidewinder and Sparrow air-to-air missiles for their usual load of air-to-ground weapons, and flew *Tally Ho* offensive strikes in the North Vietnamese panhandle and *Steel Tiger/Tiger Hound* sorties in Laos. However, until their deployment to Thailand in 1972, the F-4s did not encounter enemy air opposition during air defence sorties or during strikes over the North.

## Crusader replacement

Although by 1965 most Marine fighter squadrons had already exchanged their Vought F-8s for McDonnell F-4s, the older aircraft, unlike those in service with the Navy, had been modified to serve as fighter-bombers and were the only Marine aircraft which could carry a pair of 2,000-lb (907-kg) bombs. As this was an asset for operations in Vietnam, VMF(AW)-312 was deployed to Da Nang in December 1965, and was followed in February 1966 by VMF(AW)-235 and in November of that year by VMF(AW)-232. Finally, at the end of a second combat tour by VMF(AW)-235 during the first half of 1967, the F-8s were returned to CONUS for overhaul and modernization prior to their transfer to Navy squadrons operating from the smaller carriers and to Marine reserve fighter squadrons.

Particularly rugged, light enough to operate effectively from SATS, and easy to maintain even when proper facilities were not available, the Douglas A-4 had the added advantage of equipping numerous Marine attack squadrons. With so many attributes to commend them the diminutive A-4Cs and A-4Es became the Marines' workhorse in Vietnam and consistently maintained a high sortie rate. After the arrival of VMA-224 at Chu Lai in October 1965, seven A-4 squadrons (VMA-121, -211, -214, -223, -224, -225, and -311) took turns for nearly six years in operating from that base and from Da Nang. Following the progressive withdrawal of Marines begun during the summer of 1969, the number of Skyhawk squadrons was reduced. Nevertheless, combat operations continued in support of ARVN troops (with VMA-311 distinguishing itself during *Lam Song 719*) until May 1971, when VMA-311 departed Da Nang for MCAS Iwakuni, Japan, at the conclusion of its fourth combat tour. One year later, however, VMA-311 returned to Vietnam to help bolster allied forces repulsing the North Vietnamese invasion which had begun six weeks earlier. This last tour, during which VMA-311 operated from Bien Hoa AB, lasted until 19 January 1973. On the previous day one of their aircraft had dropped the last Marine bomb of the war during a mission in Cambodia.

## Weather troubles

Low ceilings and tropical downpours too often (and particularly during the monsoon season) limited the ability of F-4s and A-4s to continue close air support operations. As the Viet Cong and the NVA were prone to exploit this situation, the Marines were forced to devise various ways of delivering ordnance under adverse weather conditions. Like the Air Force fast movers, the Marine tactical jets soon learned to rely on ground-based bombing radars and on small radar beacons deployed by ground FACs. On occasion they also bombed through the overcast, under the guidance of Air Force F-4Ds which were equipped with LORAN. However, the ultimate answer to the quest for all-weather ground support operations was provided by the deployment of Grumman A-6As.

Arriving at Da Nang on 1 November 1966, VMA(AW)-242 soon proved that the A-6, in spite of the initial unreliability of its complex weapon system computer, was without equal in bad

Marine F-4 awaits its crew for a mission in support of the 'grunts'. The aircraft is loaded with standard bombs. As the war progressed, more and more aircraft were housed in purpose-built revetments, replacing the barrel structures.

VMFA-542 was one of the eleven squadrons which flew Phantoms in the theatre. F-4B Phantoms were used almost exclusively, but towards war's end a few F-4Js found their way on to the arena.

weather. In fact, during the worst monsoon rains in December 1966 the squadron, which had only 12 aircraft, delivered 38 percent of the ordnance dropped by all Marine aircraft. Pleased with the type's combat début, the Marines wanted to deploy additional A-6s; however, the limited number of aircraft produced and the Navy Department's preference to assign those available to carrier-based units for operations against the North and along the Ho Chi Minh Trail, meant that the build-up of VMA(AW)s proceeded more slowly than desired. Only two other A-6 squadrons were deployed to Vietnam, with VMA(AW)-533 arriving at Chu Lai in April 1967 (after the base's permanent runway had been completed) and VMA(AW)-223 following in October 1968. In four years of combat operations under difficult conditions, the contribution made by the few aircraft of these squadrons far exceeded their number.

## ECM coverage

When sustained operations against North Vietnam were initiated in February 1965, neither the Air Force, which had too few Douglas RB-66Cs to satisfy the needs of both USAFE and PACAF, nor the Navy which still relied on propeller-driven Douglas EA-1Fs (with insufficient performance to operate along with jet-powered strike aircraft), possessed an adequate force of ECM aircraft. On the other hand, the Marines had been given limited responsibilities for operations over the North but had in the Douglas EF-10B an effective jet-powered ECM aircraft. Accordingly, in April 1965 VMCJ-1 rushed a detachment of EF-10Bs to Da Nang to support the operations of both the Air Force and the Navy. During these *Fogbound* missions, ELINT activities enroute to and from targets were combined with direct jamming for the benefit of the other services' aircraft. So effective was the jamming provided by these elderly jets (the EF-10B was a modification of the first Navy all-weather fighter which had entered service in 1950), that the Air Force specially requestesd that a detachment from VMCJ-1 be part of its first anti-SAM strikes in July 1965. Similarly, while continuing to use its slow EA-1Fs for stand-off jamming, whenever feasible the Navy insisted that VMCJ-1 aircraft be on station before its Alpha strikes attempted to penetrate the better defended targets in North Vietnam. Even though its aircraft were fast approaching the end of their airframe life, VMCJ-1 continued its good work during 1966 with its EF-10Bs flying 1,547 sorties over the North and 214 in-country sorties (a particularly impressive rate as the unit never had more than ten EF-10Bs operating from Da Nang!) Fortunately by then the Air Force had acquired a sufficient number of EB-66s to take care of its needs, the Navy was about to receive its first EKA-3Bs, and the VMCJ-1 detachment at Da Nang received its first Grumman EA-6As in November 1966. Nevertheless, the EF-10B, which was affectionately nicknamed 'Willie the Whale' and less nicely the 'DRUT' (an euphimism obtained by reversing the letters), remained in Vietnam until 1969. Thereafter, as both the Air Force and the Navy had their own ECM aircraft, VMCJ-1 employed its EA-6As almost exclusively in support of Marine operations and for ELINT missions over and above the DMZ. After the Marines returned to Vietnam in 1972, ECM/ESM sorties were performed by the EA-6As of VMCJ-1 and VMCJ-2, and these two units provided valuable service during the two *Linebacker* phases.

Obsolete as a combat aircraft, the Douglas F3D-2 Skyknight was modified to the F3D-2Q configuration for use by the USMC as the world's first jet-powered electronic-countermeasures aircraft. Redesignated EF-10B in September 1962, this type filled a major void in the US inventory, and the few available EF-10Bs saw much use in Vietnam from April 1965 until 1969.

## Grumman A-6A Intruder

**VMA(AW)-242 was the first Marine Corps squadron to deploy to the war zone with the Grumman A-6A Intruder, followed later by VMA(AW)-223 and VMA(AW)-533. VMA(AW)-224 also served aboard the USS *Coral Sea*. Despite the small numbers present, the A-6 force flying from Da Nang and Chu Lai proved an excellent asset, being able to operate in some of the worst weather the South East Asian climate could throw at it. Despite initial problems with the nav/attack system, the Intruder was to prove its capability time and time again, delivering a disproportionate amount of ordnance during times of inclement weather.**

10
DT
152595
VMA-(AW)-242
MARINES

**Above: Tactical reconnaissance for the Marines was handled by the McDonnell RF-4C Phantom, flying with VMCJ-1. These had been preceded by a small number of RF-8As. This RF-4C has the luxury of a hardened shelter to protect it.**

**Above right: A year before the siege, the infamous strip at Khe Sanh is about to be used by this KC-130F. These tanker Hercs were used on supply duties as well as their primary refueling function. The helicopters are UH-1Es.**

**Marine OV-10A Bronco in flight displays the 7.62-mm machine-guns carried in sponsons under the fuselage, and four rocket pods underneath the sponsons. FAC missions were the main tasking for the type, augmenting a force of Cessna O-1Fs.**

As its designation indicates, Marine Composite Reconnaissance Squadron One operated more than one type of aircraft to fulfil its missions, with the EF-10B detachment at Da Nang being complemented by an RF-8A detachment. Also operating from Da Nang, the Marine RF-8As supported the Marines, as well as the Air Force, the Army, the Navy, and the RVNAF, by supplying aerial photos of targets in South Vietnam (and occasionally of targets in Laos and North Vietnam). For both in-country and out-of-country photographic reconnaissance activities VMCJ-1 began replacing its RF-8As with RF-4Bs in October 1966 as, on one hand, the newer aircraft were fitted for night as well as day photography and, on the other hand, the RF-8s were needed by the Navy as attrition replacements for VFP-63. Departing for MCAS Iwakuni in the spring of 1971, VMCJ-1 brought its RF-4Bs and EA-6Bs back to Vietnam one year later when it returned in answer to the North Vietnamese spring offensive. Having served in Vietnam longer than any other Marine unit, VMCJ-1 made its final departure in January 1973.

When it began sending ground forces to Vietnam, the Marine Corps was no longer allowed to have its own transport squadrons and had only a few elderly aircraft operated by H&MS for staff transport and liaison. The Corps, however, had been authorized to acquire KC-130Fs as this version of the ubiquitous Lockheed Hercules was primarily configured for inflight refueling with hose-and-drogue pods beneath the wing. Indeed, during the South East Asia War the Marines made extensive use of these aircraft in their professed role and operated them to facilitate the ferrying/deployment of tactical aircraft to and from the war zone, to refuel A-4s from Chu Lai (until the extension of the SATS runway enabled the Skyhawks to take off at full weight), and to support the strike aircraft operating over North Vietnam and Laos. In addition, the KC-130Fs of the Okinawa-based VMGR-152, supplemented by detachments from VMGR-353, were extensively used to haul men and supplies between major bases and isolated outposts, and to provide radio relay, airborne control and flare dropping capabilities. For intra-theatre logistic support, the Hercules were supplemented by a handful of less capable transport

**Above: In addition to operating low performance aircraft for conventional Forward Air Controllers (Airborne) duties, the Marine Corps used two-seat advanced jet trainers in the TAC(A), or Tactical Air Control (Airborne) role. Bearing the tail code of H&MS-13 (Headquarters & Maintenance Squadron Thirteen), this Grumman TF-9J flown by Major Robert Roche was photographed during a combat sortie over South Vietnam in February 1967.**

**Right: The success obtained in the TAC(A) role with obsolescent TF-9Js led the Marines to select the brand new Douglas TA-4F to operate in this role. This two-seat Skyhawk of H&MS-11 was photographed departing Chu Lai on 1 January 1971.**

aircraft (Beech UC-45Js; Douglas C-47H/Js, C-54Qs and C-117Ds; and Grumman US-2Bs and C1As) assigned to the Headquarters & Maintenance Squadron in each of the Marine Air Groups. Among this motley group of ancient aircraft, the Douglas C-117D (a rebuilt version of the C-47/R4D brought up to Super DC-3 standards, with more powerful engines and cleaned-up wing and tail sections) had the greatest longevity and operated in Vietnam until early 1973.

## *Eyes of the strike force*

To locate targets for tactical aircraft and to ensure accurate delivery of ordnance (at times as close as 15 m/50 ft from friendly lines), the Marines relied on three types of air controllers. In Corps terminology, Forward Air Controllers (FACs) were those operating on the ground from mobile radio vehicles or from fixed emplacements. The Forward Air Controllers (Airborne) (FAC(A)s) performed their duty from light aircraft (O-1Fs and OV-10As) or helicopters, while the Tactical Air Controllers (Airborne), (TAC(A)s) flew in high performance TF-9Js or TA-4Fs. As the few Cessna OE-1s which had been deployed with the *Shufly* helicopters were no longer flyable when Marine ground forces began fighting in Vietnam, the FAC(A)s flew in Huey helicopters and ex-Army Cessna O-1Cs of Marine Observation Squadrons until the arrival of the first North American OV-10As of VMO-2 in July 1968. Faster, well protected and armed (four M-60 machine-guns being supplemented by external stores to mark targets and suppress enemy fire), the OV-10A became one of the most effective Marine aircraft, with VMO-2 and VMO-6 operating detachments close to the battle (including Quang Nam and Dong Ha airstrips near the DMZ).

**Waiting to taxi, this well-armed OV-10A carries a Minigun pod under the centre-section, augmenting the internal weapons and rocket pods for fire suppression and target marking. OV-10s operated from strips close to the battlezone.**

**This VMA(AW)-242 A-6A displays the normal bomb carriage of the type with multiple ejector racks on wing and centreline pylons. Each rack carries six Mk 82 227-kg (500-lb) 'slick' bombs. When delivered with the accuracy obtained by the sophisticated onboard equipment, the A-6 became a much feared weapon.**

**Right: VMCJ-1 crewmen remove film and check cameras in an RF-4B Phantom.**

Whereas the Air Force only briefly experimented with F-100F two-seat fighters in the forward air control role, the Marine TAC(A)s obtained great success with their two-seat jet trainers. The use of Grumman TF-9Js, in which the backseater acted as the TAC(A), was pioneered in 1966 by H&MS-11 from Da Nang and by H&MS-13 from Chu Lai. Carrying rocket pods and armed with a 20-mm cannon, the Cougars demonstrated conclusively that jets were effective in the TAC(A) role. Thereafter, the old TF-9Js were replaced by new TA-4Fs which not only operated in-country but also went up North to direct naval gunfire against coastal targets. The success of these operations led to the present use of Douglas OA-4Ms (modernized TA-4Js fitted with specialized electronics).

### *Marines join the Air Force*

In-country operations having bogged down into a drawn-out land war, the Marine Corps (which had always insisted on controlling its aircraft as part of the integral ground-air team considered essential for its usual amphibious assaults) was pressured by Gen. William C. Westmoreland, Commander, US Military Assistance Command, to release its aviation units to a single manager for tactical aviation throughout South Vietnam, the Seventh Air Force. This change, however, had not yet been implemented when Operation *Niagara* was launched to support the Marine garrison at Khe Sanh. Located 10 miles (16 km) from the Laotian border and 16 miles (26 km) south of the DMZ, Khe Sanh had become a major Marine combat base from which search and destroy operations were mounted to control North Vietnamese infiltrations. Evidence that the enemy was preparing a major assault to remove this obstacle was uncovered at the end of 1967 and a three-month long battle, one of the most ferocious and famous actions during the South East Asia War, began in January 1968.

First operating independently, Marine combat aircraft, transports and helicopters, with effective support by Navy and Air Force aircraft (including B-52s), put on a major effort to stun the NVA offensive. The high level of activities continued unabated even after 8 March when Marine aircraft and its air control system came under the 'single management' of Gen William W. Momyer, USAF, and during *Niagara* some 100,000 tons of bombs were dropped by all US aircraft, with transports and helicopters delivering 12,500 tons of supplies. Thanks in great part to the massive air effort, the siege of Khe Sanh was lifted on 6 April. American casualties included 200 dead and 1,600 wounded; Viet Cong and North Vietnamese casualties were estimated at 10,000. Tragically, the heavy loss of

**Grumman EA-6As began supplementing EF-10Bs in the electronic-countermeasure role beginning in November 1966 when a VMCJ-1 detachment arrived at Da Nang. The EA-6A proved most successful and was operated not only during in-country operations but also to support Air Force, Navy, and Marine missions over North Vietnam and Laos.**

A-6A Intruders sometimes led A-4 Skyhawks on blind-bombing raids, using their superior navigation and attack systems to allow the Skyhawks to drop on command over the target. These four are on a medium-level bombing mission, using 'slick' iron bombs.

human lives was futile; on 23 June 1968 US political changes achieved what the Communists had failed to do, dismantle the combat base at Khe Sanh!

Under Air Force single management, the level of in-country Marine air operations continued high during the remainder of 1968 and most of 1969. Thereafter, in compliance with the reduction of US forces in Vietnam which had been initiated by the Nixon Administration, Marine Aviation units were progressively redeployed to Japan, Okinawa, Hawaii, and CONUS. However, in the spring of 1972 they returned to Da Nang (VMFA-115, -212, and -232 bringing Phantoms, VMA(AW)-533 flying A-6As, and a combined detachment of VMCJ-1 and VMCJ-2 operating EA-6As) and to Bien Hoa (VMA-211 and VMA-311 with A-4s) to provide in-country support for the RVNAF and to fly interdiction sorties over enemy LOCs in Laos. To reduce airfield congestion in Vietnam and place the strike aircraft closer to their targets, Phantoms and Intruders were soon transferred to Nam Phong (it was while operating from this Thai base that VMFA-232 lost the only Marine aircraft to be shot down by MiGs). In addition, the VMCJ-1/VMCJ-2 detachment flew ECM missions over the North in support of Navy and Air Force *Linebacker* operations (notably to provide jamming during the heavy B-52 raids). All these units departed South East Asia shortly after the Paris Agreement.

During the war the Marine Corps lost 194 fixed-wing aircraft and 270 helicopters to enemy action; 82 fixed-wing aircraft and 154 helicopters were lost to operational causes. One hundred eighty-eight Marine pilots and 391 other flying personnel had been killed in action or in air accidents.

Photographed at NAS Alameda, California, on 3 January 1972, this EA-6A was in the United States between two combat deployments. Most Marine aircraft had been brought back to CONUS in 1970 but, in answer to the North Vietnamese offensive in the spring of 1972, EA-6A detachments of VMCJ-1 and VMCJ-2 returned to Da Nang. During *Linebacker*, the EA-6As flew ECM missions over the North in support of Air Force and Navy operations.

# US Army Aviation in South East Asia

For most of the war veterans, as well as for many of the armchair strategists who watched their daily dosage of television newscasts from the safety of their home, the war in Vietnam will be remembered for its massive use of helicopters. This was not, however, the first instance of military use of rotary-wing aircraft; this claim goes to the Kriegsmarine which had assigned in mid-1942 Focke Achgelis Fa 330 gyro kites to submarines operating in the South Atlantic. As World War II went on, Germany also made limited use of helicopters, with Flettner Fl 282s flying convoy protection in the Mediterranean and Aegean, and Focke Achgelis Fa 223s being flown on rescue sorties. In US military service the pioneering efforts of Igor Sikorsky had been rewarded by the employment of R-4 helicopters, beginning in late 1944, in the CBI theatre of operations. Japan also experimented with military operation of rotary-wing aircraft and became the first nation to assign a combat role to this type of machine when the Imperial Japanese Army flew Kayaba Ka-1 autogyros on anti-submarine patrols from the escort carrier *Akitsu Maru* late in the war.

During the fifties more significant military use of helicopters was made by US forces in Korea, British forces in Malaya and during the Suez Canal operation, and French forces in Indochina and Algeria, with helicopters being employed for aeromedical evacuation, combat rescue, resupply of isolated outposts, and transportation of small combat teams. However, it was the war in Vietnam that brought helicopters to the forefront of combat equipment.

Without a doubt, ever since Air America first used 16 Sikorsky H-34 Choctaws for covert operations, helicopters came into their own during the South East Asia conflict when they were used in large numbers not only in what had become their traditional roles (primarily medical evacuation, rescue, and observation), but also to give a new degree of mobility to ground forces and to provide these forces with effective close air support. Clearly, airmobile operations dominated the Vietnam battlefield during the US involvement, and Army and Marine battalions became highly skilled in the use of the helicopter to surprise and outmanoeuver the enemy. Not only were large numbers of troops transported to the battlefront, but the technique was perfected of shifting light and medium artillery pieces by helicopter to provide continuous fire support to units involved in rapidly changing engagements. Even more significant was the large-scale employment of gunships.

The importance of helicopters during the war can be gauged by the fact that in July 1969, at the peak of its strength, the 1st Aviation Brigade, which operated the majority of the aircraft available to the US Army in Vietnam, had no fewer than 3,589 helicopters (2,202 UH-1s, 635 OH-6As, 441 AH-1Gs, and 311 CH-47s), in addition to its 641 fixed-wing aircraft.

**Covert war, 1963: Schmeisser MP42-armed Americans stand guard as a Sikorsky CH-37B tries (unsuccessfully) to lift a Piasecki CH-21 from the mud of a Vietnamese swamp. The CH-21 had been forced down by groundfire while transporting Vietnamese army units.**

Shown in clean configuration, without any armament, this Bell UH-1B bears the markings of 'A' Company, 1st Aviation Battalion, 1st Infantry Division (with its 'Big One' insignia on the vertical fin). It is typical of early transport versions of the Huey.

## *US Army Helicopter Operations*

Following President John F. Kennedy's decision on 11 November 1961 to increase US support to the Government of President Ngo Dinh Diem, the US Army undertook to deploy two Transportation Companies from Ft. Bragg and Ft. Lewis to Vietnam. Equipped with Piasecki H-21B Shawnee single-engined, twin-rotor helicopters, the 8th Transportation Company arrived at Qui Nhon on 11 December 1961, while on the same day the 57th Transportation Company set up base at Camp Bear Cat. Primarily intended to support Vietnamese ground forces and their US advisers, these two companies initiated the air mobile operations which became so characteristic of the Vietnam War. During 1962 three other companies flying H-21Bs, the 33rd, 81st and 93rd, were added to this initial commitment.

Also deployed during 1962 were the first Bell UH-1 Iroquois (although officially named Iroquois, this outstanding single-turbine Bell helicopter became better known by its nickname, Huey), with the UH-1As of the 57th Medical Detachment (Helicopter Ambulance) arriving early in the year. The build-up of the Huey force was rapid and, by early 1964, 250 UH-1s were already in Vietnam.

Below: Piasecki H-21 helicopters were the first to be deployed to Vietnam. Here a CH-21 is seen operating in the jungle of neighbouring Thailand.

Below: The door-gunners had their own peculiar style of dealing with groundfire, displayed here by this intrepid 'Razorback' crewman. The aircraft is a UH-1B gunship, with forward-firing machine-guns and rocket pods.

**Above: The 1st Cavalry arrive in tight landing formation, troopers ready to leap from the helos as soon as they are in jumping distance of the ground.**

**Above right: One man and his dog . . . when the Army moved camp, the Hueys shifted absolutely anything that could be carried.**

**If a single picture were to be selected to illustrate activities in Vietnam, it would arguably have to show airmobile operations. The foremost component of such commonplace activities was the Huey helicopter.**

The UH-1, in both its transport ('slick') and armed ('hog') versions, went on to play an extremely important part in the war. Even though proponents of fixed-wing aircraft have good reason to argue against this claim, the ubiquitous Huey can be regarded as the most important aircraft of the South East Asia War. Whatever other claims can be made for fixed-wing aircraft, there is no arguing the fact that more Hueys were operated and, unfortunately, lost during this war (1,213 to hostile actions and 1,380 to operational causes) than any other type of rotary- or fixed-wing aircraft.

Air mobility introduced a new dimension in flexibility, with the infantry/cavalry and helicopter combination soon dominating the Army's and Marine Corps' tactical doctrines. Both services relied on helicopters for insertion of troops into and extraction out of combat, for provision of supplies, artillery spotting, liaison, command and control, communications relay, night illumination, and medical evacuation. But, above all, the US Army soon learned to depend on armed helicopters to escort its transport helicopters and road/rail convoys, to clear landing zones (LZ) just prior to arrival of the transport helicopters, and to supplement and extend the range of conventional artillery. In addition, armed helicopters proved to be effective weapons during anti-armour operations.

## *Helos displace paras*

The success obtained with airmobile operations, made possible by the deployment of helicopters in great number, rendered World War II-style parachute assaults unnecessary. The only major US combat parachute assault of the war took place on 22 February 1967, at the onset of Operation *Junction City*, when 845 paratroopers of the 173rd Airborne Brigade jumped from USAF C-130s into War Zone C. On four other occasions in 1967-68 small teams of US advisers from the 5th Special Forces Group were parachuted, along with 300 to 500 Vietnamese paratroopers.

In support of airmobile operations the US Army operated three main categories of helicopters:

Prominently marked with a Red Cross, this Bell UH-1D was photographed near the DMZ on 16 October 1969 as it was landing in a clearing to pick up wounded personnel from the 101st Airborne Division. Nicknamed 'Dustoff', medical evacuations by helicopters saved a great number of lives by enabling wounded troops to be rapidly transported to medical facilities.

The Sikorsky CH-54A Tarhe was capable of lifting swung loads of up to 20,000 pounds. This capability enabled the type to retrieve more than $210 million worth of downed aircraft, such as this de Havilland Canada C-7A Caribou being transported from An Khe to Qhi Nhon on 10 December 1965 by a CH-54A of the 478th Aviation Company, 1st Cavalry Division (Airmobile).

Below right: Troops of the C Co, 1st Bn, 50th Mech, 1st Cavalry Division (Airmobile) are seen unloading from a CH-47A at a peak-top landing zone to begin a search and destroy mission.

Below: A Boeing-Vertol CH-47A lands in a cloud of dust on the chopper pad at Fire Support Base 'Bastogne' during a resupply mission on 16 April 1968.

transport, observation, and fire support. After disposing of its obsolete Piasecki CH-21s (previously designated H-21s) and Sikorsky UH-19s (formerly H-19s), the Army relied upon various models of the Bell UH-1 and Vertol CH-47 to carry troops, ammunition and equipment into combat. In addition to their crew of three (pilot, co-pilot, and crew chief/gunner), the UH-1A and UH-1B versions carried only six troops; hence, for combat operations in Vietnam, they were rapidly supplanted by the larger UH-1D and UH-1H versions, which carried 10. The twin-engined, twin-rotor Boeing-Vertol CH-47 Chinook was also sent to Vietnam in large numbers. The CH-47A, CH-47B and CH-47C versions, with progressively more powerful turboshaft engines, were used not only to carry up to 33 troops, but also to recover downed aircraft and carry large loads underslung externally.

For heavy lift, including the transportation of artillery pieces and Airmobile Surgical Centers, and recovery of downed aircraft, the 355th and 478th Aviation Companies employed a relatively small number of Sikorsky CH-54A and CH-54B Tarhes. Specially built for this purpose, the single-rotor CH-54 was powered by two 4,500 or 4,800 shp (3356 or 3579 kW) turboshaft engines and carried virtually all of its payload externally. Prior to its availability, the US Army had operated the less successful Sikorsky CH-37B Mojave in Vietnam.

## Scout helicopters

The Army had initially sent some Bell OH-13 Sioux and Hiller OH-23 Ravens for the observation role and the evacuation of wounded personnel. However, these obsolescent helicopters were later replaced in these two roles first by the more capable Bell UH-1A and UH-1B, and then by the Bell OH-58A Kiowa and Hughes OH-6A Cayuse (the winners of the 1960 Light Observation Helicopter competition). The importance of the OH-6 in the war's effort is evidenced by the fact that 658 were lost in combat and 297 in operational accidents.

Throughout the war transport helicopters, and to a lesser extent observation helicopters, were fitted with a variety of armament to suppress enemy gunfire and provide a better chance of safely landing the troops. However, it was the

The light and nimble Hughes OH-6A Cayuse, better known to the troops as the 'Loach', was extensively used by the Army as its standard scout helicopter. Frequently, as shown on this drawing, the doors were removed, a pilot-fired 7.62-mm minigun was mounted on the left side, and a flexible 0.60-calibre gun was provided for the gunner on the right side.

employment of helicopter gunships which revolutionized operational concepts. Initial evaluation of armed helicopters had been undertaken by the Utility Tactical Transport Company which, with its 15 UH-1As armed with two Browning .30 caliber flexible machine-guns and up to 16 2.75-in rockets, had arrived at Tan Son Nhut on 16 October 1962. The success of this evaluation was quickly followed by the large-scale use of specialized helicopter gunships and armed helicopters (one of which made history over Laos on 12 January 1968 when it became the first rotary-wing aircraft to shoot down a fixed-wing aircraft, an Antonov An-2 utility transport, and to force down a second aircraft of this type).

The first of these specialized machines was the UH-1C version of the Huey. Standard armament systems for the UH-1C included the M21 with one forward-firing 7.62-mm XM134 Minigun and an XM158 seven-tube 2.75-in rocket launcher mounted externally on each side of the fuselage; the XM16 system in which four 7.62-mm M60C machine-guns replaced the Miniguns of the other system; and the all-rocket XM3 system which was made up of two 24-tube launchers. In addition, like other helicopters, the UH-1C was fitted (frequently as the result of field modifications) with a variety of weapons, including a chin-mounted M5 40-mm grenade launcher, M60 machine-gun or XM134 Minigun on flexible mounts, MAD (Mortar Air Delivery) system, M24A1 20-mm cannon pods, smoke generators, etc. The weight of the armament, however, proved detrimental and the UH-1C 'hog' gunships had difficulty keeping up with the UH-1B 'slick' transport helicopters. This deficiency, partially solved by fitting more powerful engines in UH-1C airframes to obtain the UH-1M version, finally disappeared with the entry into service of the AH-1G Cobra.

On the strength of its initial experience with armed helicopters, in late 1964 the US Army had initiated the AAFSS design competition for fast, armoured and heavily-armed helicopters. In addition, realizing that the development of the AAFSS gunship would be a protracted affair, the Army

Next to the Hughes OH-6A, the Bell OH-58A was numerically the most important Army observation helicopter. This Kiowa is seen firing its door-mounted XM-58 armament kit during a practice sortie on 2 December 1969.

The small Hughes OH-6A Cayuse saw much use in the observation role. The type, however, suffered many losses with 635 OH-6As being lost to AAA and small arms fire.

**Right: Three shark-mouthed AH-1Gs cruise purposefully towards their operational area. Each is armed with a fairly typical Cobra load of two Minigun pods and two rocket pods on the stub wings, and a gun and grenade launcher in the nose turret.**

**Left: An early UH-1 gunship ('hog') displays the carriage of rocket pods and guns. UH-1s were found to be underpowered in the gunship role, and virtually disappeared on the introduction into service of the AH-1.**

took an early interest in a Bell proposal to develop an interim AAFSS helicopter from the combat-proven Huey. The result was the privately-developed Bell Model 209 which made its initial flight on 7 September 1965. Retaining the engine, rotor and transmission system of the UH-1C, the Model 209 had a completely new, lower-drag fuselage with gunner and pilot in tandem. Armament consisted of a nose turret (with either one or two Miniguns, one or two 40-mm grenade launchers, or one Minigun and one grenade launcher) and external loads mounted beneath stub wings. Performance of the new gunship was greatly increased, with top speed in clean condition exceeding that of the similarly-powered UH-1H version by some 72 per cent. In March 1966 the Army ordered the Model 209 into production as the AH-1G Cobra, with production Cobras reaching Vietnam later that same year. Soon the AH-1G built up an impressive combat record and helped reduce transport helicopter losses, but 173 were lost to hostile actions and 109 to operational causes.

To help stem the flow of tanks during the North Vietnamese spring 1972 offensive, two experimental UH-1Hs armed with TOW anti-tank missiles were rushed to Vietnam. Their spectacular success (73 hits out of the first 89 missiles fired) not only bolstered allied defences in Vietnam but also led to renewed interest in the use of helicopters against armour.

## *Unit equipment*

During the war, a typical Airmobile/Assault Helicopter Company was equiped with six UH-1Cs and 23 UH-1Ds. The typical complement of a Medium Helicopter Company/Assault Support Helicopter company, on the other hand, consisted of 16 CH-47A/B/C cargo helicopters and two OH-6A observation helicopters, and that of an Armored Cavalry Squadron was made up of nine AH-1G attack helicopters, nine OH-6A observation helicopters, and two UH-1B utility helicopters.

Army helicopter losses during operations in Vietnam were heavy (a total of 2,249 being lost to

**The first Huey gunships were the UH-1As which had arrived in Vietnam during 1962, armed with a .30 caliber Browning machine-gun and rocket pods. This UH-1A is seen in February 1963, with the flat colour scheme typical of the period.**

hostile actions and 2,075 in operational accidents) and, between 1966 and 1971, averaged one helicopter loss for every 7.9 sorties. In terms of human lives, the price paid by the US Army was even more grievous. Five hundred and sixty-four helicopter pilots, 1,155 crew members and 682 passengers were killed in non-hostile helicopter accidents.

Army helicopter units operating in South East Asia were too numerous to list in this overview; however, let it be noted that the 180th Aviation Company became the last of these units to leave Vietnam when it departed Phu Hiep on 29 March 1973.

**Above: Nicknamed 'Leprecaun', this Bell AH-1G was photographed while hot refueling at Katum in May 1970 during the Cambodian Offensive. Tactically successful, operations in Cambodia resulted in the capture of individual weapons sufficient to equip 55 full-strength VC battalions.**

**Below: Bell AH-1G hovers in its burm, ready to move off on a mission. It is in 'thumper ship' configuration, with two 40-mm grenade launchers mounted in the nose turret. The place is Bien Hoa.**

**Right: A Bell AH-1G Cobra is partially hidden by smoke and dust from its attack, probably during the 1968 Tet offensive. The gunship introduced great accuracy to counter-insurgency operations.**

Squatter
Swatter

**Bell AH-1G Hueycobra**

Resplendent in tigermouth markings, this Hueycobra gunship is armed with a 40-mm grenade launcher and a 7.62-mm Minigun in the nose turret, and 52 rockets in four pods beneath the stub wings. Developed by Bell as the private venture Model 209, this specialized gunship version of the ubiquitous Huey built up an impressive combat record and helped reduce transport helicopter losses by providing effective fire suppression during airmobile operations. The gunner sat in the forward seat, with the pilot sitting higher up to retain good visibility forward.

Far left: Also based at Long Than North, the Beech U-21As of the 2nd Signal Group Aviation Detachment were used for radio relay and transportation of priority personnel between locations in Vietnam. Similar to the civil Beech King Air, these U-21As were fitted with special radio equipment but could still carry six to ten passengers.

Left: Among the odd experiments resulting from the need to find better ways to track guerrillas moving stealthily under the cover of a jungle canopy, the Army sponsored the development of a very quiet aircraft with a muffler-equipped engine and slow-turning propeller. Using airframes from Schweizer SGS 2-32 sailplanes, Lockheed built two QT-2PCs which underwent operational evaluation under the code name *Prize Crew* in 1967-68.

Right: The successful operational evaluation of the QT-2PCs in Vietnam led to the ordering of 14 more advanced Lockheed YO-3As as part of the STANO (Surveillance, Target Acquisition and Night Observation) system. Thirteen YO-3As were operated from Long Than North by the 1st (Special Aircraft) Aviation Company, 224th Army Security Agency Battalion (Aviation), starting in early 1970.

## *US Army Fixed-wing Operations*

If helicopters were the primary air vehicles of the US Army, they were not the only flying machines to be employed by that service. In the transport role, the Army initially operated de Havilland Canada CV-2 and CV-2A Caribou twin-engined transports to resupply isolated outposts and to fly personnel and supplies from major airports to forward landing strips, from which helicopters would take them into combat. Carrying either 32 combat troops or 5,000 lb (2268 kg) of cargo, and possessing good shortfield characteristics, a single Caribou had been tested in Vietnam during the second half of 1961 and had proved well-suited to Army requirements. Accordingly, the Army pressed its demand for deployment of Caribou units. The first of these units, the 1st Aviation Company, departed Fort Benning, Georgia, on 31 May 1962 on its way to South East Asia. Initially providing non-scheduled logistics missions on behalf of American forces in Thailand, the 1st Aviation Company began operating in South Vietnam in July. Subsequently, the Caribou-equipped 19th, 57th, 61st, 92nd, 134th, and 135th Aviation Companies were also sent to Vietnam where they were found to be ideal for resupplying isolated Special Forces camps. The Air Force, however, sought to obtain control of all airlift activities in the war zone and, following the DOD decision to transfer all large fixed-wing aircraft to the USAF, the US Army lost its Caribous on 1 January 1967. Throughout the war, smaller utility transports, the use of which was not affected by this re-organisation of the US Armed Forces, were operated by Army Aviation Companies for liaison, light cargo, and passenger services. They included a variety of single-engined aircraft, such as de Havilland Canada U-1 Otters and U-6 Beavers, and light twin-engined aircraft, such as Beech U-8 Seminoles and U-21 Utes.

Fixed-wing observation aircraft of the US Army varied greatly in size and capabilities. At the lower end of the scale was the Cessna O-1 Bird Dog which, like its USAF counterpart, was also used by forward air controllers to coordinate air strikes. Other types of light single-engined observation aircraft operated by the Army were the unique Lockheed QT-2PC and YO-3A. Two experimental QT-2PCs were deployed to Vietnam in December 1967 as part of the *Prize Crew* operational evaluation programme for this extremely quiet aircraft. These aircraft were fitted with a slow-turning propeller and a muffler system to reduce their audio-detectability characteristics. Their successful use in covertly detecting Viet Cong movements led to the deployment of 13 YO-3As by the 1st (Special Aircraft) Aviation Company, 224th US Army Security Agency Battalion (Aviation), at Long Than North.

### *Observation platform*

The largest observation aircraft operated by Army units was the twin-turboprop Grumman Mohawk. Specially developed to meet joint Army and Marine Corps requirements for a battlefield surveillance aircraft, the OV-1A Mohawk saw considerable use with numerous Aviation Companies. Special versions of the Mohawk (the OV-1B, carrying side-looking airborne radar in a long

Grumman OV-1A Mohawks were used for observation duties, but could also pack some offensive punch themselves, either for light attack or target marking. This aircraft looses off unguided rockets at a ground target.

pod under the forward fuselage, and the OV-1C fitted with cameras and an infra-red sensor) were also operated by the 138th, 144th, 146th, and 156th Aviation Companies, 224th US Army Security Agency Battalion (Aviation) for intelligence gathering. Other classified electronic reconnaissance missions were flown by Army aircrews aboard Beech RU-21s carrying a variety of avionic equipment and fitted with external aerials. Finally, the largest and heaviest aircraft used by the US Army during the war were the Lockheed AP-2Es, ex-US Navy P2V-5s modified to serve as airborne radio relays, which were operated by the 1st Radio Research Company from Cam Ranh Bay, Pleiku, and other stations.

**Left: Several U-21 variants were used for electronic surveillance, characterised by large dipole antennas. This is an RU-21D.**

**Developed to meet Army and Marine Corps requirements for a battlefield surveillance aircraft, the basic OV-1A version of the Grumman Mohawk was first deployed to Vietnam during the summer of 1962. This first version was later supplemented by two more capable models: the OV-1B, with pod-mounted side-looking airborne radar as shown on this aircraft, and the OV-1C, with cameras and an infra-red sensor system.**

# The Vietnamese Air Force

Following a long-established policy of incorporating indigenous personnel in its colonial troops, France had progressively increased the number of Vietnamese serving in its C.E.F.E.O. (Corps Expéditionnaire Français d'Extrême-Orient) until they eventually accounted for nearly one-third of the Corps' strength. During this period, when French officers and NCOs provided the cadres, Vietnamese seldom rose above the non-commissioned rank. There were exceptions, however. Nguyen Van Hinh, for example, rose to the rank of captain as a B-26 pilot in the Armée de l'Air. Electing to stay in the Armée de l'air at the end of the Indochina War, Nguyen Van Hinh was subsequently promoted to the rank of Général de Division (Lieutenant General) and, just prior to his retirement in the seventies, commanded the 1er Groupement de Missiles Stratégiques (French Strategic Missile Force).

With the establishment of the State of Vietnam on 5 June 1948, and the need for ever increasing numbers of troops to fight the Communist insurgency, France began to set up the Vietnamese Army. After a slow start, this army grew rapidly with its strength surging from 35,000 regular and 35,000 auxiliary troops in 1951, to 150,000 regulars and 50,000 auxiliaries in 1953. Notwithstanding the fact that Vietnamese officers (including aircrews) and other ranks were already serving in the Armée de l'Air, the Vietnamese Army was not initially provided with its own aviation.

## *Birth of an Air Force*

The first positive step toward the creation of the Vietnamese Air Force was taken on 9 June 1951 when the organisation of an Air Training Center at Nha Tran was authorized. Staffed by French personnel and equipped with Morane-Saulnier M.S. 500 Criquets, the Nha Trang Air Training Center first trained Vietnamese instructors selected from personnel previously trained in the Armée de l'Air's flying schools in France, Algeria, and French Morocco, accepting its first group of students on 31 March 1952.

By then the Air Department of the Joint General Staff of the State of Vietnam already had two operational squadrons manned by personnel trained in French schools. The 1st Observation Squadron had been organized in July 1951 to fly Morane-Saulnier M.S. 500 Criquets from Nha Trang (later from Hue). During the following month the French had supplied an initial batch of Dassault MD 312 Flamant twin-engined light transports to equip the 312th Special Missions Squadron at Tan Son Nhut. Fitted with underwing bomb racks, the Flamants became the first VNA aircraft to have limited combat capability. Subsequently, as aircrews graduated from the Nha Trang Air Training Center, they were assigned to make up attrition in these two Vietnamese squadrons and in the 21ème, 22ème and 23ème G.A.O.A.s of the Armée de l'Air, with other aircrews later being assigned to form a second VNAF observation squadron.

Following the end of the Indochina War and in preparation for the final withdrawal of its forces from the country, France, with the concurrence of the United States, undertook to provide additional aircraft to the VNAF by transferring a number of US-supplied aircraft. While Criquets continued to be operated by the observation squadrons and the Nha Trang flight school, these old aircraft were supplemented by the VNAF's first 20 Cessna L-19s; the Flamants were replaced in the liaison and transport roles by 10 Beech C-45s, 16 Douglas C-47s and a single Republic Seabee amphibian. At

**Morane-Saulnier M.S.500 Criquets fly over other aircraft from the 1st Observation Squadron, and a civilian Douglas DC-3. The F-V registration was that of Vietnam at the time, forming part of the French civil register.**

The Morane-Saulnier M.S. 500 Criquet was an excellent craft for the hilly and jungled terrain covering much of Vietnam. Its exceptional short-field capabilities and low-speed manoeuvrability enabled it to use the smallest and roughest of strips.

the same time, the VNAF took over control of the air bases at Bien Hoa, Da Nang (known as Tourane under the French), Nha Trang, Pleiku, and Tan Son Nhut. In addition, France provided 28 Grumman F8F-1 Bearcats and started a pilot transition course at Cap Saint Jacques (Vung Tau Airfield) in preparation for the activation of the VNAF's 1er Groupe de Chasse (1st Fighter Squadron) at Bien Hoa in June 1956.

## *The Americanization of the VNAF*

Until early 1955, Vietnamese destined to become transport or fighter pilots had received advanced training in flying schools in France, as the Nha Trang Air Training Center possessed only Criquets and L-19s. Thus, at the time of the independence it became necessary to boost the training capabilities of the VNAF and, to that end, French instructors were first supplemented by US personnel. The US took over the responsibility for all Vietnamese military training on 12 February 1955 and supplied 55 North American T-6G advanced trainers. Slowly, additional training facilities were set up for maintenance personnel, and a complete support programme (including the creation of an Air Depot at Bien Hoa, an Air Traffic Center, an Air Medical Center, etc.) was implemented.

South Vietnam's refusal to conduct elections to reunify the two Vietnams in accordance with the Geneva Agreement had led American officials to expect a North Vietnamese invasion sometime after July 1956, the date by which the elections should have taken place. Even though the feared invasion did not then take place, the decision was made to help the Republic of South Vietnam strengthen its armed forces under the supervision of MAAG (Military Assistance Advisory Group) personnel in Saigon. As far as the VNAF was concerned, this build-up took the form of 16 additional Douglas C-47s and 10 ex-French Sikorsky H-19Bs. The former aircraft were to form a second transport squadron in June 1956, while the latter were to provide the initial equipment for the 1st Helicopter Squadron, established in June 1957. To gain experience, the crews of the helicopter squadron had flown H-13s and H-19s which the French had been operating in support of the International Control Commission. Thus, by the summer of 1958, the seven VNAF oprational units were distributed between Bien Hoa (1st Fighter Squadron with 25 Bearcats), Hue (1st Liaison Squadron with Cessna L-19s), Nha Trang (2nd Liaison Squadron with L-19s), and Tan Son Nhut (1st and 2nd Transport Squadrons with 32 Douglas C-47s; 1st Helicopter Squadron with 10 Sikorsky H-19Bs; and Special Air Mission Squadron with one Aero Commander L-26, three Beech C-45s, and three Douglas C-47s). However, as the Bearcats of its 1st Fighter Squadron were seldom serviceable, the VNAF was effectively a non-combat force operating unarmed transports, liaison aircraft, and helicopters. More importantly, being weak in command and staff experience, and still lacking adequate logistic support, the VNAF was not yet ready to shore up resistance against the initial North Vietnamese attack.

Three M.S. 500s of the 1st Observation Squadron fly along the South Vietnamese coast during 1951. The squadron had formed at Nha Trang, in July of that year.

### *Political backlash*

The long-feared North Vietnamese retaliation against the refusal to hold reunification elections began to materialize itself in the spring of 1959. In May of that year the North Vietnamese Communist Party again called publicly for the reunification of Vietnam and secretly undertook to obtain the reunification through armed struggle. General Vo Bam, instructed to infiltrate men and supplies into the south, immediately opened the first sections of the Ho Chi Minh Trail across the Demilitarized Zone and planned the extension of the trail system through Laos and Cambodia to reach An Loc, 75 miles (121 km) west of Saigon, and the main Viet

One of the first Vietnamese military pilots to be trained in France, Lt. N'Guyen Than Tong flew Bearcats for the VNAF until 1958, when he sought political asylum in France.

**Lt. N'Guyen Than Tong climbs aboard his Bearcat. After serving in the Légion Etrangère to acquire French citizenship more quickly, he joined the Armée de l'Air from which he retired in the early 1980s after last flying Dassault Mirage F.1Cs.**

Cong base at Cu Chi, nearer the capital. Even before the completion of the first sections of the Ho Chi Minh Trail, the Diem government, which had by then succeeded in stimulating economic growth and internal stability by eliminating the private armies of various religious sects, was suddenly faced with a much more serious threat. In September 1959 the Viet Cong ambushed two companies of the ARVN in the marshy Plain of Reeds southwest of Saigon. This first significant Viet Cong operation was to be followed by continuous fighting for over 15 years.

One month before this first major engagement, the VNAF had lost its only combat aircraft when its Bearcats were grounded due to structural deficiencies. Albeit ill-timed, the grounding of the VNAF's only fighters had been expected as a lack of spares and the aircraft's obsolescence had long pointed to the need for their eventual replacement. The VNAF had hoped to obtain jet aircraft for that purpose but, as on one hand its personnel still lacked the required maintenance skills and on the other hand the Geneva Agreement precluded the introduction of such advanced weapons, this expectation was dashed with an announcement that the contemplated transfer of two Lockheed T-33A jet trainers and four RT-33A reconnaissance aircraft would not take place. In their place, the VNAF initially received well-armed (four 20-mm cannon and up to 8,000 lb/3692 kg of external stores) and well protected ex-US Navy Douglas AD-6 piston-powered attack aircraft. The first six AD-6s, which arrived in Vietnam in September 1960 and were followed by an additional 25 aircraft in May 1961, were used to re-equip the 1st Fighter Squadron at Bien Hoa. Concurrently with arrival of the Skyraiders, the VNAF also took delivery of 11 Sikorsky H-34s to replace the surviving H-19s of its 1st Helicopter Squadron.

### *Trojan enters service*

To equip new combat units, the VNAF was also scheduled to receive North American T-28 armed trainers. Although cruising at only 200 mph (322 km/h) in clean condition and lacking protection against even light weapons, but carrying two underwing gun pods and fitted with bomb racks, the T-28Bs were well adapted to the counter-insurgency role. Moreover, being relatively easy to fly and maintain, the first 15 T-28Bs were introduced smoothly into VNAF operations, with the 2nd Fighter Squadron being activated at Nha Trang in December 1961. Six months later, one of these T-28Bs became the first VNAF aircraft to be lost in combat when on 13 June 1962 it was hit by ground fire during a bomb run on a target 36 miles (58 km) SSW of Da Nang. The aircraft crashed, killing the two crewmen. Later, the VNAF received more capable T-28Ds (rebuilt T-28As with a more powerful engine and heavier armament) as well as a handful of RT-28Bs with a camera pack in a ventral fairing.

In spite of this influx of more modern aircraft and the activation in 1961 of two additional units at Da Nang (the 2nd Helicopter Squadron in October and the 3rd Liaison Squadron in Decem-

**Grumman F8F-1 Bearcats of the 1er Groupe de Chasse (1st Fighter Squadron) at Bien Hoa in 1958. The Bearcats were the first combat aircraft of the Vietnamese Air Force and were operated by that service from June 1956 until August 1959. Formerly operated by the French Air Force, these aircraft have all servicing instructions applied in French.**

**When France withdrew from Indochina, the Republic of Vietnam received 28 Bearcats to equip its newly organized air force. Activated at Cap Saint Jacques in June 1956 and later moved to Bien Hoa, the VNAF's 1st Fighter Squadron flew F8F-1s and F8F-1Bs (as illustrated) until August 1958.**

ber), the VNAF had only some 70 aircraft on strength at the end of 1961. By then its capabilities were stretched to the limit by the need to counter rapidly increasing Viet Cong activities throughout South Vietnam. In particular, its two transport squadrons and two helicopter squadrons could not provide all the logistic support required by the ARVN, and its training facilities at Nha Trang could not keep up with increased demand for aircrews and other air force personnel. By then, however, more direct US help was on its way with the USAF sending its first *Farm Gate* detachment to Tan Son Nhut in November 1961, the US Army deploying its first helicopters to Qui Nhom and to Camp Bear Cat in December 1961, and the first *Shufly* helicopters of the US Marine Corps arriving at Soc Trang in April 1962. Intratheatre logistics were further boosted in 1962 with the arrival in January of the *Mule Train* Fairchild C-123s of the 346th Troop Carrier Squadron and, shortly thereafter, of the C-123s of the 777th TCS and the de Havilland Canada CV-2s of the US Army's 1st Aviation Company. Moreover, as the VNAF had not enough crews to man its C-47s, the USAF sent 30 pilots to serve as co-pilots with otherwise all-Vietnamese C-47 crews. Known as the 'Dirty Thirty', these USAF crews left South Vietnam on 3 December 1963 after logging more than 20,000 hours in VNAF C-47s. Other USAF aircrews seconded to the VNAF included experienced forward air controllers, with the first five FACs arriving in South Vietnam on 15 February 1962.

**A VNAF T-28B makes a napalm delivery on Viet Cong targets along a canal in May 1962. The VNAF received its first 15 North American T-28Bs in December 1961.**

With more A-1Hs (as the AD-6s were redesignated in 1962), T-28Ds and H-34s scheduled to be delivered to the VNAF, aircrew and maintenance personnel training underwent a major revision. In January 1962 all flight training at the Nha Trang Air Training Center was temporarily terminated, with aircrew training being transferred to US facilities in the United States. At that time the Air Training Center continued to provide a minimum of eight weeks of basic military training for cadets and airmen. Moreover, in September 1962 the

**The VNAF flew the North American RT-28B on reconnaissance missions, with a ventral camera pack. This example is from the 314th Special Missions Squadron, seen at Tan Son Nhut in February 1964.**

Loaded with anti-personnel bombs and rocket pods, this 514th Fighter Squadron Douglas A-1H is pre-flighted prior to a mission from Tan Son Nhut.

VC and NVA attacks against allied air bases in South East Asia, mostly in the Republic of Vietnam, were responsible for the destruction of 145 US fixed-wing aircraft and 205 helicopters, plus an undetermined number of VNAF aircraft and helicopters. This VNAF C-47 was destroyed in a VC mortar attack against Tan Son Nhut AB during the night of 14 April 1966.

USAF dispatched a Mobile Training Unit to instruct VNAF personnel in preparation for the resumption of flight training at the Air Training Center following the delivery of 25 Cessna U-17s. Other changes implemented at Nha Trang during the early sixties included the organization of a Communications and Electronics School and the transfer of Air Traffic Control and Forward Air Control training to other VNAF facilities.

During the early sixties, with USAF personnel flying as combat instructors and taking an active part in combat operations, the VNAF increasingly proved itself while flying interdiction, close air support, reconnaissance, train and convoy escort (a role for which the T-28 was well-suited as long as the Viet Cong lacked effective antiaircraft weapons), flare dropping, and resupply sorties. The VNAF also began taking over responsibility from the USAF for aerial psychological operations (leaflet dropping and broadcasting from aircraft). For that purpose, it first used a modified C-47 in June 1962, and later went on to operate specially fitted de Havilland Canada U-6As and Cessna U-17As.

In addition to these normal in-country operations, in April 1961 the VNAF began to take the war to the enemy by flying clandestine missions deep into North Vietnam. For these covert activities, crews and C-47s from the 1st and 2nd Transport squadrons were specially selected to fly night missions from Nha Trang to the Cao Bang, Lang Son and Phat Diem areas north of Hanoi, where sabotage teams were dropped to blow up roads, bridges, and power plants. Undertaken under the

Right: Skyraider in low-visibility scheme for both day and night operations. The figure on the cowling is a Chinese figure from a pack of cards.

Below right: Based at Tan Son Nhut AB, the 112th Liaison Squadron was one of the VNAF units flying Cessna Bird Dogs in the FAC role. Armed with marker rockets, this O-1A was photographed during a sortie in September 1971.

command of Major Nguyen Cao Ky, who eventually rose to the rank of Air Vice Marshal and after the 18 June 1965 military coup became the nation's Prime Minister, these forays continued until July 1962 and resulted in the loss of three C-47s.

During 1963-64 the combined effect of deliveries of larger numbers of aircraft and helicopters, stepped up training and better command organization, enabled the VNAF to increase substantially both its combat strength and effectiveness. With more units being organized, the original single digit squadron identification system gave place in January 1963 to a new triple digit system. The first digit identified the type of unit (1 for liaison, 2 for helicopter, 3 for special missions, 4 for transpsort, 5 for fighter and attack, 7 for reconnaissance, 8 for combat/gunship, and 9 for training). Accordingly, older units were redesignated under this new system with the 1st, 2nd and 3rd Liaison Squadrons being renumbered 110th, 112th and 114th; the 1st and 2nd Helicopter squadrons becoming the 211th and 213th; the 1st and 2nd Transpsort Squadrons being changed to the 413th and 415th; and the 1st and 2nd Fighter Squadrons becoming the 514th and 516th Fighter Squadrons. Newly organized units adopted the triple digit designation from the onset. Noteworthy among the new units was the 716th Composite Reconnaissance Squadron, which was activated at Tan Son Nhut in December 1963 as the first reconnaissance unit of the VNAF. Initially receiving two Beech C-45s fitted with cameras, the 716th was scheduled to receive three Douglas RC-47s and 18 North American RT-28Bs; however, in June 1964, as this unit was becoming fully operational, the decision was taken to reorganize it at Bien Hoa as the 520th Fighter Squadron.

Not content with making its strength increas-

Large numbers of Skyraiders were transferred to the VNAF as the war progressed, and these fought until the very last day of the war. This trio is carrying anti-personnel bombs and napalm, a devastating combination for troop concentrations.

**Two-seat A-1E and A-1G Skyraiders served both as conversion trainers and as full combat aircraft. This A-1G is from the 518th Fighter Squadron, 23rd Tactical Wing at Bien Hoa.**

ingly felt over the battlefields, the VNAF joined with other military forces to plot a coup against the government of Ngo Dinh Diem. Hatching on 1 November 1963, the coup succeeded in two days, with four A-1Hs and two T-28Ds supporting the rebels with gun and rocket strikes against the presidential compound and turning away troops which had remained loyal to Diem. A Military Revolutionary Council immediately organized a provisional government which was recognized by the United States on 8 November. Meanwhile, taking advantage of the confusion created by the coup, the Viet Cong stepped up its attacks and the VNAF was soon again devoting its full attention to the war effort.

### *Reorganization*

As the number of squadrons increased, it became necessary for the VNAF to regroup them into wings. Taking the number of the air bases at which they were organized, the 23rd, 33rd, 41st, 63rd, and 74th Tactical Wings were activated respectively at Bien Hoa, Tan Son Nhut, Da Nang, Pleiku, and Can Tho during the first half of 1964. Thus, at the end of that year the four Tactical Wings had 285 aircraft in four Fighter Squadrons (the 514th, 516th, 518th and 520th, equipped with A-1Hs and some T-28Ds); four Liaison Squadrons with O-1s (the 110th, 112th, 114th and 116th); three Helicopter Squadrons with H-34s (the 211th, 213th and 217th); and two Transport Squadrons with C-47s (the 413th and 415th). In addition, an elite unit (the 83rd Special Squadron, later expanded into the 83rd Special Operations Group, and finally becoming the 83rd Tactical Group (Special Operations) on 1 January 1966) had been organized in 1964 under the direct command of the VNAF Chief of Staff, then Colonel Nguyen Cao Ky. Initially equipped with Douglas C-47 and Fairchild C-123B transports, as well as a single Cessna U-17A single-engined utility aircraft (a type which, as previously noted, was also used at the Nha Trang Air Training Center for pilot training), the 83rd SOG acquired the 522nd Fighter Squadron and its Douglas A-1Hs in April 1965.

In 1966, with continued growth requiring still larger command and control organizations, the VNAF added Air Divisions to its force structure. Numbered after the Corps Area in which they were assigned, the First. Second, Third, and Fourth Air Divisions were respectively headquartered at Da Nang, Nha Trang, Bien Hoa and Binh Thuy. Later were added the 5th Air Division at Tan Son Nhut and the 6th Air Division at Pleiku.

If the qualifications and dedication of the 83rd SOG personnel could not be questioned, the same could not yet be said about other Vietnamese airmen. American advisers complained that the VNAF was unable to undertake fast reaction strikes and that its crews were showing great reluctance to fly at night or during weekends. Increased OJT (On the Job Training) under the guidance of US advisers and a determined effort on the part of Nguyen Cao Ky to shape up his air force soon produced the desired results. By early 1965 the VNAF had become capable of undertaking more adventurous operations.

On Christmas Eve 1964, Viet Cong saboteurs in Saigon killed two American advisers and injured 64 Americans and 43 Vietnamese, while the Viet Cong itself stepped up its attacks against hamlets and outposts throughout South vietnam. This offensive, which culminated in attacks on a US advisory detachment and the headquarters of the US Army 52nd Aviation Battalion at Camp Holloway near Pleiku, led President Johnson to authorize Operation *Flaming Dart*, a series of retaliatory air strikes against North Vietnam. Led by Nguyen Cao Ky, A-1Hs from all four VNAF fighter squadrons joined USAF and US Navy aircraft on 8 February 1965 in raids against barracks near Dong Hoi just north of the DMZ (*Flaming Dart I*) and, three days later, in strikes over the North Vietnamese panhandle (*Flaming Dart II*). Meanwhile, the VNAF Skyraiders continued their operations in the south. On 16 February one of these aircraft sank a steel-hulled vessel transporting weapons for two Viet Cong regiments which were threatening Saigon. Once again, however, the VNAF was called to intervene in the political affairs of the Republic of Vietnam, with Ky lending the support of his A-1Hs to a military revolt which resulted on 19 February in the removal of General Nguyen Khanh as the nation's President.

### *Jets at last*

The good performance of the VNAF during *Flaming Dart*, and in particular of its 514th Fighter Squadron which was awarded the Presidential Unit Citation from the United States, finally led the United States to consent to Nguyen Cao Ky's insistent request for jet aircraft. Aircrew training had in fact started in the late spring of 1964, when three Vietnamese officers began receiving instruction on USAF Martin B-57C twinjet bombers at Clark AB in the Philippines. Soon followed by additional Vietnamese flights and ground personnel, including their commander, General Nguyen Cao Ky, the initial VNAF jet crews had to wait until 9 August 1965 to get their first B-57Bs. Thereafter, these crews flew a small number of missions from Da Nang AB in aircraft from the 3rd Bombardment Wing, USAF, and in B-57s temporarily painted in VNAF markings. However, following a training accident at NAS Cubi Point in the Philippines and an operational accident at Pleiku, the Vietnamese B-57 programme was terminated in February 1966 without having contributed much to the war's effort.

**During the fall of 1972, the VNAF received a large quantity of aircraft under the *Enhance Plus* programme. These included 120 Northrop F-5As, F-5Bs and RF-5As transferred by the USAF, Iran, South Korea, and Taiwan. The desert type camouflage of this F-5A identifies it as an ex-Imperial Iranian Air Force aircraft.**

Much more significant for the future of the VNAF was the transfer on 1 June 1967 of 17 Northrop F-5A single-seat and two F-5B two-seat twinjet fighters from the 4503rd Tactical Fighter Squadron (*Skoshi Tiger*), USAF. The delivery of Northrop F-5As to the VNAF had first been proposed as far back as 1963 by Brig. Gen. Robert R. Rowland, then chief of the MAAG Air Force Section, but had been opposed by the Department of State until 1965. Finally, in anticipation of this transfer, 33 VNAF pilots had been sent to Williams AFB, Arizona, in August 1966 for jet training and conversion to the Northrop fighters. Following conversion training in the United States the aircrews returned to Bien Hoa, where a few sorties were flown prior to official acceptance of the F-5s on 1 June 1967. Manned by VNAF combat veterans, the 522nd Fighter Squadron immediately began flying operational missions with the number of monthly F-5 sorties increasing from 388 in June 1967 to 527 in December of the same year, and to 683 in March 1968. In spite of this achievement, the VNAF was not allowed to add more F-5 squadrons until 1972. In 1968, however, it obtained Cessna A-37Bs as its next jet combat aircraft.

## *Jets gain acceptance*

When the F-5s of the 522nd Fighter Squadron had become operational in June 1967, the VNAF also had the 514th, 516th, 518th, 520th, and 524th Fighters Squadrons flying propeller-driven A-1Hs and A-1Gs (a version of the Skyraider fitted with dual control and used by USAF advisers to provide combat training to new VNAF pilots) and had gained increased acceptance by field commanders. The Vietnamese Air force, however, remained weak in its transport and helicopter elements, with the United States, and to a much smaller extent the Royal Australian Air Force, operating the only modern aircraft in these two categories. The modernization of the VNAF transport fleet which, with the activation of the 417th Transport Squadron on 1 January 1967 was made up of three C-47 squadrons, began in March 1968 with the conversion of the 413th Transport Squadron to Fairchild C-119Gs, but did not gain speed until the massive transfer of aircraft in late 1972 as part of *Enhance Plus*. In spite of the progressive transfer of H-34s from US Army and Marine Corps units in Vietnam, the VNAF was suffering even more from a chronic lack of helicopters. Already in August 1964 its fourth helicopter squadron, the 293rd, had had to be inactivated and its H-34s and personnel transferred to keep the other three squadrons close to authorized strength. Modest gains were made in March 1968 when a final batch of H-34s were received and, for the first time, the three squadrons were at full strength. On a longer term basis improvements were to come only two years later, with the transfer of Bell UH-1s and Boeing-Vertol CH-47s.

On the eve of the 1968 Tet (Vietnamese Lunar New Year) holiday truce, the VNAF's strike capability was provided by 86 operationally ready fighters (17 F-5A/Bs, and 69 A-1G/Hs). However, when the 1968 Tet Offensive commenced on 30 January, and the Viet Cong and North Vietnamese army launched violent attacks against Saigon, all 34 provincial capitals, and numerous cities, towns, villages and military installations throughout South Vietnam, the VNAF was not able to react in force as nearly 60 percent of its personnel had been sent on leave for the Lunar New Year. Nevertheless the VNAF reacted quickly, with aircrews on duty bearing the brunt of the initial air activities until personnel on leave were able to rejoin their units. Throwing every available aircraft into the battle the VNAF finally established itself as a very effective air force, taking the offensive to the enemy, supporting hard-pressed ARVN units capably, and maintaining higher levels of strike performance in terms of sorties flown and ordnance expended than in earlier periods. When the Tet Offensive was finally broken at the end of February 1968, with the Viet Cong ceasing to exist as an effective force, the VNAF could show an impressive record. It had flown 7,213 sorties in

**Cessna A-37B Dragonfly of the 518th Fighter Squadron operating out of Da Nang AB. In addition to its tip tanks, the aircraft carries two external wing tanks and four 500-lb Mk 82 bombs. VNAF squadron identification markings, such as the 518th FS star-studded blue band around the aft fuselage of the A-37B, tended to be rather colourful.**

**The VNAF's first operational jet fighter unit, the 522nd Fighter Squadron, became operational in June 1967. Its initial equipment consisted of 17 F-5As (one of which is seen in a revetment at Bien Hoa AB as it is readied for a sortie) and two F-5Bs previously flown by the USAF during the *Skoshi Tiger* evaluation of the Northrop lightweight fighter.**

**These Fairchild C-119Gs are seen shortly after being turned over to the VNAF. They served with the 413th Transport Squadron from March 1968 onwards, the beginning of a steadily-increasing modernisation of VNAF transport forces.**

**Above right: Bell UH-1H (US serial 66-17394) in VNAF markings. As part of the Vietnamization Programme, the VNAF received an initial batch of 170 Hueys in 1969-70; substantial additional deliveries were made in later years, notably as part of *Enhance Plus*.**

**Tactical reconnaissance requirements for the VNAF rested on the Northrop RF-5A. The modified nose contained forward- and oblique-looking cameras.**

four weeks, during which it had expended 6,700 tonnes of ammunition, and transported 12,200 troops and 230 tonnes of equipment and supplies. In the process, it had lost ten aircraft on the ground and seven in the air. Notwithstanding these losses, the VNAF came out of the Tet Offensive stronger than ever, with morale at its peak and an operational strength of 375 aircraft (21 F-5s, 82 A-1s, 48 transports, 111 observation/liaison aircraft, 101 helicopters, and 12 sundry aircraft).

Initiated in January 1968, when the 524th Fighter Squadron stood down at Nha Trang, the conversion of VNAF units to the Cessna A-37B was temporarily interrupted during the Tet Offensive as all available pilots were thrown into the battle. However, after the military situation in South Vietnam had been stabilized, the conversion programme was resumed and pilots were sent to England AFB, Louisiana, to receive the necessary training. Initial delivery of A-37Bs was made in November 1968, with the 524th Fighter Squadron becoming operational on the type in March 1969 and being quickly followed by the 520th and 516th Fighter Squadrons. In a sense not as effective as the old Skyraiders, being armed with a single 7.62-mm Minigun instead of four 20-mm cannon and carrying only about half the bomb load, the A-37Bs had the distinct advantage of being new aircraft for which parts were readily available. Easy to fly and providing good weapon-firing platforms, the A-37Bs were slated to become the most numerous aircraft in the VNAF inventory.

## The Vietnamization Programme

Following a series of victories over the Viet Cong during the first part of 1968 (first during the Tet Offensive, then in the A Shau Valley in April, around Saigon in July, and at Duc Lap and Ban Me Thuot in August) and the start of the peace talks in Paris, it appeared that the threat to South Vietnam was no longer critical. Moreover, the sterling performance of the ARVN and the VNAF during the 1968 battles gave high hopes that the South Vietnamese would soon be able to take care of the in-country fighting by themselves. At the same time, in the United States the antiwar movement

had become a major political factor and President Lyndon B. Johnson was forced not to seek re-election. During the ensuing presidential campaign the Republican candidate, Richard M. Nixon, pledged to bring American ground troops home and to seek an honourable peace; a campaign pledge which he undertook to carry out after his election.

To do so the Nixon Administration decided to capitalize on the newly-found strength of the South Vietnamese Armed Forces and to beef them up, so that on 9 June 1969 President Nixon could announce a plan to withdraw progressively US ground combat troops and, at a slower pace, US air units. Concurrently with this withdrawal a Vietnamization Programme was to be implemented, with training of South Vietnamese military forces being stepped up and additional weapons and materials provided to equip new Vietnamese units.

At that time Major General Tran Van Minh (who in 1967 had succeeded Nguyen Cao Ky as the VNAF Commander and who, rising to the rank of Lieutenant General, remained in that position until the end) reconfirmed the role of the VNAF as follows:

- To conduct tactical air reconnaissance, interdiction and close air support operations to defeat Communist insurgency in the Republic of Vietnam, and assist as appropriate in maintaining internal security.
- To deter external aggression and, in conjunction with US/Free World Forces, provide tactical air reconnaissance, interdiction, and close air support in support of defensive and counteroffensive operations against overt invasion.
- To participate in the air defence of the Republic of Vietnam.
- To provide airlift and re-supply for RVN forces within limitations of equipment.
- To develop, operate, and maintain minimum essential ground environment to accommodate air operations.

**The elderly Sikorsky UH-34 struggled on with the VNAF throughout most of the war, being used on many missions including defoliant spraying flights. This example is seen at Da Nang.**

Since 1963, most of the training of VNAF personnel had been accomplished through the expensive process of sending them to the United States. However, in-country training was then progressively stressed. This undertaking was accelerated first after the appointment in June 1967 of Colonel Nguyen Ngoc Oanh as the new commander of the Nha Trang Air Training Center, and then again after the start of the Vietnamization Programme. With USAF assistance in an advisory capacity and in procuring materials and supplies, Colonel Oanh set out to improve the morale of the Center's personnel and the facilities of the base. At the same time, the mission of the Air Training Center was redefined to include military, technical and flying training for officers and airmen (all volunteers, whereas the bulk of the ARVN was made up of conscripts). After receiving four months of basic military training, cadets selected to become aircrews underwent either 290 hours of ground school and 146 hours of flying training in Cessna

**During late 1972, the project *Enhance Plus* pumped many aircraft into the VNAF, important among these being 32 Lockheed C-130 Hercules transports. This line-up is seen just after delivery at Tan Son Nhut, along with a pair of Fairchild C-123s.**

**Principal FAC platform for the VNAF was the Cessna O-1 Bird Dog. The whip aerials affixed to each wing served the communications systems.**

U-17s prior to being sent to the United States for advanced training, or 155 hours of ground school and 110 hours of flight before becoming liaison pilots. In addition, all received appropriate training in the Center's English Language School, with students scheduled for pilot training in the United States receiving another six weeks at the Defense Language Institute at Lackland AFB, Texas. Other schools at the Nha Trang Air Training Center included the Technical School for maintenance personnel, the Communications and Electronics School, and the General Services School for support personnel. For flight training the scope of the Center's activities was later substantially increased to reduce the dependence on US training, and by the early seventies primary training was provided by the 912th Flying Training Squadron with Cessna T-41As, while advanced training was the responsibility of the 920th Flying Training Squadron with Cessna T-37A/Cs. An idea of the magnitude of the Nha Trang Air Training Center's task, supplemented by USAF schools, can be gauged from the fact that the VNAF strength grew from 16,277 personnel and 362 aircraft in 17 squadrons in February 1968, to 61,147 personnel and 2,075 aircraft in 65 squadrons in January 1973.

As the Vietnamization of the war went on, the VNAF not only received additional aircraft of the types already in service, but was also provided with new types. Foremost among the new aircraft were 150 Bell UH-1Hs and 20 Boeing-Vertol CH-47As which were delivered in 1969-1970, and two types of fixed-wing gunships. Consideration had been given in the fall of 1967 to converting C-47s of the 417th Transport Squadron to the gunship configuration, but an insufficient supply of 7.62-mm Miniguns and related equipment had prevented the implementation of this modification programme. However, after the USAF obtained more capable gunships, the decision was made to transfer 16 Douglas AC-47s to equip a new VNAF unit, the 817th Combat Squadron, at Tan Son Nhut. The VNAF received its first five AC-47s on 2 July 1969 and immediately placed them in service. Manned by experienced personnel, the 817th Combat Squadron soon proved itself the equal of its USAF mentors and demonstrated a firm grasp of all facets of its mission. A second gunship unit, the 819th Combat Squadron, was activated in September 1971 when the USAF transferred 16 Fairchild AC-119Gs to the VNAF. Subsequently, the VNAF obtained additional AC-119Gs and AC-119Ks to make up attrition in the 819th Combat Squadron, to convert the 817th from the AC-47 to the more potent gunship, and to organize the 821st Combat Squadron. Meanwhile, the modernization of the VNAF transport force had begun in 1970-71 with the transfer of 48 Fairchild C-123Ks to re-equip the 421st and 423rd Transport Squadrons.

### *Strength and capability*

The increased strength and combat capability of the VNAF, still supplemented by US air power, and the much reduced threat posed by the Viet Cong, enabled the ARVN to take the brunt of offensive (or to use the vernacular of the time, counteroffensive) operations in Cambodia beginning in April 1970, and in Laos in February-March 1971. The tacit tolerance of Communist sanctuaries in Cambodia, if not their more overt acceptance by the government of Prince Norodom Sihanouk, had long been a stiletto pointed at the heart of the Republic of Vietnam. Protracted diplomatic manoeuvering by the United States, and the eventual recognition by Prince Sihanouk of the threat posed to his government by an estimated 40,000 North Vietnamese and Viet Cong troops, had led the Cambodian leader to inform the US Ambassador in Phnom Penh in January 1969 that "he would not object to the United States engaging in 'hot pursuit' in unpopulated areas of

**Light communications, liaison and transport duties were handled by the Cessna U-17. This was a military version of the Model 185, used widely by commercial pilots in difficult terrain around the world.**

The Cessna U-17 could also perform FAC duties. This aircraft carries radio equipment for this and pylons under the wings for mounting smoke rockets.

Cambodia" and to seek, in March 1970, international assistance in removing foreign Communist troops from Cambodian soil. As a result of Prince Sihanouk's communication, the Strategic Air Command began on 18 March 1969 to fly B-52s bombing sorties against enemy base camps and headquarters in Cambodia. Nevertheless, the threat posed by Communist forces poised along the border of South Vietnam remained great. More effective action was finally taken as Cambodia had become pro-American following the March 1970 overthrow of Prince Sihanouk by his Prime Minister, Lieutenant General Lon Nol.

On 1 May 1970, after VNAF and USAF tactical aircraft had struck at Communist targets in Cambodia for one week, 48,000 ARVN and 42,000 US troops crossed the border into Cambodia with a dual objective. They were to (1) shore up the weak army of the Khmer Republic struggling with North Vietnamese units and (2) destroy the enemy forces and supplies long stored in numerous base camps. Within 60 days all American and most ARVN troops had withdrawn back into South Vietnam after inflicting heavy losses to the North Vietnamese Army and the remnants of the Viet Cong, and capturing large quantities of weapons and ammunition. In great part much of this success had been achieved through effective air support of the allied ground forces, with the VNAF's A-1, A-37 and F-5 pilots proving both aggressive and accurate. However, the tactical success of the Cambodian venture was a political failure as antiwar protests reached new highs in the United States, and also a strategic fiasco for as soon as the ground forces were withdrawn the North Vietnamese began sending replacement troops and supplies

With loudspeakers mounted on the left-hand side, these VNAF de Havilland Canada U-6As were photographed during an operational sortie over the Mekong Delta in August 1971. This psychological warfare aircraft was operated from Tan Son Nhut AB by the 314th Special Missions Squadron, 33rd Tactical Wing, VNAF.

**Communist troops storm Tan Son Nhut airport during the final move on Saigon. Many US-built aircraft were captured intact by the North, and used by the newly-united Vietnamese air force. VNAF Bell UH-1s are captured intact here in their shelters.**

along the Ho Chi Minh Trail. Within six months the Communists had seized back nearly one-half of Cambodia's territory and had restocked their dépots. Consequently, during 1971 and 1972, the ARVN was repeatedly forced to send its troops back into Cambodia in vain attempts to sanitize the border area and help the weak Khmer army. In support of these more limited South Vietnamese operations, the VNAF and the USAF continued striking Communist targets in Cambodia even after the January 1973 cease fire in Vietnam. Finally, all air operations in Cambodia were suspended on 15 August 1973.

## Laotian involvement

In Laos, where government forces and CIA-trained Meo tribesmen had been battling against the Pathet Lao ever since the early fifties, both the United States and North Vietnam were heavily enmeshed in support of their respective sides. In addition to providing equipment, training and advisers for the Royal Lao Army and Royal Lao Air Force, the United States had flown air combat operations in Laos since June 1964 and had established a network of temporary landing strips (*Lima Sites*) for use by helicopters and STOL aircraft (notably those operated by Air America). The extent of American involvement in Laos was, however, much smaller than that of North Vietnam, as the Hanoi government was maintaining a large number of troops in that supposedly neutral country. More importantly, the Laotian territory was criss-crossed by sections of the Ho Chi Minh Trail over which North Vietnamese troops and supplies were transported to Cambodia and South Vietnam. It was in an attempt to foil an anticipated North Vietnamese offensive that on 8 February 1971 the ARVN moved into Laos to cut the Ho Chi Minh Trail.

With the United States providing most of the airlift (including 600 helicopters) and American ground forces taking part in initial operations on the Vietnamese side of the border, some 5,000 ARVN and Vietnamese Marine Corps troops went on the offensive with air support provided by the VNAF and the US air forces. Once again VNAF's aircrews did themselves proud, even though for the first time they were faced with intense AAA fire, including radar-controlled guns, SA-2 surface-to-air missiles and portable SA-7 Strella missiles. During Operation *Lam Son 719/Dewey Canyon II*, which ended on 6 April 1971 with the hasty return of South Vietnamese forces to within the nation's borders, some 14,500 enemy troops were killed and 106 of their tanks were destroyed; allied losses were also high with 2,400 KIAs and MIAs, and 114 helicopters and eight fixed-wing aircraft shot down.

By the first quarter of 1972, allied intelligence was well aware that North Vietnam, in spite of its losses during the Cambodian and Laotian operations, had succeeded in rebuilding its forces in and around the Republic of Vietnam. In particular, Communist forces in the south were believed to include over 40,000 regular troops equipped with substantial numbers of heavy artillery pieces (120- and 130-mm guns of recent Soviet design), tanks and armoured fighting vehicles, Sagger wire-guided anti-tank missiles, and SA-7 Strella anti-aircraft missiles. As expected, the enemy offensive began on 30 March with a heavy thrust against the Quang Tri and Thua Thien provinces near the DMZ, an assault against Kontum and Pleiku in the Central Highlands, a multi-pronged attack from the regained sanctuary in Cambodia, and harassment operations around the major cities. By then the number of USAF aircraft in Vietnam had been reduced from 737 in June 1968 to 277 in December 1971 and over half of the in-country sorties were being provided by the VNAF. The scale of the Communist offensive was such that these resources were known to be insufficient to provide the number of sorties required. Accordingly, the USAF and the Marine Corps quickly tripled their air strength through the massive redeployment of aircraft from PACAF and CONUS bases, while carrier-based aircraft stepped up their operations from Dixie Station. In spite of the initial poor performance of the ARVN, but thanks to the rapid increase in American air power and the valor of the VNAF (which, during the first month lost 36 aircraft as its A-1s and A-37s did not have the survivability and performance to sustain operations where the enemy deployed AAA and SAMs), the North Vietnamese offensive was finally checked in June 1972. More than anything else, however, it was Operation *Linebacker I* (the American retaliatory raids against the north which had begun on 8 May 1972 and included mining the port of Haiphong) which convinced the North Vietnamese to instruct Vo Nguyen Giap to stop his offensive in the south and Le Duc Tho to show willingness to reach a compromise at the Paris peace talk negotiations. Temporarily, the Republic of Vietnam had been saved once again.

## Vietnamization effectiveness

At this point it is necessary to quote a few statistics to demonstrate the effectiveness of the Vietnamization Programme. Between January 1968 and December 1972 the number of VNAF combat aircraft increased from 89 to a high of 334 (with a low of 48 aircraft being recorded in October

**The VNAF fought right to the end. This Cessna O-1 Bird Dog was shot down and crashed in the streets of Saigon literally minutes before the surrender on 30 April 1975.**

North Vietnamese troops take the VNAF transport area at Tan Son Nhut, capturing de Havilland Canada C-7s and Douglas C-47s intact. The VNAF transport fleet served Vietnam well after the war for a number of years, but spares difficulties led to an increasing reliance on Soviet equipment.

and November 1968 due to losses earlier in that year) while the number of US combat aircraft in South East Asia decreased from 992 to 623 (with a low of 384 aircraft in August/September 1971, and a high of 1,199 combat aircraft in July 1968). Over the same period the VNAF helicopter inventory increased from 71 to 521 machines (with a low of 36 in April 1969 and a high of 542 in September 1972) while the number of US helicopters in the Republic of Vietnam went down from 2,984 to a low of 482 (with a high of 3,571 in April 1970).

In terms of operations, VNAF combat aircraft accounted for an 11.6 percent share of Allied sorties in the Republic of Vietnam during January 1968 and for a 41.6 percent share during December 1972. For helicopter sorties the VNAF share went up from a mere 1.2 percent during January 1968 to 53.5 percent during December 1972. Finally, by November 1972 VNAF transport carried 90.8 percent of all Vietnamese military passengers and paratroopers airlifted within the country; during the following month this percentage dropped to 47.9 percent as transport crews stood down for C-130A conversion training.

## *Heavy losses*

These gratifying results, however, were reached at a high human and material price with the VNAF losing 136 combat aircraft (60 in the air, 10 on the ground, and 66 to operational causes) and 183 helicopters (127 in the air, nine on the ground, and 47 to operational causes) between January 1968 and December 1972.

Notwithstanding the newfound strength of the VNAF, US and South Vietnamese leaders were painfully aware of how close to succeeding the spring 1972 Communist offensive had come. Moreover, as progress toward the negotiation of a peace agreement was still slow, it became clear that the Republic of Vietnam Armed Forces would have to be increased substantially if they were to have a chance to hold off North Vietnam on their own after the full and complete US withdrawal. In addition, time was running out as the necessary weapons and supplies had to be delivered prior to a final agreement being reached by the Paris negotiators. Accordingly, in the fall of 1972 the United States organized project *Enhance Plus*, an unprecedented air and sea lift of supplies, ammunition, tanks, artillery and aircraft.

For the VNAF, this final infusion of equipment meant the rapid delivery of 569 helicopters (549 UH-1s and 20 CH-47s); over 100 transports (mostly C-7s, some C-119s and, more importantly, 32 Lockheed C-130As which had been quickly withdrawn from Air National Guard units in the United States and became the VNAF's first four-engined turbine transports); 110 attack aircraft (20 A-1Hs withdrawn from USAF service in Thailand and 90 A-37Bs); 20 ex-USAF AC-119K gunships; five Douglas EC-47 twin-engined transports fitted for ECM warfare; and 120 F-5 fighters. While most of these aircraft could quickly be transferred by the USAF and the US Army or, in the case of some of the UH-1s and A-37Bs, had already been set aside for delivery to the VNAF, this was not the case for the F-5s. As part of the previously planned expansion of the VNAF fighter force, four additional squadrons had been scheduled to be formed and equipped with 126 F-5E single-seaters and F-5F two-seaters. However, as the new version of the Northrop fighter could not be supplied prior to the expected conclusion of the Paris peace talks, it was decided to loan F-5As, RF-5As, and F-5Bs to the VNAF, with the intent of later replacing them on a one-for-one basis. Accordingly, the USAF provided 20 F-5As and F-5Bs from its training unit at Williams AFB, Arizona, while 100 more (including RF-5A reconnaissance fighters) were obtained from Iran, South Korea, and Taiwan. Eventually, beginning in May 1974 when a first VNAF squadron received its full complement of 18 F-5Es, sufficient numbers of F-5Es were delivered in 1974-75 to enable the conversion of three squadrons and the return of some of the loaned F-5As.

The timely completion of *Enhance Plus* prior to the signing of the Paris Agreement on 27 January 1973 left the RVNAF, and particularly its air force, with ample supplies of weapons. The VNAF, however, still lacked the types of high-performance aircraft, sophisticated ECM equipment, and precision ammunition ('smart' bombs) needed for operations in SAM and AAAs threat areas and to fly interdiction sorties against the enemy supply

Dramatic action as a Vietnamese pilot jumps from his Huey near the US Navy carriers sailing off Saigon. Such desperate scenes were commonplace through the last days of Vietnam.

lines along the Ho Chi Minh Trail. During the following 27 months this deficiency became increasingly more obvious and finally contributed heavily to the final collapse of the Republic of Vietnam.

## The VNAF's Last Stand

Despite the extensive equipment and training provided to the RVNAF in general, and the VNAF in particular, under the Vietnamization Programme and *Enhance Plus*, the South Vietnamese found themselves in a continuously defensive posture as soon as the complete withdrawal of US forces had been accomplished. Initially the North Vietnamese probed the defences of the South rather gingerly, fearing that the United States would be compelled to come back to the rescue of South Vietnam. However, emboldened by their early success and the lack of US military response, they kept bolstering their strength and brought in more and more regular troops as well as anti-aircraft guns and missiles. The latter development proved particularly costly for the VNAF which notably, between February and December 1973, lost 154 of its 959 helicopters and half of its RF-5A reconnaissance aircraft. At the same time, the hastily trained personnel flying and maintaining the large number of aircraft received during *Enhance Plus* were not up to the task. Aircraft availability and bombing precision dropped sharply, compared to the results obtained between 1968 and 1972 when the VNAF had reached the peak of its performance. As for the ARVN, the situation was even worse; without American advisers watching over, corruption and desertion reached alarming levels. Finally when the US Congress (tired of supporting the government of President Nguyen Van Thieu and worried by the effects of the 1973 Arab oil embargo) imposed restrictions on the supply of fuel and ammunition to South Vietnam, and with President Nixon removed from the White House following the Watergate scandal, North Vietnam jumped at the opportunity of realizing its long sought after reunification of the country.

In the final hours of South Vietnam, military personnel and their families scrambled aboard helicopters and headed for the Task Force covering the Saigon evacuation. After depositing its passengers, this VNAF UH-1 deliberately ditched, the boat standing by to rescue the pilot.

### Order of battle

When the North Vietnamese Army began to prod the South Vietnamese defences in preparation for the full-scale invasion of the Republic of Vietnam, the VNAF had 1,994 aircraft in service with a further 224 aircraft, mostly obsolete Douglas A-1Hs, in storage. The First Division, headquartered at Da Nang, was comprised of the 41st and 51st Tactical Wings with two Fighter Squadrons (the 532nd and the 538th with F-5Es); four Attack Squadrons (the 516th, 528th and 550th with A-37Bs, and the 534th with A-1Hs); two Observation Squadrons (the 110th and the 120th with O-1s, O-2s and U-17s); and six Helicopter Squadrons (the 213th, 219th, 233rd, 239th and 257th with UH-1s, and the 247th with CH-47s). Headquartered at Nha Trang, where it had two Training Squadrons (the 912th with T-41s and the 920th with T-37s), the 2nd Air Division also controlled the 62nd Tactical Wing at Phan Rang which operated two A-37 Attack Squadrons (the 524th and 580th with A-37Bs); the 114th Observation Squadron with O-1s, O-2s and U-17s; and the 215th Helicopter Squadron with UH-1s. At Bien Hoa, the 3rd Air Division was made up of the 23rd and 43rd Tactical Wings and their four Fighter Squadrons (522nd, 536th, 542nd and 544th with F-5As); two Attack Squadrons with A-37Bs (the 514th and 518th); two Observation Squadrons (the 112th and 124th) with the usual assortment of aircraft; and six Helicopter Squadrons (five with UH-1s, the 221st, 223rd, 231st, 245th and 251st, and the 237th with CH-47s). At Binh Thuy, the 4th Air Division had the 74th Tactical Wing with three Attack Squadrons (the 520th, 526th and 546th) flying A-37Bs, and the 116th and 122nd Observation Squadrons. In addition, based at Soc Trang, the 4th Air Division's 84th Tactical Wing was comprised of six Helicopter Squadrons (the 249th with CH-47s, and the 211th, 217th, 225th, 227th and 255th with UH-1s). The 33rd and 53rd Tactical Wings were assigned to the 5th Air Division at Tan Son Nhut and included the 259th Helicopter Squadron with UH-1s, the 314th Special Missions Squadron with VC-47Ds and UH-1s, nine Transport Squadrons (the 415th with C-47s; the 417th, 419th and 427th with C-7s; the 413th with C-119s; the 421st and 423rd with C-123s; and the 435th and 437th with C-130s), two Reconnaissance Squadrons (the 718th with EC-47s and the 720th with RC-119Ls) and two Combat Squadrons (the 819th and 821st) with AC-119 gunships. Finally, the 6th Air Division at Pleiku was comprised of the 72nd Tactical Wing with the 530th Attack Squadron (A-1Hs), the 118th Observation Squadron (O-1s, O-2s and U-17s), and the 229th and 235th Helicopter Squadrons (UH-1s) at Pleiku, and of the 82nd Tactical Wing at Phu Cat with the 540th Fighter Squadron (F-5Es), the 817th Combat Squadron (AC-119s), the 241st Helicopter Squadron (CH-47s), and the 243rd Helicopter Squadron (UH-1s).

At the end of February 1975 (eight weeks after Phoc Long had become the first South Vietnamese province to fall to the Communists), the balance of forces in the south still appeared to favour the Republic of Vietnam as it had 662,000 troops and 880 tanks versus 375,000 troops and 600 tanks for the North Vietnamese and their local supporters. However, in terms of regular troops, the North Vietnamese held a slight advantage (225,000 versus 180,000). Moreover, the North benefited from better military leadership and the will to win. After nine more weeks of fighting the Republic of Vietnam ceased to exist.

The quick and final Communist offensive began on 8 March 1975 with co-ordinated country-wide attacks, with the Central Highlands being selected as the main battlefield in an attempt to cut South Vietnam in two. Albeit the ARVN, with strong air support provided by the VNAF, fought well in some sectors, the bulk of its forces crumbled quickly. Ban Me Thuot fell on 10 March, Pleiku on the 16th, Da Nang on the 29th, Qhui Nhon on the 31st, and Nha Trang on 1 April, as the offensive of the North Vietnamese Army succeeded beyond the wildest expectations of the Political Bureau of the Democratic Republic of Vietnam. For the VNAF the losses were staggering, as in addition to the numerous aircraft shot down in combat operations or destroyed on the ground during Communist rocket attacks against air bases, it had been forced to abandon large numbers of aircraft at Pleiku (64 aircraft), Da Nang (130) and Nha Trang. The end was in sight and the evacuation of US and other foreign nationals from Saigon was ordered on 1 April 1975.

Still possessing some 1,600 aircraft in early April the VNAF fought on, but as the ARVN kept falling back in complete disarray it was forced to abandon its base at Phan Rang on the 16th. By then the VNAF was left with only 976 operationally ready aircraft, including 169 A-37Bs and 109 F-5A/F-5Es. To supplement its fighters, gunships and attack aircraft in providing whatever air support could be mustered, the VNAF was even forced to fly C-130As as 'bombers' by dropping daisy cutters (HE bombs fitted with fuse extender), 55-US gallon (208-litre) fuel drums and 15,000-lb (6804-kg) BLU-82 bombs through the rear loading ramp.

### Tan Son Nhut attack

As the war was drawing to a close it appeared that the VNAF harboured in its ranks a number of traitors as, on the evening of 28 April, three A-37Bs had created much confusion during a straffing and bombing attack on Tan Son Nhut. Later, however, Senior General Van Tien Dung, the principal architect of North Vietnam's final offensive, admitted that this attack had been made by North Vietnamese pilots flying captured aircraft. VNAF airmen, in fact, were still carrying on the fight, with the final combat sorties being flown on the morning of 30 April and the VNAF losing an A-1H and an AC-119K to SA-7s on the last day of the war. By then, however, it was all over, and those who could or wanted to do so had taken their aircraft out of the country, preferring exile to Communist rule.

The bravery and devotion of the last VNAF crews to lose their lives in combat was unfortunately not matched by the sad, and even ugly, behaviour of some of those who sought refuge abroad. Panicking and no longer caring for the safety of others, some fighter and attack pilots jettisoned their external tanks and ordnance on the active runway at Tan Son Nhut, while helicopter pilots failed to show proper airmanship in trying to settle their overloaded aircraft aboard US Navy ships steaming off the coast. In the final count, whether they acted properly or not, VNAF aircrews managed to take some 90 aircraft out of the country including 11 A-1s, eight A-37s, five C-7s, 13 C-47s, three C-119s, six C-130s, and 30 F-5s which reached Thailand. In addition a number of helicopters and at least one O-1 were recovered on board US Navy ships. On the other hand, after Duong Van Minh (the last President of the Republic of Vietnam) surrendered on 30 April 1975, the Communists obtained some 1,100 aircraft including 87 F-5s, 95 A-37s, 37 AC-119s, and 23 C-130s, as well as a complete air base network.

### Final bravery

From its modest début with hand-me-down aircraft the VNAF had grown into a well-rounded organization which, in terms of number of aircraft, ranked fourth among the world's air forces. Nevertheless, even though it was at war for most of its existence, the VNAF never shot down an enemy aircraft as its operations were almost exclusively conducted in support of ground operations within the borders of the Republic of South Vietnam. In doing so, its aircrews had progressed from dilettante status in the fifties to seasoned veterans in the late sixties and early seventies. However, after the Republic of Vietnam was left alone, the quality of VNAF aircrews became uneven as the veterans were joined by hastily trained crews. For our part, we prefer to remember the VNAF for the courage of the aircrews who, in the last 24 hours of the war, 'trolled' for enemy fire so that aircraft operating on the evacuation airlift could have a chance to depart safely.

**As more and more helicopters arrived from the mainland, the decks of the carriers became so crowded that no further machines could land. As soon as they arrived, they were unceremoniously dumped over the side to make room for more. The US Navy deck crew handled the panic admirably, all aircraft landing safely, including a Cessna O-1 which made a radio-silent landing on *Midway*.**

**On 29th April 1975, Nguyen Cao Ky, the former South Vietnamese Premier and head of the VNAF was flown to the carrier USS *Midway* by Air America Huey. Later in the day, 29 UH-1s, 2 CH-47s and a single O-1 appeared heading for the carriers in a giant armada, a dramatic finale to the 30-year air war.**

# Other Allied Air Forces in South East Asia

Albeit the air forces of France, the United States and the Republic of Vietnam successively played the leading role during the 30-year air war over South East Asia, those of Australia, Cambodia, the Republic of China, Laos, New Zealand and Thailand also supported allied operations. The activities of these smaller air forces are briefly described anon.

This Bell 47B-1 of No. 9 Squadron of the Australian Army Aviation Corps was used by the Commander, 1st Battalion, 5th Royal Australian Regiment.

## *The Royal Australian Air Force*

As a founding SEATO member, Australia had long committed resources to the common defence, with the RAAF first deploying Commonwealth CA-27 Sabre fighters to Butterworth, Malaya, in December 1958. Thus, when less than four years later the Republic of Vietnam requested assistance in fighting Communist guerrillas, the Commonwealth quickly answered this call by sending the Australian Army Training Team, Vietnam (AATTV). The first AATTV personnel arrived in Vietnam at the end of July 1962 and strength was increased progressively until over 100 army officers and warrant officers served as ARVN advisors and led their trainees into combat. Then, in the spring of 1965, Australia committed additional ground forces to the war, with Special Air Service (SAS) commandoes and two infantry battalions, along with supporting artillery, armoured personnel carriers and engineers being assigned first to the Australian Army Forces, Vietnam (AAFV) and then, from May 1966, to the 1st Australian Task Force (ATF). The last of these combat troops departed from Vietnam in March 1972, but an Australian Army Assistance Group,

RAAF Sabres line up at Don Muang at Bangkok, sharing the ramp with a USAF C-124 and C-133, both on the trans-Pacific air bridge.

**Above:** The only RAAF combat aircraft to take part in the air war over South East Asia were the Australian-built Canberra B.Mk 20 tactical bombers of No. 2 Squadron. This squadron flew 11,963 sorties for the loss of only 2 aircraft.

**Below:** The most visible form of Australian support were the heliborne units operating alongside US Army units. They too used the Bell UH-1 as their main form of transport. This UH-1D is armed with rocket pods and guns.

**Royal Australian Air Force Bell UH-1 sets down a party of troops on a road in South Vietnam. The Huey is equipped with a door-mounted M60 machine gun for suppressive fire, especially useful for landing in 'hot' LZs.**

**In-country air transport for the 1st ATF was provided by de Havilland Wallabies (similarly to the C-7A Caribous operated by the USA and USAF) of No. 35 Squadron, RAAF. These Wallabies are seen at Tan Son Nhut AB where in July 1967 they shared the crowded ramp area with USAF C-130s. The last four Wallabies departed South Vietnam in February 1972.**

Vietnam (AAAGV) continued to provide advisors until 31 January 1973.

For logistic and personnel support of the successive Australian army organizations in Vietnam, jet airliners chartered from Qantas Airways and RAAF transports provided airlift between Australia and Vietnam, with the Lockheed C-130As originally used by No. 36 Squadron for that purpose being supplemented in 1966 by the C-130Es of No. 37 Squadron. For in-country operations the RAAF also provided Bell UH-1B helicopters and the de Havilland Canada DHC-4 Caribous of No. 35 Squadron. The first of these aircraft (which were the same as the C-7As flown in Vietnam by US Army and USAF units, and which the Australians called Wallabies) arrived at Vung Tau AB in August 1964. Soon the Wallabies provided direct support for Australian ground troops and also supplemented US Army and USAF transport aircraft assigned to the allied Common Service Airlift System. The last four Wallabies were withdrawn from Vietnam in February 1972.

For combat operations the RAAF deployed its No. 2 Squadron. Equipped with Australian-built Canberra B.Mk 20 jet bombers, this unit arrived at Phan Rang AB in April 1967 and was placed under the operational control of the 35th TFW, USAF, prior to flying its first sorties on 23 April. Like the Martin B-57B, the Canberra B.Mk 20 was a licence-built version of the English Electric twinjet bomber, but the American B-57B had been optimized for tactical operations. The Australian Canberra was better suited for level bombing operations as it lacked two key features of the US version, namely wing-mounted guns and underwing store attachment points (however, during short duration sorties the Canberra B.Mk 20 could carry a 500-lb (227-kg) or 750-lb (340-kg) bomb beneath each wing tip in place of its usual external tanks). Accordingly, No. 2 Squadron flew mainly in the latter role, both during daylight operations and at night for *Combat Skyspot/Combat Proof* missions. Earning the respect of their USAF associates and the gratitude of allied ground troops, the Australian airmen built up an impressive record of 11,963 sorties, for the loss of only two aircraft and two crewmen, prior to their departure from Vietnam on 4 June 1971.

Mikoyan-Gurevich MiG-17 'Fresco' fighters of the Royal Khmer Air Force line up at Phnom Penh in 1970, while an Antonov An-2 'Colt' is just visible in the hangar behind. The MiG-17s represented the sharp end of the Cambodian forces, but did not see action during the war.

## The Khmer Air Force

Since gaining its independence in the mid-fifties, Cambodia (now renamed Kampuchea) has changed sides several times as internal violence and foreign interventions have progressively brought that small nation to chaos and slaughter. After France had been forced to leave its former colonies in Indochina, the Kingdom of Cambodia left the Union Française. Nevertheless, France continued to provide assistance and instructors for the Aviation Royale Khmer (Royal Khmer Aviation) which was organized in early 1954. Initial equipment for this service consisted of seven Toyo-built Fletcher FD-25A and FD-25B Defender light aircraft ordered from Japan, seven Morane-Saulnier M.S. 733 Alcyon basic trainers acquired from France, five Dassault MD 315s, and small numbers of Douglas C-47s, de Havilland Canada Beavers and Cessna L-19s supplied by the United States. Most of these aircraft were unarmed, but gunnery training and internal policing duties were undertaken by a handful of FD-25B Defenders and M.S. 733 Alcyons which carried light armament. In the early sixties these ineffective aircraft were supplemented by a small batch of North American T-28As fitted with wing guns and underwing weapons racks.

### Cambodia turns to Moscow

Soon after the delivery of these T-28As, relations between Cambodia and the United States took a turn for the worse as the result of incidents along the border with South Vietnam, where ARVN forces and their US advisers were fighting Viet Cong troops operating from Cambodian sanctuaries. Prince Norodom Sihanouk, Cambodia's Premier and former King, and his Popular Social Communist Party then increasingly aligned Cambodia with Communist nations and obtained a first batch of four MiG-15 jet fighters from the USSR in November 1963. However, it was a US-supplied T-28A which on 19 March 1964 obtained the Royal Khmer Aviation's only air victory when one of these aircraft shot down a USAF O-1, killing its US pilot and Vietnamese observer. Two months earlier the US Military Assistance Advisory Group had left the country, and in August 1964 Cambodia broke diplomatic relations with both the Republic of Vietnam and the United States.

Renamed the Royal Khmer Air Force, Cambodia's diminutive air service then sought to boost its capabilities to defend the nation's border against feared crossings by South Vietnamese troops. Additional equipment, in the form of MiG-15 (NATO reporting name 'Fagot') and MiG-17 'Fresco' fighters, and Antonov An-2 'Colt' and Ilyushin Il-14 'Crate' transports, was received from the USSR and the PRC during the mid-sixties, but it was France's contribution which most infuriated the United States. In 1965, ignoring strong American protests, President General Charles de Gaulle approved the transfer of 15 ex-Armée de l'Air Douglas AD-4NA Skyraider attack aircraft (then designated A-1Ds by the US Navy) which France had obtained during the fighting in Algeria. However, neither Communist nor French help could do much to increase the effective strength of the Royal Khmer Air Force as Cambodia lacked the

Seven Morane-Saulnier M.S.733 Alcyons were acquired from France during the initial equipping of the Aviation Royale Khmer. These were used for basic training, and on occasion, could be fitted with light guns and racks for weapons training.

**Although the concept of using light armed STOL aircraft as *Pave Coin* 'mini gunships' was not retained by the USAF, the *Credible Chase* evaluation pitted the Fairchild AU-23 Peacemaker against the Helio AU-24 Stallion. This AU-24A was photographed on 1 June 1971 in Bangkok, Thailand, prior to being transferred to the Khmer Air Force.**

personnel and facilities to maintain these aircraft. By 1970 only a few of the Cambodian transports and trainers remained airworthy.

On 18 March 1970 the ousting of Prince Nordom Sihanouk as Cambodia's chief of State heralded a new era; General Lon Nol proclaimed a republic and sought US assistance in eliminating Communist troops and safe-havens from his country. Soon thereafter training of aircrews and ground personnel for the restyled Khmer Air Force began, and new equipment was provided by the United States (Cessna T-41A Mescalero basic trainers, de Havilland Canada U-6 and Douglas C-47 transports, and North American T-28B counter-insurgency aircraft) and Australia (C-47s). Later additions from US sources included Bell Huey helicopters (including some gunships), Fairchild C-123K transports (the first five arriving in April 1973 after being overhauled in Taiwan), Cessna A-37B light attack aircraft, Fairchild AU-24A mini gunships, Cessna O-1 observation aircraft and more C-47 transports. Known as *Project Flycatcher*, the supply of aircraft to the Khmer Air Force was terminated on 30 June 1974.

Notwithstanding the quantitative improvement of the Khmer Air Force, air support by USAF aircraft from the spring of 1970 until August 1973, and massive logistic support by USAF transports and chartered American airliners, the country was slowly overrun by Khmer Rouge insurgents. In the end the Khmer Government surrendered to the Communists. Neither the US airlift nor the good performance put up by Khmer aircrews (particularly those flying transport aircraft in support of ground operations, and bringing supplies to Pnom Penh once the Mekong river was controlled by enemy forces), could have prevented the fall of the capital city on 17 April 1975. At that time several Khmer Air Force aircraft, including 10 of its 17 C-123s, escaped to Thailand with crews and their family members and friends who were unwilling to submit to Communist rule.

## *The Chinese Nationalist Air Force*

Virulently anti-Communist, the Republic of China was eager to join allied forces in Vietnam. However, fearing a strong reaction from the People's Republic of China, the US Government pressured the Republic of Vietnam to reject help from Taiwanese sources. Hence, with the exception of participation in covert operations (including the provision of pilots for C-123s used for 'unconventional' warfare) and the use of its Ching Chuan Kang AB by USAF transports and tankers taking part in operations in South East Asia, the Republic of China's only contribution to the war effort was made in 1962 when aircrews and two Curtiss C-46Ds of the CNAF flew in support of USAID activities.

## *The Republic of Korea Air Force*

Having first sent a Survey Team to South Vietnam in August 1964, the Republic of Korea subsequently made a major contribution to the ground battle. It provided two Army divisions (the Capital Division which was stationed in Binh Dinh Province from September 1966 until March 1973, and the 9th Infantry Division which operated around Ninh Hoa during the same period) and its 2nd Marine Corps Brigade which was successively engaged around Cam Ranh Bay, Tuy Hoa, Phu Bai and Hoi An from October 1965 until February 1972. Both of the Army divisions brought with them their aviation sections which, along with the semi-independent 11th Aviation Company, flew Bell UH-1 helicopters and three fixed-wing utility aircraft. Moreover, beginning in July 1967, two Curtiss C-46s of the ROKAF were based at Tan Son Nhut AB for in-country support of Korean forces; in early 1970 this duty was taken over by three Douglas C-54s. Airlift between South Korea and Vietnam was provided by USAF C-130s and, from July 1966, by C-54 transports of the ROKAF. In addition, Korean Air Lines and Air Korea flew resupply missions.

Other Korean support came in the shape of civil-registered aircraft which flew in support of Korean troops in the theatre. One type of aircraft operated in the war zone was a Cessna 337 (civil version of the O-2 FAC platform). Other civil Korean aircraft may have performed clandestine ferry flights, alongside those of Taiwan.

Very rarely illustrated is this Morane-Saulnier M.S. 500 Criquet of the newly established Royal Laotian Air Force being pushed out of its hangar at Vientiane, Laos, in 1955. Of interest is the red roundel of Laos with the three white elephants of the royal dynasty.

## *The Royal Lao Air Force*

Like the VNAF and the Aviation Royale Khmer, the Aviation Royale Laotienne (Royal Lao Aviation) was organized after France was forced to leave Indochina. Initial training of its aircrews and ground personnel was undertaken in the mid-fifties in France and French Morocco, and initial equipment (Cessna L-19 and Morane-Saulnier M.S. 500 Criquet observation aircraft, de Havilland Canada Beaver and Aero Commander 520 light transport and liaison aircraft, and Douglas C-47 transports) was drawn from French inventory in Indochina.

In 1961 the United States opened a Military Assistance Advisory Group in Vietiane and supplied a small number of North American T-6 armed trainers. However, following Prince Souvanna Phouma's attempt at grouping representatives of the Lao Neutralists, Rightists, and the Pathet Lao in a coalition government, MAAG personnel were withdrawn from Laos in October 1962. Even though the major powers then guaranteed the neutrality of Laos the Soviets, less scrupulous, moved in to fill the vacuum, bringing with them nine Lisunov Li-2s (Soviet-built versions of the Douglas DC-3, also known by their NATO reporting name 'Cab') for the RLAF. Russian mistakes, and the increasing militancy of the Pathet Lao, finally led to the break-up of the fragile coalition and in the spring of 1964 Prince Souvanna Phouma requested US assistance. As noted in Chapter 3, this request led to USAF intervention in support of the Laotian government. Moreover, for the Royal Lao Air Force, it marked the beginning of an 11-year period of Americanization.

As part of Project *Water Pump*, Detachment 6, 1st Air Commando Wing, USAF, moved to Udorn RTAFB in March 1964 to begin training RLAF crews to fly North American T-28Ds. Equipped with four of these aircraft, Laotian pilots flew their first operations against the Pathet Lao on 17 May. Later, additional T-28Ds were obtained from the USAF and the VNAF, and the type became the most important combat aircraft of the Royal Lao Air Force (some 50 were in service when a dozen were destroyed in a Communist raid against the airfield at Luang Prabang on 16 July 1966). Other aircraft then flown in significant number by the RLAF included the ubiquitous C-47, with some of these aircraft being used as makeshift bombers beginning in 1965. During the same period, Laos also received Sikorsky H-34 helicopters and soon its Army and Meo irregulars became quite adept at mounting air mobile operations (notably in August 1969 when RLAF H-34s helped win a major battle on the southern fringes of the Plain of Jars).

All along it was American fast movers and B-52s which provided the heavy fire support for operations against the Pathet Lao and their North Viet-

The North American T-28D was the major combat type of the Royal Lao Air Force throughout the conflict, and these were used in action against Pathet Lao forces.

**Making only a relatively small contribution to the war effort, the RNZAF flew logistic support missions from New Zealand to South Vietnam with the Handley Page Hastings C.3s of No. 41 Squadron and Lockheed C-130H Hercules of No. 40 Squadron. Earlier, Bristol 170 Freighters of No. 1 Squadron, such as this aircraft seen at Don Muang Airport in June 1962, flew missions to Thailand.**

namese ally. Thus, as President Nixon tried to end the United States' direct participation in the war, it became necessary to provide more aircraft to the Royal Lao Air Force. The lack of a sufficient number of Laotian skilled personnel meant, however, that C-47s and T-28Ds would have to continue as the primary types, with AC-47 gunships being considered particularly desirable. Initially, it was intended to convert four RLAF C-47s by installing .50-caliber (12.7-mm) machine guns; however, this jury-rigged installation was not expected to be satisfactory and during the summer of 1969 the RLAF received five ex-VNAF C-47s which were converted to full AC-47 standard with three 7.62-mm SUU-11 Miniguns. Finally, in 1970 these early gunships were replaced with ex-USAF AC-47s with the latest and more reliable MXU-479/A gun pods. A final type entered RLAF service in February 1973 when five ex-Air America C-123s were handed over prior to the 22 February cease-fire.

### Communist victory

Once more a coalition government was formed but soon numerous violations were reported. Loyal troops, with support from the RLAF, attempted to resist as best they could until August 1975 when the Pathet Lao finally gained complete control of the country. By then few US-supplied aircraft remained airworthy; however, some did manage to reach safety by escaping to Thailand. Four months later the Communists forced the King to abdicate, and the 600-year old monarchy gave place to the Democratic Republic of Laos.

## The Royal New Zealand Air Force

New Zealand ground troops fought in Vietnam from July 1965 until June 1972 as part of the ANZAC (Australian-New Zealand Army Corps) and, at peak strength, were comprised of two infantry companies, one artillery battery and a platoon of SAS commandoes. No aircraft were provided for use in South Vietnam but the RNZAF flew logistic flights between home bases and the war front, first using Bristol Freighter Mk 31s and Handley Page Hastings C.3s of No. 41 Squadron and then Lockheed C-130H Hercules of No. 40 Squadron.

## The Royal Thai Air Force

In the case of Thai military personnel, airmen preceded ground troops in Vietnam as, beginning in September 1964, a 17-man task force worked

**The MiG-15UTI 'Midget' was used by both Cambodia and North Vietnam for advanced and weapons training. Seen in June 1970, this Cambodian aircraft is standing in front of an Ilyushin Il-14 'Crate', both types having been supplied by the Soviet Union.**

and flew as part of VNAF C-47 units, whereas troops did not arrive until three years later when an infantry regiment was first posted to Camp Bear Cat. Although this contingent was withdrawn 11 months later, it was followed in February 1969 by forces in divisional strength (the Royal Thai Army Expeditionary Division, which was redesignated the Royal Thai Army Volunteer Force in September 1971, eventually comprised nine infantry and three artillery battalions, one armoured cavalry squadron, support forces, and one aviation company). Rotation of Thai military personnel and logistic support was provided by USAF transports.

Although not allowed to serve as aircraft commanders, the RTAF pilots, navigators, and maintenance personnel who had first joined VNAF C-47 units in 1964 proved to be most valuable; they not only provided experience to these units but also enabled the VNAF to assign more of its still meager aircrew strength to squadrons flying combat aircraft. So successful was this programme of supplying personnel that in July 1966 the RTAF assigned its *Victory Flight* personnel to fly with the USAF 19th Air Commando Squadron (later redesignated 19th Tactical Airlift Squadron). In fact, two of the C-123Ks from this USAF unit were specially repainted in Thai markings. Upon inactivation of the 19th TAS in May 1971, the Thai aircrews and their two aircraft were transferred to the 421st Transport Squadron, VNAF. Later in that year the RTAF C-47 and C-123K crews returned to Thailand.

The large US Air Force presence in Thailand meant that many bases were shared with RTAF units. Air defence for these bases was provided by Thai aircraft, usually North American F-86 Sabres. Thai aircraft also patrolled the borders with Cambodia and Laos, and were well versed in counter-insurgency operations, although these were not needed with respect to the war with North Vietnam.

**Above: RTAF Fairchild C-123Ks provided some airlift capability in the war zone.**

**Above left: OV-10 Broncos were used by the RTAF for light strike and FAC duties.**

**Although not contributing combat aircraft during the South East Asia War, the Royal Thai Air Force worked closely with USAF units in Thailand. Here two North American F-86Ds of the Thai 12th Fighter Wing are seen from the cockpit of a USAF TF-102A. The Thai Sabre Dogs were Sidewinder-capable.**

# The Vietnam People's Air Force

Upon wresting its independence from France in 1954, the Democratic Republic of Vietnam inherited a fairly adequate aviation infrastructure, with major airfields at Bach Mai and Gia Lam, near Hanoi, and at Cat Bi and Do Son, near Haiphon, and with numerous airstrips located throughout Tonkin and the northern part of Annam under its control. The new nation, however, was willing neither to receive aircraft from France nor to have its aircrews and ground personnel trained by its former rulers. Although some help was soon provided by the Soviet Union and the People's Democratic Republic of China, for ten years the fledgling Vietnam People's Air Force (soon to become better known as the North Vietnamese Air Force or, simply, as the NVNAF) was equipped only with piston-powered trainers (Yakovlev Yak-18 'Max' for primary training and Yak-11 'Moose' for basic training) and transports (Antonov An-2 'Colt', Ilyushin Il-12 'Coach' and Il-14 'Crate', and Lisunov Li-2 'Cab'). In the early sixties, flying alongside Soviet-crewed aircraft, NVNAF transports began flying air resupply sorties for the Pathet Lao and may have been used at least once to drop paratroopers over Laos. At about the same time, training of NVNAF jet crews was initiated in China and the USSR.

The timely initiation of this training programme enabled the NVNAF to react within days of the Gulf of Tonkin Incident and the subsequent retaliatory air strikes, and some 36 MiG-15 'Fagot' and MiG-17 'Fresco' jet fighters arrived from nearby Chinese bases at the Phuc Yen airfield, NNW from Hanoi. Nevertheless, it was fortunate for North Vietnam that the United States did not then mount full-scale offensive operations as its meager force of MiGs, manned by still inexperienced crews and lacking the necessary GCI facilities, would have been quickly put out of action. Washington was unwilling to escalate the war but Hanoi could not chance its future and forged ahead with the implementation of an integrated air defence system, complete with GCI network, improved air bases, radar-controlled antiaircraft artillery, and SAMs. In the spring of 1965, less than two months after the first *Flaming Dart* strikes and just as *Rolling Thunder* was launched, the NVNAF was still small but was ready to fight.

## *Initial success*

Going into action on 3 April 1965, the North Vietnamese MiG-17s at first took the best of their opponents; on that day they damaged a US Navy F-8E and the next day shot down two USAF F-105Ds, without incurring a loss. During the remainder of 1965 the NVNAF was unable to match its initial success and, on the contrary, lost six MiG-17s (three confirmed and one probable by Navy aircraft, and two confirmed by USAF aircraft). Obviously, GCI controllers and aircrews were insufficiently trained, and from August 1965 until April 1966, the NVNAF stood down to hone its skills and most of its aircraft and aircrews were pulled back to China for further training. During

**North Vietnamese pilots in Soviet anti-G suits discuss their forthcoming mission. The MiGs operated under close GCI control throughout the war, limiting their capability to strictly controlled intercepts, often involving slashing high-speed attacks.**

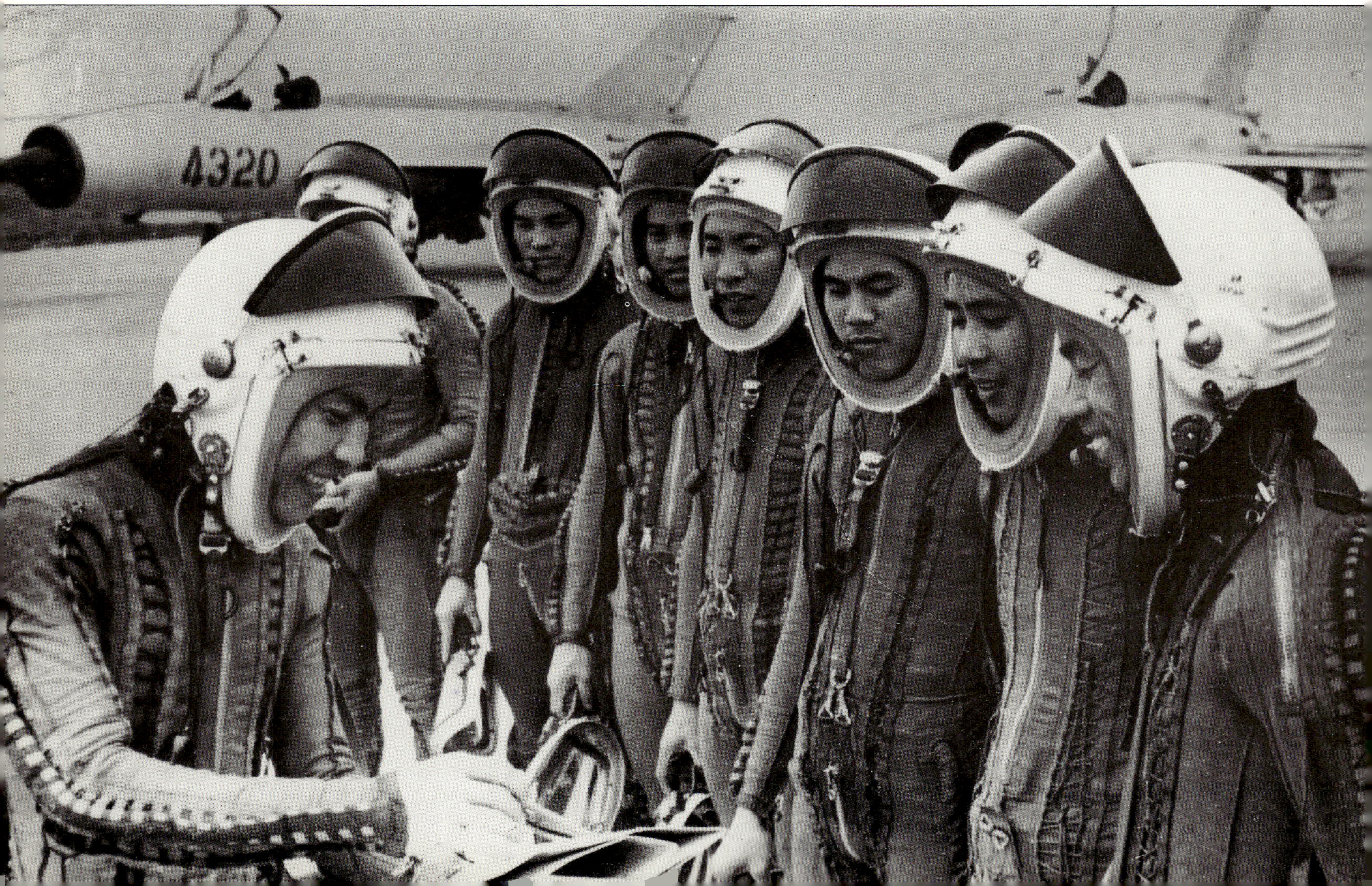

**Highly manoeuvrable at transonic speeds, MiG-17Fs proved difficult foes. When operating under GCI control, thus alleviating their lack of radar, Frescoes were particularly effective against heavily laden strike aircraft. Soviet- and Chinese-built MiG-17s were the most numerous NVNAF fighters throughout most of the war.**

this period the NVNAF also introduced into service its first MiG-21 'Fishbed' supersonic fighters and Ilyushin Il-28 'Beagle' jet bombers. The Il-28s, however, were not to take an active part in the air war and their only contribution to the defence of North Vietnam was as a deterrent which forced both the USAF and the US Navy to keep back a number of fighters to intercept feared NVNAF bombing operations.

From the onset it appears that the NVNAF realized that its limited fighter force should not be wasted in vain attempts to obtain the maximum number of victories in air combat against US fighters but, rather, should be used to force the bomb-laden strike aircraft to jettison their bombs prematurely. Accordingly, when in April 1966 the NVNAF returned to the fray (it then had an estimated 63 MiG-17s and 15 MiG-21s), its GCI controllers, who had a precise idea of the likely routes to be followed by USAF aircraft from their bases in Thailand to their main objectives in the heart of North Vietnam, usually vectored the MiG-17s for stern attacks from below. When this tactic was successful (as it was during the last quarter of 1966 when over 55 percent of the US strike aircraft were forced to jettison their ordnance prior to reaching their targets), the subsonic MiG-17s remained at low altitude where their tighter turning radius, combined with the reduced effectiveness of the radar and the missiles of US fighters when operating in ground clutter, gave them a fair chance of success in dogfights. Whenever they could, the 'Fresco' pilots would then form a 'wagon wheel' (a modified 'Lufberry Circle' tactic in which four or more fighters fly in a tight circle to provide 6 o'clock coverage for each other) to lure the F-4s. This tactice, however, was soon countered as US fighters refused to be drawn into further dogfights and, co-ordinating their attacks, only made hit-and-run passes at the MiG's wagon wheel.

While MiG-17s had to rely on their superior maneuverability and low altitude tactics to offset the higher speed and missile armament of US fighters, MiG-21s were much more capable combat aircraft. Slightly slower than F-105s at low altitude and than F-4s at high altitude, MiG-21s were more maneuverable than US aircraft, with the possible exception of F-8s. Moreover, when their built-in cannon armament was supplemented by K-13A 'Atoll' infrared-guided missiles (with which a first kill was scored on 14 December 1966), MiG-21s were adequately armed, and their only shortcoming was their relatively short endurance. First entering combat on 23 April 1966, the NVNAF MiG-21s initially did not achieve the hoped for

**23-mm, 37-mm and 57-mm calibre anti-aircraft guns were the constant enemies of US fliers throughout the war. This crew blasts away with their camouflaged gun at bombers overhead. Note the novel flak jackets.**

**Above: Trying to stay out of the launch parameters of the Sidewinder missiles of an F-4C, a MiG-17F takes violent evasive action at low altitude during a combat in the vicinity of Hanoi. The high visibility of the North Vietnamese national markings is noteworthy.**

**Pilots walk away from their MiG fighters. The MiG-21 'Fishbed' was a supersonic fighter with high manoeuvrability. However, North Vietnamese tactics rarely allowed the pilots to exploit this facet of the MiG-21's capabilities.**

**North Vietnamese pilots rush to their MiG-21s in a posed scramble. The MiGs are the MiG-21PF 'Fishbed-D' version, armed with two AA-2 'Atolls' each. This missile was a direct copy of the US AIM-9 Sidewinder.**

success. The first 'Fishbed' was shot down by an F-4C of the 480th TFS/35th TFW on 26 April; four more fell to USAF fighters during the year and another was shot down by a Navy F-8E. According to American sources, during 1966 the NVNAF lost six MiG-21s and 23 MiG-17s in air-to-air combat while it was credited with the destruction of only six US aircraft (three each from the Air Force and the Navy); North Vietnam, however, claimed that one of its pilots, Captain Nguyen Van Bay, had scored seven kills against F-4s, F-100s and F-105s, thus becoming the war's first ace.

## *Concern over figures*

Even though North Vietnamese results were inflated for propaganda reasons (the discrepancy between the conflicting claims being also explained in part by the fact that some of the aircraft which the United States admitted losing to unknown causes were brought down by MiGs rather than by AAA or SAMs), they did cause much concern to American officials. Accordingly, on 2 January 1967 the USAF mounted *Operation Bolo* during which F-4Cs decoyed the NVNAF by flying mission profiles similar to those of bomb-laden F-105Ds. As their GCI controllers had failed to recognize the American ruse, a strong force of MiG-21s rose below cloud cover to attack the expected strike force. In a furious battle fought close to its Phuc Yen airfield, the NVNAF lost seven 'Fishbeds' (nearly half of its operational inventory of MiG-21s) without inflicting a loss to the USAF. Two more MiG-21s were shot down four days later and the NVNAF was forced to stand down while its losses were made up by additional Soviet deliveries of aircraft and its personnel received further training in China. Soon the NVNAF was again posing too great a threat, forcing Washington finally to relent on its long-standing ban against attacks on North Vietnamese airfields.

American strikes against some of its airfields did not prove a serious problem for the NVNAF as its aircraft were kept in widely separated and bunkered dispersals, and as US aircraft were still precluded from attacking either the Gia Lam airport in Hanoi or Chinese bases near the North Vietnamese border. More troublesome were roving groups of US fighters which attempted to intercept the short-ranged MiGs as they returned to their bases, thus forcing the NVNAF to implement coordinated tactics. First sending its MiG-17s for hit-and-run attacks to break up formations of US aircraft, the NVNAF had them quickly break off the engagement to mount low altitude patrols near airfields to protect the MiG-21s returning to base. For their part, the 'Fishbed' interceptors were primarily used to engage US aircraft which had been separated from the main force as a result of the MiG-17s' passes. While this tactic could not hope to stop the American air offensive, it did

**Below right: SA-2 'Guideline' missiles on their launcher. Although much feared, the SAMs did not have the impact that might have been expected, largely due to US countermeasures (in particular *Wild Weasel* defence-suppression missions).**

**Below: Vietnamese pilot in the cockpit of his MiG-21. All stencilling around the cockpit is in Cyrillic.**

**Like the US air forces, the NVNAF made extensive use of revetments to protect its aircraft. Of earthen construction, this revetment at Kep Airfield may have proven effective against bomb and straffing attacks but did not prevent an RF-101C from spotting two MiG-17s.**

succeed in forcing the USAF and USN to increase the number of fighters which were either assigned directly to MIGCAPs or instructed to jettison ordnance as soon as the MiGs appeared in order to protect the main force of strike aircraft. Moreover, after the lopsided losses it had suffered early in 1967, the NVNAF was able to achieve a more favourable kill-to-loss ratio later in the year. The United States admitted the loss of five F-4s, 17 F-105s and numerous strike and support aircraft, but claimed to have shct down 75 MiGs and to have reduced the NVNAF operational inventory to only 28 MiG-17s and 12 MiG-21s by the end of 1967. Eight additional MiGs were destroyed by the USAF during the first quarter of 1968, while the Navy claimed the destruction of six aircraft during the summer. For all practical purposes, the NVNAF had ceased to exist when strikes against the North were discontinued.

Although air bases with runways suitable for MiG operations had been built at Bai Thuong, Quan Lang and Vinh, the NVNAF seldom de-

**The MiGs were active at night as well, operating with ground radars almost totally. During *Linebacker II*, the MiGs were used to trail the bombers and relay altitude and speed information to SAM sites.**

**Above: An AAA battery in Hanoi blasts away at US bombers during the December 1972 *Linebacker II* raids. The guns accounted for nearly 60 percent of US combat losses.**

**Left: SA-2 on its launcher and (inset) launching. The SAMs accounted for only 5 percent of US combat losses. Regular Elint flights kept pace with any developments and effective ECM was maintained from 1965 onwards.**

ployed its fighters to these bases in the northern portion of the panhandle as its first task was to protect the Red River area. However, after President Johnson had ordered a suspension of bombing operations north of the 20th parallel, MiGs began operating as far south as the 19th parallel and occasionally over the Gulf of Tonkin. These overwater sorties never posed a serious threat to US Navy ships, but during the war at least seven MiGs were lost to Talos surface-to-air missiles fired from warships of Task Force 77. NVNAF operations outside the borders of North Vietnam were even less frequent and, with the exception of a small number of air resupply sorties in Laos, the NVNAF did not support Communist ground operations. Hence the reported sighting of one of its Mi-6 'Hook' helicopters near Pleiku in April 1969 was probably a case of inaccurate identification.

The halt of all American bombing operations on 1 November 1968 again enabled North Vietnam to rebuild its air force, with intensive training taking place not only at home but also in China and the Soviet Union. Thus, by the spring of 1972 the service had an adequate number of qualified aircrews and maintenance personnel to man Soviet-supplied MiG-17s and MiG-21s, including versions of these aircraft fitted with search and track airborne radar for all-weather operations, and Chinese-supplied Shenyang F 6s (Chinese-built MiG-19 'Farmers'). Its inventory was then estimated by the United States to include 80 MiG-17s, 33 MiG-19s (American sources do not differentiate between Soviet-built 'Farmers' and their Chinese versions), and 93 MiG-21s.

### *Further action*

Once again feeling strong, the NVNAF had begun in early 1972 to send its fighters to the Laotian border, and in February and March two MiGs were lost for the destruction of a USAF F-4D. These skirmishes were soon followed by the largest air battles of the war, as on 6 April 1972 the United States resumed air operations over the North. During *Freedom Train* and *Linebacker I* the NVNAF lost large numbers of aircraft (three in April, 27 in May, five in June, six in July, five in

**MiG-21PF of the VPAF, armed with AA-2 'Atolls'. The 'star and bar' insignia of the VPAF may have caused some confusion with the VNAF and USAF, but the distinctive shape of the MiGs could not be confused with any aircraft flying from the South.**

**Claimed to be the aircraft of Col. Toon, the top-scoring NVNAF pilot, this MiG-17F bore seven small red stars for victories against US aircraft when it was shown to Japanese journalists. It is claimed that Col. Toon obtained six more kills before being shot down on 10 May 1972 by Lt. Cunningham and Lt(jg) Driscoll.**

August, nine in September, and eight during the first half of October); nevertheless, against the USAF it succeeded in limiting its loss-to-kill ratio to an acceptable 2-to-3 level. More significantly from the American point of view was the fact that during that period MiGs accounted for over 60 percent of the USAF losses, thus reflecting the better proficiency of North Vietnamese pilots. Against the US Navy the NVNAF did not fare as well as, since the autumn of 1968, American naval aircrews had received intensive air combat training as part of the *Topgun* programme. Notably, this training enabled Lt. Randy Cunningham and Lt (jg) William Driscoll to shoot down three MiG-17s on 10 May 1972, with the last of their victories being obtained against the top scoring NVNAF pilot, Col. Toon, who at the time of his death was credited by the North Vietnamese propaganda with 13 victories. (Should this claim be accurate, Col. Toon would have outscored the top American ace by better than 2-to-1 and would have scored 16 percent of the NVNAF kills.)

Having lost at least 58 fighters in air combat in less than seven months, plus an undetermined number of others in operational accidents and during US attacks on its airfields, the NVNAF was expected to have been greatly reduced in strength. However, by then it had an adequate supply of aircrews and the aircraft which it had lost were for the most part replaced by the PRC. In particular, North Vietnam received additional F 4s, F 5s and F 6s (Chinese-built MiG-17Fs, MiG-17PFs and MiG-19PFs), so that at the end of October 1972 its operational inventory was estimated to incldue 66 'Frescoes', 40 'Farmers', but only 39 of the more capable 'Fishbeds'.

### *Linebacker II*

In spite of this strength, the NVNAF was unable to stop renewed American air operations during *Linebacker II*, as the United States then enjoyed massive numerical superiority and because weather conditions often prevented NVNAF day fighters from operating against the better equipped USAF and US Navy. During night operations by B-52s the NVNAF used its fighters to shadow the US heavy bombers, reporting their altitude and course to AAA and SAM controllers, but lost two MiG-21s to the bombers' gunners without scoring a kill. Five other MiG-21s were shot down by US fighters during the last weeks of the war, and the NVNAF incurred its last loss on 12 January 1973 when one of its MiG-17s was shot down by an F-4B from VF-161.

After the signing of the January 1973 Paris Agreement, the NVNAF was able to recoup and undertake a programme of air base construction (significantly, the airfields at Do Khe, Khe Phat, and Dong Hoi, in the southern part of the panhandle close to the DMZ, were upgraded for jet operation) in preparation for the planned offensive against the Republic of Vietnam. Nevertheless, when the time came for Hanoi to launch its long expected offensive in the spring of 1975, NVNAF operations in support of the victorious Communist ground forces were rendered unnecessary by the quick collapse of the ARVN and few, if any, sorties were flown by its MiGs over the South. However, the NVNAF scored a psychological victory when it quickly turned around three US-built Cessna A-37Bs which had been captured at Pleiku and used them to bomb and strafe Tan Son Nhut AB in the evening of 28 April 1975.

This ability to operate captured aircraft in spite of the lack of support by manufacturer's technical representatives was soon to enable the NVNAF to reach its numerical peak, for large numbers of aircraft fell into North Vietnamese hands when Saigon capitulated. As large supplies of spare parts were also captured, the NVNAF went on to fly these US-built aircraft, along with its Soviet-built and Chinese-built aircraft, during operations in Kampuchea and border incidents with its former Chinese ally, the Air Force of the People's Liberation Army. Over ten years later, notwithstanding cannibalization and substitution of locally built components, it is doubtful that more than a handful of the captured Cessna A-37Bs, Lockheed C-130As, and Northrop F-5A/F-5Es remains airworthy.

**MiG-21PFs line-up with their crews for inspection. North Vietnam claimed many more US aircraft than the US admitted, using the world stage for typical communist propaganda exercises.**

**The most potent aircraft 'left behind' were the Northrop F-5s. This weary-looking F-5B is seen with Vietnamese markings in its US-built shelter. Aircraft could only be kept airworthy by cannibalisation, and it is unlikely that many survived the decade in service.**

582

# Appendices

**Appendix A: US Fixed-wing and Helicopter Losses**

**Appendix B: Aircraft of the South East Asia Wars**

# Appendix A

## US FIXED-WING AIRCRAFT AND HELICOPTER LOSSES

The US fixed-wing aircraft and helicopter losses summarized in the following tables, and quoted elsewhere in this book, are based on Joint Chiefs of Staff data as summarized in a report prepared in October 1973 by the Directorate for Information Operations, OASD (Comptroller), Department of Defense. This report includes all combat and operational losses up to 15 August 1973, the date on which all offensive operations in South East Asia were ended in compliance with a Congressional mandate.

Data for all services are summarized in Table 1, which shows that total US losses reached 8,588 fixed-wing aircraft and helicopters. Tables 2, 3, 4, and 5 present the same data respectively for the USAF, USN, USMC, and USA. For each of the four services, losses are further broken down, by aircraft and year, in six categories:

A. Losses to MiGs
B. Losses to SAMs
C. Losses to AAA and small arms fire
D. Losses on the ground during enemy attacks against allied air bases
E. Combat losses (the sum of losses in the first four categories)
F. Operational losses (i.e., non-combat losses due to accidents, pilot error, etc.)

It is interesting to note that AAA and small arms fire accounted for the largest portion of the losses. For fixed-wing aircraft, the percentages of total losses by cause were as follows:

| | USAF | USN | USMC | USA | All services |
|---|---|---|---|---|---|
| To MiGs | 2.8 | 1.8 | 0.4 | 0.2 | 2.1 |
| To SAMs | 5.2 | 9.8 | 1.4 | 0 | 5.3 |
| To AAA | 64.7 | 52.3 | 64.1 | 27.6 | 57.5 |
| At Air Bases | 4.5 | 0 | 4.4 | 7.8 | 3.9 |
| Sub-Total | 77.2 | 63.9 | 70.3 | 35.6 | 68.8 |
| Operational | 22.8 | 36.1 | 29.7 | 64.4 | 31.2 |
| Total | 100.0 | 100.0 | 100.0 | 100.0 | 100.0 |

Corresponding percentages for helicopter losses were as follows:

| | USAF | USN | USMC | USA | All services |
|---|---|---|---|---|---|
| To MiGs | 1.3 | 0 | 0 | 0.1 | 0.1 |
| To SAMs | 0 | 0 | 0.2 | 0.2 | 0.2 |
| To AAA | 69.7 | 27.1 | 56.2 | 47.9 | 48.7 |
| At Air Bases | 5.3 | 0 | 7.3 | 3.8 | 4.2 |
| Sub-Total | 76.3 | 27.1 | 63.7 | 52.0 | 53.2 |
| Operational | 23.7 | 72.9 | 36.3 | 48.0 | 46.8 |
| Total | 100.0 | 100.0 | 100.0 | 100.0 | 100.0 |

As regards the geographical area in which fixed-wing aircraft combat losses occurred, the percentage breakdown for each of the services was as follows:

| | USAF | USN | USMC | USA | All services |
|---|---|---|---|---|---|
| N. Vietnam | 36.9 | 83.6 | 17.0 | 0 | 42.8 |
| Laos | 23.9 | 10.7 | 8.8 | 1.3 | 18.6 |
| S. Vietnam | 37.1 | 4.9 | 74.2 | 96.8 | 36.9 |
| Cambodia & others | 2.1 | 0.8 | 0 | 1.9 | 1.7 |

The geographical distribution of helicopter combat losses was as follows:

| | USAF | USN | USMC | USA | All services |
|---|---|---|---|---|---|
| N. Vietnam | 10.3 | 38.5 | 0.4 | 0 | 0.5 |
| Laos | 37.9 | 0 | 3.7 | 4.2 | 4.9 |
| S. Vietnam | 48.3 | 61.5 | 95.9 | 92.7 | 91.9 |
| Cambodia & Others | 3.5 | 0 | 0 | 3.1 | 2.7 |

### Table 1

### US AIRCRAFT AND HELICOPTERS LOST TO ALL CAUSES (Summary)

| | 1962 | 1963 | 1964 | 1965 | 1966 | 1967 | 1968 | 1969 | 1970 | 1971 | 1972 | 1973 | Total 1962-1973 |
|---|---|---|---|---|---|---|---|---|---|---|---|---|---|
| **FIXED-WING AIRCRAFT** | | | | | | | | | | | | | |
| Combat Losses | | | | | | | | | | | | | |
| To MiGs | – | – | – | 4 | 12 | 27 | 12 | 1 | – | 1 | 22 | – | 79 |
| To SAMs | – | – | – | 11 | 34 | 60 | 11 | – | – | 5 | 73 | 3 | 197 |
| To AAA and Small Arms Fire | 7 | 14 | 33 | 245 | 413 | 397 | 377 | 266 | 154 | 81 | 141 | 12 | 2,140 |
| In Enemy Attacks on Air Bases | – | – | 5 | 13 | 6 | 31 | 59 | 21 | 2 | 3 | 5 | – | 145 |
| Sub-total | 7 | 14 | 38 | 273 | 465 | 515 | 459 | 288 | 156 | 90 | 241 | 15 | 2,561 |
| Operational Losses | 3 | 13 | 30 | 119 | 169 | 213 | 198 | 178 | 106 | 55 | 59 | 15 | 1,158 |
| Total Aircraft Losses | 10 | 27 | 68 | 392 | 634 | 728 | 657 | 466 | 262 | 145 | 300 | 30 | 3,719 |
| **HELICOPTERS** | | | | | | | | | | | | | |
| Combat Losses | | | | | | | | | | | | | |
| To MiGs | – | – | – | – | – | – | – | – | 1 | 1 | – | – | 2 |
| To SAMs | – | – | – | – | – | – | – | – | – | – | 7 | – | 7 |
| To AAA and Small Arms Fire | 4 | 9 | 21 | 61 | 125 | 269 | 502 | 493 | 442 | 324 | 119 | 4 | 2,373 |
| In Enemy Attacks on Air Bases | – | – | 1 | 20 | 4 | 16 | 60 | 50 | 30 | 19 | 5 | – | 205 |
| Sub-total | 4 | 9 | 22 | 81 | 129 | 285 | 562 | 543 | 473 | 344 | 131 | 4 | 2,587 |
| Operational Losses | 17 | 25 | 37 | 87 | 192 | 378 | 450 | 505 | 380 | 158 | 48 | 5 | 2,282 |
| Total Helicopter Losses | 21 | 34 | 59 | 168 | 321 | 663 | 1012 | 1048 | 853 | 502 | 179 | 9 | 4,869 |
| TOTAL US AIRCRAFT LOSSES | 31 | 61 | 127 | 560 | 955 | 1391 | 1669 | 1514 | 1115 | 647 | 479 | 39 | 8,588 |

### Table 2

### USAF LOSSES TO ALL CAUSES (Summary)

| | 1962 | 1963 | 1964 | 1965 | 1966 | 1967 | 1968 | 1969 | 1970 | 1971 | 1972 | 1973 | Total 1962-1973 |
|---|---|---|---|---|---|---|---|---|---|---|---|---|---|
| **FIXED-WING AIRCRAFT** | | | | | | | | | | | | | |
| Combat Losses | | | | | | | | | | | | | |
| To MiGs | – | – | – | 3 | 8 | 22 | 9 | – | – | 1 | 19 | – | 62 |
| To SAMs | – | – | – | 5 | 18 | 28 | 3 | – | – | 4 | 51 | 3 | 112 |
| To AAA and Small Arms Fire | 7 | 12 | 24 | 139 | 265 | 252 | 248 | 189 | 117 | 61 | 84 | 8 | 1,406 |
| In Enemy Attacks on Air Bases | – | – | 5 | 11 | 5 | 23 | 35 | 12 | 2 | 1 | 5 | – | 99 |
| Sub-total | 7 | 12 | 29 | 158 | 296 | 325 | 295 | 201 | 119 | 67 | 159 | 11 | 1,679 |
| Operational Losses | 3 | 5 | 10 | 66 | 78 | 86 | 85 | 68 | 41 | 16 | 30 | 7 | 495 |
| Total Aircraft Losses | 10 | 17 | 39 | 224 | 374 | 411 | 380 | 269 | 160 | 83 | 189 | 18 | 2,174 |
| **HELICOPTERS** | | | | | | | | | | | | | |
| Combat Losses | | | | | | | | | | | | | |
| To MiGs | – | – | – | – | – | – | – | – | 1 | – | – | – | 1 |
| To SAMs | – | – | – | – | – | – | – | – | – | – | – | – | 0 |
| To AAA and Small Arms Fire | – | – | – | 3 | 2 | 9 | 9 | 16 | 7 | 4 | 3 | – | 53 |
| In Enemy Attacks on Air Bases | – | – | 1 | – | 1 | – | – | 1 | – | – | 1 | – | 4 |
| Sub-total | – | – | 1 | 3 | 3 | 9 | 9 | 17 | 8 | 4 | 4 | – | 58 |
| Operational Losses | – | – | – | – | 2 | 1 | 2 | 8 | 3 | 1 | – | 1 | 18 |
| Total Helicopter Losses | – | – | 1 | 3 | 5 | 10 | 11 | 25 | 11 | 5 | 4 | 1 | 76 |
| TOTAL USAF LOSSES | 10 | 17 | 40 | 227 | 379 | 421 | 391 | 294 | 171 | 88 | 193 | 19 | 2,250 |

## Table 2A

### USAF LOSSES TO MIGS (by aircraft type and year)

| | 1962 | 1963 | 1964 | 1965 | 1966 | 1967 | 1968 | 1969 | 1970 | 1971 | 1972 | 1973 | Total 1962-1973 |
|---|---|---|---|---|---|---|---|---|---|---|---|---|---|
| A-1 | – | – | – | – | 1 | 1 | – | – | – | – | – | – | 2 |
| EB-66 | – | – | – | – | – | – | 1 | – | – | – | – | – | 1 |
| RC-47 | – | – | – | – | 1 | – | – | – | – | – | – | – | 1 |
| F-4 | – | – | – | – | 3 | 9 | 3 | – | – | 1 | 17 | – | 33 |
| RF-101 | – | – | – | – | – | 1 | – | – | – | – | – | – | 1 |
| F-102 | – | – | – | – | – | – | 1 | – | – | – | – | – | 1 |
| F-105 | – | – | – | 3 | 3 | 11 | 4 | – | – | – | 2 | – | 23 |
| Sub-total fixed-wing | – | – | – | 3 | 8 | 22 | 9 | – | – | 1 | 19 | – | 62 |
| HH-53 | – | – | – | – | – | – | – | – | 1 | – | – | – | 1 |
| Sub-total helicopters | – | – | – | – | – | – | – | – | 1 | – | – | – | 1 |
| TOTAL USAF AIRCRAFT LOST TO MIGS | – | – | – | 3 | 8 | 22 | 9 | – | 1 | 1 | 19 | – | 63 |

## Table 2B

### USAF LOSSES TO SAMS (by aircraft type and year)

| | 1962 | 1963 | 1964 | 1965 | 1966 | 1967 | 1968 | 1969 | 1970 | 1971 | 1972 | 1973 | Total 1962-1973 |
|---|---|---|---|---|---|---|---|---|---|---|---|---|---|
| A-1 | – | – | – | – | – | – | – | – | – | – | 3 | – | 3 |
| B-52 | – | – | – | – | – | – | – | – | – | – | 16 | 2 | 18 |
| EB-66 | – | – | – | – | 2 | 1 | – | – | – | – | 1 | – | 4 |
| AC-130 | – | – | – | – | – | – | – | – | – | – | 2 | – | 2 |
| F-4 | – | – | – | 2 | 6 | 3 | 1 | – | – | 2 | 16 | – | 30 |
| RF-4 | – | – | – | – | – | 4 | – | – | – | – | 3 | – | 7 |
| RF-101 | – | – | – | – | 3 | 2 | – | – | – | – | – | – | 5 |
| F-104 | – | – | – | – | 2 | – | – | – | – | – | – | – | 2 |
| F-105 | – | – | – | 3 | 5 | 17 | 2 | – | – | 1 | 4 | – | 32 |
| O-1 | – | – | – | – | – | 1 | – | – | – | – | – | – | 1 |
| O-2 | – | – | – | – | – | – | – | – | – | 1 | 2 | – | 3 |
| OV-10 | – | – | – | – | – | – | – | – | – | – | 4 | 1 | 5 |
| Sub-total fixed-wing | – | – | – | 5 | 18 | 28 | 3 | – | – | 4 | 51 | 3 | 112 |
| Sub-total helicopters | – | – | – | – | – | – | – | – | – | – | – | – | 0 |
| TOTAL USAF AIRCRAFT LOST TO SAMS | – | – | – | 5 | 18 | 28 | 3 | – | – | 4 | 51 | 3 | 112 |

## Table 2C

### USAF LOSSES TO AAA AND SMALL ARMS FIRE (by aircraft type and year)

| | 1962 | 1963 | 1964 | 1965 | 1966 | 1967 | 1968 | 1969 | 1970 | 1971 | 1972 | 1973 | Total 1962-1973 |
|---|---|---|---|---|---|---|---|---|---|---|---|---|---|
| A-1 | – | – | 7 | 13 | 33 | 14 | 30 | 20 | 17 | 9 | 3 | – | 146 |
| A-7 | – | – | – | – | – | – | – | – | – | – | 2 | 2 | 4 |
| A-26/B-26 | 1 | 7 | 1 | – | 2 | 5 | 1 | 2 | – | – | – | – | 19 |
| A-37 | – | – | – | – | – | 1 | 4 | 1 | 1 | 4 | 3 | – | 14 |
| B-57 | – | – | 1 | 9 | 9 | 6 | 5 | 4 | 1 | – | – | – | 35 |
| EB-66 | – | – | – | 1 | – | – | – | – | – | – | – | – | 1 |
| C-7 | – | – | – | – | – | 1 | 1 | 2 | 3 | – | – | – | 7 |
| C-47/EC-47/RC-47/SC-47 | 1 | – | – | – | – | 1 | 1 | 1 | 1 | – | – | 1 | 6 |
| AC-47 | – | – | – | 2 | 4 | 4 | 4 | 1 | – | – | – | – | 15 |
| AC-119 | – | – | – | – | – | – | – | – | – | – | 1 | – | 1 |
| C-123 | 1 | 1 | 1 | 1 | 6 | 2 | 4 | 1 | – | – | – | – | 17 |
| C-130 | – | – | – | 1 | 3 | 1 | 7 | 5 | – | – | 5 | – | 22 |
| AC-130 | – | – | – | – | – | – | – | 1 | 1 | – | 2 | – | 4 |
| F-4 | – | – | – | 10 | 33 | 63 | 50 | 57 | 30 | 22 | 38 | 4 | 307 |
| RF-4 | – | – | – | – | 7 | 16 | 19 | 8 | 9 | 3 | 3 | – | 65 |
| F-5 | – | – | – | 1 | 6 | – | – | – | – | – | – | – | 7 |
| F-100 | – | – | 2 | 21 | 19 | 30 | 48 | 41 | 17 | 8 | – | – | 186 |
| RF-101 | – | – | 1 | 9 | 13 | 7 | 1 | – | – | – | – | – | 31 |
| F-102 | – | – | – | 1 | 1 | – | – | – | – | – | – | – | 2 |
| F-104 | – | – | – | 3 | 3 | – | – | – | – | – | – | – | 6 |
| F-105 | – | – | 1 | 54 | 103 | 69 | 28 | 16 | 7 | – | 1 | – | 279 |
| F-111 | – | – | – | – | – | – | 2 | – | – | – | 6 | – | 8 |
| O-1 | – | 1 | 3 | 13 | 21 | 24 | 20 | 6 | 4 | 1 | – | – | 93 |
| O-2 | – | – | – | – | – | 4 | 22 | 16 | 11 | 5 | 11 | – | 69 |
| OV-10 | – | – | – | – | – | – | 1 | 6 | 15 | 9 | 9 | 1 | 41 |
| T-28 | 3 | 3 | 7 | – | – | 4 | – | – | – | – | – | – | 17 |
| U-10 | 1 | – | – | – | – | – | – | 1 | – | – | – | – | 2 |
| HU-16 | – | – | – | – | 2 | – | – | – | – | – | – | – | 2 |
| Sub-total fixed-wing | 7 | 12 | 24 | 139 | 265 | 252 | 248 | 189 | 117 | 61 | 84 | 8 | 1,406 |
| UH-1 | – | – | – | – | – | 2 | 2 | 6 | 3 | – | – | – | 13 |
| CH-3/HH-3 | – | – | – | 1 | 1 | 5 | 6 | 7 | 3 | – | – | – | 23 |
| HH-43 | – | – | – | 2 | 1 | 2 | 1 | 2 | – | – | – | – | 8 |
| CH-53/HH-53 | – | – | – | – | – | – | – | 1 | 1 | 4 | 3 | – | 9 |
| Sub-total helicopters | – | – | – | 3 | 2 | 9 | 9 | 16 | 7 | 4 | 3 | – | 53 |
| TOTAL USAF AIRCRAFT LOST TO AAA AND SMALL ARMS | 7 | 12 | 24 | 142 | 267 | 261 | 257 | 205 | 124 | 65 | 87 | 8 | 1,459 |

## Table 2D

## USAF LOSSES DURING ENEMY ATTACKS AGAINST AIR BASES (by aircraft type and year)

| | 1962 | 1963 | 1964 | 1965 | 1966 | 1967 | 1968 | 1969 | 1970 | 1971 | 1972 | 1973 | Total 1962-1973 |
|---|---|---|---|---|---|---|---|---|---|---|---|---|---|
| A-1 | – | – | – | – | 2 | – | – | – | – | – | – | – | 2 |
| A-37 | – | – | – | – | – | – | 1 | – | – | – | 1 | – | 2 |
| B-57 | – | – | 5 | – | – | – | – | – | – | – | – | – | 5 |
| C-7 | – | – | – | – | – | – | 1 | – | – | – | – | – | 1 |
| AC-47 | – | – | – | – | – | – | 2 | – | – | – | – | – | 2 |
| EC-47 | – | – | – | – | – | – | – | – | 1 | – | – | – | 1 |
| AC-119 | – | – | – | – | – | – | – | – | – | – | 1 | – | 1 |
| C-123 | – | – | – | – | 2 | – | 2 | – | – | – | – | – | 4 |
| C-130 | – | – | – | 3 | – | 5 | 1 | 1 | – | 1 | 1 | – | 12 |
| HC-130 | – | – | – | – | – | – | 2 | – | – | – | – | – | 2 |
| F-4 | – | – | – | – | – | 6 | 3 | – | – | – | – | – | 9 |
| RF-4 | – | – | – | – | – | – | 4 | – | – | – | – | – | 4 |
| F-100 | – | – | – | – | – | 1 | 2 | 4 | – | – | – | – | 7 |
| RF-101 | – | – | – | – | – | – | 1 | – | – | – | – | – | 1 |
| F-102 | – | – | – | 3 | – | 1 | – | – | – | – | – | – | 4 |
| O-1 | – | – | – | 5 | 1 | 8 | 8 | 5 | 1 | – | – | – | 28 |
| O-2 | – | – | – | – | – | 2 | 6 | 1 | – | – | 1 | – | 10 |
| OV-10 | – | – | – | – | – | – | – | – | – | – | 1 | – | 1 |
| U-3 | – | – | – | – | – | – | 1 | – | – | – | – | – | 1 |
| U-10 | – | – | – | – | – | – | 1 | 1 | – | – | – | – | 2 |
| Sub-total fixed-wing | – | – | 5 | 11 | 5 | 23 | 35 | 12 | 2 | 1 | 5 | – | 99 |
| CH-3 | – | – | – | – | – | – | – | 1 | – | – | – | – | 1 |
| HH-43 | – | – | 1 | – | 1 | – | – | – | – | – | – | – | 2 |
| HH-53 | – | – | – | – | – | – | – | – | – | – | 1 | – | 1 |
| Sub-total helicopters | – | – | 1 | – | 1 | – | – | 1 | – | – | 1 | – | 4 |
| TOTAL USAF AIRCRAFT LOST AT AIR BASES | – | – | 6 | 11 | 6 | 23 | 35 | 13 | 2 | 1 | 6 | – | 103 |

## Table 2E

## USAF COMBAT LOSSES (by aircraft type and year)

| | 1962 | 1963 | 1964 | 1965 | 1966 | 1967 | 1968 | 1969 | 1970 | 1971 | 1972 | 1973 | Total 1962-1973 |
|---|---|---|---|---|---|---|---|---|---|---|---|---|---|
| A-1 | – | – | 7 | 13 | 36 | 15 | 30 | 20 | 17 | 9 | 6 | – | 153 |
| A-7 | – | – | – | – | – | – | – | – | – | – | 2 | 2 | 4 |
| A-26/B-26 | 1 | 7 | 1 | – | 2 | 5 | 1 | 2 | – | – | – | – | 19 |
| A-37 | – | – | – | – | – | 1 | 5 | 1 | 1 | 4 | 4 | – | 16 |
| B-52 | – | – | – | – | – | – | – | – | – | – | 16 | 2 | 18 |
| B-57 | – | – | 6 | 9 | 9 | 6 | 5 | 4 | 1 | – | – | – | 40 |
| EB-66 | – | – | – | 1 | 2 | 1 | 1 | – | – | – | 1 | – | 6 |
| C-7 | – | – | – | – | – | 1 | 2 | 2 | 3 | – | – | – | 8 |
| C-47/EC-47/RC-47/SC-47 | 1 | – | – | – | 1 | 1 | 1 | 1 | 2 | – | – | 1 | 8 |
| AC-47 | – | – | – | 2 | 4 | 4 | 6 | 1 | – | – | – | – | 17 |
| AC-119 | – | – | – | – | – | – | – | – | – | – | 2 | – | 2 |
| C-123 | 1 | 1 | 1 | 1 | 8 | 2 | 6 | 1 | – | – | – | – | 21 |
| C-130 | – | – | – | 4 | 3 | 6 | 8 | 6 | – | 1 | 6 | – | 34 |
| AC-130 | – | – | – | – | – | – | – | 1 | 1 | – | 4 | – | 6 |
| HC-130 | – | – | – | – | – | – | 2 | – | – | – | – | – | 2 |
| F-4 | – | – | – | 12 | 42 | 81 | 57 | 57 | 30 | 25 | 71 | 4 | 379 |
| RF-4 | – | – | – | – | 7 | 20 | 23 | 8 | 9 | 3 | 6 | – | 76 |
| F-5 | – | – | – | 1 | 6 | – | – | – | – | – | – | – | 7 |
| F-100 | – | – | 2 | 21 | 22 | 33 | 50 | 45 | 17 | 8 | – | – | 198 |
| RF-101 | – | – | 1 | 9 | 13 | 8 | 2 | – | – | – | – | – | 33 |
| F-102 | – | – | – | 4 | 1 | 1 | 1 | – | – | – | – | – | 7 |
| F-104 | – | – | – | 3 | 5 | – | – | – | – | – | – | – | 8 |
| F-105 | – | – | 1 | 60 | 111 | 97 | 34 | 16 | 7 | 1 | 7 | – | 334 |
| F-111 | – | – | – | – | – | – | 2 | – | – | – | 6 | – | 8 |
| O-1 | – | 1 | 3 | 18 | 22 | 33 | 28 | 11 | 5 | 1 | – | – | 122 |
| O-2 | – | – | – | – | – | 6 | 28 | 17 | 11 | 6 | 14 | – | 82 |
| OV-10 | – | – | – | – | – | – | 1 | 6 | 15 | 9 | 14 | 2 | 47 |
| T-28 | 3 | 3 | 7 | – | – | 4 | – | – | – | – | – | – | 17 |
| U-3 | – | – | – | – | – | – | 1 | – | – | – | – | – | 1 |
| U-10 | 1 | – | – | – | – | – | 1 | 2 | – | – | – | – | 4 |
| HU-16 | – | – | – | – | 2 | – | – | – | – | – | – | – | 2 |
| Sub-total fixed-wing | 7 | 12 | 29 | 158 | 296 | 325 | 295 | 201 | 119 | 67 | 159 | 11 | 1,679 |
| UH-1 | – | – | – | – | – | 2 | 2 | 6 | 3 | – | – | – | 13 |
| CH-3/HH-3 | – | – | – | 1 | 1 | 5 | 6 | 8 | 3 | – | – | – | 24 |
| HH-43 | – | – | 1 | 2 | 2 | 2 | 1 | 2 | – | – | – | – | 10 |
| CH-53/HH-53 | – | – | – | – | – | – | – | 1 | 2 | 4 | 4 | – | 11 |
| Sub-total helicopters | – | – | 1 | 3 | 3 | 9 | 9 | 17 | 8 | 4 | 4 | – | 58 |
| TOTAL USAF AIRCRAFT COMBAT LOSSES | 7 | 12 | 30 | 161 | 299 | 334 | 304 | 218 | 127 | 71 | 163 | 11 | 1,737 |

## Table 2F
## USAF OPERATIONAL LOSSES (by aircraft type and year)

| | 1962 | 1963 | 1964 | 1965 | 1966 | 1967 | 1968 | 1969 | 1970 | 1971 | 1972 | 1973 | Total 1962-1973 |
|---|---|---|---|---|---|---|---|---|---|---|---|---|---|
| A-1 | – | – | 1 | 12 | 5 | 1 | 6 | 9 | 4 | 2 | 1 | – | 41 |
| A-7 | – | – | – | – | – | – | – | – | – | – | – | 2 | 2 |
| A-26/B-26 | – | – | – | – | 1 | – | – | 1 | – | – | – | – | 2 |
| A-37 | – | – | – | – | – | 1 | 2 | 1 | – | – | 2 | – | 6 |
| KB-50 | – | – | 1 | – | – | – | – | – | – | – | – | – | 1 |
| B-52 | – | – | – | 2 | – | 3 | – | 1 | – | – | 2 | – | 8 |
| B-57 | – | – | 1 | 12 | 4 | – | 1 | – | – | – | – | – | 18 |
| EB-66 | – | – | – | – | – | 2 | 2 | 1 | 1 | 2 | 1 | – | 9 |
| C-7 | – | – | – | – | – | 2 | 5 | 3 | 1 | 1 | – | – | 12 |
| C-47/EC-47/RC-47/SC-47 | – | 1 | 1 | 1 | 2 | 1 | 2 | 3 | 1 | – | 1 | – | 13 |
| AC-47 | – | – | – | – | – | 2 | – | – | – | – | – | – | 2 |
| AC-119 | – | – | – | – | – | – | – | 1 | 3 | – | – | – | 4 |
| EC-121 | – | – | – | – | – | – | – | 2 | – | – | – | – | 2 |
| C-123 | 3 | 2 | 1 | 6 | 3 | 5 | 4 | 2 | 4 | 2 | – | – | 32 |
| C-130 | – | – | – | 3 | 3 | 8 | 6 | 1 | – | – | – | – | 21 |
| KC-135 | – | – | – | – | – | – | 1 | – | – | – | – | – | 1 |
| C-141 | – | – | – | – | – | 2 | – | – | – | – | – | – | 2 |
| F-4 | – | – | 1 | 1 | 14 | 16 | 6 | 7 | 3 | 2 | 11 | 2 | 63 |
| RF-4 | – | – | – | – | – | 3 | 2 | 2 | – | – | – | – | 7 |
| F-5 | – | – | – | – | 1 | 1 | – | – | – | – | – | – | 2 |
| F-100 | – | – | – | 5 | 4 | 3 | 12 | 9 | 9 | 3 | – | – | 45 |
| RF-101 | – | – | – | – | 3 | 3 | – | – | – | – | – | – | 6 |
| F-102 | – | – | 1 | – | 2 | 2 | 2 | 1 | – | – | – | – | 8 |
| F-104 | – | – | – | 2 | – | 4 | – | – | – | – | – | – | 6 |
| F-105 | – | – | – | 8 | 15 | 16 | 13 | 5 | 3 | – | 3 | – | 63 |
| F-111 | – | – | – | – | – | – | 1 | – | – | – | – | 2 | 3 |
| O-1 | – | 1 | – | 11 | 16 | 7 | 10 | 3 | 2 | – | – | – | 50 |
| O-2 | – | – | – | – | – | 1 | 7 | 8 | 5 | 1 | – | – | 22 |
| OV-10 | – | – | – | – | – | – | 1 | 5 | 4 | 1 | 4 | 1 | 16 |
| U-2 | – | – | – | – | 1 | – | – | – | – | – | – | – | 1 |
| U-6 | – | – | – | – | 1 | – | – | – | – | – | – | – | 1 |
| U-10 | – | – | 1 | 1 | 2 | 3 | – | 1 | – | – | – | – | 8 |
| HU-16 | – | – | – | 2 | – | – | – | – | – | – | – | – | 2 |
| QU-22 | – | – | – | – | – | – | – | 2 | 1 | 2 | 5 | – | 10 |
| T-28 | – | 1 | 2 | – | 1 | – | 2 | – | – | – | – | – | 6 |
| Sub-total fixed-wing | 3 | 5 | 10 | 66 | 78 | 86 | 85 | 68 | 41 | 16 | 30 | 7 | 495 |
| UH-1 | – | – | – | – | – | 1 | – | 3 | 1 | 1 | – | – | 6 |
| CH-3/HH-3 | – | – | – | – | 2 | – | 1 | 2 | 2 | – | – | – | 7 |
| HH-43 | – | – | – | – | – | – | – | 3 | – | – | – | – | 3 |
| HH-53 | – | – | – | – | – | – | 1 | – | – | – | – | 1 | 2 |
| Sub-total helicopters | – | – | – | – | 2 | 1 | 2 | 8 | 3 | 1 | – | 1 | 18 |
| TOTAL USAF OPERATIONAL LOSSES | 3 | 5 | 10 | 66 | 80 | 87 | 87 | 76 | 44 | 17 | 30 | 8 | 513 |

## Table 3
## USN LOSSES TO ALL CAUSES (Summary)

| | 1962 | 1963 | 1964 | 1965 | 1966 | 1967 | 1968 | 1969 | 1970 | 1971 | 1972 | 1973 | Total 1962-1973 |
|---|---|---|---|---|---|---|---|---|---|---|---|---|---|
| **FIXED-WING AIRCRAFT** | | | | | | | | | | | | | |
| Combat Losses | | | | | | | | | | | | | |
| To MiGs | – | – | – | 1 | 4 | 5 | 3 | – | – | – | 2 | – | 15 |
| To SAMs | – | – | – | 6 | 15 | 30 | 7 | – | – | 1 | 22 | – | 81 |
| To AAA and Small Arms Fire | – | – | 4 | 91 | 105 | 99 | 55 | 16 | 14 | 4 | 43 | 4 | 435 |
| In Enemy Attacks on Air Bases | – | – | – | – | – | – | – | – | – | – | – | – | 0 |
| Sub-total | – | – | 4 | 98 | 124 | 134 | 65 | 16 | 14 | 5 | 67 | 4 | 531 |
| Operational Losses | – | – | 15 | 27 | 39 | 52 | 43 | 45 | 30 | 16 | 24 | 8 | 299 |
| Total Aircraft Losses | – | – | 19 | 125 | 163 | 186 | 108 | 61 | 44 | 21 | 91 | 12 | 830 |
| **HELICOPTERS** | | | | | | | | | | | | | |
| Combat Losses | | | | | | | | | | | | | |
| To MiGs | – | – | – | – | – | – | – | – | – | – | – | – | 0 |
| To SAMs | – | – | – | – | – | – | – | – | – | – | – | – | 0 |
| To AAA and Small Arms Fire | – | – | – | 1 | 3 | 5 | 4 | – | – | – | – | – | 13 |
| In Enemy Attacks on Air Bases | – | – | – | – | – | – | – | – | – | – | – | – | 0 |
| Sub-total | – | – | – | 1 | 3 | 5 | 4 | – | – | – | – | – | 13 |
| Operational Losses | – | – | 3 | 3 | 8 | 9 | 5 | 3 | 1 | – | 2 | 1 | 35 |
| Total Helicopter Losses | – | – | 3 | 4 | 11 | 14 | 9 | 3 | 1 | – | 2 | 1 | 48 |
| TOTAL USN LOSSES | – | – | 22 | 129 | 174 | 200 | 117 | 64 | 45 | 21 | 93 | 13 | 878 |

## Table 3A
## USN LOSSES TO MIGS (by aircraft type and year)

| | 1962 | 1963 | 1964 | 1965 | 1966 | 1967 | 1968 | 1969 | 1970 | 1971 | 1972 | 1973 | Total 1962-1973 |
|---|---|---|---|---|---|---|---|---|---|---|---|---|---|
| A-1 | – | – | – | – | – | – | 1 | – | – | – | – | – | 1 |
| A-3 | – | – | – | – | 1 | – | – | – | – | – | – | – | 1 |
| A-4 | – | – | – | – | – | 1 | – | – | – | – | 1 | – | 2 |
| A-6 | – | – | – | – | – | 2 | – | – | – | – | – | – | 2 |
| F-4 | – | – | – | 1 | – | 1 | 2 | – | – | – | 1 | – | 5 |
| F-8 | – | – | – | – | 3 | 1 | – | – | – | – | – | – | 4 |
| Sub-total fixed-wing | – | – | – | 1 | 4 | 5 | 3 | – | – | – | 2 | – | 15 |
| Sub-total helicopters | – | – | – | – | – | – | – | – | – | – | – | – | 0 |
| TOTAL USN AIRCRAFT LOST TO MIGS | – | – | – | 1 | 4 | 5 | 3 | – | – | – | 2 | – | 15 |

## Table 3B

### USN LOSSES TO SAMS (by aircraft type and year)

| | 1962 | 1963 | 1964 | 1965 | 1966 | 1967 | 1968 | 1969 | 1970 | 1971 | 1972 | 1973 | Total 1962-1973 |
|---|---|---|---|---|---|---|---|---|---|---|---|---|---|
| A-1 | – | – | – | – | 2 | – | – | – | – | – | – | – | 2 |
| A-4 | – | – | – | 1 | 9 | 18 | 2 | – | – | – | 1 | – | 31 |
| RA-5C | – | – | – | 1 | 1 | – | – | – | – | – | 1 | – | 3 |
| A-6 | – | – | – | 1 | 1 | 2 | 1 | – | – | – | 1 | – | 6 |
| A-7 | – | – | – | – | – | 1 | 1 | – | – | – | 14 | – | 16 |
| F-4 | – | – | – | 1 | – | 5 | 1 | – | – | 1 | 5 | – | 13 |
| F-8 | – | – | – | 2 | 2 | 4 | 2 | – | – | – | – | – | 10 |
| Sub-total fixed-wing | – | – | – | 6 | 15 | 30 | 7 | – | – | 1 | 22 | – | 81 |
| Sub-total helicopters | – | – | – | – | – | – | – | – | – | – | – | – | 0 |
| TOTAL USN AIRCRAFT LOST TO SAMS | – | – | – | 6 | 15 | 30 | 7 | – | – | 1 | 22 | – | 81 |

## Table 3C

### USN LOSSES TO AAA AND SMALL ARMS FIRE (by aircraft type and year)

| | 1962 | 1963 | 1964 | 1965 | 1966 | 1967 | 1968 | 1969 | 1970 | 1971 | 1972 | 1973 | Total 1962-1973 |
|---|---|---|---|---|---|---|---|---|---|---|---|---|---|
| A-1/EA-1 | – | – | 1 | 19 | 18 | 7 | – | – | – | – | – | – | 45 |
| A-3/EA-3/EKA-3/KA-3/RA-3 | – | – | – | – | 1 | 3 | 1 | – | – | – | – | – | 5 |
| A-4 | – | – | 1 | 35 | 46 | 49 | 20 | 5 | 3 | – | 4 | – | 163 |
| RA-5 | – | – | – | 3 | 2 | 4 | 3 | 1 | – | – | 2 | – | 15 |
| A-6/EA-6/KA-6 | – | – | – | 4 | 6 | 5 | 12 | 3 | 2 | 1 | 8 | 2 | 43 |
| A-7 | – | – | – | – | – | – | 6 | 4 | 6 | 2 | 20 | – | 38 |
| F-4 | – | – | – | 8 | 15 | 17 | 5 | 1 | – | – | 5 | 2 | 53 |
| F-8 | – | – | 1 | 15 | 10 | 12 | 2 | – | – | – | 2 | – | 42 |
| RF-8 | – | – | 1 | 7 | 6 | 2 | 2 | – | – | – | 2 | – | 20 |
| OV-10 | – | – | – | – | – | – | – | 2 | 3 | 1 | – | – | 6 |
| P-2/OP-2 | – | – | – | – | – | – | 3 | – | – | – | – | – | 3 |
| P-3 | – | – | – | – | – | – | 1 | – | – | – | – | – | 1 |
| S-2 | – | – | – | – | 1 | – | – | – | – | – | – | – | 1 |
| Sub-total fixed-wing | – | – | 4 | 91 | 105 | 99 | 55 | 16 | 14 | 4 | 43 | 4 | 435 |
| UH-2 | – | – | – | – | – | 1 | – | – | – | – | – | – | 1 |
| SH-3 | – | – | – | 1 | 1 | 2 | – | – | – | – | – | – | 4 |
| UH-34 | – | – | – | – | 2 | 2 | 2 | – | – | – | – | – | 6 |
| CH-46 | – | – | – | – | – | – | 2 | – | – | – | – | – | 2 |
| Sub-total helicopters | – | – | – | 1 | 3 | 5 | 4 | – | – | – | – | – | 13 |
| TOTAL USN AIRCRAFT LOST TO AAA AND SMALL ARMS | – | – | 4 | 92 | 108 | 104 | 59 | 16 | 14 | 4 | 43 | 4 | 448 |

## Table 3D

### USN LOSSES DURING ENEMY ATTACKS AGAINST AIR BASES (by aircraft type and year)

| 1962 | 1963 | 1964 | 1965 | 1966 | 1967 | 1968 | 1969 | 1970 | 1971 | 1972 | 1973 | Total 1962-1973 |
|---|---|---|---|---|---|---|---|---|---|---|---|---|

* * * NONE * * *

## Table 3E

### USN COMBAT LOSSES (by aircraft type and year)

| | 1962 | 1963 | 1964 | 1965 | 1966 | 1967 | 1968 | 1969 | 1970 | 1971 | 1972 | 1973 | Total 1962-1973 |
|---|---|---|---|---|---|---|---|---|---|---|---|---|---|
| A-1/EA-1 | – | – | 1 | 19 | 20 | 7 | 1 | – | – | – | – | – | 48 |
| A-3/EA-3/EKA-3/KA-3/RA-3 | – | – | – | – | 2 | 3 | 1 | – | – | – | – | – | 6 |
| A-4 | – | – | 1 | 36 | 55 | 68 | 22 | 5 | 3 | – | 6 | – | 196 |
| RA-5 | – | – | – | 4 | 3 | 4 | 3 | 1 | – | – | 3 | – | 18 |
| A-6/EA-6/KA-6 | – | – | – | 5 | 7 | 9 | 13 | 3 | 2 | 1 | 9 | 2 | 51 |
| A-7 | – | – | – | – | – | 1 | 7 | 4 | 6 | 2 | 34 | – | 54 |
| F-4 | – | – | – | 10 | 15 | 23 | 8 | 1 | – | 1 | 11 | 2 | 71 |
| F-8 | – | – | 1 | 17 | 15 | 17 | 4 | – | – | – | 2 | – | 56 |
| RF-8 | – | – | 1 | 7 | 6 | 2 | 2 | – | – | – | 2 | – | 20 |
| OV-10 | – | – | – | – | – | – | – | 2 | 3 | 1 | – | – | 6 |
| P-2/OP-2 | – | – | – | – | – | – | 3 | – | – | – | – | – | 3 |
| P-3 | – | – | – | – | – | – | 1 | – | – | – | – | – | 1 |
| S-2 | – | – | – | – | 1 | – | – | – | – | – | – | – | 1 |
| Sub-total fixed-wing | – | – | 4 | 98 | 124 | 134 | 65 | 16 | 14 | 5 | 67 | 4 | 531 |
| UH-2 | – | – | – | – | – | 1 | – | – | – | – | – | – | 1 |
| SH-3 | – | – | – | 1 | 1 | 2 | – | – | – | – | – | – | 4 |
| UH-34 | – | – | – | – | 2 | 2 | 2 | – | – | – | – | – | 6 |
| CH-46 | – | – | – | – | – | – | 2 | – | – | – | – | – | 2 |
| Sub-total helicopters | – | – | – | 1 | 3 | 5 | 4 | – | – | – | – | – | 13 |
| TOTAL USN AIRCRAFT COMBAT LOSSES | – | – | 4 | 99 | 127 | 139 | 69 | 16 | 14 | 5 | 67 | 4 | 544 |

## Table 3F

### USN OPERATIONAL LOSSES (by aircraft type and year)

| | 1962 | 1963 | 1964 | 1965 | 1966 | 1967 | 1968 | 1969 | 1970 | 1971 | 1972 | 1973 | Total 1962-1973 |
|---|---|---|---|---|---|---|---|---|---|---|---|---|---|
| A-1 | – | – | 1 | 5 | 9 | 3 | – | – | – | – | – | – | 18 |
| A-3/EA-3/EKA-3/KA-3/RA-3 | – | – | – | 1 | 1 | 3 | – | 2 | 2 | 1 | – | 1 | 11 |
| A-4 | – | – | 6 | 5 | 19 | 18 | 9 | 10 | 8 | 1 | 1 | – | 77 |
| RA-5C | – | – | 1 | 1 | 1 | 4 | – | – | – | 1 | – | 1 | 9 |
| A-6/EA-6/KA-6 | – | – | – | – | 1 | – | 3 | 1 | – | 3 | 3 | – | 11 |
| A-7 | – | – | – | – | – | – | 7 | 10 | 8 | 5 | 10 | 2 | 42 |
| C-1 | – | – | – | – | – | – | 1 | – | – | – | – | – | 1 |
| C-47 | – | – | – | – | – | 1 | – | – | – | – | – | – | 1 |
| E-1 | – | – | – | 1 | 1 | 1 | – | – | – | – | – | – | 3 |
| E-2 | – | – | – | – | – | – | – | – | 1 | – | – | – | 1 |
| F-4 | – | – | 1 | 4 | 3 | 13 | 12 | 5 | 5 | 2 | 5 | 4 | 54 |
| F-8 | – | – | 3 | 9 | 3 | 9 | 9 | 15 | 5 | 3 | 2 | – | 58 |
| RF-8 | – | – | 1 | 1 | 1 | – | 1 | 2 | 1 | – | 2 | – | 9 |
| OV-10 | – | – | – | – | – | – | – | – | – | – | 1 | – | 1 |
| P-2 | – | – | 1 | – | – | – | – | – | – | – | – | – | 1 |
| P-3 | – | – | – | – | – | – | 1 | – | – | – | – | – | 1 |
| S-2 | – | – | 1 | – | – | – | – | – | – | – | – | – | 1 |
| Sub-total fixed-wing | – | – | 15 | 27 | 39 | 52 | 43 | 45 | 30 | 16 | 24 | 8 | 299 |
| UH-2 | – | – | 3 | – | 2 | 1 | 2 | 2 | – | – | – | – | 10 |
| SH-3 | – | – | – | – | 1 | 2 | – | – | 1 | – | 2 | – | 6 |
| UH-34 | – | – | – | 3 | 5 | 5 | 1 | – | – | – | – | – | 14 |
| CH-46 | – | – | – | – | – | 1 | 2 | 1 | – | – | – | – | 4 |
| CH-53 | – | – | – | – | – | – | – | – | – | – | – | 1 | 1 |
| Sub-total helicopters | – | – | 3 | 3 | 8 | 9 | 5 | 3 | 1 | – | 2 | 1 | 35 |
| TOTAL USN OPERATIONAL LOSSES | – | – | 18 | 30 | 47 | 61 | 48 | 48 | 31 | 16 | 26 | 9 | 334 |

## Table 4

### USMC LOSSES TO ALL CAUSES (Summary)

| | 1962 | 1963 | 1964 | 1965 | 1966 | 1967 | 1968 | 1969 | 1970 | 1971 | 1972 | 1973 | Total 1962-1973 |
|---|---|---|---|---|---|---|---|---|---|---|---|---|---|
| **FIXED-WING AIRCRAFT** | | | | | | | | | | | | | |
| Combat Losses | | | | | | | | | | | | | |
| To MiGs | – | – | – | – | – | – | – | – | – | – | 1 | – | 1 |
| To SAMs | – | – | – | – | 1 | 2 | 1 | – | – | – | – | – | 4 |
| To AAA and Small Arms Fire | – | – | – | 4 | 23 | 35 | 50 | 34 | 17 | 1 | 13 | – | 177 |
| In Enemy Attacks on Air Bases | – | – | – | 2 | – | 2 | 8 | – | – | – | – | – | 12 |
| Sub-total | – | – | – | 6 | 24 | 39 | 59 | 34 | 17 | 1 | 14 | – | 194 |
| Operational Losses | – | – | 1 | 10 | 12 | 23 | 15 | 13 | 5 | – | 3 | – | 82 |
| Total Aircraft Losses | – | – | 1 | 16 | 36 | 62 | 74 | 47 | 22 | 1 | 17 | – | 276 |
| **HELICOPTERS** | | | | | | | | | | | | | |
| Combat Losses | | | | | | | | | | | | | |
| To MiGs | – | – | – | – | – | – | – | – | – | – | – | – | 0 |
| To SAMs | – | – | – | – | – | – | – | – | – | – | 1 | – | 1 |
| To AAA and Small Arms Fire | – | 1 | 4 | 15 | 29 | 50 | 68 | 42 | 24 | 4 | 1 | – | 238 |
| In Enemy Attacks on Air Bases | – | – | – | 20 | – | 5 | 6 | – | – | – | – | – | 31 |
| Sub-total | – | 1 | 4 | 35 | 29 | 55 | 74 | 42 | 24 | 4 | 2 | – | 270 |
| Operational Losses | 2 | 6 | 5 | 12 | 16 | 33 | 29 | 29 | 17 | 2 | 2 | 1 | 154 |
| Total Helicopter Losses | 2 | 7 | 9 | 47 | 45 | 88 | 103 | 71 | 41 | 6 | 4 | 1 | 424 |
| TOTAL USMC LOSSES | 2 | 7 | 10 | 63 | 81 | 150 | 177 | 118 | 63 | 7 | 21 | 1 | 700 |

## Table 4A

### USMC LOSSES TO MIGS (by aircraft type and year)

| | 1962 | 1963 | 1964 | 1965 | 1966 | 1967 | 1968 | 1969 | 1970 | 1971 | 1972 | 1973 | Total 1962-1973 |
|---|---|---|---|---|---|---|---|---|---|---|---|---|---|
| F-4 | – | – | – | – | – | – | – | – | – | – | 1 | – | 1 |
| TOTAL USMC AIRCRAFT LOST TO MIGS | – | – | – | – | – | – | – | – | – | – | 1 | – | 1 |

## Table 4B

### USMC LOSSES TO SAMS (by aircraft type and year)

| | 1962 | 1963 | 1964 | 1965 | 1966 | 1967 | 1968 | 1969 | 1970 | 1971 | 1972 | 1973 | Total 1962-1973 |
|---|---|---|---|---|---|---|---|---|---|---|---|---|---|
| A-4 | – | – | – | – | – | 2 | – | – | – | – | – | – | 2 |
| A-6 | – | – | – | – | – | – | 1 | – | – | – | – | – | 1 |
| EF-10 | – | – | – | – | 1 | – | – | – | – | – | – | – | 1 |
| Sub-total fixed-wing | – | – | – | – | 1 | 2 | 1 | – | – | – | – | – | 4 |
| CH-53 | – | – | – | – | – | – | – | – | – | – | 1 | – | 1 |
| Sub-total helicopters | – | – | – | – | – | – | – | – | – | – | 1 | – | 1 |
| TOTAL USMC AIRCRAFT LOST TO SAMS | – | – | – | – | 1 | 2 | 1 | – | – | – | 1 | – | 5 |

## Table 4C
## USMC LOSSES TO AAA AND SMALL ARMS FIRE (by aircraft type and year)

| | 1962 | 1963 | 1964 | 1965 | 1966 | 1967 | 1968 | 1969 | 1970 | 1971 | 1972 | 1973 | Total 1962-1973 |
|---|---|---|---|---|---|---|---|---|---|---|---|---|---|
| A-4/TA-4 | – | – | – | 1 | 9 | 14 | 19 | 13 | 7 | – | 3 | – | 66 |
| A-6/EA-6 | – | – | – | – | – | 4 | 3 | 4 | – | – | 4 | – | 15 |
| KC-130 | – | – | – | – | 1 | – | 1 | – | – | – | – | – | 2 |
| F-4 | – | – | – | 1 | 10 | 10 | 16 | 13 | 9 | – | 6 | – | 65 |
| RF-4 | – | – | – | – | – | 1 | 2 | – | – | – | – | – | 3 |
| F-8 | – | – | – | 2 | 3 | 4 | 3 | – | – | – | – | – | 12 |
| TF-9 | – | – | – | – | – | 1 | – | – | – | – | – | – | 1 |
| EF-10 | – | – | – | – | – | 1 | 2 | – | – | – | – | – | 3 |
| O-1 | – | – | – | – | – | – | 1 | 1 | – | – | – | – | 2 |
| OV-10 | – | – | – | – | – | – | 3 | 3 | 1 | 1 | – | – | 8 |
| Sub-total fixed-wing | – | – | – | 4 | 23 | 35 | 50 | 34 | 17 | 1 | 13 | – | 177 |
| AH-1 | – | – | – | – | – | – | – | 2 | 5 | – | – | – | 7 |
| UH-1 | – | – | – | 3 | 4 | 13 | 18 | 9 | 5 | 1 | – | – | 53 |
| UH-34 | – | 1 | 4 | 11 | 17 | 20 | 11 | – | – | – | – | – | 64 |
| CH-37 | – | – | – | 1 | – | – | – | – | – | – | – | – | 1 |
| CH-46 | – | – | – | – | 8 | 17 | 36 | 30 | 12 | 3 | – | – | 106 |
| CH-53 | – | – | – | – | – | – | 3 | 1 | 2 | – | 1 | – | 7 |
| Sub-total helicopters | – | 1 | 4 | 15 | 29 | 50 | 68 | 42 | 24 | 4 | 1 | – | 238 |
| TOTAL USMC AIRCRAFT LOST TO AAA AND SMALL ARMS | – | 1 | 4 | 19 | 52 | 85 | 118 | 76 | 41 | 5 | 14 | – | 415 |

## Table 4D
## USMC LOSSES DURING ENEMY ATTACKS AGAINST AIR BASES (by aircraft type and year)

| | 1962 | 1963 | 1964 | 1965 | 1966 | 1967 | 1968 | 1969 | 1970 | 1971 | 1972 | 1973 | Total 1962-1973 |
|---|---|---|---|---|---|---|---|---|---|---|---|---|---|
| A-4 | – | – | – | 2 | – | – | – | – | – | – | – | – | 2 |
| A-6 | – | – | – | – | – | – | 2 | – | – | – | – | – | 2 |
| F-4 | – | – | – | – | – | – | 6 | – | – | – | – | – | 6 |
| F-8 | – | – | – | – | – | 2 | – | – | – | – | – | – | 2 |
| Sub-total fixed-wing | – | – | – | 2 | – | 2 | 8 | – | – | – | – | – | 12 |
| UH-1 | – | – | – | 13 | – | 2 | 1 | – | – | – | – | – | 16 |
| UH-34 | – | – | – | 7 | – | 2 | 2 | – | – | – | – | – | 11 |
| CH-46 | – | – | – | – | – | 1 | 2 | – | – | – | – | – | 3 |
| CH-53 | – | – | – | – | – | – | 1 | – | – | – | – | – | 1 |
| Sub-total helicopters | – | – | – | 20 | – | 5 | 6 | – | – | – | – | – | 31 |
| TOTAL USMC AIRCRAFT LOST AT AIR BASES | – | – | – | 22 | – | 7 | 14 | – | – | – | – | – | 43 |

## Table 4E
## USMC COMBAT LOSSES (by aircraft type and year)

| | 1962 | 1963 | 1964 | 1965 | 1966 | 1967 | 1968 | 1969 | 1970 | 1971 | 1972 | 1973 | Total 1962-1973 |
|---|---|---|---|---|---|---|---|---|---|---|---|---|---|
| A-4/TA-4 | – | – | – | 3 | 9 | 16 | 19 | 13 | 7 | – | 3 | – | 70 |
| A-6/EA-6 | – | – | – | – | – | 4 | 6 | 4 | – | – | 4 | – | 18 |
| KC-130 | – | – | – | – | 1 | – | 1 | – | – | – | – | – | 2 |
| F-4 | – | – | – | 1 | 10 | 10 | 22 | 13 | 9 | – | 7 | – | 72 |
| RF-4 | – | – | – | – | – | 1 | 2 | – | – | – | – | – | 3 |
| F-8 | – | – | – | 2 | 3 | 6 | 3 | – | – | – | – | – | 14 |
| TF-9 | – | – | – | – | – | 1 | – | – | – | – | – | – | 1 |
| EF-10 | – | – | – | – | 1 | 1 | 2 | – | – | – | – | – | 4 |
| O-1 | – | – | – | – | – | – | 1 | 1 | – | – | – | – | 2 |
| OV-10 | – | – | – | – | – | – | 3 | 3 | 1 | 1 | – | – | 8 |
| Sub-total fixed-wing | – | – | – | 6 | 24 | 39 | 59 | 34 | 17 | 1 | 14 | – | 194 |
| AH-1 | – | – | – | – | – | – | – | 2 | 5 | – | – | – | 7 |
| UH-1 | – | – | – | 16 | 4 | 15 | 19 | 9 | 5 | 1 | – | – | 69 |
| UH-34 | – | 1 | 4 | 18 | 17 | 22 | 13 | – | – | – | – | – | 75 |
| CH-37 | – | – | – | 1 | – | – | – | – | – | – | – | – | 1 |
| CH-46 | – | – | – | – | 8 | 18 | 38 | 30 | 12 | 3 | – | – | 109 |
| CH-53 | – | – | – | – | – | – | 4 | 1 | 2 | – | 2 | – | 9 |
| Sub-total helicopters | – | 1 | 4 | 35 | 29 | 55 | 74 | 42 | 24 | 4 | 2 | – | 270 |
| TOTAL USMC AIRCRAFT COMBAT LOSSES | – | 1 | 4 | 41 | 53 | 94 | 133 | 76 | 41 | 5 | 16 | – | 464 |

## Table 4F
## USMC OPERATIONAL LOSSES (by aircraft type and year)

| | 1962 | 1963 | 1964 | 1965 | 1966 | 1967 | 1968 | 1969 | 1970 | 1971 | 1972 | 1973 | Total 1962-1973 |
|---|---|---|---|---|---|---|---|---|---|---|---|---|---|
| A-4/TA-4 | – | – | – | 2 | 6 | 9 | 10 | 2 | 1 | – | 1 | – | 31 |
| A-6/EA-6 | – | – | – | – | – | 2 | 2 | 2 | – | – | – | – | 6 |
| C-117 | – | – | – | – | 1 | – | – | 1 | – | – | – | – | 2 |
| KC-130 | – | – | – | 1 | – | – | – | 1 | – | – | – | – | 2 |
| F-4 | – | – | – | 2 | 2 | 6 | 2 | 5 | 4 | – | 2 | – | 23 |
| RF-4 | – | – | – | – | – | 1 | – | – | – | – | – | – | 1 |
| F-8 | – | – | – | 2 | 2 | 3 | 1 | – | – | – | – | – | 8 |
| RF-8 | – | – | – | 1 | – | – | – | – | – | – | – | – | 1 |
| EF-10 | – | – | – | 1 | – | – | – | – | – | – | – | – | 1 |
| O-1 | – | – | 1 | 1 | 1 | 2 | – | – | – | – | – | – | 5 |
| OV-10 | – | – | – | – | – | – | – | 2 | – | – | – | – | 2 |
| Sub-total fixed-wing | – | – | 1 | 10 | 12 | 23 | 15 | 13 | 5 | – | 3 | – | 82 |
| AH-1 | – | – | – | – | – | – | – | – | 3 | – | – | – | 3 |
| UH-1 | – | – | – | – | – | 10 | 6 | 8 | 6 | – | 2 | – | 32 |
| UH-34 | 2 | 6 | 5 | 12 | 13 | 11 | 7 | 3 | – | – | – | – | 59 |
| CH-46 | – | – | – | – | 3 | 12 | 12 | 15 | 7 | 1 | – | – | 50 |
| CH-53 | – | – | – | – | – | – | 4 | 3 | 1 | 1 | – | 1 | 10 |
| Sub-total helicopters | 2 | 6 | 5 | 12 | 16 | 33 | 29 | 29 | 17 | 2 | 2 | 1 | 154 |
| TOTAL USMC OPERATIONAL LOSSES | 2 | 6 | 6 | 22 | 28 | 56 | 44 | 42 | 22 | 2 | 5 | 1 | 236 |

## Table 5

## USA LOSSES TO ALL CAUSES (Summary)

| | 1962 | 1963 | 1964 | 1965 | 1966 | 1967 | 1968 | 1969 | 1970 | 1971 | 1972 | 1973 | Total 1962-1973 |
|---|---|---|---|---|---|---|---|---|---|---|---|---|---|
| **FIXED-WING AIRCRAFT** | | | | | | | | | | | | | |
| Combat Losses | | | | | | | | | | | | | |
| To MiGs | – | – | – | – | – | – | – | 1 | – | – | – | – | 1 |
| To SAMs | – | – | – | – | – | – | – | – | – | – | – | – | 0 |
| To AAA and Small Arms Fire | – | 2 | 5 | 11 | 20 | 11 | 24 | 27 | 6 | 15 | 1 | – | 122 |
| In Enemy Attacks on Air Bases | – | – | – | – | 1 | 6 | 16 | 9 | – | 2 | – | – | 34 |
| Sub-total | – | 2 | 5 | 11 | 21 | 17 | 40 | 37 | 6 | 17 | 1 | – | 157 |
| Operational Losses | – | 8 | 4 | 16 | 40 | 52 | 55 | 52 | 30 | 23 | 2 | – | 282 |
| Total Aircraft Losses | – | 10 | 9 | 27 | 61 | 69 | 95 | 89 | 36 | 40 | 3 | – | 439 |
| **HELICOPTERS** | | | | | | | | | | | | | |
| Combat Losses | | | | | | | | | | | | | |
| To MiGs | – | – | – | – | – | – | – | – | – | 1 | – | – | 1 |
| To SAMs | – | – | – | – | – | – | – | – | – | – | 6 | – | 6 |
| To AAA and Small Arms Fire | 4 | 8 | 17 | 42 | 91 | 205 | 421 | 435 | 411 | 316 | 115 | 4 | 2,069 |
| In Enemy Attacks on Air Bases | – | – | – | – | 3 | 11 | 54 | 49 | 30 | 19 | 4 | – | 170 |
| Sub-total | 4 | 8 | 17 | 42 | 94 | 216 | 475 | 484 | 441 | 336 | 125 | 4 | 2,246 |
| Operational Losses | 15 | 19 | 29 | 72 | 166 | 335 | 414 | 465 | 359 | 155 | 44 | 2 | 2,075 |
| Total Helicopter Losses | 19 | 27 | 46 | 114 | 260 | 551 | 889 | 949 | 800 | 491 | 169 | 6 | 4,321 |
| TOTAL USA LOSSES | 19 | 37 | 55 | 141 | 321 | 620 | 984 | 1038 | 836 | 531 | 172 | 6 | 4,760 |

## Table 5A

## USA LOSSES TO MIGS (by aircraft type and year)

| | 1962 | 1963 | 1964 | 1965 | 1966 | 1967 | 1968 | 1969 | 1970 | 1971 | 1972 | 1973 | Total 1962-1973 |
|---|---|---|---|---|---|---|---|---|---|---|---|---|---|
| OV-1 | – | – | – | – | – | – | – | 1 | – | – | – | – | 1 |
| Sub-total fixed-wing | – | – | – | – | – | – | – | 1 | – | – | – | – | 1 |
| UH-1 | – | – | – | – | – | – | – | – | – | 1 | – | – | 1 |
| Sub-total helicopters | – | – | – | – | – | – | – | – | – | 1 | – | – | 1 |
| TOTAL USA AIRCRAFT LOST TO MIGS | – | – | – | – | – | – | – | 1 | – | 1 | – | – | 2 |

## Table 5B

## USA LOSSES TO SAMS (by aircraft type and year)

| | 1962 | 1963 | 1964 | 1965 | 1966 | 1967 | 1968 | 1969 | 1970 | 1971 | 1972 | 1973 | Total 1962-1973 |
|---|---|---|---|---|---|---|---|---|---|---|---|---|---|
| AH-1 | – | – | – | – | – | – | – | – | – | – | 4 | – | 4 |
| UH-1 | – | – | – | – | – | – | – | – | – | – | 1 | – | 1 |
| CH-47 | – | – | – | – | – | – | – | – | – | – | 1 | – | 1 |
| TOTAL USA HELICOPTERS LOST TO SAMS | – | – | – | – | – | – | – | – | – | – | 6 | – | 6 |

## Table 5C

## USA LOSSES TO AAA AND SMALL ARMS FIRE (by aircraft type and year)

| | 1962 | 1963 | 1964 | 1965 | 1966 | 1967 | 1968 | 1969 | 1970 | 1971 | 1972 | 1973 | Total 1962-1973 |
|---|---|---|---|---|---|---|---|---|---|---|---|---|---|
| CV-2 | – | – | 1 | – | 1 | – | – | – | – | – | – | – | 2 |
| O-1 | – | – | 2 | 8 | 12 | 8 | 16 | 19 | 5 | 12 | – | – | 82 |
| OV-1 | – | 2 | 2 | 2 | 7 | – | 7 | 4 | – | 2 | 1 | – | 27 |
| U-1 | – | – | – | – | – | 2 | – | 2 | 1 | – | – | – | 5 |
| U-6 | – | – | – | 1 | – | 1 | 1 | 1 | – | – | – | – | 4 |
| U-8 | – | – | – | – | – | – | – | – | – | – | – | – | 0 |
| U-21 | – | – | – | – | – | – | – | 1 | – | 1 | – | – | 2 |
| Sub-total fixed-wing | – | 2 | 5 | 11 | 20 | 11 | 24 | 27 | 6 | 15 | 1 | – | 122 |
| AH-1 | – | – | – | – | – | – | 16 | 39 | 34 | 39 | 28 | 1 | 157 |
| UH-1 | – | 2 | 17 | 39 | 72 | 164 | 243 | 196 | 196 | 135 | 30 | 1 | 1,095 |
| OH-6 | – | – | – | – | – | 3 | 103 | 191 | 161 | 123 | 53 | 1 | 635 |
| OH-13 | – | – | – | 3 | 15 | 20 | 26 | 1 | – | – | – | – | 65 |
| CH-21 | 4 | 5 | – | – | – | – | – | – | – | – | – | – | 9 |
| OH-23 | – | – | – | – | 1 | 12 | 16 | – | – | – | – | – | 29 |
| CH-37 | – | 1 | – | – | 1 | – | – | – | – | – | – | – | 2 |
| CH-47 | – | – | – | – | 2 | 6 | 16 | 8 | 9 | 4 | 3 | 1 | 49 |
| CH-54 | – | – | – | – | – | – | 1 | – | – | – | – | – | 1 |
| OH-58 | – | – | – | – | – | – | – | – | 11 | 15 | 1 | – | 27 |
| Sub-total helicopters | 4 | 8 | 17 | 42 | 91 | 205 | 421 | 435 | 411 | 316 | 115 | 4 | 2,069 |
| TOTAL USA AIRCRAFT LOST TO AAA AND SMALL ARMS | 4 | 10 | 22 | 53 | 111 | 216 | 445 | 462 | 417 | 331 | 116 | 4 | 2,191 |

## Table 5D

## USA LOSSES DURING ENEMY ATTACKS AGAINST AIR BASES (by aircraft type and year)

| | 1962 | 1963 | 1964 | 1965 | 1966 | 1967 | 1968 | 1969 | 1970 | 1971 | 1972 | 1973 | Total 1962-1973 |
|---|---|---|---|---|---|---|---|---|---|---|---|---|---|
| C-7 | – | – | – | – | 1 | – | – | – | – | – | – | – | 1 |
| O-1 | – | – | – | – | – | 4 | 12 | 9 | – | 2 | – | – | 27 |
| OV-1 | – | – | – | – | – | – | 1 | – | – | – | – | – | 1 |
| U-1 | – | – | – | – | – | – | 1 | – | – | – | – | – | 1 |
| U-6 | – | – | – | – | – | 1 | 1 | – | – | – | – | – | 2 |
| U-8 | – | – | – | – | – | 1 | – | – | – | – | – | – | 1 |
| U-21 | – | – | – | – | – | – | 1 | – | – | – | – | – | 1 |
| Sub-total fixed-wing | – | – | – | – | 1 | 6 | 16 | 9 | – | 2 | – | – | 34 |
| AH-1 | – | – | – | – | – | – | – | 2 | 5 | 4 | 1 | – | 12 |
| UH-1 | – | – | – | – | 3 | 10 | 45 | 26 | 17 | 12 | 1 | – | 114 |
| OH-6 | – | – | – | – | – | – | 1 | 11 | 7 | 2 | 2 | – | 23 |
| OH-13 | – | – | – | – | – | – | 5 | – | – | – | – | – | 5 |
| OH-23 | – | – | – | – | – | 1 | 1 | – | – | – | – | – | 2 |
| CH-47 | – | – | – | – | – | – | 2 | 10 | 1 | – | – | – | 13 |
| OH-58 | – | – | – | – | – | – | – | – | – | 1 | – | – | 1 |
| Sub-total helicopters | – | – | – | – | 3 | 11 | 54 | 49 | 30 | 19 | 4 | – | 170 |
| TOTAL USA AIRCRAFT LOST AT AIR BASES | – | – | – | – | 4 | 17 | 70 | 58 | 30 | 21 | 4 | – | 204 |

## Table 5E

## USA COMBAT LOSSES (by aircraft type and year)

| | 1962 | 1963 | 1964 | 1965 | 1966 | 1967 | 1968 | 1969 | 1970 | 1971 | 1972 | 1973 | Total 1962-1973 |
|---|---|---|---|---|---|---|---|---|---|---|---|---|---|
| CV-2 | – | – | 1 | – | 2 | – | – | – | – | – | – | – | 3 |
| O-1 | – | – | 2 | 8 | 12 | 12 | 28 | 28 | 5 | 14 | – | – | 109 |
| OV-1 | – | 2 | 2 | 2 | 7 | – | 8 | 5 | – | 2 | 1 | – | 29 |
| U-1 | – | – | – | – | – | 2 | 1 | 2 | 1 | – | – | – | 6 |
| U-6 | – | – | – | 1 | – | 2 | 2 | 1 | – | – | – | – | 6 |
| U-8 | – | – | – | – | – | 1 | – | – | – | – | – | – | 1 |
| U-21 | – | – | – | – | – | – | 1 | 1 | – | 1 | – | – | 3 |
| Sub-total fixed-wing | – | 2 | 5 | 11 | 21 | 17 | 40 | 37 | 6 | 17 | 1 | – | 157 |
| AH-1 | – | – | – | – | – | – | 16 | 41 | 39 | 43 | 33 | 1 | 173 |
| UH-1 | – | 2 | 17 | 39 | 75 | 174 | 288 | 222 | 213 | 148 | 32 | 1 | 1,211 |
| OH-6 | – | – | – | – | – | 3 | 104 | 202 | 168 | 125 | 55 | 1 | 658 |
| OH-13 | – | – | – | 3 | 15 | 20 | 31 | 1 | – | – | – | – | 70 |
| CH-21 | 4 | 5 | – | – | – | – | – | – | – | – | – | – | 9 |
| OH-23 | – | – | – | – | 1 | 13 | 17 | – | – | – | – | – | 31 |
| CH-37 | – | 1 | – | – | 1 | – | – | – | – | – | – | – | 2 |
| CH-47 | – | – | – | – | 2 | 6 | 18 | 18 | 10 | 4 | 4 | 1 | 63 |
| CH-54 | – | – | – | – | – | – | 1 | – | – | – | – | – | 1 |
| OH-58 | – | – | – | – | – | – | – | – | 11 | 16 | 1 | – | 28 |
| Sub-total helicopters | 4 | 8 | 17 | 42 | 94 | 216 | 475 | 484 | 441 | 336 | 125 | 4 | 2,246 |
| TOTAL USA AIRCRAFT COMBAT LOSSES | 4 | 10 | 22 | 53 | 115 | 233 | 515 | 521 | 447 | 353 | 126 | 4 | 2,403 |

## Table 5F

## USA OPERATIONAL LOSSES (by aircraft type and year)

| | 1962 | 1963 | 1964 | 1965 | 1966 | 1967 | 1968 | 1969 | 1970 | 1971 | 1972 | 1973 | Total 1962-1973 |
|---|---|---|---|---|---|---|---|---|---|---|---|---|---|
| CV-2 | – | 2 | 1 | 1 | 8 | – | – | – | – | – | – | – | 12 |
| O-1 | – | – | 3 | 9 | 21 | 35 | 41 | 33 | 19 | 14 | – | – | 175 |
| OV-1 | – | 3 | – | 1 | 3 | 7 | 6 | 9 | 3 | 3 | 1 | – | 36 |
| YO-3 | – | – | – | – | – | – | – | – | – | 2 | – | – | 2 |
| U-1 | – | 3 | – | 2 | 2 | 2 | 3 | 3 | 2 | – | – | – | 17 |
| U-6 | – | – | – | 3 | 4 | 5 | 4 | 5 | 4 | 3 | – | – | 28 |
| U-8 | – | – | – | – | 2 | 2 | – | 2 | 1 | – | 1 | – | 8 |
| U-21 | – | – | – | – | – | 1 | 1 | – | 1 | 1 | – | – | 4 |
| Sub-total fixed-wing | – | 8 | 4 | 16 | 40 | 52 | 55 | 52 | 30 | 23 | 2 | – | 282 |
| AH-1 | – | – | – | – | – | – | 6 | 37 | 38 | 22 | 6 | – | 109 |
| UH-1 | – | 7 | 28 | 64 | 127 | 255 | 284 | 280 | 220 | 90 | 24 | 1 | 1,380 |
| OH-6 | – | – | – | – | – | 2 | 58 | 129 | 71 | 27 | 9 | 1 | 297 |
| OH-13 | 1 | – | – | 7 | 25 | 47 | 19 | – | 1 | – | – | – | 100 |
| CH-21 | 14 | 12 | 1 | – | – | – | – | – | – | 3 | – | – | 30 |
| OH-23 | – | – | – | – | 3 | 23 | 34 | 3 | 1 | – | – | – | 64 |
| CH-37 | – | – | – | – | 1 | – | – | – | – | – | – | – | 1 |
| CH-47 | – | – | – | 1 | 8 | 6 | 13 | 15 | 17 | 12 | 1 | – | 73 |
| CH-54 | – | – | – | – | 2 | 2 | – | 1 | 1 | 1 | 1 | – | 8 |
| OH-58 | – | – | – | – | – | – | – | – | 10 | – | 3 | – | 13 |
| Sub-total helicopters | 15 | 19 | 29 | 72 | 166 | 335 | 414 | 465 | 359 | 155 | 44 | 2 | 2,075 |
| TOTAL USA OPERATIONAL LOSSES | 15 | 27 | 33 | 88 | 206 | 387 | 469 | 517 | 389 | 178 | 46 | 2 | 2,357 |

A Douglas EB-66B Destroyer creates a double image in the boom operator's window as it noses in for a refuelling session. These ECM platforms were vital in keeping losses to SAMs to a minimum. Six were lost to enemy action during the war.

# Appendix B

## AIRCRAFT OF THE SOUTH EAST ASIA WARS

The following historical synopses and brief specifications are provided as a quick reference for the military aircraft mentioned in this book.

### AAC.1 Toucan

Following the end of World War II, manufacture of the German-designed Junkers Ju 52/3M g7e continued in France and, as the AAC.1 Toucan, the type was selected to re-equip some of the postwar French transport units. The aircraft's rugged construction and minimal field requirements led to its large-scale employment by units of the Armée de l'Air operating in Indochina. There, the aircraft was used as a transport and as a makeshift bomber until supplanted by more modern types.

**Specification**
**Type:** 18-seat military transport
**Powerplant:** three 830-hp (619kW) BMW 132A radial piston engines
**Performance:** maximum speed 165 mph (266 km/h) at sea level; service ceiling 18,000 ft (5485 m); combat range 800 miles (1285 km)
**Weights:** empty 14,325 lb (6498 kg); loaded 24,200 lb (10977 kg)
**Dimensions:** span 95 ft 10 in (29.21 m); length 62 ft (18.90 m); height 14 ft 10 in (4.52 m); wing area 1,184 sq ft (110 m$^2$)
**Armament:** could carry up to 2,205 lb (1000 kg) of bombs when used as a bomber

**Toucans were widely used in Indochina for transport duties, their rugged structure serving the French well in the primitive conditions prevailing in the theatre.**

### Aero Commander 520

This American-built twin-engined light transport saw limited service with the VNAF and the Royal Lao Air Force during the fifties and early sixties.

**Specification**
**Type:** five/seven-seat light transport
**Powerplant:** two 260-hp (194-kW) Lycoming GO-435-C2 six-cylinder horizontally-opposed air-cooled engines
**Performance:** maximum speed 211 mph (340 km/h) at sea level; climb rate 1,800 ft/min (550 m/min); service ceiling 24,400 ft (7440 m); range 850 miles (1368 km)
**Weights:** empty 3,970 lb (1801 kg); loaded 6,000 lb (2722 kg)
**Dimensions:** span 44 ft (13.41 m); length 36 ft (10.97 m); height 14 ft (4.27 m); wing area 242 sq ft (22.5 m$^2$)
**Armament:** none

**The Aero Commander served the US forces in a number of variants, but its use in the combat zone was confined to that of the VNAF and Royal Lao Air Force. It was employed for light intra-theatre transport of key staff.**

### Aichi E13A1a Jake

Eight of these Japanese single-engined floatplanes, which had been left in Indochina by the Imperial Japanese Navy, were used by Escadrille 8S of the Aéronautique Navale between the end of 1945 and the summer of 1947.

**Specification**
**Type:** twin-float reconnaissance seaplane
**Powerplant:** one 1,060-hp (790-kW) Mitsubishi Kinsei 43 radial piston engine
**Performance:** maximum speed 234 mph (377 km/h) at 7,155 ft (2180 m); climb rate 9,845 ft (3000 m) in 6 min 5 sec; service ceiling 28,640 ft (8730 m); combat range 1,300 miles (2090 km)
**Weights:** empty 5,825 lb (2642 kg); loaded 8,025 lb (3640 kg)
**Dimensions:** span 47 ft 7 in (14.50 m); length 37 ft 1 in (11.30 m); height 24 ft 3.5 in (7.40 m); wing area 387.5 sq ft (36 m$^2$)
**Armament:** one 0.303-in (7.7-mm) flexible rear-firing machine-gun, plus a bombload of 550 lb (250 kg)

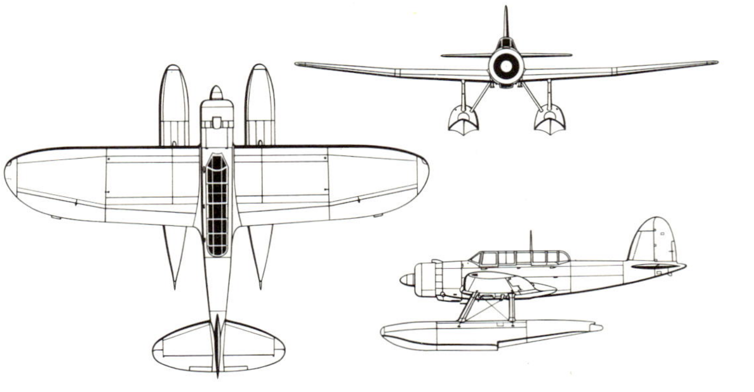

**One of the several types of Japanese aircraft that were adopted for French use in the theatre was the E13A. Its floatplane configuration made it useful for coastal patrol until other more capable types became available.**

### Antonov An-2 Colt

Rugged and possessing good STOL characteristics, this large Soviet single-engined biplane proved well suited to operations in the less developed areas of North Vietnam and neighbouring countries. As such, it was used by the NVNAF for the resupply of isolated outposts and Pathet Lao forces. One of these aircraft gained the doubtful distinction of becoming the first confirmed 'kill' by helicopters. The Royal Khmer Air Force also received a handful of An-2s.

**Specification**
**Type:** 14-troop transport biplane
**Powerplant:** one 1,000-hp (746-kW) Shvetsov ASh-62M radial piston engine
**Performance:** maximum speed 157 mph (253 km/h) at 5,740 ft (1750 m); climb rate 550 ft/min (168 m/min); service ceiling 14,270 ft (4350 m); range 560 miles (900 km)
**Weights:** loaded 12,125 lb (5500 kg)
**Dimensions:** span 59 ft 7.7 in (18.18 m); length 41 ft 9.6 in (12.74 m); height 13 ft 1.5 in (4.00 m); wing area, total 770.7 sq ft (71.60 m$^2$)
**Armament:** none

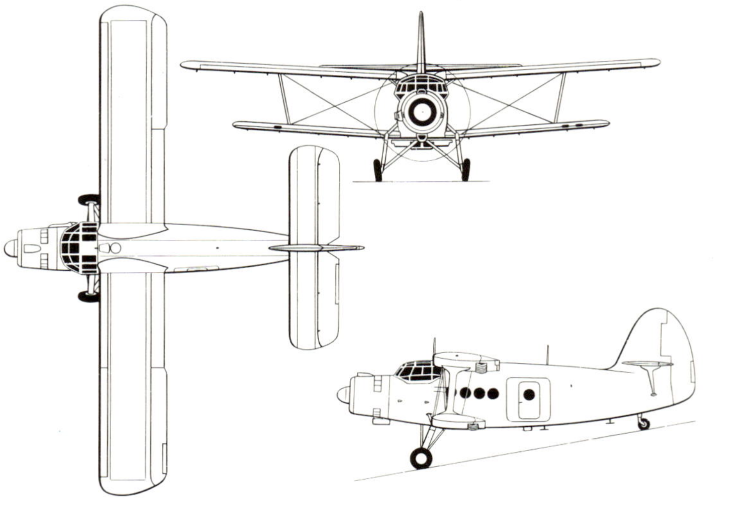

**The immensely sturdy An-2 has been the standard light utility transport for Soviet-supplied air arms for many years. The North Vietnamese used theirs widely for supply duties, some venturing outside Vietnam into Laos.**

## Beech C-45G Expediter

Among the aircraft rushed to Indochina by the United States to help the French at the time of the Dien Bien Phu battle were 10 C-45Gs. Taken over by the VNAF in 1955, these aircraft were used briefly for communications and staff transport. The Marines also flew a few UC-45Js in Vietnam.

**Specification**
**Type:** 7-passenger light transport
**Powerplant:** two 450-hp (336-kW) Pratt & Whitney R-985-AN-1 radial piston engines
**Performance:** maximum speed 215 mph (346 km/h) at 5,000 ft (1525 m); climb rate 10,000 ft (3050 m) in 8.6 min; service ceiling 20,000 ft (6095 m); range 700 miles (1127 km)
**Weights:** empty 5,890 lb (2672 kg); loaded 7,850 lb (3560 kg)
**Dimensions:** span 47 ft 8 in (14.53 m); length 34 ft 3 in (10.44 m); height 9 ft 8 in (2.95 m); wing area 349 sq ft (32.42 m$^2$)
**Armament:** none

**Beech's classic light twin transport appeared in both radial-powered (illustrated) and turboprop-powered versions.**

## Beech U-8 Seminole

Military equivalent of the Beech Twin Bonanza executive aircraft, the U-8 was operated in South East Asia by the US Army for staff transport and general liaison work.

**Specification** (U-8F)
**Type:** 6-seat staff transport
**Powerplant:** two 340-hp (254-kW) Lycoming IGSO-480-A1A6 air-cooled piston engines
**Performance:** maximum speed 240 mph (386 km/h); climb rate 1,300 ft/min (396 m/min); service ceiling 27,000 ft (8230 m); range 1,370 miles (2205 km)
**Weights:** empty 4,996 lb (2266 kg); loaded 7,700 lb (3493 kg)
**Dimensions:** span 45 ft 10.5 in (13.98 m); length 33 ft 4 in (10.16 m); height 14 ft 2 in (4.32 m); wing area 277 sq ft (25.73 m$^2$)
**Armament:** none

**The U-8 Seminole was based on the civil Model 50 Twin Bonanza. Shown is the U-8F, based on the larger Queen Air 65, also used for liaison duties. This aircraft was the forerunner of the extensive U-21/C-12 family.**

## Beech U-21

In addition to operating U-21As to supplement its U-8 staff transports, the US Army made extensive use in Vietnam of a specially fitted version of this light twin-turboprop aircraft for battlefield reconnaissance and electronic surveillance duties.

**Specification** (RU-21C)
**Type:** special reconnaissance transport
**Powerplant:** two 550-shp (410-kW) Pratt & Whitney T74-CP-700 turboprops
**Performance:** maximum speed 249 mph (401 km/h) at 11,000 ft (3350 m); climb rate 2,000 ft/min (610 m/min); service ceiling 25,500 ft (7775 m); range 1,170 miles (1885 km)
**Weights:** empty 5,464 lb (2478 kg); loaded 9,650 lb (4377 kg)
**Dimensions:** span 45 ft 10.5 in (13.98 m); length 35 ft 6 in (10.82 m); height 14 ft 2.5 in (4.33 m); wing area 279.7 sq ft (25.98 m$^2$)
**Armament:** none

**The U-21A was the standard liaison transport for the Army during the war. Many versions appeared with electronic surveillance gear, the type's good loiter making it ideal for monitoring battlefield communications and emissions.**

## Beech QU-22

Derived from the popular Beech Bonanza private aircraft, the QU-22B was an electronic intelligence-gathering drone used by the USAF to relay data collected by the *Igloo White* sensors.

**Specification** (QU-22B)
**Type:** electronic intelligence-gathering drone
**Powerplant:** one 285-hp (213-kW) Continental IO-520-B air-cooled piston engine
**Performance:** maximum speed 204 mph (328 km/h)
**Weight:** loaded 3,600 lb (1633 kg)
**Dimensions:** span 32 ft 10 in (10.01 m); length 26 ft 4 in (8.03 m)
**Armament:** none

**The QU-22B could be flown either manned or unmanned, on relay duties for the *Igloo White* programme. The U-22 featured a geared propeller with characteristic nose profile.**

## Bell AH-1 HueyCobra

The design of the HueyCobra helicopter gunship, undertaken by Bell as a private venture, proved an outstanding success. During the war, AH-1Gs were used in large number by US Army units while the Marine Corps operated both single-engined AH-1Gs and twin-engined AH-1Js.

**Specification** (AH-1G)
**Type:** two-seat attack helicopter
**Powerplant:** one 1,400-shp (1044-kW) Lycoming T53-L-13 turboshaft
**Performance:** maximum speed 219 mph (352 km/h) at sea level; climb rate 1,580 ft/min (482 m/min); service ceiling 10,000 ft (3050 m); combat range 257 miles (414 km)
**Weights:** empty 6,096 lb (2765 kg); loaded 9,500 lb (4310 kg)
**Dimensions:** rotor diameter 44 ft (13.41 m); fuselage length 44 ft 5 in (13.54 m); height 13 ft 5.4 in (4.10 m)
**Armament:** XM-28 nose turret with twin 0.30-in (7.62-mm) miniguns and four rocket launchers

**Principal helicopter gunship of the war, the AH-1 could carry a variety of weapons, including rocket pods, guns and grenade launchers. This example is seen in an attack dive, armed with four pods of rockets.**

## Bell UH-1 Iroquois

Perhaps the most representative aircraft of the Vietnam War era, the Huey made its appearance in the theatre in 1962 with the US Army's 57th Medical Detachment. Subsequently, short fuselage (UH-1A, UH-1B, UH-1C, UH-1E, and UH-1P) and long fuselage (UH-1D, UH-1F, UH-1H, and UH-1N) versions became numerically the most important helicopters in South East Asia where they were used for a great variety of missions (troop transport, observation, medical evacuation, search and rescue, fire support, staff transport, etc.) by the Army, the Air Force, the Navy, and the Marine Corps, as well as by the air forces of the Republic of Vietnam, Australia, and Cambodia.

**Specification** (UH-1H)
**Type:** 15-seat utility helicopter
**Powerplant:** one 1,400-shp (1044-kW) Lycoming T53-L-13A turboshaft
**Performance:** maximum speed 127 mph (204 km/h) at sea level; climb rate 1,680 ft/min (512 m/min); service ceiling 19,700 ft (6005 m); combat range 345 miles (555 km)
**Weights:** empty 5,082 lb (2305 kg); loaded 9,500 lb (4309 kg)
**Dimensions:** rotor diameter 48 ft (14.63 m); fuselage length 41 ft 6 in (12.65 m); height 14 ft 6 in (4.42 m)
**Armament:** two 0.30-in (7.62-mm) M-60 flexible machine-guns

**UH-1s depart on a combat assault mission. The Huey displaced parachuting and other methods of troop insertion during the war, flying in tightly formated lines. The door-mounted machine-gun was for suppressive fire during assaults.**

## Bell OH-13 Sioux

When the US Army began fighting in Vietnam, OH-13s were used for observation duties. This obsolete type, however, was soon replaced by more modern types, the Bell OH-58 and Hughes OH-6.

**Specification** (OH-13S)
**Type:** 3-seat utility and observation helicopter
**Powerplant:** one 260-hp (194-kW) Lycoming TVO-435 A1A air-cooled piston engine
**Performance:** maximum speed 105 mph (169 km/h) at sea level; climb rate 1,190 ft/min (363 m/min); service ceiling 13,200 ft (4025 m); range 325 miles (525 km)
**Weights:** empty 1,936 lb (877 kg); loaded 2,850 lb (1295 kg)
**Dimensions:** rotor diameter 37 ft 1.5 in (11.31 m); fuselage length 32 ft 6 in (9.91 m); height 9 ft 3 in (2.82 m)
**Armament:** none

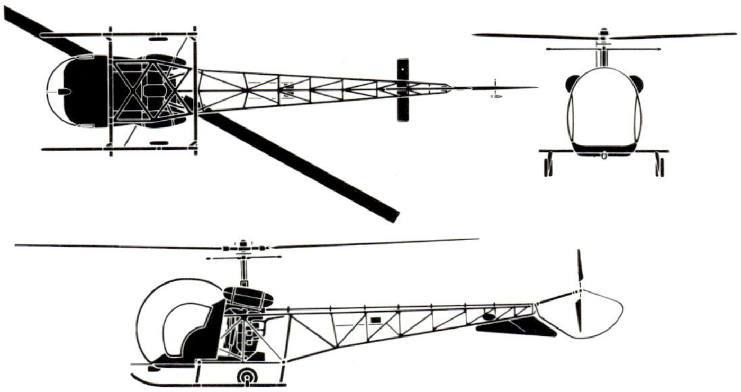

**One of the earliest effective helicopters, the Bell Model 47 has been used for many duties, including medevac, scouting and liaison. As well as early use with the US Army, the Australians employed the type as part of their contribution to the war.**

## Bell OH-58 Kiowa

Co-winner of the 1960 Army competition for Light Observation Helicopters, this five-seat turboshaft-powered observation helicopter made its combat début in 1970.

**Specification** (OH-58A)
**Type:** five-seat utility and observation helicopter
**Powerplant:** one 400-shp (298-kW) Allison T63-A-700 turboshaft
**Performance:** maximum speed 138 mph (222 km/h) at sea level; climb rate 1,780 ft/min (543 m/min); service ceiling 19,000 ft (5790 m); range 355 miles (570 km)
**Weights:** empty 1,583 lb (718 kg); loaded 3,000 lb (1360 kg)
**Dimensions:** rotor diameter 35 ft 4 in (10.77 m); fuselage length 31 ft 2 in (9.50 m); height 9 ft 6.5 in (2.91 m)
**Armament:** one XM-27 kit with an 0.30-in (7.62-mm) Minigun

**The OH-58 has been the standard light helicopter of the US Army since 1970. Based on the civil JetRanger, good speed and agility have led to a successful career as a scout. This aircraft carries a Minigun on the port side for suppressive fire.**

## Bell P-63 Kingcobra

Three hundred P-63Cs were received by France to help equip the Armée de l'Air at the end of World War II. The type was obsolete for use in Europe, but its heavy armament and metal construction appeared to suit it for operations in Indochina. In this theatre, however, the Kingcobra's reliance on well-prepared airfields limited its usefulness.

**Specification** (P-63C)
**Type:** single-seat fighter
**Powerplant:** one 1,425-hp (1063-kW) Allison V-1710-109 inline liquid-cooled piston engine
**Performance:** maximum speed 410 mph (660 km/h) at 25,000 ft (7620 m); climb rate 28,000 ft (8535 m) in 8.6 min; service ceiling 38,600 ft (11765 m); combat range 320 miles (515 km)
**Weights:** empty 6,800 lb (3084 kg); loaded 9,300 lb (4218 kg)
**Dimensions:** span 38 ft 4 in (11.68 m); length 32 ft 8 in (9.96 m); height 12 ft 7 in (3.84 m); wing area 248 sq ft (23.04 m$^2$)
**Armament:** one 37-mm cannon and four 0.50-in (12.7-mm) machine-guns, plus three 500-lb (227-kg) bombs

**Seen at Hanoi in June 1950, this line-up of P-63Cs is from GC I/5 'Vendee'.**

## Boeing RB-47H Stratojet

Being phased out from the SAC inventory when the United States went to war in South East Asia, the RB-47H was operated only briefly by the 55th Strategic Reconnaissance Wing to relay electronic signals gathered over North Vietnam by Ryan 147D and 147E drones.

### Specification

**Type:** 6-seat electronic reconnaissance aircraft
**Powerplant:** six 7,200-lb (3266-kg) thrust General Electric J47-GE-25 turbojets
**Performance:** maximum speed 594 mph (956 km/h) at 15,000 ft (4570 m); climb rate 3,700 ft/min (1128 m/min); service ceiling 31,500 ft (9600 m); combat range 3,040 miles (4890 km)
**Weights:** empty 89,230 lb (40474 kg); loaded 191,135 lb (86697 kg)
**Dimensions:** span 116 ft 4 in (35.46 m); length 108 ft 8.4 in (33.13 m); height 28 ft (8.53 m); wing area 1,428 sq ft (132.67 m²)
**Armament:** none

**SAC's primary Sigint gatherer until the advent of the capable RC-135 was the RB-47, characterised by the lengthened nose and additional aerials. As well as co-operation with drones, the RB-47 also provided Sigint coverage during the early days.**

## Boeing KB-50J

When in June 1964 the first tactical strikes were made in Laos, the only tankers available to support the F-100s and RF-101s were the jet-augmentec KB-50Js of the 421st ARefS. These obsolete aircraft served for another seven months prior to the inactivation of PACAF's only Air Refuelling Squadron.

### Specification

**Type:** inflight refuelling tanker
**Powerplant:** four 3,500-hp (2610-kW) Pratt & Whitney R-4360-35 radial piston engines and two 5,620-lb (2549-kg) thrust General Electric J47-GE-23 turbojets
**Performance:** maximum speed 444 mph (714 km/h) at 17,000 ft (5180 m); climb rate 3,260 ft/min (994 m/min); service ceiling 39,700 ft (12100 m); combat range 2,300 miles (3700 km)
**Weights:** empty 93,200 lb (42275 kg); loaded 179,500lb (81420 kg)
**Dimensions:** span 141 ft 3 in (43.05 m); length 105 ft 1 in (32.03 m); height 33 ft 7 in (10.24 m); wing area 1,720 sq ft (159.79m²)
**Armament:** none

**At the outbreak of war, the KB-50 was the only available tanker. Their wartime career was brief, but they did perform sterling work until replaced by KC-135s. This example demonstrates the probe and drogue technique with a pair of RF-101Cs.**

## Boeing B-52 Stratofortress

The BUFFs were used during most of the war for saturation raids against suspected enemy camps and concentrations in South Vietnam, Laos and Cambodia, and for the interdiction campaign a ong the Ho Chi Minh Trail in Laos and the North Vietnamese panhandle. If their effectiveness in these roles is somewhat questionable, there is no doubt that B-52s proved highly effective during *Linebacker II* when they dropped nearly three-fourths of the bombs in this 11-day attack. The B-52Fs initially used in South East Asia had bomb bays optimized for carrying nuclear stores and were soon supplanted by 'Big Belly' B-52Ds modified to carry internally and externally an increased load of conventional bombs. B-52Gs were added to the force in time for the *Linebacker II* offensive.

### Specification (B-52D)

**Type:** strategic bomber
**Powerplant:** eight 12,100-lb (5488-kg) thrust Pratt & Whitney J57-P-19W turbojets
**Performance:** maximum speed 628 mph (1010 km/h); climb rate 2,460 ft/min (750 m/min); service ceiling 38,050 ft (11600 m); combat range 7,290 miles (11730 km)
**Weights:** empty 165,110 lb (74893 kg); loaded 450,000 lb (204117 kg)
**Dimensions:** span 185 ft (56.39 m); length 156 ft 7.25 in (47.73 m); height 48 ft 4 in (14.73 m); wing area 4,000 sq ft (371.60 m²)
**Armament:** four 0.50-in (12.7-mm) machine-guns in tail turret and up to 60,000 lb (27215 kg) of bombs

**'Big Belly' B-52Ds bore the brunt of the bombing campaign in South East Asia, also supported by B-52Fs and B-52Gs. The B-52D had a manned tail turret with four 0.50-in machine-guns, and two MiGs were downed in this way. As the war progressed, the ECM fit of the D-model became ever more capable, and by flying in cells of three, the BUFFs managed to avoid most of the hundreds of SAMs fired at them during their operations.**

## Boeing KC-135 Stratotanker

The KC-135A tanker made tactical operations with adequate offensive loads possible and provided support for B-52 *Arc Light* operations. Its greatest value, however, was its direct contribution to saving aircrews and aircraft which were running out of fuel either due to operational problems or battle damage. The specially configured KC-135Q also provided air refuelling for SR-71s. Other missions undertaken during the war by specialized versions of the Stratotanker included *Combat Lightning* radio relay sorties by KC-135As and EC-135Ls, and *Combat Apple* electronic intelligence-gathering sorties by RC-135Cs, RC-135Ds, and RC-135Ms.

**Specification** (KC-135A)
**Type:** inflight refuelling tanker
**Powerplant:** four 13,750-lb (6237-kg) thrust Pratt & Whitney J57-P-59W turbojets
**Performance:** maximum speed 585 mph (941 km/h) at 30,000 ft (9145 m); climb rate 2,000 ft/min (610 m/min); service ceiling 50,000 ft (15240 m); range 1,150 miles (1850 km) carrying 120,000 lb (54430 kg) of transfer fuel
**Weights:** empty 98,446 lb (44654 kg); loaded 297,000 lb (134717 kg)
**Dimensions:** span 130 ft 10 in (39.88 m); length 136 ft 3 in (41.53 m); height 38 ft 4 in (11.68 m); wing area 2,433 sq ft (226.03 $m^2$)
**Armament:** none

**As the only tanker asset throughout most of the conflict, the KC-135 was tasked with many different aircraft types to refuel. Along with bomber support, the main job was to tank strike aircraft heading North, such as these Phantoms.**

## Boeing-Vertol CH-46 Sea Knight

After suffering more than their fair share of teething problems, the Marine CH-46 twin-rotor helicopters became effective medium transport vehicles. Their last employment in the war was during *Frequent Wind*, the final evacuation of Saigon on 29-30 April 1975.

**Specification** (CH-46A)
**Type:** medium transport (17 troops) helicopter
**Powerplant:** two 1,250-shp (932-kW) General Electric T58-GE-8B turboshafts
**Performance:** maximum speed 160 mph (257 km/h) at sea level; climb rate 1,540 ft/min (469 m/min); service ceiling 12,800 ft (3900 m); combat range 245 miles (395 km)
**Weights:** empty 11,708 lb (5311 kg); loaded 18,700 lb (8482 kg)
**Dimensions:** rotor diameter (each) 50 ft (15.24 m); fuselage length 44 ft 10 in (13.66 m); height 16 ft 8.5 in (5.09 m)

**Marine assault was largely handled by the Sea Knight, a role in which it continues today. The good load-carrying ability, and damage absorption made it ideal for landing Marine units quickly and effectively in 'hot' areas. These aircraft are from HMH-161, operating south of Da Nang.**

## Boeing-Vertol CH-47 Chinook

Resembling a larger CH-46, the Chinook was the main Army medium transport helicopter and was also operated by the VNAF.

**Specification** (CH-47C)
**Type:** medium transport (44 troops) helicopter
**Powerplant:** two 3,750-shp (2796-kW) Lycoming T55-L-11 turboshafts
**Performance:** maximum speed 190 mph (306 km/h) at sea level; climb rate 2,880 ft/min (878 m/min); service ceiling 15,000 ft (4570 m); combat range 230 miles (370 km)
**Weights:** empty 20,378 lb (9243 kg); loaded 46,000 lb (20865 kg)
**Dimensions:** rotor diameter (each) 60 ft (18.29 m); fuselage length 51 ft (15.54 m); height 18 ft 7 in (5.66 m)
**Armament:** one door-mounted 0.30-in (7.62-mm) flexible machine-gun

**The CH-47 was widely used by the US Army for transport of heavy items such as artillery and fuel bladders. Troop assault was also undertaken, sometimes using rope ladders to descend into difficult spots.**

## Cessna A-37 Dragonfly

Following the successful combat evaluation of the A-37A, an armed version of the T-37 trainer, the more powerful A-37B was extensively used by the USAF in South Vietnam for close support and convoy escort. As a result of the Vietnamization Programme, A-37Bs became the most numerous combat aircraft in the VNAF inventory; a few were also delivered to the Khmer Air Force.

**Specification** (A-37B)
**Type:** light strike aircraft
**Powerplant:** two 2,850-lb (1293-kg) thrust General Electric J85-GE-17A turbojets
**Performance:** maximum speed 507 mph (816 km/h) at 16,000 ft (4875 m); climb rate 6,990 ft/min (2130 m/min); service ceiling 41,765 ft (12730 m); combat range 460 miles (740 km)
**Weights:** empty 6,211 lb (2817 kg); loaded 14,000 lb (6350 kg)
**Dimensions:** span 35 ft 10.5 in (10.93 m); length 29 ft 3 in (8.92 m); height 8 ft 10.5 in (2.70 m); wing area 184 sq ft (17.10 $m^2$)
**Armament:** one 0.30-in (7.62-mm) Minigun and up to 5,680 lb (2576 kg) of external stores

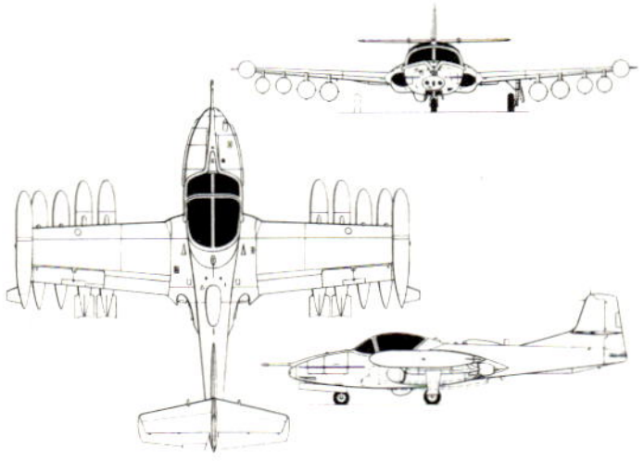

**The A-37 Dragonfly could count on eight pylons for weapons and fuel carriage. The type packed a considerable punch for its small size.**

**Bomb-laden A-37 heads for its target in South Vietnam. The A-37 was used on all forms of light strike missions, including rescue escort, counter-insurgency and FAC. A-37s were widely used by the Vietnamese.**

## Cessna O-1 Bird Dog

Upon reaching full independence, the Republic of Vietnam took over from the French inventory 20 of the L-19s which had been supplied by the United States at the time of the Dien Bien Phu emergency. Redesignated O-1 in 1962, this observation aircraft went on to see extensive service not only with the VNAF, but also with the USAF, the USA, the USMC, and the Royal Khmer Aviation/Khmer Air Force.

**O-1F Bird Dog armed with marker rockets flies over featureless jungle in South Vietnam. Note hastily-applied 'star and bar' which has been inverted.**

**Specification** (O-1E)
**Type:** two-seat observation and forward air control aircraft
**Powerplant:** one 213-hp (159-kW) Continental O-470-11 air-cooled piston engine
**Performance:** maximum speed 115 mph (185 km/h) at sea level; climb rate 1,150 ft/min (351 m/min); service ceiling 18,500 ft (5640 m); range 530 miles (850 km)
**Weights:** empty 1,614 lb (732 kg); loaded 2,400 lb (1088 kg)
**Dimensions:** span 36 ft (10.97 m); length 25 ft 10 in (7.87 m); height 7 ft 4 in (2.23 m); wing area 174 sq ft (16.16 $m^2$)
**Armament:** four target-marking rockets

## Cessna O-2

To supplement its O-1s in the FAC role, the USAF began acquiring push-pull twin-engined O-2As in 1967. These aircraft were joined in Vietnam by 31 generally similar O-2B psychological warfare aircraft fitted with air-to-ground broadcasting equipment and a leaflet dispenser.

**Specification** (O-2A)
**Type:** two-seat observation and forward air control aircraft
**Powerplant:** two 210-hp (157-kW) Continental IO-360C/D air-cooled piston engines
**Performance:** maximum speed 199 mph (320 km/h) at sea level; climb rate 1,100 ft/min (335 m/min); service ceiling 18,000 ft (5490 m); range 1,060 miles (1705 km)
**Weights:** empty 2,848 lb (1291 kg); loaded 4,630 lb (2100 kg)
**Dimensions:** span 38 ft 2 in (11.63 m); length 29 ft 9 in (9.07 m); height 9 ft 4 in (2.84 m); wing area 202.5 sq ft (18.81 $m^2$)
**Armament:** four underwing hard points for target-marking rockets or 0.30-in (7.62-mm) Minigun pods

**This O-2A carries the typical weapon load for a FAC mission. Two Minigun pods provide suppressive fire while two white phosphorus rocket pods are used for marking targets. The O-2s speed and agility made it less vulnerable than the O-1 in the FAC role, but it was larger and noisier.**

## Cessna T-37

In addition to being extensively used in the United States for training USAF and VNAF aircrews, this light twinjet trainer was operated by the 920th Training Squadron of the VNAF at Nha Trang.

**Specification** (T-37C)
**Type:** two-seat basic trainer
**Powerplant:** two 1,025-lb (465-kg) thrust Continental T69-T-25 turbojets
**Performance:** maximum speed 425 mph (684 km/h) at 20,000 ft (6100 m); climb rate 3,370 ft/min (1027 m/min); service ceiling 39,200 ft (11950 m); range 930 miles (1495 km)
**Weights:** empty 4,480 lb (2032 kg); loaded 8,007 lb (3632 kg)
**Dimensions:** span 33 ft 9.25 in (10.29 m); length 29 ft 3.5 in (8.93 m); height 9 ft 2 in (2.79 m); wing area 183.9 sq ft (17.08 $m^2$)
**Armament:** two underwing hard points for gun pods

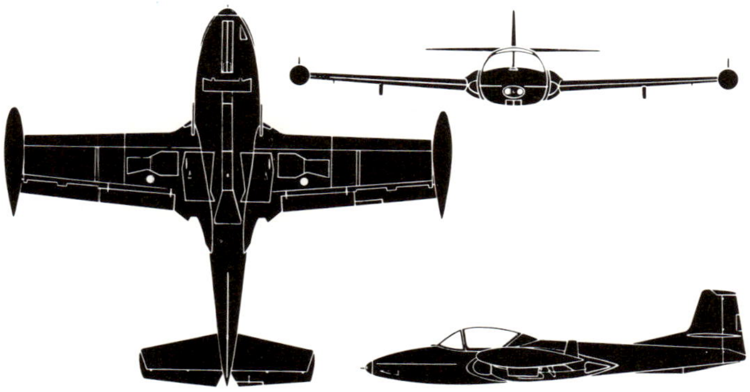

**The USAF's basic jet trainer is the Cessna T-37, and these were supplied to South Vietnam to perform the same function.**

## Cessna T-41A Mescalero

The military version of the Cessna 172 light aircraft was operated by the USAF Air Training Command in its Undergraduate Pilot Training Program, by the VNAF's 912th Training Squadron, and by the Khmer Air Force.

**Specification**
**Type:** two-seat primary trainer
**Powerplant:** one 150-hp (112-kW) Lycoming O-320-E2D air-cooled piston engine
**Performance:** maximum speed 153 mph (246 km/h) at sea level; climb rate 880 ft/min (268 m/min); service ceiling 17,000 ft (5180 m); range 1,010 miles (1625 km)
**Weights:** empty 1,405 lb (637 kg); loaded 2,550 lb (1156 kg)
**Dimensions:** span 35 ft 10 in (10.92 m); length 26 ft 11 in (8.20 m); height 8 ft 9.5 in (2.68 m); wing area 174 sq ft (16.16 $m^2$)
**Armament:** none

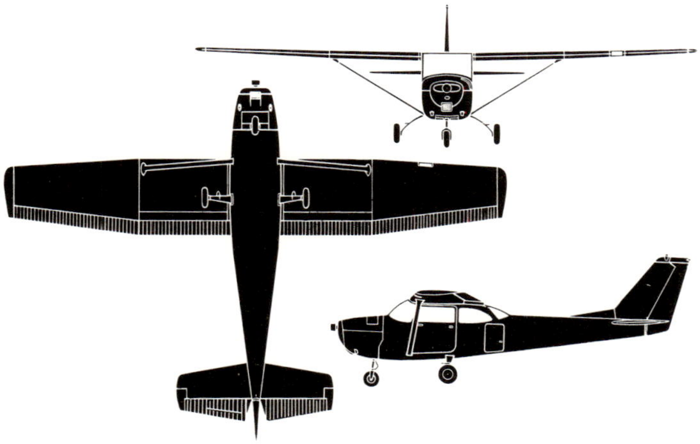

**Another USAF aircraft which was employed for training by the VNAF was the T-41A. The type's stability and forgiving qualities make it ideal as an initial trainer.**

## Cessna U-3 'Blue Canoe'

Deriving its nickname from its colourful paint scheme, the 'Blue Canoe' was a staff transport evolved from the Cessna 310 executive aircraft. In South East Asia the USAF flew both U-3As with conventional vertical tail surfaces and U-3Bs with swept fin and rudder.

**Specification** (U-3A)
**Type:** five-seat staff transport
**Powerplant:** two 240-hp (179-kW) Continental O-470-M air-cooled piston engines
**Performance:** maximum speed 231 mph (372 km/h) at sea level; climb rate 1,640 ft/min (500 m/min); service ceiling 28,100 ft (8565 m); range 1,400 miles (2250 km)
**Weights:** empty 2,965 lb (1345 kg); loaded 4,830 lb (2190 kg)
**Dimensions:** span 36 ft 1 in (11.0 m); length 27 ft 1 in (8.25 m); height 10 ft 5 in (3.17 m); wing area 175 sq ft (16.26 m$^2$)
**Armament:** none

**Staff transport and liaison for the USAF was the domain of the Cessna U-3. This aircraft is a U-3B, seen at Tan Son Nhut in 1964, in front of *Mule Train* C-123 transports.**

## Cessna U-17 Skywagon

For light utility work and flight training the VNAF and the Royal Lao Air Force received some U-17s (military equivalent of the civil Cessna 185). A small number of the Vietnamese aircraft were fitted out for psychological warfare with air-to-ground broadcasting equipment and leaflet dispensers.

**Specification** (U-17A)
**Type:** six-seat utility aircraft
**Powerplant:** one 300-hp (224-kW) Continental IO-520-D air-cooled piston engine
**Performance:** maximum speed 178 mph (286 km/h) at sea level; climb rate 1,010 ft/min (308 m/min); service ceiling 17,150 ft (5230 m); range 1,075 miles (1730 km)
**Weights:** empty 1,585 lb (719 kg); loaded 3,350 lb (1519 kg)
**Dimensions:** span 35 ft 10 in (10.92 m); length 25 ft 9 in (7.85 m); height 7 ft 9 in (2.36 m); wing area 174 sq ft (16.16m$^2$)
**Armament:** none

**Cessna U-17A on a test-hop prior to delivery to the VNAF for liaison duties.**

## Chance Vought AU-1 Corsair

Trained on the F4U-7, the last version of the famous World War II Corsair, the Flottille 14F of the French Navy was sent to Indochina without aircraft during the fight for Dien Bien Phu. There the unit flew another version of the Corsair, the AU-1, as 25 of these aircraft were loaned to France during the closing year of the Indochina War.

**Specification**
**Type:** carrier-based fighter
**Powerplant:** one 2,300-hp (1715-kW) Pratt & Whitney R-2800-83W radial piston engine
**Performance:** maximum speed 438 mph (705 km/h) at 9,500 ft (2895 m); climb rate 2,920 ft/min (890 m/min); service ceiling 39,500 ft (12040 m); combat range 485 miles (780 km)
**Weights:** empty 9,835 lb (4461 kg); loaded 19,400 lb (8800 kg)
**Dimensions:** span 41 ft (12.50 m); length 34 ft 1 in (10.39 m); height 14 ft 10 in (4.52 m); wing area 314 sq ft (29.17 m$^2$)
**Armament:** four 20-mm cannon and 4,000 lb (1814 kg) of external stores

**Aéronavale F4U-7 undergoes engine tests. The Corsair arrived late in the Indochina war but was heavily employed on attack duties against Viet Minh forces during the abortive French efforts at Dien Bien Phu. Like its carrierborne cousin the F8F Bearcat, the Corsairs flew all of their missions from land bases.**

## Consolidated PBY-5A Catalina

In 1945 these old and slow amphibians were the first aircraft taken to Indochina by France's Aéronautique Navale. There they served in their intended maritime patrol role and also performed bombing and medical evacuation missions until phased out in 1950.

**Specification**
**Type:** maritime patrol amphibian
**Powerplant:** two 1,200-hp (895-kW) Pratt & Whitney R-1830-92 radial piston engines
**Performance:** maximum speed 196 mph (315 km/h) at 7,000 ft (2135 m); climb rate 620 ft/min (189 m/min); service ceiling 13,000 ft (3960 m); range 2,350 miles (3780 km)
**Weights:** empty 20,910 lb (9485 kg); loaded 35,420 lb (16066 kg)
**Dimensions:** span 104 ft (31.70 m); length 63 ft 10 in (19.46 m); height 20 ft 2 in (6.15 m); wing area 1,400 sq ft (130.06 m$^2$)
**Armament:** three 0.30-in (7.7-mm) flexible machine-guns and two 0.50-in (12.7-mm) machine-guns, plus 4,000 lb (1814 kg) of bombs

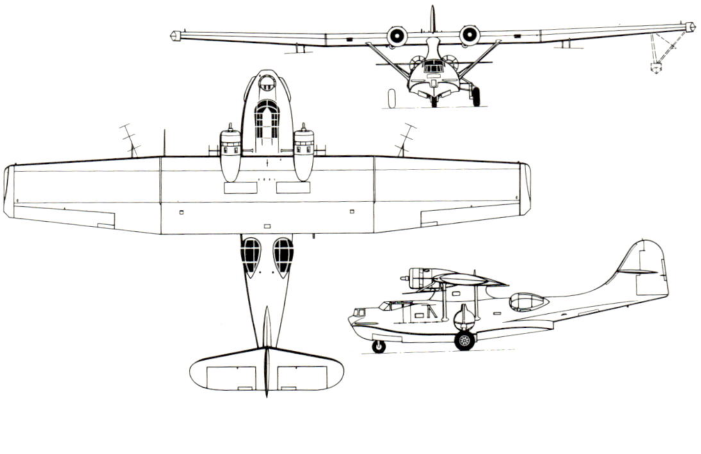

**The venerable Catalina provided maritime patrol and a few bombing missions in the theatre until phased out in favour of land-based aircraft.**

## Consolidated PB4Y Privateer

The largest aircraft flown by French forces in Indochina, the PB4Y-2S land-based maritime patrol aircraft were operated by Flottille 8F/28F in the bombing role from the fall of 1950 until the French withdrawal from their former colony.

**Specification** (PB4Y-2S)
**Type:** four-engined bomber
**Powerplant:** four 1,350-hp (1007-kW) Pratt & Whitney R-1830-94 radial piston engines
**Performance:** maximum speed 237 mph (381 km/h) at 13,750 ft (4190 m); climb rate 1,090 ft/min (332 m/min); service ceiling 20,700 ft (6310 m); combat range 2,800 miles (4505 km)
**Weights:** empty 37,485 lb (17003 kg); loaded 65,000 lb (29484 kg)
**Dimensions:** span 110 ft (33.53 m); length 74 ft 7 in (22.73 m); height 30 ft 1 in (9.17 m); wing area 1,048 sq ft (97.36 m$^2$)
**Armament:** twelve 0.50-in (12.7-mm) machine-guns in one nose, two dorsal, two waist, and one tail turrets, plus up to 12,800 lb (5805 kg) of bombs

**Replacing the Catalinas, the Privateer introduced greater bombing capability to the theatre and were the largest aircraft to be operated by the French. This Flotille 28F aircraft displays the heavy defensive armament carried by the type, the two dorsal turrets covered with protective sheets. The waist blisters contained a pair of guns each. The Privateer had grown out of the well-known Liberator bomber.**

## Convair F-102 Delta Dagger

Initially deployed to South Vietnam to serve in the air defence role, F-102s also flew escort for B-52s flying against targets in the North Vietnamese panhandle. Rarely noted is the fact that during one of the latter missions, an F-102A of the 509th FIS was brought down on 3 February 1968 by an 'Atoll' air-to-air missile fired by a MiG-21.

**Specification** (F-102A)
**Type:** single-seat interceptor fighter
**Powerplant:** one 11,700-lb (5307-kg) dry thrust and 17,200-lb (7802-kg) afterburning thrust Pratt & Whitney J57-P-23 turbojet
**Performance:** maximum speed 825 mph (1328 km/h) at 40,000 ft (12190 m); climb rate 13,000 ft/min (3962 m/min); service ceiling 54,000 ft (16460 m); combat range 670 miles (1080 km)
**Weights:** empty 19,350 lb (8777 kg); loaded 31,276 lb (14187 kg)
**Dimensions:** span 38 ft 1.5 in (11.62 m); length 68 ft 4.5 in (20.84 m); height 21 ft 2.5 in (6.46 m); wing area 661.5 sq ft (61.45 m$^2$)
**Armament:** six AIM-4 Falcon air-to-air missiles

**Standard PACAF fighter of the day, detachments served in Vietnam from the F-102 force based at Clark AB in the Philippines. No air-to-ground weaponry could be carried.**

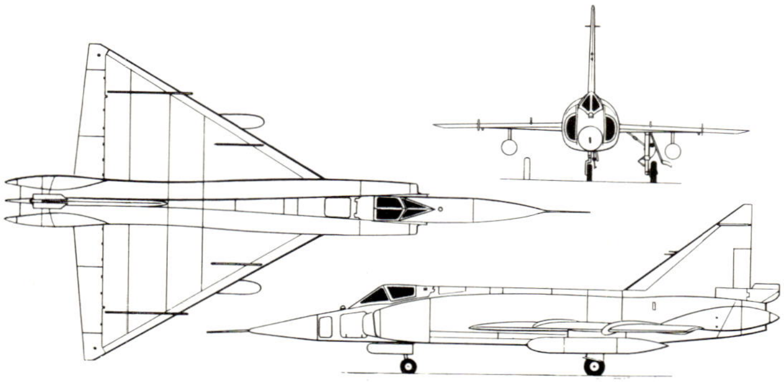

## Curtiss SB2C-5 Helldiver

Standard carrier-borne bomber of the Aéronautique Navale, the SB2C-5 operated in Indochina from the decks of the *Arromanches, La Fayette*, and *Bois Belleau*, as well as from shore bases.

**Specification**
**Type:** two-seat carrier-based dive bomber
**Powerplant:** one 1,900-hp (1417-kW) Wright R-2600-20 radial piston engine
**Performance:** maximum speed 290 mph (467 km/h) at 16,500 ft (5030 m); climb rate 1,850 ft/min (564 m/min); service ceiling 27,600 ft (8410 m); combat range 1,165 miles (1875 km)
**Weights:** empty 10,589 lb (4803 kg); loaded 14,415 lb (6539 kg)
**Dimensions:** span 49 ft 9 in (15.16 m); length 36 ft 8 in (11.18 m); height 13 ft 2 in (4.01 m); wing area 422 sq ft (39.20 m$^2$)
**Armament:** two wing-mounted 20-mm cannon and two 0.303-in (7.7-mm) flexible machine-guns, plus up to 2,000 lb (907 kg) of bombs

**Seeing widespread service throughout the Pacific during the later years of World War II, the Helldiver continued its combat record in Indochina, flying bombing missions from French carriers. These aircraft are from Flotille 3F, embarked aboard *Arromanches*.**

## Dassault MD 312 and MD 315 Flamant

As one of the first post-World War II aircraft of French design to enter service with the Armée de L'Air, the Flamant was too late to see much use in Indochina. In the mid-fifties five MD 315s were delivered to the Royal Khmer Aviation and a few MD 312s were briefly operated by the VNAF before being returned to France.

**Specification**
**Type:** six-seat liaison aircraft
**Powerplant:** two 580-hp (433-kW) SNECMA-Renault 12S 02-201 inline liquid-cooled engines
**Performance:** maximum speed 236 mph (380 km/h); climb rate 984 ft/min (300 m/min); service ceiling 26,245 ft (8000 m); range 746 miles (1200 km)
**Weights:** empty 9,347 lb (4240 kg); loaded 12,754 lb (5785 kg)
**Dimensions:** span 67 ft 9 in (20.65 m); length 41 ft (12.50 m); height 14 ft 9.2 in (4.50 m); wing area 508 sq ft (47.20 m$^2$)
**Armament:** none

**Various versions of the indigenous Flamant were employed by French forces during the war in Indochina. Used primarily for liaison and staff transport, the type could also perform medevac duties. Later the Flamant served in small numbers with Cambodia and South Vietnam.**

## De Havilland Mosquito

Aware of the good results obtained with Mosquitoes by the RAF in India-Burma during World War II and later in Malaya, the Armée de l'Air entertained high hopes for the Mosquitoes of G.C. I/3 'Corse.' Heavily armed and possessing adequate range for operations in Indochina, the British-built twin-engined aircraft appeared to be an excellent choice. Unfortunately, a combination of problems with the aircraft's wooden structures and the age of its airframe led to serious maintenance difficulties, thus forcing the French Mosquito out of operation after only six months in Indochina.

**Specification** (Mosquito F.B.Mk VI)
**Type:** two-seat fighter-bomber
**Powerplant:** two 1,635-hp (1219-kW) Rolls-Royce Merlin 25 inline liquid-cooled engines
**Performance:** maximum speed 378mph (608 km/h); climb rate 2,850 ft/min (869 m/min); service ceiling 33,000 ft (10060 m); combat range 1,205 miles (1940 km)
**Weights:** empty 14,344 lb (6506 kg); loaded 22,258 lb (10096 kg)
**Dimensions:** span 54 ft 2 in (16.51 m); length 40 ft 6 in (12.34 m); height 12 ft 6 in (3.81 m); wing area 454 sq ft (42.18 m²)
**Armament:** four 0.303-in (7.7-mm) machine-guns and four 20-mm cannon, plus eight 60-lb (27.2-kg) rockets

**The excellent Mosquito suffered the same fate with the French as it had with British units during World War II; its wooden structure could not really cope with the hot and humid climate of South East Asia.**

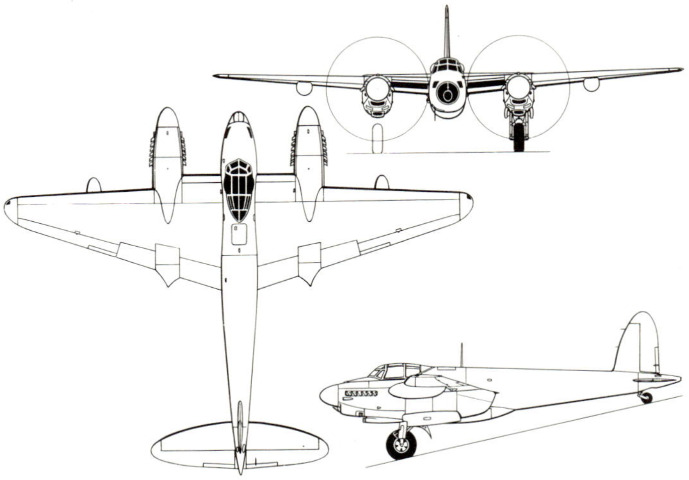

## De Havilland Canada C-7 Caribou

Initially operated in South East Asia by Army Aviation Companies, the Caribous were taken over by the USAF in January 1967. The 'Boos', which the USAF had considered less capable than its C-123s, soon proved themselves in Air Force service. Under the name of Wallabies, Caribous were operated in Vietnam between August 1964 and February 1972 by No. 35 Squadron, RAAF. The VNAF also received 48 of these aircraft during 1972.

**Specification** (C-7A)
**Type:** tactical transport (32 troops or 8,740 lb/3965 kg of cargo)
**Powerplant:** two 1,450-hp (1081-kW) Pratt & Whitney R-2000-7M2 radial piston engines
**Performance:** maximum speed 216 mph (347 km/h) at 6,500 ft (1980 m); climb rate 1,355 ft/min (413 m/min); service ceiling 24,800 ft (7560 m); range with maximum payload 242 miles (390 km)
**Weights:** empty 18,260 lb (8283 kg); loaded 28,500 lb (12928 kg)
**Dimensions:** span 95 ft 7.5 in (29.15 m); length 72 ft 7 in (22.12 m); height 31 ft 9 in (9.68 m); wing area 912 sq ft (84.72 m²)
**Armament:** none

**Possessing excellent short and rough field capability, the Caribou was used widely in the war zone. Its primary job for the US Army and Air Force was the supply of outlying Special Forces camps which could not handle C-130 transports.**

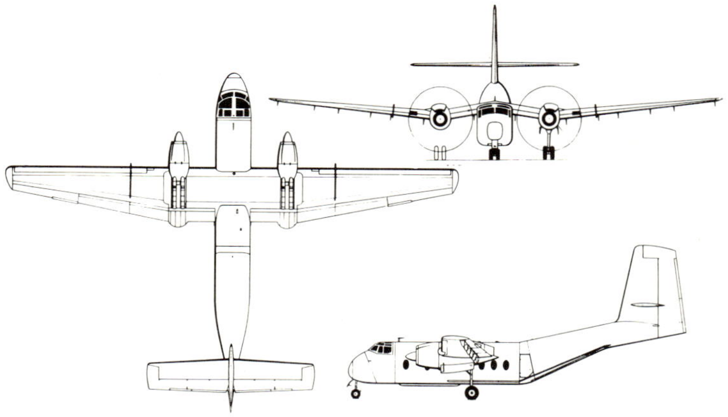

## De Havilland Canada U-1A Otter

Nearly one-half of the Canadian production of this large single-engined STOL aircraft was absorbed by the US military. Most of them were operated by the USA, with 23 aircraft being lost in Vietnam as a result of hostile actions or operational accidents between 1963 and 1970.

**Specification**
**Type:** nine-passenger utility transport
**Powerplant:** one 600-hp (447-kW) Pratt & Whitney R-1340-S1H1-G radial piston engine
**Performance:** maximum speed 160 mph (257 km/h) at 5,000 ft (1525 m); climb rate 735 ft/min (224 m/min); service ceiling 18,800 ft (5730 m); range 960 miles (1545 km)
**Weights:** empty 4,168 lb (1891 kg); loaded 8,000 lb (3629 kg)
**Dimensions:** span 58 ft (17.68 m); length 41 ft 10 in (12.75 m); height 12 ft 7 in (3.84 m); wing area 375 sq ft (34.84 m²)
**Armament:** none

**The US Army was the major operator of the Otter in South East Asia, employing the type for light transport. A number of RU-1s were used by Radio Research Companies for direction-finding duties.**

## De Havilland Canada U-6A Beaver

This Canadian-designed bush aircraft was first acquired by US military forces during the Korean War under the L-20 designation. A few were transferred to France in 1954 for use in Indochina. Later, the STOL characteristics of this aircraft (which was redesignated U-6 in 1962) were put to good use in Vietnam by the USA and the VNAF, with the latter also using the type for psychological warfare.

**Specification**
**Type:** seven passenger utility aircraft
**Powerplant:** one 450-hp (336-kW) Pratt & Whitney R-985-AN-1 radial piston engine
**Performance:** maximum speed 163 mph (262 km/h) at 5,000 ft (1525 m); climb rate 1,020 ft/min (311 m/min); service ceiling 18,000 ft (5485 m); range 455 miles (730 km)
**Weights:** empty 2,850 lb (1293 kg); loaded 5,100 lb (2313 kg)
**Dimensions:** span 48 ft (14.63 m); length 30 ft 3 in (9.22 m); height 9 ft (2.74 m); wing area 250 sq ft (23.23 m²)
**Armament:** none

**The type of aircraft operated in the far north of Canada had great application to the rough mountainous areas of Vietnam, the Beaver fitting the bill perfectly. In common with its larger sister, the Otter, the Beaver was also used for electronic surveillance purposes, such aircraft being designated RU-6.**

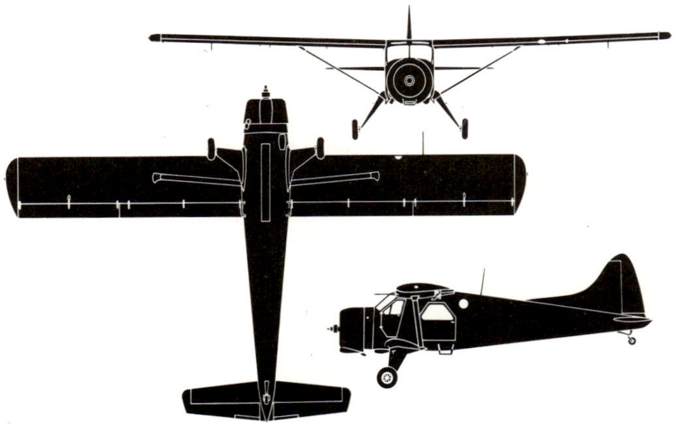

## Douglas A-1 Skyraider

Still equipping numerous Navy attack squadrons at the time of the Gulf of Tonkin Incident, A-1Hs and A-1Js played an active role during the early offensive against the North. Progressively replaced by A-6s aboard the large carriers, and by A-4s or A-7s aboard the smaller carriers, these single-seat Skyraiders were last deployed by VA-25 in 1967-68. During that period, detachments of four-seat EA-1Fs provided ECM support for CTF-77, with the last of these detachments leaving the Gulf of Tonkin in January 1969 aboard the USS *Intrepid*.

After the Skyraider had been adopted in 1964 to equip Air Commando Squadrons, single-seat A-1Hs and A-1Js and two-seat A-1Es and A-1Gs saw considerable service with the USAF in providing close support, flying interdiction missions along the Ho Chi Minh Trail, and escorting rescue helicopters. In this last role the Air Force flew Skyraiders until the fall of 1972. The VNAF received its first AD-6s (A-1Hs) in 1960 and operated both single-seat and two-seat versions of the Skyraider until 1975. Fifteen AD-4NAs (A-1Ds), which had been supplied to the Khmer Air Force by France in spite of US Government opposition to their transfer, saw much less use as Cambodia then lacked personnel to fly and maintain these aircraft.

**Specification** (A-1H)
**Type:** single-seat attack aircraft
**Powerplant:** one 2,700-hp (2013-kW) Wright R-3350-26WA radial piston engine
**Performance:** maximum speed 322 mph (518 km/h) at 18,000 ft (5485 m); climb rate 2,850 ft/min (869 m/min); service ceiling 28,500 ft (8685 m); combat range 1,315 miles (2115 km)
**Weights:** empty 11,968 lb (5429 kg); loaded 18,106 lb (8213 kg)
**Dimensions:** span 50 ft 0.25 in (15.25 m); length 38 ft 10 in (11.84 m); height 15 ft 8.25 in (4.78 m); wing area 400.33 sq ft (37.19 m$^2$)
**Armament:** four wing-mounted 20-mm cannon, plus up to 8,000 lb (3630 kg) of external stores

**VA-176 flew this A-1H Skyraider on attack missions over North Vietnam. During the early years of the war the tough and hard-hitting Skyraider still had much to offer the US Navy.**

**Breathing noise, dirt and power, the Skyraider found a new customer in the US Air Force during the conflict. Its most famous USAF role was that of 'Sandy' escort to rescue helicopters, for which its long loiter, ability to take fire and heavy weapons load made it unsurpassable. Although replaced by jets, these had great difficulty in staying with the helicopter throughout rescues.**

## Douglas A-3 Skywarrior

Although A-3Bs of VAH squadrons flew some bombing missions over the North and the South in 1965-66, it was their secondary capability as a tanker that was by then of greater interest to the Navy. Accordingly, in 1967 the removable air refuelling pack of the A-3Bs was replaced at NARF Alameda with a permanent tanker package to obtain the KA-3B version. The same overhaul and repair facility converted a number of A-3Bs and KA-3Bs into EKA-3Bs by adding electronic countermeasures systems to serve in the dual role of tanker and electronic support aircraft. During the South East Asia War, VAP-61, and VAP-62 flew RA-3Bs while VQ-1 sent detachments of EA-3Bs.

**Specification** (KA-3B)
**Type:** three-seat carrier-based tanker
**Powerplant:** two 10,500-lb (4763-kg) dry thrust and 12,400-lb (5625-kg) thrust with water injection Pratt & Whitney J57-P-10 turbojets
**Performance:** maximum speed 620 mph (998 km/h) at sea level; service ceiling 41,100 ft (12525 m); climb rate 5,620 ft/min (1713 m/min); combat range 2,100 miles (3380 km)
**Weights:** empty 37,329 lb (16932 kg); loaded 70,000 lb (31751 kg)
**Dimensions:** span 72 ft 6 in (22.10 m); length 76 ft 4 in (23.27 m); height 22 ft 9.5 in (6.95 m); wing area 812 sq ft (75.44 m$^2$)
**Armament:** none

**Among the support aircraft operated by the US Navy, none were more important than the various forms of A-3 Skywarrior, supplying ECM, Elint and tanking. This is a KA-3B tanker, seen on *Kitty Hawk* wearing experimental camouflage.**

## Douglas A-4 Skyhawk

Single-seat versions of the Skyhawk, a carrier-based light attack aircraft powered by a Wright J65 turbojet (A-4B and A-4C) or Pratt & Whitney J52 (A-4E and A-4F), bore the brunt of the Navy offensive against the North until 1968. Thereafter, replaced aboard the larger carriers by A-7s, Skyhawks continued in operation aboard the older carriers until the US withdrawal. As a result of their long and active combat life, more A-4s were lost during the South East Asia War than any other types of carrier-based aircraft and accounted for nearly 37 percent of Navy combat losses (compared with just above 10 percent for the A-7s). Likewise, 36 percent of the Marine combat losses were accounted for by single-seat A-4s and two-seat TA-4Fs, the latter being flown in the TAC(A) role.

**Specification** (A-4E)
**Type:** single-seat carrier-based attack aircraft
**Powerplant:** one 8,500-lb (3856-kg) thrust Pratt & Whitney J52-P-6A turbojet
**Performance:** maximum speed 673 mph (1083 km/h) at sea level; climb rate 5,750 ft/min (1753 m/min); service ceiling 42,700 ft (13015 m); combat range 1,160 miles (1865 km)
**Weights:** empty 9,853 lb (4469 kg); loaded 16,216 lkb (7355 kg)
**Dimensions:** span 27 ft 6 in (8.38 m); length 40 ft 1.5 in (12.23 m); height 15 ft 2 in (4.62 m); wing area 260 sq ft (24.15 m$^2$)
**Armament:** two 20-mm cannon, plus up to 8,200 lb (3719 kg) of external stores

**Standard attack bomber for both the Navy and Marines was the Douglas A-4, 'Heinemann's Hotrod'. The type had an amazing weapons carrying ability for its size, combined with high agility. Nevertheless, the Skyhawk suffered many losses.**

## Douglas B-26 (A-26) Invader

Fast, long-legged, rugged and heavily armed (up to 14 forward-firing 0.50-in machine-guns in its 'solid nose' B-26B version, or eight guns in the B-26C version, plus 5,000 lb of bombs, napalm cannisters or rockets), the Invader was undoubtedly the most effectve combat aircraft operated by the Armée de l'Air in Indochina. These same qualities led to its use by the *Farm Gate* detachment beginning in 1961. Fatigue-induced structural failures led to the type being withdrawn from use in 1964. The A-26A (initially designated B-26K) was a modernized version with strengthened structure which was used by the USAF for interdiction missions over the Ho Chi Minh Trail between 1966 and 1969.

**Specification** (A-26A)
**Type:** twin-engined counter-insurgency attack aircraft
**Powerplant:** two 2,500-hp (1864-kW) Pratt & Whitney R-2800-52W radial piston engines
**Performance:** maximum speed 327 mph (526 km/h) at 15,000 ft (4570 m); climb rate 2,050 ft/min (625 m/min); service ceiling 30,500 ft (9295 m); combat range 1,480 miles (2380 km)
**Weights:** empty 25,130 lb (11399 kg); loaded 37,000 lb (16783 kg)
**Dimensions:** span 71 ft 6 in (21.79 m); length 51 ft 7.3 in (15.73 m); height 19 ft (5.79 m); wing area 541 sq ft (50.26 m$^2$)
**Armament:** eight 0.50 in (12.7-mm) forward-firing machine-guns, plus 8,000 lb (3629 kg) of internal and external stores

**First use of the B-26 in South East Asia was by the French, which used it on bombing missions against the Viet Minh. Both B-26B and C models were flown, one of the former depicted here. It is from GB I/19 'Gascogne', which flew from Tourane.**

## Douglas B-66 Destroyer

Developed from the Navy A-3 Skywarrior, the tactical reconnaissance bomber B-/RB-66 series saw only limited service with the USAF. However, its EB-66C version was the only type of ESM/ECM aircraft in the Air Force inventory when operations over North Vietnam resulted in an urgent need for electronic countermeasures aircraft. Accordingly, the EB-66Cs were soon supplemented in South East Asia by EB-66Bs and EB-66Es obtained by modifying B-/RB-66Bs for ECM warfare.

**Specification** (EB-66C)
**Type:** seven-seat electronic warfare aircraft
**Powerplant:** two 10,200-lb (4627-kg) thrust Allison J71-A-13 turbojets
**Performance:** maximum speed 641 mph (1032 km/h) at 3,000 ft (915 m); climb rate 3,950 ft/min (1204 m/min); service ceiling 35,700 ft (10880 m); combat range 2,035 miles (3275 km)
**Weights:** empty 44,771 lb (20308 kg); loaded 76,967 lb (34912 kg)
**Dimensions:** span 74 ft 7 in (22.73 m); length 75 ft 2 in (22.91 m); height 23 ft 7 in (7.19 m); wing area 781 sq ft (72.55 m$^2$)
**Armament:** none

**The Air Force equivalent of the A-3 was not used in the same variety of roles, but did provide both ECM and ESM coverage for northbound strike forces, as well as accurate navigation for blind medium-level bombing missions. Flying from bases in Thailand, the B-66 force was kept busy in these roles until the advent of effective ECM carriage by the strikers themselves.**

## Douglas C-9A Nightingale

Specially acquired by the Air Force for aeromedical evacuation, the C-9A was a military version of the DC-9-32CF jetliner. Beginning in 1972, C-9As were flown in their intended role in South East Asia and within CONUS where they provided an efficient link between specialized military hospitals.

**Specification**
**Type:** aeromedical evacuation transport
**Powerplant:** two 14,500-lb (6577-kg) thrust Pratt & Whitney JT8D-9 turbofans
**Performance:** maximum speed 575 mph (925 km/h); range 1,245 miles (2005 km)
**Weight:** loaded 108,000 lb (48988 kg)
**Dimensions:** span 93 ft 5 in (28.47 m); length 119 ft 4 in (36.37 m); height 27 ft 6 in (8.38 m); wing area 1,000.7 sq ft (92.97 m²)
**Armament:** none

**Douglas C-9s were used for evacuation of wounded personnel from bases in South East Asia to Clark AB in the Philippines. This aircraft is seen on the last such flight of the war, taxiing out of Ubon.**

## Douglas C-47

Used to transport the first French troops to return to Indochina in 1945, the ubiquitous C-47 was to be seen throughout the next 30 years of fighting in Indochina and was operated by all combatants (the NVNAF, the Royal Khmer Air Force, and the Royal Lao Air Force flying a small number of Lisunov Li-2 transports, a Soviet-built derivative of the pre-World War II Douglas DC-3.) In addition to its transport role, this famous Douglas aircraft was used as a makeshift bomber by the French and South Vietnamese, for psychological warfare and for conventional and reconnaissance duties (SC-47D, EC-47P, EC-47Q, and EC-47N) by the USAF and the VNAF, and as a gunship (AC-47D, the 'A' prefix officially indicating the aircraft's role but jokingly being 'translated' as A for Ancient) by the USAF, and VNAF, the Khmer Air Force and the RLAF.

**Specification** (C-117D)
**Type:** twin-engined personnel (33 troops) or cargo transport
**Powerplant:** two 1,475-hp (1100-kW) Wright R-1820-80 radial piston engines
**Performance:** maximum speed 270 mph (435 km/h) at 5,900 ft (1800 m); climb rate 1,300 ft/min (396 m/min); range 1,750 miles (2815 km)
**Weights:** empty 19,537 lb (8862 kg); loaded 31,000 lb (14061 kg)
**Dimensions:** span 90 ft (27.43 m); length 67 ft 9 in (20.65 m); height 18 ft 3 in (5.56 m); wing area 969 sq ft (90.02 m²)
**Armament:** none

**Throughout the wars in Southeast Asia, the C-47 has played a major role. During the French involvement, they provided the backbone of the transport fleet. These shown here are from Air France, brought in to aid Armee de l'Air units.**

## Douglas C-54 Skymaster

Until 1955, France utilized Douglas DC-4 commercial transports and C-54 military versions for logistic support between the Métropole and Indochina. Use of this obsolete transport by US forces was limited, with Navy reserve crews and Marine H&MS squadrons flying C-54s in the transport role, while the USAF briefly flew specially-fitted versions for air rescue (SC-54D) and infrared reconnaissance (*Hilo Hattie*).

**Specification** (C-54G)
**Type:** military personnel (50 troops) or cargo (max. payload of 32,000 lb/14515 kg) transport
**Powerplant:** four 1,450-hp (1081-kW) Pratt & Whitney R-2000-9 radial piston engines
**Performance:** maximum speed 275 mph (442 km/h) at 17,500 ft (5335 m); climb rate 10,000 ft (3048 m) in 11 min; service ceiling 26,000 ft (7925 m); range 3,500 miles (5630 km) with payload of 10,000 lb (4535 kg)
**Weights:** empty 38,930 lb (17659 kg); loaded 62,000 lb (28123 kg)
**Dimensions:** span 117 ft 6 in (35.81 m); length 93 ft 10 in (28.60 m); height 27 ft 6 in (8.38 m); wing area 1,460 sq ft (135.63 m²)
**Armament:** none

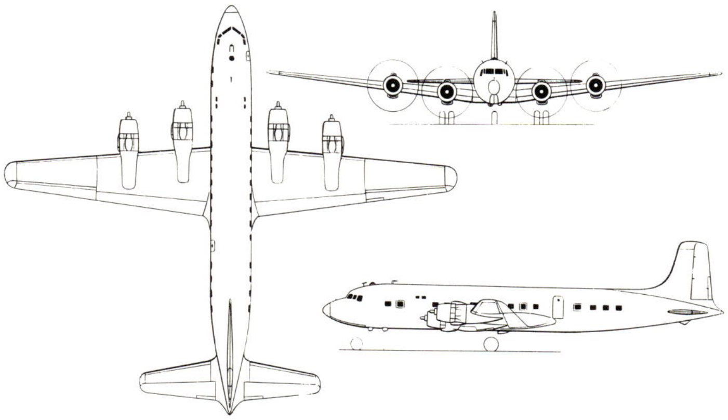

**The DC-4 and its military C-54 counterpart were sparingly used on transport and specialized duties. Among the latter were rescue and infra-red reconnaissance.**

## Douglas C-118 Liftmaster

In South East Asia the ageing C-118A (a military version of the Douglas DC-6A airliner) was primarily used for staff transport and aeromedical evacuation.

**Specification** (C-118A)
**Type:** military personnel (74 troops) or cargo (maximum payload of 27,000 lb/12247 kg) military transport
**Powerplant:** four 2,500-hp (1864-kW) Pratt & Whitney R-2800-52W radial piston engines
**Performance:** maximum speed 315 mph (507 km/h); climb rate 1,120 ft/min (341 m/min); range 3,005 miles (4835 km) with payload of 24,565 lb (11142 kg)
**Weights:** empty 55,357 lb (25110 kg); loaded 107,000 lb (48534 kg)
**Dimensions:** span 117 ft 6 in (35.81 m); length 106 ft 10 in (32.56 m); height 28 ft 8 in (8.74 m); wing area 1,463 sq ft (135.92 m²)
**Armament:** none

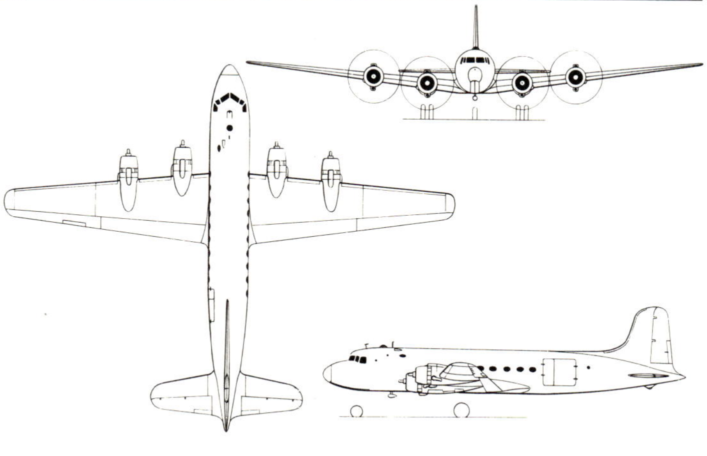

**A natural enlargement of the DC-4/C-54 layout, the DC-6/C-118 was used on support missions during the early years of the US involvement. Primary role was casualty evacuation, but this was lost to the C-9A.**

## Douglas C-124 Globemaster II

USAF Globemaster IIs flew logistics missions between France and Indochina to rush troops and equipment to the hard-pressed French forces during 1954-55. When the United States became fully involved in the Vietnamese conflict the capacious Globemaster II, although it was slow and obsolete, proved invaluable; it was the only USAF transport capable of carrying large combat vehicles and bulky pieces of construction equipment until the Lockheed C-5A entered service.

**Specification** (C-124C)
**Type:** military cargo transport (maximum payload of 74,000 lb/33565 kg) or personnel transport (200 troops or 168 patients and 15 medical attendants)
**Powerplant:** four 3,800-hp (2834-kW) Pratt & Whitney R-4360-63A radial piston engines
**Performance:** maximum speed 304 mph (489 km/h) at 20,800 ft (6340 m); climb rate 760 ft/min (232 m/min); service ceiling 21,800 ft (6645 m); range 4,030 miles (6585 km) with a payload of 26,375 lb (11963 kg)
**Weights:** empty 101,165 lb (45888 kg); loaded 185,000 lb (83915 kg)
**Dimensions:** span 174 ft 1.5 in (53.07 m); length 130 ft 5 in (39.75 m); height 48 ft 3.5 in (14.72 m); wing area 2,506 sq ft (232.82 $m^2$)
**Armament:** none

**The remarkable Globemaster served on the trans-Pacific air bridge, bringing in outsize items to the war zone. Such items were loaded and unloaded via clamshell doors which opened up the bottom half of the fuselage while personnel occupied the upper deck. This example is seen pulling on to the ramp at Tan Son Nhut in 1966.**

## Douglas C-133 Cargomaster

Plagued by engine unreliability and fatigue problems the C-133, which had a capacious fuselage, was nevertheless much needed for logistic support of operations in South East Asia. The type was withdrawn from use in 1971 after the entry into service of the Lockheed C-5A.

**Specification** (C-133B)
**Type:** military cargo transport
**Powerplant:** four7,500-eshp (5593-ekW) Pratt & Whitney T34-P-9W turboprops
**Performance:** maximum speed 359 mph (578 km/h) at 8,70 ft (2650 m); climb rate 1,280 ft/min (390 m/min); service ceiling 29,950 ft (9130 m); range 4,000 miles (6435 km) with payload of 52,000 lb (23587 kg)
**Weights:** empty 120,263 lb (54550 kg); loaded 275,000 lb (124738 kg)
**Dimensions:** span 179 ft 8 in (54.76m); length 157 ft 6 in (48.01 m); height 48 ft 3 in (14.71 m); wing area 2,673 sq ft (248.33 $m^2$)
**Armament:** none

**The C-133 was much swifter than the Globemaster for the transport of large goods, but it suffered from reliability problems. Tan Son Nhut was the major airfield for such transport flights into South Vietnam, this C-133 landing there in 1969.**

## Douglas EF-10B Skynight

Although the Navy's first jet fighter was no longer suitable for combat operations in the early sixties, its EF-10B version became much needed a few years later as it was the only jet-powered ECM aircraft in naval aviation service. In this role, the type was operated in Vietnam by VMCJ-1 from 1965 until 1969.

**Specification**
**Type:** two-seat electronic warfare aircraft
**Powerplant:** two 3,400-lb (1542-kg) thrust Westinghouse J34-WE-36 turbojets
**Performance:** maximum speed 565 mph (909 km/h) at 20,000 ft (6095 m); climb rate 4,000 ft/min (1219 m/min); service ceiling 38,300 ft (11675 m); maximum range 1,540 miles (2480 km)
**Weights:** empty 18,160 lb (8237 kg); loaded 23,575 lb (10693 kg)
**Dimensions:** span 50 ft (15.24 m); length 45 ft 6 in (13.87 m); height 16 ft 1 in (4.90 m); wing area 400 sq ft (37.16 $m^2$)
**Armament:** four 20-mm cannon in the nose

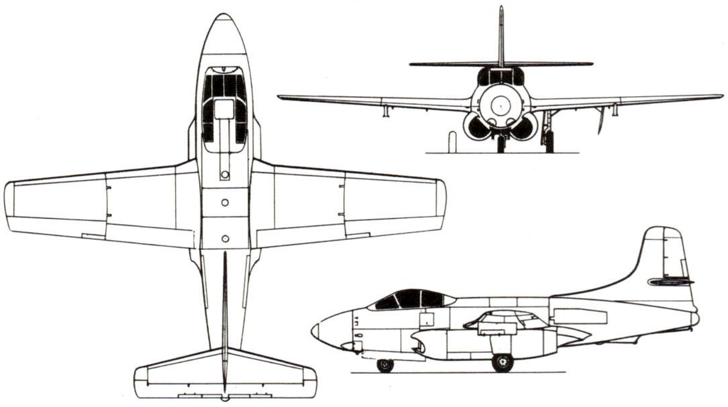

**Until the arrival of the dedicated Grumman EA-6A, the EF-10B Skyknight flew ECM protection missions for Marine Corps strike aircraft, operating with VMCJ-1 from Da Nang.**

## Douglas SBD-5 Dauntless

The famous Dauntless (the winner of the Battle of Midway in June 1942) was already obsolete when the Aéronautique Navale received its first SBD-5s in 1944. Nevertheless, Dauntlesses made three deployments to Indochina in 1947-48 aboard the escort carrier *Dixmude* and the light carrier *Arromanches*.

**Specification**
**Type:** two-seat carrier-based dive bomber
**Powerplant:** one 1,200-hp (895-kW) Wright R-1820-60 radial piston engine
**Performance:** maximum speed 255 mph (410 km/h) at 14,000 ft (4265 m); climb rate 1,700 ft/min (518 m/min); service ceiling 25,530 ft (7780 m); combat range 1,115 miles (1795 km)
**Weights:** empty 6,404 lb (2905 kg); loaded 9,359 lb (4245 kg)
**Dimensions:** span 41 ft 6.4 in (12.66 m); length 33 ft 1.25 in (10.09 m); height 13 ft 7 in (4.14 m); wing area 325 sq ft (30.19 $m^2$)
**Armament:** two 0.50-in (12.7-mm) forward-firing machine-guns and two 0.303-in (7.7-mm) flexible machine-guns, plus a maximum bomb load of 2,250 lb (1020 kg)

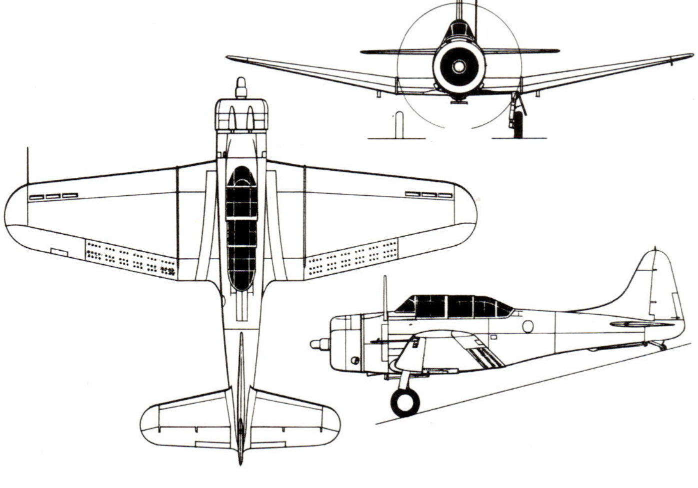

**Despite its obsolescence, the Dauntless flew on with Aeronavale units after the end of World War II, and was used during the early campaigns against the Viet Minh, flying from French carriers. The Dauntless made up for its light bombload by being highly accurate.**

## English Electric Canberra B.Mk 20 (see Martin B-57)

## Fairchild C-119 Flying Boxcar

To help make up shortages in the French military transport system in Indochina, in 1954 the United States temporarily lent a number of C-119Cs. These aircraft were returned to the USAF in 1955 and the type was not operated in Vietnam again until January 1969 when AC-119Gs were deployed. Later in the same year, these gunships were joined in USAF service by jet-augmented AC-119Ks. Subsequently the VNAF also flew C-119G/L transports and AC-119G/K gunships. On 30 April 1975 an AC-119K became the last VNAF aircraft to be lost in combat.

**Specification** (AC-119K)
**Type:** gunship
**Powerplant:** two 3,700-hp (2759-kW) Wright R-3350-89B radial piston engines and two 2,850-lb (1293-kg) thrust General Electric J85-GE-17 turbojets
**Performance:** maximum speed 243 mph (391 km/h) at 10,000 ft (3050 m); combat range 990 miles (1595 km)
**Weights:** empty 44,747 lb (20300 kg); loaded 77,000 lb (34925 kg)
**Dimensions:** span 109 ft 3 in (33.29 m); length 86 ft 6 in (26.36 m); height 26 ft 6 in (8.08 m); wing area 1,447 sq ft (134.43 m²)
**Armament:** four 0.30-in (7.62-mm) Miniguns and two 20-mm six-barrel cannon

**Last of the gunship conversions was the Fairchild AC-119K 'Stinger'. These aircraft featured jet augmentation, APQ-133 beacon tracking radar and an armament of four Miniguns and two Vulcans.**

## Fairchild C-123 Provider

For ten and one half years, beginning in January 1962, USAF C-123Bs and C-123Ks (the latter being a jet-augmented version which arrived in Vietnam in May 1967) contributed a substantial share of in-country airlift and resupply operations. Provider transports were also operated in South East Asia by Air America, the VNAF, the Khmer Air Force, the Royal Lao Air Force and the Royal Thai Air Force. Moreover, the USAF *Ranch Hand* unit used UC-123Bs and UC-123Ks for chemical spraying.

**Specification** (C-123K)
**Type:** tactical assault transport (60 troops or 15,000 lb/6800 kg of cargo)
**Powerplant:** two 2,500-hp (1864-kW) Pratt & Whitney R-2800-99W radial piston engines and two 2,850-lb (1293-kg) thrust General Electric J85-GE-17 turbojets.
**Performance:** maximum speed 228 mph (367 km/h) at 10,000 ft (3050 m); climb rate 1,220 ft/min (372 m/min); service ceiling 21,100 ft (6430 m); combat range 1,470 miles (2365 km)
**Weights:** empty 35,366 lb (16042 kg); loaded 60,000 lb (27215 kg)
**Dimensions:** span 110 ft (33.53 m); length 76 ft 3 in (23.24 m); height 34 ft 1 in (10.39 m); wing area 1,223 sq ft (113.62 m²)
**Armament:** none

**Although performing sterling work in the transport role, the C-123s are best remembered for their defoliation spraying missions under the *Ranch Hand* programme.**

## Fairchild AU-23A Peacemaker

As part of the *Credible Chase* project the Air Force evaluated both the AU-23A and the Helio AU-24A as mini-gunships. Neither was retained for service with the USAF but a few AU-23As (the gunship version of the Swiss-designed Pilatus Turbo-Porter built under licence by Fairchild Industries) were delivered to the Khmer Air Force in 1974 as part of *Project Flycatcher*. Fairchild-built Turbo-Porters were also used by Air America as STOL transports.

**Specification**
**Type:** mini gunship
**Powerplant:** one 576-eshp (430-ekW) AiResearch TPE 331-1-101 turboprop
**Performance:** maximum speed 164 mph (264 km/h) at 10,000 ft (3050 m); climb rate 1,607 ft/min (490 m/min); service ceiling 27,875 ft (8500 m); combat range 683 miles (1100 km)
**Weights:** empty 2,612 lb (1185 kg); loaded 4,850 lb (2200 kg)
**Dimensions:** span 49 ft 8 in (15.13 m); length 35 ft 9 in (10.90 m); height 10 ft 6 in (3.20 m); wing area 310 sq ft (28.80 m²)
**Armament:** one 20-mm XM-197 cannon in aft cabin, plus up to 2,000 lb (907 kg) of external stores

**The Fairchild-built version of the Porter formed the basis for the AU-23 gunship project. Other Porters were operated in South East Asia on covert insertion missions by Air America, the CIA's airline.**

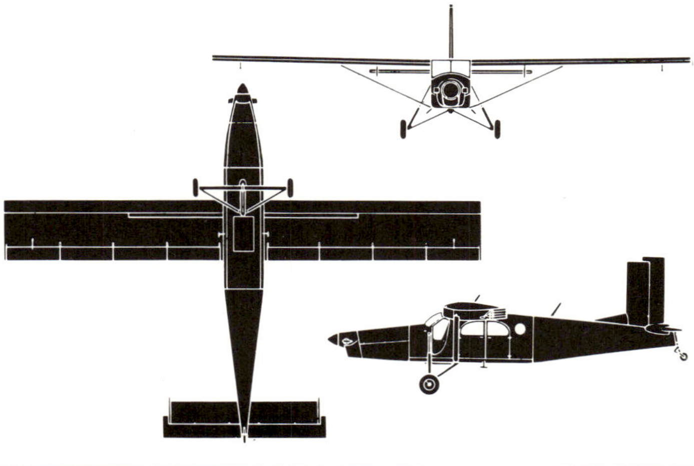

## Fletcher FD-25 Defender

Designed in the United States as a light ground support aircraft for use by small air forces, the Defender was built under licence by Toyo Aircraft Company. Japanese-built Defenders (FD-25A two-seaters and FD-25B single-seaters) were among the first aircraft acquired by the Royal Khmer Aviation.

**Specification** (FD-25B)
**Type:** light counterinsurgency aircraft
**Powerplant:** one 225-hp (168-kW) Continental E-225-8 air-cooled piston engine
**Performance:** maximum speed 187 mph (301 km/h); climb rate 1,725 ft/min (526 m/min); range 630 miles (1015 km)
**Weights:** empty 1,428 lb (648 kg); loaded 2,700 lb (1225 kg)
**Dimensions:** span 30 ft (9.14 m); length 20 ft 11 in (6.38 m); height 6 ft 3 in (1.91 m); wing area 150 sq ft (13.94 m²)
**Armament:** two 0.30-in (7.62-mm) machine-guns and an external load of up to 500lb (227 kg)

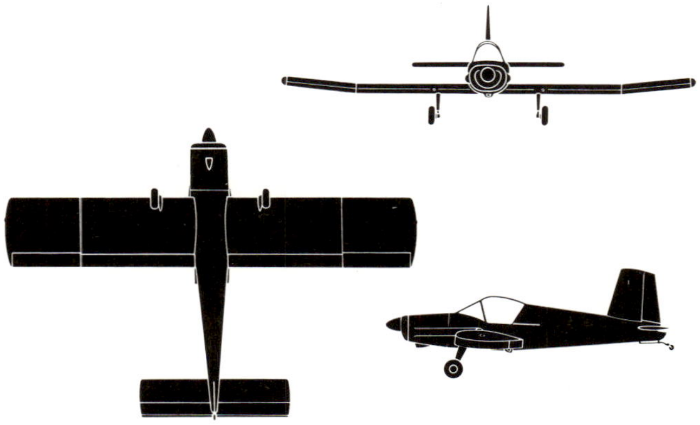

**The light attack Fletcher Defender was used only by the Royal Khmer Air Force during the conflict. They had little impact on proceedings.**

## General Dynamics F-111A

In 1968, following the loss of three aircraft, the initial *Combat Lancer* deployment of F-111As to South East Asia was terminated abruptly. F-111As were again sent to Thailand four years later and, this time, performed with great success during *Linebacker II* when their highly sophisticated terrain-following and blind-bombing radar enabled them to hit difficult targets accurately even under appalling weather conditions.

### Specification

**Type:** two-seat tactical strike fighter
**Powerplant:** two 12,000-lb (5443-kg) dry thrust and 18,500-lb (8391-kg) afterburning thrust Pratt & Whitney TF30-P-3 turbojets
**Performance:** maximum speed 1,650 mph (2655 km/h) at 40,000 ft (12190 m); combat range 1,500 miles (2415 km) with maximum weapons load
**Weights:** empty 42,500 lb (19278 kg); loaded 92,500 lb (41957 kg)
**Dimensions:** span (unswept) 63 ft (19.20 m) and (swept) 31 ft 11.4 in (9.74 m); length 73 ft 6 in (22.40 m); height 17 ft 1.5 in (5.22 m); wing area 525 sq ft (48.77 m²)
**Armament:** one 20-mm M-61 six-barrel cannon and up to 30,000 lb (13608 kg) of internal and external stores

**F-111A seen during the *Combat Lancer* evaluation deployment, preparing for launch on a bombing mission. After the disastrous deployment, it was to be 1972 before the F-111 graced Asian skies again.**

## Grumman A-6 Intruder

Capable of all-weather operations, the A-6A proved to be an outstanding aircraft when it began combat operations in July 1965 with VA-75 from the USS *Independence*. The type then quickly became the standard carrier-based medium attack aircraft of the US Navy and was also flown by VMA(AW) squadrons operating from land bases and from the USS *Coral Sea*. Specialized attack versions included the A-6B, fitted to fire Standard ARMs (anti-radiation missiles), and the A-6C, with sensors for detecting and attacking truck convoys. The KA-6D, a tanker version, saw extensive service with carrier-based units. Electronic countermeasures versions were the two-seat EA-6A operated by the Marines and the four-seat EA-6B flown by Navy squadrons.

### Specification (A-6A)

**Type:** carrier-based all-weather attack aircraft
**Powerplant:** two 9,300-lb (4218-kg) thrust Pratt & Whitney J52-P-8A turbojets
**Performance:** maximum speed 685 mph (1102 km) at sea level; climb rate 6,950 ft/min (2118 m/min); service ceiling 41,660 ft (12700 m); combat range 1,920 miles (3090 km)
**Weights:** empty 25,684 lb (11650 kg); loaded 60,280 lb (27343 kg)
**Dimensions:** span 53 ft (16.15 m); length 54 ft 7 in (16.64 m); height 15 ft 7 in (4.75 m); wing area 529 sq ft (49.15 m²)
**Armament:** up to 15,000 lb (6804 kg) of external stores

**Multiple-ejector rack-equipped A-6A returns post-strike to USS *Ranger*. The landing pose demonstrates arrester hook, leading edge slats, trailing edge flaps and split wingtip airbrakes, all needed for slow approach speed and speedy stopping on the deck.**

## Grumman C-1 Trader (see Grumman S-2 Tracker)

## Grumman C-2A Greyhound (see Grumman E-2 Hawkeye)

## Grumman E-1B Tracer

Although replaced aboard the larger and more modern carriers by turboprop-powered Hawkeyes, the less capable Tracer was used throughout the American phase of the war to provide airborne early warning over the Gulf of Tonkin.

### Specification

**Type:** carrier-based airborne early warning aircraft
**Powerplant:** two 1,525-hp (1137-kW) Wright R-1820-82 radial piston engines
**Performance:** maximum speed 228 mph (367 km/h) at 5,000 ft (1525 m); climb rate 1,120 ft/min (341 m/min); service ceiling 15,800 ft (4815 m); combat range 875 miles (1410 km)
**Weights:** empty 20,638 lb (9361 kg); loaded 26,600 lb (12065 kg)
**Dimensions:** span 72 ft 4.75 in (22.07 m); length 45 ft 3.5 in (13.80 m); height 16 ft 10 in (5.13 m); wing area 506 sq ft (47.01 m²)
**Armament:** none

**The E-1 Tracer was based on the C-1 Trader airframe, with twin fins and a dorsal rotodome housing APS-82 airborne early warning radar.**

## Grumman E-2 Hawkeye

Carrying a powerful radar scanner in a rotating housing ('rotodome'), the Hawkeye was a highly capable airborne early warning aircraft. E-2As were first deployed to the Gulf of Tonkin at the end of 1965 aboard the USS *Kitty Hawk*, and this and later versions progressively replaced the older Tracers aboard the larger carriers. A transport derivative, the C-2A Greyhound, supplemented the C-1A Trader in the important COD mission.

### Specification (E-2A)

**Type:** carrier-based airborne early warning aircraft
**Powerplant:** two 4,050-eshp (3020-ekW) Allison T56-A-8A turboprops
**Performance:** maximum speed 370 mph (595 km/h); service ceiling 31,700 ft (9660 m); combat range 1400 miles (2250 km)
**Weights:** empty 36,063 lb (16358 kg); loaded 49,638 lb (22515 kg)
**Dimensions:** span 80 ft 7 in (24.56 m); length 56 ft 4 in (17.17 m); height 18 ft 4 in (5.59 m); wing area 700 sq ft (65.03 m²)
**Armament:** none

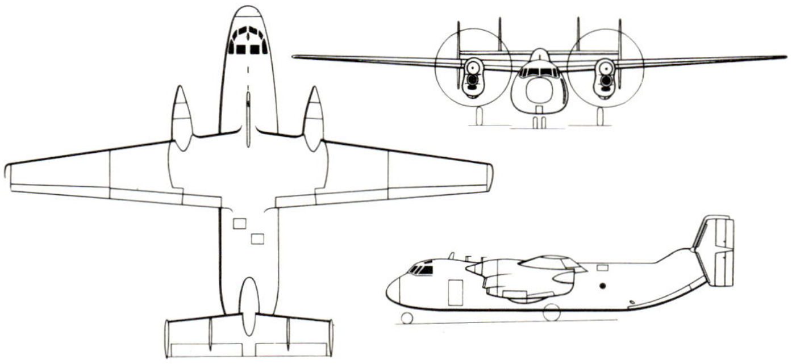

**Grumman C-2 Greyhound COD aircraft.**

## Grumman F-14A Tomcat

**VF-1 F-14A seen on its first deployment aboard *Enterprise* during April 1975.**

Tomcats, which arrived too late to be used while the US Navy was operating against North Vietnam, made a brief appearance in the theatre when VF-1 and VF-2, operating from the *Enterprise*, provided air cover during the closing days of *Frequent Wind* in April 1975.

### Specification

**Type:** two-seat carrier-based fighter
**Powerplant:** two 20,600-lb (9344-kg) afterburning thrust Pratt & Whitney TF30-P-412 turbofans
**Performance:** maximum speed 1,564 mph (2517 km/h) at 40,000 ft (12190 m); climb rate 30,000 ft/min (9144 m/min); service ceiling 60,000 ft (18290 m); combat range 2,000 miles (3220 km)
**Weights:** empty 37,500 lb (17010 kg); loaded 57,300 lb (25990 kg)
**Dimensions:** span (unswept) 64 ft 1.5 in (19.55 m) and (swept) 38 ft 2 in (11.63 m); length 62 ft 8 in (19.10 m); height 16 ft (4.87 m); wing area 565 sq ft (52.49 m²)
**Armament:** one 20-mm M-61 six-barrel cannon plus four AIM-7 Sparrow and four AIM-9 Sidewinder air-to-air missiles (or cannon and six AIM-54 Phoenix air-to-air missiles)

## Grumman F6F-5 Hellcat

After the United States began supplying military aircraft for use by French forces in Indochina, ex-US Navy Hellcats were operated by three Groupes de Chasse of the Armée de l'Air between November 1950 and January 1953. Beginning in September 1951, Hellcats of the Aéronautique Navale were also deployed to Indochina aboard the *Arromanches* and *La Fayette*.

### Specification

**Type:** carrier-based fighter
**Powerplant:** one 2,000 hp (1491-kW) Pratt & Whitney R-2800-10W radial piston engine
**Performance:** maximum speed 380 mph (611 km/h) at 23,400 ft (7130 m); climb rate 2,980 ft/min (908 m/min); service ceiling 37,300 ft (11370 m); combat range 945 miles (1520 km)
**Weights:** empty 9,238 lb (4190 kg); loaded 15,413 lb (6991 kg)
**Dimensions:** span 42 ft 10 in (13.06 m); length 33 ft 7 in (10.24 m); height 13 ft 1 in (3.99 m); wing area 334 sq ft (31.03 m²)
**Armament:** six wing-mounted 0.50-in (12.7-mm) machine-guns and 1,000 lb (454 kg) of bombs or rockets

**Deck crewman prepares to remove the run-up chock from the wheel of a Flotille 11F Hellcat as it prepares to launch from *Arromanches*.**

## Grumman F8F Bearcat

Even though designed in 1943 as a carrier-based interceptor for the US Navy, it was as a land-based fighter-bomber that the Bearcat made its combat début in March 1951 with G.C. 3/6 'Roussillon'. The type went on to become numerically the most important fighter of the Armée de l'Air in Indochina and served with distinction during the battle for Dien Bien Phu. Twenty-eight Bearcats also became the first VNAF fighters and served in Vietnamese colours until August 1959

### Specification (F8F-1B)

**Type:** carrier-based fighter
**Powerplant:** one 2,100-hp (1566-kW) Pratt & Whitney R-2800-34W radial piston engine
**Performance:** maximum speed 421 mph (677 km/h) at 19,700 ft (6005 m); climb rate 4,570 ft/min (1392 m/min); service ceiling 38,700 ft (11795 m); combat range 1,105 miles (1780 km)
**Weights:** empty 7,070 lb (3207 kg); loaded 12,947 lb (5873 kg)
**Dimensions:** span 35 ft 10 in (10.92 m); length 28 ft 3 in (8.61 m); height 13 ft 10 in (4.22 m); wing area 244 sq ft (22.67 m²)
**Armament:** four wing-mounted 20-mm cannon plus 1,000 lb (454 kg) of bombs or rockets

**Principal fighter-bomber in the Indochina war was the F8F Bearcat. Serving with Armée de l'Air units, the F8F was employed on strikes with bombs, rockets, cannon or napalm.**

## Grumman TF-9J Cougar

Having become during the late fifties the standard Navy advanced trainer, the F9F-8T (TF-9J after 1962) helped most naval pilots to hone their skills prior to joining operational squadrons and deploying to the Gulf of Tonkin. Although the type saw more limited service with the USMC, it was only with that service that the TF-9J was flown in combat in the TAC(A) role beginning in 1966.

### Specification

**Type:** two-seat advanced jet trainer and forward air control aircraft
**Powerplant:** one 7,200-lb (3266-kg) thrust Pratt & Whitney J48-P-8A turbojet
**Performance:** maximum speed 705 mph (1135 km/h) at sea level; climb rate 40,000 ft (12192 m) in 8.5 min; service ceiling 50,000 ft (15240 m); combat range 600 miles (965 km)
**Weight:** loaded 20,600 lb (9344 kg)
**Dimensions:** span 34 ft 6 in (10.52 m); length 44 ft 5 in (13.54 m); height 12 ft 3 in (3.73 m); wing area 337 sq ft (31.31 m²)
**Armament:** two 20-mm cannon and 2,000 lb (907 kg) of external stores

**The Marine Corps found the fast-mover FAC a vital piece of combat operations. First aircraft in the role for the USMC was the TF-9J Cougar.**

## Grumman JRF-5 Goose

Twelve JRF-5 light twin-engined flying-boats were operated in Indochina beginning in February 1972 by Escadrille 8S for maritime surveillance. Some of these aircraft were fitted with twin side-firing machine-guns in their left fuselage door, thus becoming the first fixed-wing gunships to be used in South East Asia.

**Specification**
**Type:** utility transport (4-7 passengers) amphibian
**Powerplant:** two 450-hp (336-kW) Pratt & Whitney R-985-AN-6 radial piston engines
**Performance:** maximum speed 201 mph (323 km/h) at 5,000 ft (1525 m); climb rate 1,100 ft/min (335 m/min); service ceiling 21,300 ft (6490 m); range 640 miles (1030 km)
**Weights:** empty 5,425 lb (2461 kg); loaded 8,000 lb (3629 kg)
**Dimensions:** span 49 ft (14.94 m); length 38 ft 6 in (11.73 m); height 16 ft 2 in (4.93 m); wing area 375 sq ft (34.84 $m^2$)
**Armament:** (French Navy modification) twin 0.50-in (12.7-mm) machine-guns firing sideways

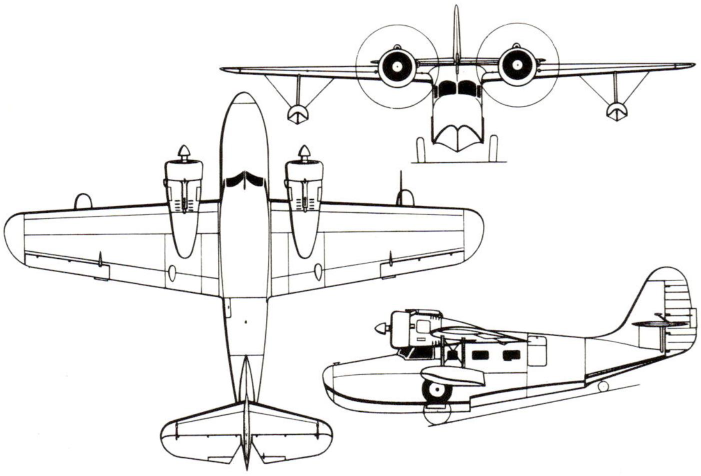

**Grumman produced a family of amphibians with similar layout but in differing sizes, the Goose being the second smallest. It proved reliable in the coastal patrol and SAR roles.**

## Grumman S-2 Tracker

During the early phases of US operations in the Gulf of Tonkin, when intervention by Chinese submarines was feared, S-2s based aboard CVS carriers provided anti-submarine cover for CTF-77. Utility versions (US-2A, US-2B and US-2C) of the Tracker were used in support of the Fleet and Marine activities, while the specialized C-1A Trader was the main COD aircraft shuttling personnel, mail, and urgently needed parts from shore bases to carriers.

**Specification** (S-2E)
**Type:** carrier-based anti-submarine aircraft
**Powerplant:** two 1,525-hp (1137-kW) R-1820-82WA radial piston engines
**Performance:** maximum speed 265 mph (426 km/h) at sea level; climb rate 1,390 ft/min (424 m/min); service ceiling 21,000 ft (6400 m); combat range 1,150 miles (1850 km)
**Weights:** empty 18,750 lb (8505 kg); loaded 26,867 lb (12187 kg)
**Dimensions:** span 72 ft 7 in (22.12 m); length 43 ft 6 in (13.26 m); height 16 ft 7.5 in (5.06 m); wing area 496 sq ft (46.08 $m^2$)
**Armament:** up to 4,810 lb (2182 kg) of depth charges, torpedoes, mines or rockets

**Grumman S-2 Tracker of VS-21, with MAD tail boom retracted.**

## Grumman HU-16B Albatross

From June 1964 until September 1967, when their duties were taken over by air-refuelable HH-3 helicopters, the Albatross amphibians were the main USAF combat rescue vehicles operating in South East Asia.

**Specification**
**Type:** six-seat air-sea rescue amphibian
**Powerplant:** two 1,425-hp (1063-kW) Wright R-1820-76B radial piston engines
**Performance:** maximum speed 236 mph (379 km/h) at sea level; climb rate 1,450 ft/min (442 m/min); service ceiling 21,500 ft (6550 m); range 2,850 miles (4585 km)
**Weights:** empty 22,883 lb (10380 kg); loaded 30,353 lb (13768 kg)
**Dimensions:** span 96 ft 8 in (29.46 m); length 62 ft 10 in (19.15 m); height 25 ft 10 in (7.87 m); wing area 1,035 sq ft (96.15 $m^2$)
**Armament:** none

**Larger than the Goose, the Albatross provided early combat rescue coverage for the USAF in South East Asia. Wearing blue-grey and light grey colour schemes, the aircraft flew from Da Nang.**

## Grumman OV-1 Mohawk

The high-performance Mohawk observation aircraft saw extensive service in Vietnam, where it was first deployed by the USA during the summer of 1962. The basic OV-1A version was complemented by the OV-1B with underfuselage SLAR (side looking airborne radar), the OV-1C with infrared sensors, and the OV-1D with either SLAR or infrared sensors. Some Mohawks were fitted to carry external stores but this practice was not standardized.

**Specification** (OV-1A)
**Type:** two-seat STOL observation aircraft
**Powerplant:** two 1,150-eshp (858-kW) Lycoming T53-L-7 turboprops
**Performance:** maximum speed 308 mph (496 km/h) at 5,000 ft (1525 m); climb rate 2,950 ft/min (899 m/min); service ceiling 30,300 ft (9235 m); range 1,230 miles (1980 m)
**Weights:** empty 9,937 lb (4507 kg); loaded 12,672 lb (5748 kg)
**Dimensions:** span 42 ft (12.80 m); length 41 ft (12.50 m); height 12 ft 8 in (3.86 m); wing area 330 sq ft (30.65 $m^2$)
**Armament:** none

**The OV-1B version of the Mohawk battlefield surveillance platform carried a SLAR in a canoe pod under the starboard fuselage. This was used to provide stand-off radar imagery of armoured units and troop movements.**

## Handley Page Hastings C.3

Three examples of this British-built transport, which had been acquired by the RNZAF in 1951, were used by its No. 41 Squadron for logistic flights between New Zealand and South Vietnam until replaced by the Lockheed C-130Hs of No. 40 Squadron.

### Specification

**Type:** military transport (50 troops) aircraft
**Powerplant:** four 1,675-hp (1249-kW) Bristol Hercules 737 radial piston engines
**Performance:** maximum speed 350 mph (564 km/h); climb rate 890 ft/min (271 m/min); service ceiling 26,500 ft (8075 m); range with maximum payload 1,690 miles (2720 km)
**Weights:** empty 48,600 lb (22045 kg); loaded 80,000 lb (36287 kg)
**Dimensions:** span 113 ft (34.44 m); length 82 ft 8 in (25.20 m); height 22 ft 6 in (6.86 m); wing area 1,408 sq ft (130.80 m²)
**Armament:** none

**Standard RAF transport of the day, the Hastings was also used in small numbers by the RNZAF, which flew these occasionally in to the war zone delivering materiel, serving alongside another British-built transport, the Bristol Freighter.**

## Helio U-10 and AU-24

U-10A STOL utility aircraft were among the types sent in late 1962 to boost the strength of the *Farm Gate* detachment. Later on, Air Commando Squadrons flew U-10As and U-10Ds, notably to resupply *Lima Sites* in Laos. Fifteen AU-24A mini-gunships, which differed from U-10s in being powered by a Pratt & Whitney PT6 turboprop and armed with a side-firing XM-197 20-mm gun, were evaluated as part of the *Credible Chase* project.

### Specification (U-10A)

**Type:** five-seat utility aircraft
**Powerplant:** one 295-hp (220-kW) Lycoming GO-480-G1D6 air-cooled piston engine
**Performance:** maximum speed 176 mph (283 km/h) at 8,200 ft (2500 m); climb rate 1,350 ft/min (411 m/min); range 670 miles (1080 km)
**Weights:** empty 2,037 lb (924 kg); loaded 3,920 lb (1778 kg)
**Dimensions:** span 39 ft (11.89 m); length 30 ft 9 in (9.37 m); height 8 ft 10 in (2.69 m); wing area 231 sq ft (21.46 m²)
**Armament:** none

**With its good STOL characteristics, the Helio U-10B was well-suited to ancillary activities such as resupply of isolated bases, psychological warfare and covert activities. The USAF had to take back aircraft from the CONUS ANG to supply its demand for the type in South East Asia.**

## Hiller OH-23 Raven

The first helicopters to be operated for war-related activities in Indochina were a pair of civil Hiller 360s acquired by the Service de Santé d'Indochine and used for medical evacuation. They were soon joined by a small number of H-23As and H-23Bs (military versions of the Hiller 360) which were supplied to the Armée de l'Air by the United States. Later on, the US Army made limited use in Vietnam of more modern versions of this light helicopter.

### Specification (OH-23G)

**Type:** three-seat utility and observation helicopter
**Powerplant:** one 305-hp (227-kW) Lycoming VO-540-A1B air-cooled piston engine
**Performance:** maximum speed 96 mph (154 km/h) at sea level; climb rate 1,290 ft/min); service ceiling 15,200 ft (4635 m); range 250 miles (400 km)
**Weights:** empty 1,755 lb (796 kg); loaded 2,800 lb (1270 kg)
**Dimensions:** rotor diameter 35 ft 5 in (10.79 m); fuselage length 28 ft 6 in (8.69 m); height 10 ft 1.5 in (3.09 m)
**Armament:** none

**This Service de Santé Hiller 360 flies out wounded during the fighting around Ninh Binh in Tonkin province in 1951. The Service de Santé was a civil organization.**

## Hughes OH-6 Cayuse

Although it was only used by the USA the OH-6 light observation helicopter was, next to the ubiquitous Huey, numerically the most important helicopter in South East Asia. Its combat and operational losses accounted for 22 percent of all US helicopter losses.

### Specification (OH-6A)

**Type:** six-seat utility and observation helicopter
**Powerplant:** one 317-shp (236-kW) Allison T63-A-5A turboshaft
**Performance:** maximum speed 150 mph (241 km/h) at sea level; climb rate 1,700 ft/min (518 m/min); service ceiling 15,800 ft (4815 m); range 380 miles (610 km)
**Weights:** empty 1,146 lb (520 kg); loaded 2,400 lb (1090 kg)
**Dimensions:** rotor diameter 26 ft 4 in (8.03 m); fuselage length 23 ft (7.01 m); height 8 ft 1.5 in (2.48 m)
**Armament:** one XM-27 kit with one 0.30-in (7.62-mm) Minigun

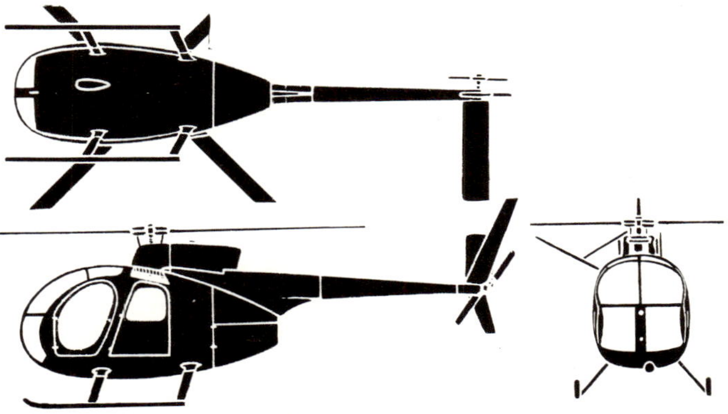

**The Cayuse, named 'Loach' in service (from a contraction of the LOH competition which it won jointly with the Bell OH-58), suffered huge losses. It often operated as hunter to the Bell AH-1 Cobra, seeking out Viet Cong forces for the gunship.**

## Ilyushin Il-12 'Coach' and Il-14 'Crate'

Standard post-World War II Soviet transports, the Il-12 'Coach' and its modernized and slightly enlarged Il-14 'Crate' derivative were widely exported by the Soviet Union to pro-communist nations. In South East Asia these transports were operated by the NVNAF and the Royal Khmer Air Force.

**Specification** (Il-14M 'Crate')
**Type:** twin-engined personnel and light cargo transport
**Powerplant:** two 1,900-hp (1417-kW) Shvetsov ASh-82T radial piston engines
**Performance:** maximum speed 261 mph (420 km/h); climb rate 1,230 ft/min (375 m/min); service ceiling 21,980 ft (6700 m); range 1,555 miles (2500 km)
**Weights:** empty 27,778 lb (12600 kg); loaded 39,683 lb (18000 kg)
**Dimensions:** span 104 ft (31.70 m); length 73 ft 2 in (22.30 m); height 25 ft 11 in (7.90 m); wing area 1,076.4 sq ft (100.0 $m^2$)
**Armament:** none

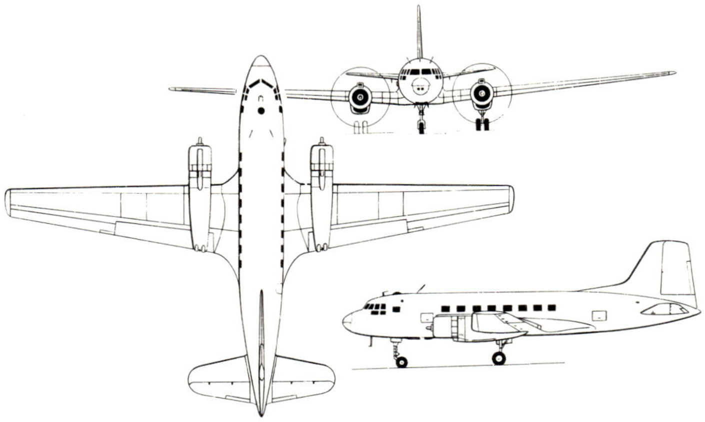

**A Soviet attempt at a DC-3 replacement, the Ilyushin Il-12 and Il-14 (illustrated) drew heavily on DC-3/Li-2 experience. Both types were flown by Communist forces in the theatre for general transport duties.**

## Ilyushin Il-28 'Beagle'

Long considered by American forces to be a potential threat to ships of CTF-77 in the Gulf of Tonkin and to installations in South Vietnam and Thailand, the few light bombers of this type possessed by the NVNAF were never thrown into the battle. In fact, they spent most of their time at Chinese bases to avoid American raids.

**Specification**
**Type:** three-seat tactical jet bomber
**Powerplant:** two 5,952-lb (2700-kg) thrust Klimov VK-1 turbojets
**Performance:** maximum speed 559 mph (900 km/h) at 14,765 ft (4500 m); climb rate 2,955 ft/min (900 m/min); service ceiling 40,355 ft (12300 m); combat range 1,365 miles (2200 km)
**Weights:** empty 28,417 lb (12890 kg); loaded 40,565 lb (18400 kg)
**Dimensions:** span 70 ft 4.5 in (21.45 m); length 57 ft 10.9 in (17.65 m); wing area 654.47 sq ft (60.80 $m^2$)
**Armament:** two fixed forward-firing 23-mm NR-23 cannon and two 23-mm NR-23 cannon in the tail turret, plus a bombload of 6,614 lb (3000 kg)

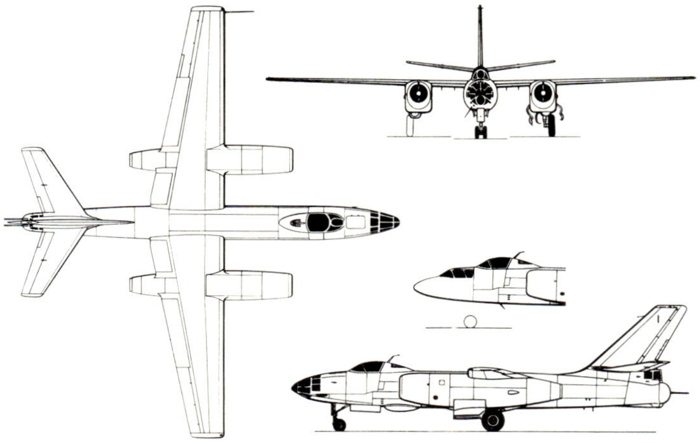

**The threat from the Ilyushin Il-28 'Beagle' bombers never materialized during the war. The Il-28 was a medium bomber roughly comparable to the Canberra/B-57, although not as manoeuvrable and lacking in altitude performance. Nevertheless, the decent bombload could have caused problems for US Navy ships if caught unguarded. (Scrap view shows two-seat Il-28U 'Mascot' trainer.)**

## Kaman HH-43 Huskie

Although initially deployed to South East Asia to provide crash rescue at various air bases, the Huskie had the scope of its activities enlarged to include combat rescue of downed crews. For this task, the unarmed HH-43Bs were quickly supplemented by armed and armoured HH-43Fs. Replaced in the combat rescue role by Jolly Greens, both versions of the Huskie were retained for base rescue operations until the US withdrawal.

**Specification** (HH-43F)
**Type:** search and rescue helicopter
**Powerplant:** One 825-shp (615-kW) Lycoming T53-L-11A turboshaft
**Performance:** maximum speed 120 mph (193 km/h); climb rate 1,800 ft/min (549 m/min); service ceiling 23,000 ft (7010 m); combat range 500 miles (810 km)
**Weights:** empty 4,619 lb (2095 kg); loaded 6,504 lb (2950 kg)
**Dimensions:** rotor diameter 47 ft (14.33 m); length 25 ft 2 in (7.67 m); height 15 ft 6.5 in (4.73 m)
**Armament:** one 0.303-in (7.7-mm) flexible machine-gun

**Early combat rescue coverage was provided by the distinctive HH-43, known by its callsign 'Pedro'. Quickly replaced by more capable helicopters, the HH-43 continued on base rescue duty, exemplified here by this aircraft carrying fire suppression equipment over Da Nang.**

## Kaman UH-2 Seasprite

Standard 'plane guard' helicopters of the US Navy in the mid-sixties, single-engined UH-2As and UH-2Bs, and later twin-engined UH-2Cs, served aboard most carriers in the Gulf of Tonkin until replaced by SH-3s. An armoured and armed version of the Seasprite, the HH-2C was used for combat rescue.

**Specification** (UH-2A)
**Type:** utility helicopter
**Powerplant:** one 1,250-shp (932-kW) General Electric T58-GE-8B turboshaft
**Performance:** maximum speed 162 mph (261 km/h) at sea level; climb rate 1,740 ft/min (530 m/min); service ceiling 17,400 ft (5305 m); combat range 670 miles (1080 km)
**Weights:** empty 6,100 lb (2767 kg); loaded 10,200 lb (4627 kg)
**Dimensions:** rotor diameter 44 ft (13.41 m); length 52 ft 2 in (15.90 m); height 13 ft 6 in (4.11 m)
**Armament:** none

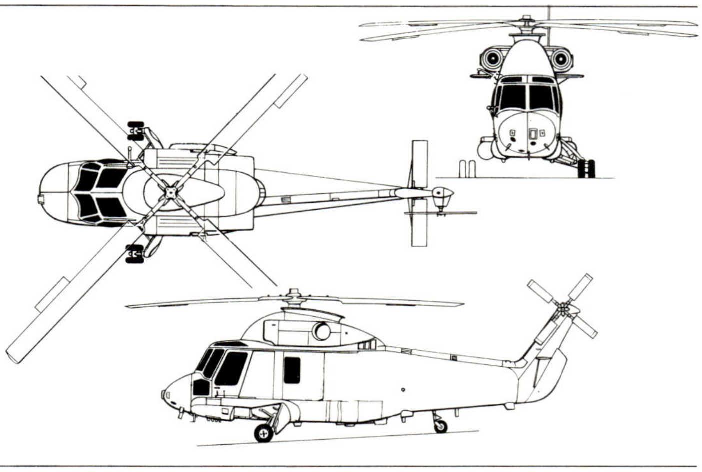

**Seasprites have performed sterling service in support duties for many years, currently being employed on anti-submarine duties. This is a UH-2C twin-engined SAR platform.**

## Lisunov Li-2 'Cab' (see Douglas C-47)

## Lockheed C-5A Galaxy

Placed in trans-Pacific service shortly after its squadron début in 1970, the C-5A provided MAC with its first jet transport capable of carrying bulky and heavy military combat vehicles. This capability became particularly useful when, in the fall of 1972, large quantities of aircraft and tanks were rushed to the ARVN prior to the signing of the Paris Agreement.

### Specification

**Type:** heavy lift (maximum payload of 265,000 lb/120200 kg) strategic freighter
**Powerplant:** four 41,100-lb (18643-kg) thrust General Electric TF39-GE-1 turbofans
**Performance:** maximum speed 564 mph (907 km/h) at 25,000 ft (7620 m); climb rate 5,840 ft/min (1780 m/min); service ceiling 47,700 ft (14540 m); range 1,875 miles (3015 km) with maximum payload
**Weights:** empty 321,000 lb (145603 kg); loaded 769,000 lb (348812 kg)
**Dimensions:** span 222 ft 8.5 in (67.88 m); length 247 ft 9.5 in (75.53 m); height 65 ft 1.25 in (19.84 m); wing area 6,200 sq ft (576 $m^2$)
**Armament:** none

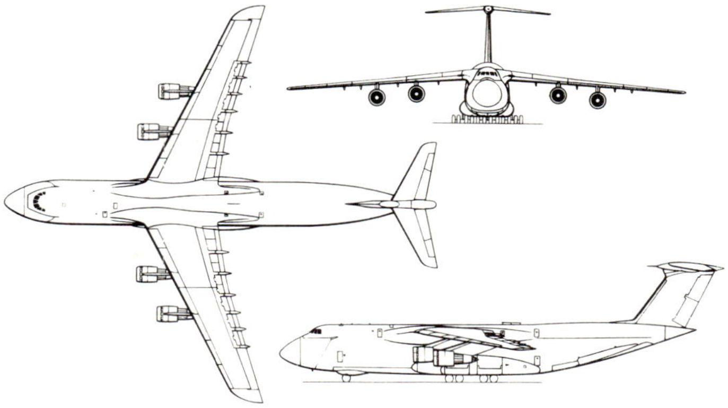

**The mighty Galaxy was the world's largest aircraft at the time of its service in South East Asia. Providing much airlift capability, the Galaxy's role in the final evacuation was cut short by a tragic crash while carrying a load of orphans destined for new homes in the States.**

---

## Lockheed EC-121 Warning Star

While airborne early warning was the primary role of military versions of the Super Constellation of the Air Force (EC-121D and EC-121M) and the Navy (EC-121K and EC-121M) during the South East Asia War, the type was also used for various special missions including television relay and broadcasting for American forces in Vietnam by Navy aircraft; aeromedical evacuation (C-121C and C-121G) and electronic reconnaissance/countermeasures (EC-121S) by the Air National Guard; and relay of data from the *Igloo White* detection network (EC-121R) by the Air Force.

### Specification (EC-121D)

**Type:** airborne early warning aircraft
**Powerplant:** four 3,400-hp (2535-kW) Wright R-3350-34 radial piston engines
**Performance:** maximum speed 321 mph (516 km/h) at 20,000 ft (6095 m); climb rate 845 ft/min (258 m/min); service ceiling 20,600 ft (6280 m); combat range 4,600 miles (7400 km)
**Weights:** empty 80,611 lb (36565 kg); loaded 143,600 lb (65136 kg)
**Dimensions:** span 123 ft 5 in (37.62 m); length 116 ft 2 in (35.41 m); height 27 ft (8.23 m); wing area 1,654 sq ft (153.66 $m^2$)
**Armament:** none

**Lockheed EC-121Ds provided airborne early warning coverage for USAF aircraft. This *Big Eye* Constellation patrols over Thailand, giving MiG warning and interception vectors to fighters operating over the North.**

---

## Lockheed C-130 Hercules

The airlift versions of the Hercules (C-130A/B/E/H) were the most important military transport aircraft during the South East Asia War and were used both for intra-theatre logistics by the USAF and the VNAF, and for strategic airlift by the USAF, the RAAF and the RNZAF. During the war the Air Force also operated its C-130 transports in the ABCCC role and to drop heavy bombs for clearing helicopter landing sites in the jungle, while the Marines used their KC-130Fs for transport and for refuelling tactical aircraft. In addition, the Air Force employed various specialized versions for drone-launching and monitoring (DC-130A and DC-130E), for air rescue work (HC-130H) and for refuelling helicopters (HC-130P). Equally important to the war's effort were the progressively improved gunship versions of the Hercules, the AC-130A and AC-130E.

### Specification (C-130A)

**Type:** military personnel (64 paratroops or 92 troops) and cargo (maximum payload of 45,000 lb/20410 kg) transport
**Powerplant:** four 3,750-eshp (2796-kW) Allison T56-A-9 turboprops
**Performance:** maximum speed 383 mph (616 km/h) at 20,400 ft (6220 m); climb rate 2,570 ft/min (783 m/min); service ceiling 41,300 ft (12590 m); range 2,090 miles (3365 km) with payload of 35,000 lb (15875 kg)
**Weights:** empty 59,328 lb (26911 kg); loaded 108,000 lb (48988 kg)
**Dimensions:** span 132 ft 7 in (40.41 m); length 97 ft 9 in (29.79 m); height 38 ft 6 in (11.73 m); wing area 1,745.5 sq ft (162.16 $m^2$)
**Armament:** none

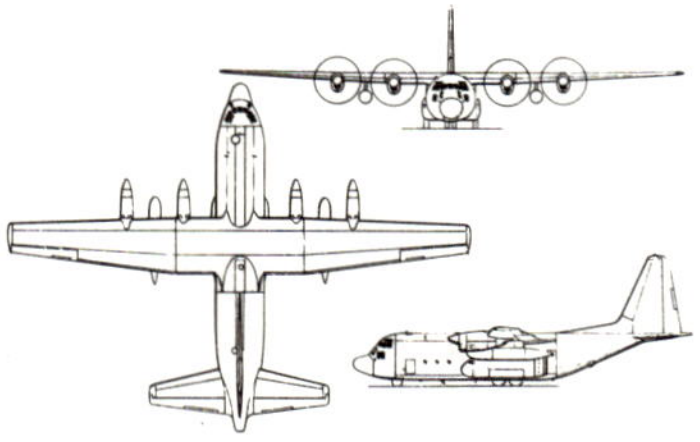

**Lockheed C-130H Hercules transport.**

**AC-130 gunship versions of the Hercules were the most effective truck-busters over the Ho Chi Minh Trail. This aircraft is an AC-130A of the 16th SOS, complete with anti-SAM ALQ-87 ECM pods under the wings.**

## Lockheed C-141A StarLifter

The Air Force's first specialized cargo jet transport began trans-Pacific logistic flights in August 1965. Over the next ten years, until taking part in the *Frequent Wind* evacuation of Saigon, StarLifters steadily gained in importance, carrying cargo and personnel on westbound flights and performing aeromedical evacuation on the return trip home.

**Specification**
**Type:** long-range personnel (123 paratroops or 154 equipped troops) or cargo (maximum payload of 62,717 lb/28448 kg) transport
**Powerplant:** four 21,000-lb (9525-kg) thrust Pratt & Whitney TF33-P-7 turbofans
**Performance:** maximum speed 565 mph (909 km/h) at 24,400 ft (7440 m); climb rate 7,925 ft/min (2416 m/min); service ceiling 51,700 ft (15760 m); range 4,155 miles (6685 km) with payload of 62,717 lb (28448 kg)
**Weights:** empty 136,900 lb (62097 kg); loaded 323,100 lb (146556 kg)
**Dimensions:** span 160 ft (48.77 m); length 145 ft (44.20 m); height 39 ft 4 in (11.99 m); wing area 3,228.1 sq ft (299.90 m$^2$)
**Armament:** none

**Lockheed's C-141A enabled the swift transport of materiel across the Pacific to be carried out with ease. StarLifters were considerably faster than other transports on the air bridge. During the final evacuation, they provided much of the capability during the early days of the airlift.**

## Lockheed F-104 Starfighter

Never quite successful in US service, the F-104C and its two-seat F-104D version did not fare well in South East Asia; for in-country operations they carried an insufficient weapon load and they lacked the range (in spite of the addition of a fixed refuelling probe) for operations over the North. Eight were lost in combat and six were destroyed in operational accidents without obtaining compensating results.

**Specification** (F-104C)
**Type:** single-seat tactical fighter
**Powerplant:** one 10,000-lb (4536-kg) dry thrust and 15,800-lb (7167-kg) afterburning thrust General Electric J79-GE-7 turbojet
**Performance:** maximum speed 1,150 mph (1850 km/h) at 50,000 ft (15240 m); climb rate 54,000 ft/min (16459 m/min); service ceiling 58,000 ft (17680 m); combat range 850 miles (1370 km)
**Weights:** empty 12,760 lb (5788 kg); loaded 19,470 lb (8831 kg)
**Dimensions:** empty span 21 ft 9 in (6.63 m); length 54 ft 8 in (16.66 m); height 13 ft 5 in (4.09 m); wing area 196.1 sq ft (18.22 m$^2$)
**Armament:** one 20-mm M-61 six-barrel cannon, plus external stores up to 4,000 lb (1814 kg)

**The Starfighter fared no better in South East Asia as it did in USAF service in general. Short on range and weapons load, the F-104 had little impact on the air war. These two F-104Cs are seen over South Vietnam early in the war, prior to adopting tactical camouflage.**

## Lockheed QT-2PC and YO-3

One of the most unique ideas to be tried during the war involved the use of low performance but extremely quiet aircraft to detect covertly enemy activities in South Vietnam. The concept was validated in 1968 when two QT-2PCs operated in Vietnam and led to the 1970 deployment of the 13 YO-3As of the 1st Army Security Agency Company. Employing a modified Schweitzer sailplane structure, the YO-3A had a slow turning propeller and was fitted with a large muffler.

**Specification** (YO-3A)
**Type:** two-seat observation aircraft
**Powerplant:** one 210-hp (157-kW) Continental IO-360D air-cooled piston engine
**Performance:** maximum speed 138 mph (222 km/h) at sea level; climb rate 615 ft/min (187 m/min); service ceiling 14,000 ft (4265 m); endurance 4.4 hr
**Weights:** empty 3,129 kg (1419 kg); loaded 3,519 lb (1596 kg)
**Dimensions:** span 57 ft (17.37 m); length 29 ft 4 in (8.94 m); height 9 ft 1 in (2.77 m); wing area 205 sq ft (19.04 m$^2$)

**Final incarnation of the Lockheed quiet-plane project was the YO-3A, featuring a conventional fuselage and engine layout allied to sailplane wings. The exhaust on the starboard side ran the length of the fuselage for noise-damping.**

## Lockheed P-2 Neptune

SP-2Hs were initially used in South East Asia by Navy patrol squadrons for *Market Time* maritime surveillance. Later on, VO-67 flew the OP-2E version of the Neptune to seed ALARS sensors along the Ho Chi Minh Trail, while VAH-21 flew AP-2Hs for night interdiction sorties over the Mekong Delta. The Army's 1st Radio Research Company employed AP-2Es for airborne radio relays and for COMINT.

**Specification** (SP-2H)
**Type:** maritime patrol aircraft
**Powerplant:** two 3,500-hp (2610-kW) Wright R-3350-32W radial piston engines and two 3,400-lb (1540-kg) thrust Westinghouse J34-WE-36 turbojets
**Performance:** maximum speed 403 mph (648 km/h) at 14,000 ft (4625 m); climb rate 1,760 ft/min (536 m/min); service ceiling 22,000 ft (6705 m); combat range 2,200 miles (3540 km)
**Weights:** empty 49,935 lb (22650 kg); loaded 73,139 lb (33175 kg)
**Dimensions:** span 103 ft 10 in (31.65 m); length 91 ft 8 in (27.94 m); height 29 ft 4 in (8.94 m); wing area 1,000 sq ft (92.90 m$^2$)
**Armament:** up to 8,000 lb (3629 kg) of bombs, torpedoes, mines, depth charges or rockets

**Standard maritime patrol SP-2H Neptune of VP-31, one of the squadrons involved with *Market Time* patrols along the coast of South Vietnam, aimed at deterring infiltration and supply by junks sailing up the many creeks and deltas of the country.**

## Lockheed P-3 Orion

Upon entering service with Navy maritime patrol squadrons, the Orion took over from the Neptune responsibility for *Market Time* operations.

**Specification** (P-3B)
**Type:** martime patrol aircraft
**Powerplant:** four 4,910-eshp (3661-ekW) Allison T56-A-14 turboprops
**Performance:** maximum speed 473 mph (761 km/h) at 15,000 ft (4570 m); climb rate 1,950 ft/min (594 m/min); service ceiling 28,300 ft (8625 m); mission radius with 3 hr on station 1,550 miles (2495 km)
**Weights:** empty 61,491 lb (27892 kg); loaded 135,000 lb (61235 kg)
**Dimensions:** span 99 ft 8 in (30.38 m); length 116 ft 10 in (35.61 m); height 33 ft 8.5 in (10.27 m); wing area 1,300 sq ft (120.77 $m^2$)
**Armament:** up to 19,250 lb (8732 kg) of bombs, torpedoes, mines, depth charges or rockets

**The Orion has been the standard land-based maritime patrol platform for the US Navy since its introduction into service in 1962, gradually replacing Neptunes as they rolled off the production line. Orions performed a similar role in the war zone.**

## Lockheed SR-71A 'Blackbird'

With their impressive speed and ceiling, SR-71s of the Air Force, and possibly A-12s of the CIA, were ideal vehicles for sensitive reconnaissance operations over the southern coast of the PRC and along the China-Vietnam border.

**Specification**
**Type:** strategic reconnaissance aircraft
**Powerplant:** two 32,500-lb (14742-kg) afterburning thrust Pratt & Whitney J58-P-20 turbojets
**Performance:** maximum speed 2,250 mph (3620 km/h); service ceiling 100,000 ft (30480 m); combat range 3,000 miles (4830 km)
**Weight:** loaded 170,000 lb (77111 kg)
**Dimensions:** span 55 ft 7 in (16.94 m); length 107 ft 5 in (32.74 m); height 18 ft 6 in (5.64 m)
**Armament:** none

**SR-71A lands at Kadena following a South East Asia mission.**

## Lockheed RT-33A

Easily passing in the eyes of the uninitiated for its less pugnacious progenitor, the T-33A advanced jet trainer, the RT-33A tactical reconnaissance aircraft was selected by the Air Force to undertake covert *Field Goal* sorties over Laos in 1961. Within a year they were supplanted by RF-101s as the need for more intelligence mandated the use of increasingly capable systems.

**Specification**
**Type:** tactical reconnaissance aircraft
**Powerplant:** one 5,200-lb (2359-kg) thrust Allison J33-A-35 turbojet
**Performance:** maximum speed 600 mph (965 km/h) at sea level; climb rate 4,870 ft/min (1484 m/min); service ceiling 48,000 ft (14630 m); combat range 1,025 miles (1650 km)
**Weights:** empty 8,365 lb (3794 kg); loaded 12,071 lb (5475 kg)
**Dimensions:** span 38 ft 10.5 in (11.85 m); length 37 ft 9 in (11.51 m); height 11 ft 8 in (3.55 m); wing area 234.8 sq ft (21.81 $m^2$)
**Armament:** none

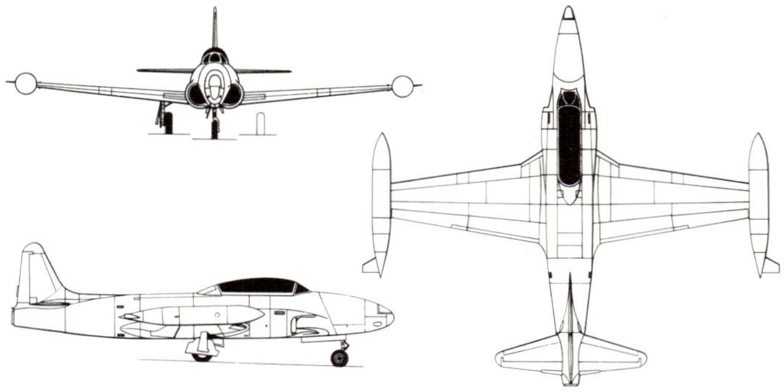

**The basic T-33A trainer version was also used by the Royal Thai Air Force for advanced training duties, although these saw no part in the fighting.**

## Lockheed U-2

Notwithstanding the large-scale use of reconnaissance drones and tactical reconnaissance aircraft, U-2s were also needed for operations over North Vietnam and across the PRC border as their high-altitude capability and effective passive defence systems enabled them to fly at will over the most difficult targets. Begun in December 1963, U-2 activities in South East Asia continued until well after the official ending of US operations over the North.

**Specification** (U-2C)
**Type:** high-altitude reconnaissance aircraft
**Powerplant:** one 17,000-lb (7711-kg) thrust Pratt & Whitney J75-P-13B turbojet
**Performance:** cruising speed 460 mph (740 km/h) at 65,000 ft (19,810 m); combat ceiling 75,100 ft (22890 m); range 4,750 miles (7645 km)
**Weights:** empty 13,870 lb (6291 kg); loaded 23,970 lb (10873 kg)
**Dimensions:** span 80 ft 2 in (24.43 m); length 49 ft 8.5 in (15.15 m); height 15 ft (4.57 m); wing area 600 sq ft (55.74 $m^2$)
**Armament:** none

**Sigint-configured U-2R of the 349th SRS, 100th SRW lands at U-Tapao in Thailand.**

## Loire 130M

Brought to Indochina prior to World War II, antiquated Loire 130 observation flying-boats fought against the Thais in 1940 and against the Japanese in 1944. Two survivors were operated by Escadrille 8S during the early phase of the Indochina War.

**Specification**
**Type:** three-seat observation flying-boat
**Powerplant:** one 720-hp (537-kW) Hispano-Suiza 12Xirsl liquid-cooled piston engine
**Performance:** maximum speed 137 mph (220 km/h) at 6,890 ft (2100 m); climb to 9,840 ft (3000 m) in 12 min; service ceiling 19,685 ft (6000 m); endurance 7.5 hr
**Weights:** empty 4,519 lb (2050 kg); loaded 7,716 lb (3500 kg)
**Dimensions:** span 52 ft 5.9 in (16.00 m); length 37 ft 0.9 in (11.30 m); height 12 ft 7.5 in (3.85 m); wing area 411.19 sq ft (38.20 $m^2$)
**Armament:** two 0.295-in (7.5-mm) machine-guns, one each in bow and dorsal positions, plus 165 lb (75 kg) bombs

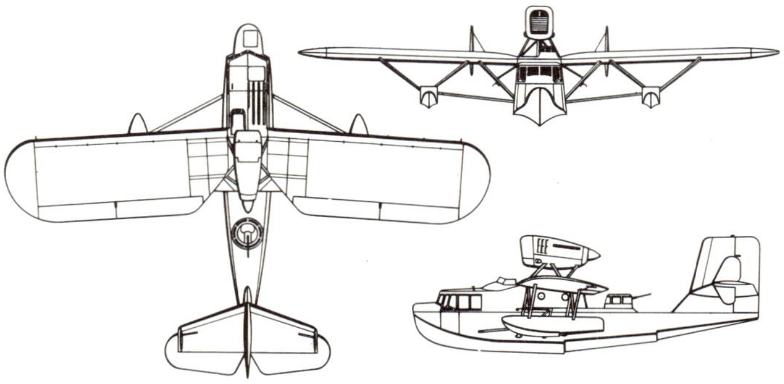

**The Loire 130M performed coastal patrol during the early days of the Indochina war. It had earlier fought with the French during World War II.**

## Martin B-57 Canberra

Flying the first USAF in-country offensive sorties on 18 February 1965, Martin B-57B and B-57C tactical bombers (American developments of the English Electric Canberra twinjet bomber) were mostly used in South Vietnam for air support. In this role, B-57s on loan from the USAF were operated for a few months by the VNAF. B-57B/C/Es were also used in the interdiction campaign along the Trail, but it was the B-57G version of the Martin bomber which was better suited to this task as it had been fitted with a variety of sensors. Longer lived than either the standard B-57 tactical bombers or the B-57G night interdiction aircraft, the *Patricia Lynn* RB-57Es were among the most effective US aircraft for locating hidden enemy bases and depots.

**Specification** (B-57B)
**Type:** two-seat tactical bomber
**Powerplant:** two 7,200-lb (3266-kg) thrust Wright J65-W-5 turbojets
**Performance:** maximum speed 582 mph (936 km/h) at 40,000 ft (12190 m); climb rate 3,500 ft/min (1067 m/min); service ceiling 48,000 ft (14630 m); combat range 2,300 miles (3700 km)
**Weights:** empty 28,793 lb (13060 kg); loaded 56,965 lb (25839 kg)
**Dimensions:** span 64 ft (19.51 m); length 65 ft 6 in (19.96 m); height 15 ft 7 in (4.75 m); wing area 960 sq ft (89.18 $m^2$)
**Armament:** eight wing-mounted 0.50-in (12.7-mm) machine-guns plus 6,000 lb (2722 kg) of internal and external stores

**Martin B-57Bs fire up for a bombing mission from Tan Son Nhut, shortly after their introduction into the combat zone. The Canberra proved particularly accurate against Viet Cong installations, and had good night capability.**

## Martin P-5 Marlin

Marlins, the last Navy combat flying-boats, flew *Market Time* patrols from seaplane tenders in the South China Sea until May 1967.

**Specification** (P-5B)
**Type:** maritime patrol flying-boat
**Powerplant:** two 3,450-hp (2573-kW) Wright R-3350-32WA radial piston engines
**Performance:** maximum speed 251 mph (404 km/h) at sea level; climb rate 1,200 ft/min (366 m/min); service ceiling 24,000 ft (7315 m); combat range 2,050 miles (3300 km)
**Weights:** empty 50,485 lb (22900 kg); loaded 85,000 lb (38555 kg)
**Dimensions:** span 118 ft 2 in (36.02 m); length 100 ft 7 in (30.66 m); height 32 ft 8.5 in (9.97 m); wing area 1,406 sq ft (130.62 $m^2$)
**Armament:** up to 8,000 lb (3629 kg) of bombs, torpedoes, depth charges, mines or rockets

**Flying-boats were a rare sight by the time of the US involvement, and the Navy's Marlins did not last long in the coastal patrol role. This is a VP-42 SP-5M.**

## McDonnell F-4 Phantom II

More F-4 fighters and RF-4 reconnaissance aircraft were lost in South East Asia than any other type of aircraft, with Phantom IIs accounting for 20.1 percent of total fixed-wing aircraft combat and operational losses. In air combat against MiGs, F-4s obtained 145.5 kills and achieved a kill-to-loss ration of 3.73 to 1. With the Navy, F-4Bs first flew combat sorties from the USS *Constellation* during the Gulf of Tonkin Incident, and F-4Js were first deployed in 1968 aboard the USS *America*; the rare F-4G version went aboard the USS *Kitty Hawk* in 1965-66. With the Marines, F-4Bs and F-4Js were primarily employed from Chu Lai and Da Nang, but also flew from Laos and from the *America*. VMCJ-1 also flew RF-4Bs in Vietnam beginning in October 1966. The first Air Force Phantom IIs in South East Asia were the F-4Cs of the 45th TFS which were sent to Ubon in April 1965. This initial fighter version was joined by F-4Ds in May 1967 and F-4Es in November 1968. RF-4C reconnaissance aircraft were first used in October 1967 by the 16th TRS and, by November 1970, had fully replaced the RF-101Cs.

**Specification** (F-4B)
**Type:** two-seat carrier-based fighter
**Powerplant:** two 10,900-lb (4944-kg) dry thrust and 17,000-lb (7711-kg) afterburning thrust General Electric J79-GE-8 turbojets
**Performance:** maximum speed 1,485 mph (2390 km/h) at 48,000 ft (14630 m); climb rate 28,000 ft/min (8534 m/min); service ceiling 62,000 ft (18900 m); combat range 800 miles (1285 km)
**Weights:** empty 28,000 lb (12701 kg); loaded 44,600 lb (20230 kg)
**Dimensions:** span 38 ft 4.9 in (11.71 m); length 58 ft 3.75 in (17.77 m); height 16 ft 3 in (4.95 m); wing area 530 sq ft (49.24 $m^2$)
**Armament:** four AIM-7 Sparrow and four AIM-9 Sidewinder air-to-air missiles, or up to 16,000 lb (7257 kg) of external stores

**Above: The Navy's Phantoms were employed on both strike and air defence duties. This VF-213 F-4B from *Kitty Hawk* bombs a target in North Vietnam, while carrying Sparrow and Sidewinder missiles for self-defence.**

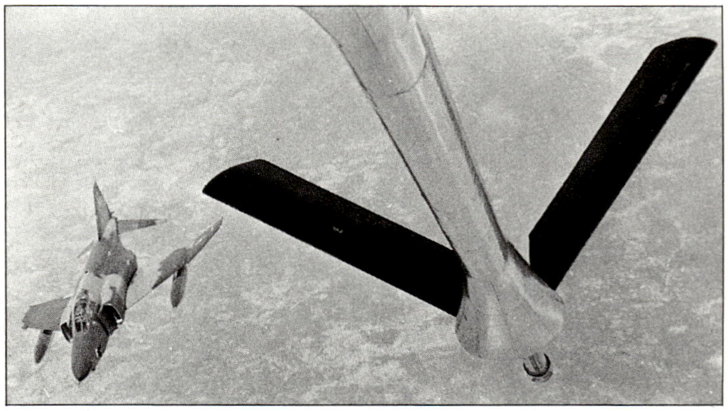

**McDonnell RF-4C approaches the boom of a KC-135 tanker over South East Asia. This type provided virtually all the tactical reconnaissance requirements of the USAF during the later years of the conflict.**

## McDonnell RF-101 Voodoo

RF-101Cs first flew reconnaissance sorties in South East Asia during the fall of 1961 when the USAF sent the *Pipe Stem* and *Able Mable* detachments to South Vietnam and Thailand respectively. Voodoos, supplemented by RF-4Cs from 1965, undertook a large share of USAF tactical reconnaissance activities until the departure of the 45th TRS from Tan Son Nhut in November 1970.

**Specification** (RF-101C)
**Type:** single-seat tactical reconnaissance aircraft
**Powerplant:** two 10,200-lb (4627-kg) dry thrust and 15,000-lb (6804-kg) afterburning thrust Pratt & Whitney J57-P-13 turbojets
**Performance:** maximum speed 1,012 mph (1629 km/h) at 35,000 ft (10670 m); climb rate 45,550 ft/min (13885 m/min); service ceiling 55,300 ft (16855 m); combat range 2,045 miles (3290 km)
**Weights:** empty 26,136 lb (11855 kg); loaded 48,133 lb (21832 kg)
**Dimensions:** span 39 ft 8 in (12.09 m); length 69 ft 4 in (21.13 m); height 18 ft (5.49 m); wing area 368 sq ft (34.19 m$^2$)
**Armament:** none

**Equipped with forward- and oblique-looking cameras, the RF-101C was a very fast reconnaissance platform. Often operating alone, RF-101s brought back much of the intelligence from the North during the early years, but suffered many losses. Gradually superseded by RF-4s, the Voodoo was a much-loved aircraft that stayed in service until 1970.**

## Mikoyan-Gurevich MiG-15 'Fagot' and MiG-15UTI

Already obsolete when the United States began air operations against North Vietnam, this famous Soviet fighter was used by the NVNAF only for advanced training (primarily at Chinese air bases), with the single-seat MiG-15bis 'Fagot' operating alongside the two-seat MiG-15UTI 'Midget'. A few MiG-15bis were also operated briefly by the Royal Khmer Air Force during the mid-sixties.

**Specification** (MiG-15UTI)
**Type:** two-seat jet trainer
**Powerplant:** one 5,952-lb (2700-kg) thrust Klimov VK-1 turbojet
**Performance:** maximum speed 630 mph (1015 km/h) at sea level; climb rate 10,235 ft/min (3120 m/min); service ceiling 47,980 ft (14625 m); range 590 miles (950 km)
**Weights:** empty 8,818 lb (4000 kg); loaded 10,692 lb (4850 kg)
**Dimensions:** span 33 ft 0.9 in (10.08 m); length 32 ft 11.3 in (10.04 m); height 12 ft 1.7 in (3.70 m); wing area 221.74 sq ft (20.6 m$^2$)
**Armament:** one 23-mm NS-23 cannon

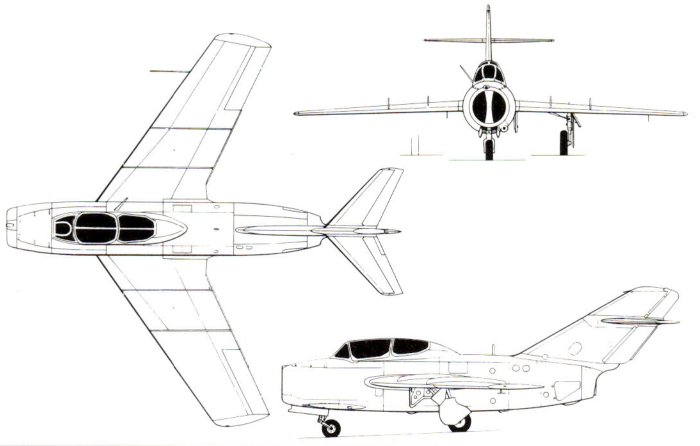

**The MiG-15 was a classic fighter which had a profound effect during the Korean war. The type saw no combat during the war in South East Asia, used only for weapons training by the North.**

## Mikoyan-Gurevich MiG-17 'Fresco'

Even though its top speed was just below Mach 1.0, the MiG-17 proved a formidable foe for US strike aircraft and their escorting fighters as it was one of the most manoeuvrable jet aircraft ever built and carried a heavy cannon armament. From 1965 onward the NVNAF primarily operated MiG-17F clear-weather interceptors (as well as some Chinese-built Shenyang F 4s); it also received some MiG-17PF limited all-weather fighters and MiG-17PFUs in which the cannon armament was replaced by a pair of AA-1 'Alkali' radar-homing air-to-air missiles. In 1964-65, a few MiG-17Fs were also supplied by the USSR to the Royal Khmer Air Force.

interceptor
**Powerplant:** one 5,732-lb (2600-kg) dry thrust and 7,452-lb (3380-kg) afterburning thrust Klimov VK-1F turbojet
**Performance:** maximum speed 711 mph (1145 km/h) at 9,840 ft (3000 m); climb rate 12,485 ft/min (3805 m/min); service ceiling 54,460 ft (16600 m); combat range 915 miles (1470 km)
**Weights:** empty 9,855 lb (4470 kg); loaded 13,382 lb (6070 kg)
**Dimensions:** span 31 ft 7.1 in (9.63 m); length 36 ft 4.6 in (11.09 m); height 12 ft 5.6 in (3.80 m); wing area 243.27 sq ft (22.6 m$^2$)
**Armament:** one 37-mm N-37 and two 23-mm NR-23 cannon

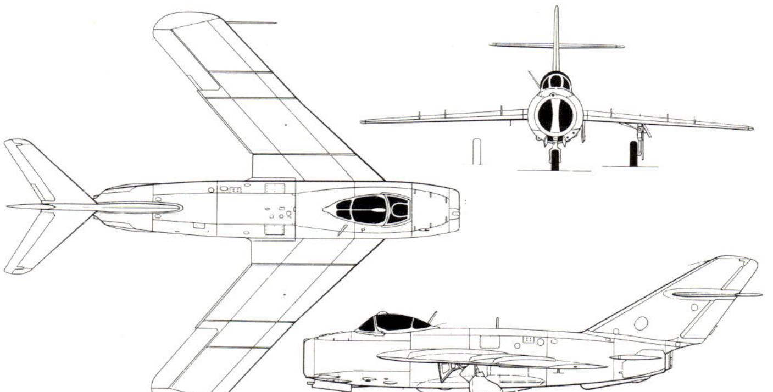

**Mikoyan-Gurevich MiG-17F 'Fresco'.**

## Mikoyan-Gurevich MiG-19 'Farmer'

Most of the aircraft of this type, which served with the NVNAF in relatively small numbers from about 1970, appear to have been Chinese-built Shenyang F 6s. Nevertheless, it can be safely assumed that the NVNAF also received examples of the Soviet-built MiG-19S (the pattern version for the F 6), as well as some MiG-19PMs in which the cannon armament was replaced by four AA-1 'Alkali' radar-homing air-to-air missiles.

**Specification** (MiG-19S 'Farmer-A')
**Type:** single-seat clear-weather interceptor
**Powerplant:** two 5,732-lb (2600-kg) dry thrust and 7,165-lb (3250-kg) afterburning thrust Tumansky RD-9B turbojets
**Performance:** maximum speed 901 mph (1450 km/h) at 32,810 ft (10000 m); climb rate 22,640 ft/min (6900 m/min); service ceiling 54,135 ft (16500 m); combat range 870 miles (1400 km)
**Weights:** empty 12,699 lb (5760 kg); loaded 16,755 lb (7600 kg)
**Dimensions:** span 29 ft 6.3 in (9.00 m); length 42 ft 11.75 in (13.10 m); height 13 ft 2.3 in (4.02 m); wing area 269.1 sq ft (25.00 m$^2$)
**Armament:** three 30-mm NR-30 cannon

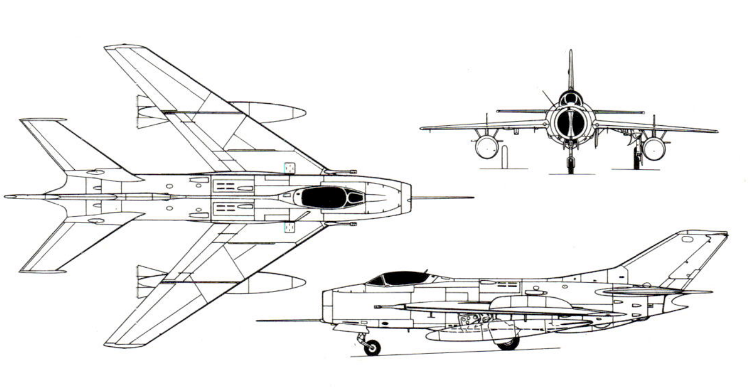

**Twin-engined growth from the MiG-17, the MiG-19 was a fast and extremely tough opponent. The NR-30 cannon were hard-hitting weapons with high muzzle velocity. Most Vietnamese MiG-19s did not have missile capability.**

## Mikoyan-Gurevich MiG-21 'Fishbed'

First encountered over North Vietnam in April 1966, the MiG-21 progressively became the most important interceptor in NVNAF service. Lighter and nimbler than contemporary American fighters, the type was highly respected by US airmen and proved to be a formidable foe. Principal versions used in Vietnam were the MiG-21F 'Fishbed-C' clear-weather interceptor, the MiG-21PF 'Fishbed-D' and MiG-21PFS 'Fishbed-E' limited all-weather interceptors, and the MiG-21PFMA 'Fishbed-J' which incorporated numerous improvements and featured a heavier missile armament.

**Specification** (MiG-21PFS 'Fishbed-E')
**Type:** single-seat limited all-weather interceptor
**Powerplant:** one 8,598-lb (3900-kg) dry thrust and 13,669-lb (6200-kg) afterburning thrust Tumansky R-11-F2S-300 turbojet
**Performance:** maximum speed 1,386 mph (2230 km/h) at 36,090 ft (11000 m); climb rate 24,605 ft/min (7500 m/min); service ceiling 59,055 ft (18000 m); combat range 930 miles (1500 km)
**Weights:** empty 11,464 lb (5200 kg); loaded 18,740 lb (8500 kg)
**Dimensions:** span 23 ft 5.5 in (7.15 m); length 46 ft 11 in (14.30 m); height 14 ft 9 in (4.50 m); wing area 247.57 sq ft (23.0 $m^2$)
**Armament:** twin barrel 23-mm GSh-23 cannon and two K-13A 'Atoll' infrared-homing air-to-air missiles

**Vietnamese MiG-21 seen manoeuvring hard during a dogfight over North Vietnam. This classic fighter became the sharp end of the Vietnamese interceptor forces, its excellent agility and high speed making it a difficult opponent to catch or escape from.**

## Morane-Saulnier M.S. 500 Criquet

As part of their scheme to make use of aircraft production facilities in occupied Europe, during World War II the Germans had ordered Morane-Saulnier to undertake the manufacture of Fieseler Fi 156 Storch observation aircraft. After the liberation of France, the type remained in production as the M.S. 500 powered by an Argus As 410C engine, the M.S. 501 with a Renault 6Q, and the M.S. 502 with a Salmson 9AB. In addition to being extensively used by the Armée de l'Air in Indochina, Criquets were the first aircraft delivered in 1941 to the newly organized Vietnamese Air Training Center at Nha Trang.

**Specification** (M.S. 502)
**Type:** three-seat artillery spotting and observation aircraft
**Powerplant:** one 230-hp (172-kW) Salmson 9AB radial piston engine
**Performance:** maximum speed 106 mph (170 km/h) at sea level; climb rate 3,280 ft (1000 m) in 5.5 min; service ceiling 14,110 ft (4300 m); combat range 435 miles (700 km)
**Weights:** empty 2,094 lb (950 kg); loaded 3,142 lb (1425 kg)
**Dimensions:** span 46 ft 9 in (14.25 m); length 31 ft 8 in (9.65 m); height 10 ft 2 in (3.10 m); wing area 279.9 sq ft (26.0 $m^2$)
**Armament:** none

**Used for a variety of purposes, including liaison, observation and artillery spotting, the M.S. 500 was widely employed by French forces during the Indochina war and was later used by the South Vietnamese. Full-span slats and flaps bestowed extraordinary short field performance.**

## Morane-Saulnier M.S. 733 Alcyon

In 1955, as a gift to the newly formed Aviation Royale Khmer, France gave seven Alcyons (four of which were fitted with light armament for gunnery training and police duties) to Cambodia.

**Specification**
**Type:** two/three-seat basic trainer
**Powerplant:** one 240-hp (179-kW) Potez 6D.30 air-cooled inline piston engine
**Performance:** maximum speed 162 mph (260 km/h) at sea level; climb rate 820 ft/min (250 m/min); service ceiling 15,750 ft (4800 m); endurance 4 hr
**Weights:** empty 2,778 lb (1260 kg); loaded 3,682 lb (1670 kg)
**Dimensions:** span 37 ft 0.9 in (11.30 m); length 30 ft 6.1 in (9.30 m); height 8 ft (2.44 m); wing area 235.7 sq ft (21.90 $m^2$)
**Armament:** four 3-in (76.2-mm) unguided rockets

**France's basic trainer was supplied to Cambodian forces for the same role. Some were fitted with light armament for weapons training.**

## Nakajima A6M-2N 'Rufe'

One of the floatplane fighters, which the Japanese had left in Indochina, was impressed into service with the Aéronautique Navale but crashed almost immediately after being overhauled.

**Specification**
**Type:** single-seat floatplane fighter
**Powerplant:** one 940-hp (701-kW) Nakajima NK1C Sakae 12 radial piston engine
**Performance:** maximum speed 270 mph (435 km/h) at 16,405 ft (5000 m); climb rate 16,405 ft (5000 m) in 6 min 43 sec; service ceiling 32,810 ft (10000 m); combat range 715 miles (1150 km)
**Weights:** empty 4,215 lb (1912 kg); loaded 5,423 lb (2460 kg)
**Dimensions:** span 39 ft 4.4 in (12.0 m); length 33 ft 1.6 in (10.10 m); height 14 ft 1.3 in (4.30 m); wing area 241.5 sq ft (22.44 $m^2$)
**Armament:** two fuselage-mounted 0.303-in (7.7-mm) machine-guns and two wing-mounted 20-mm cannon, plus two 132 lb (60 kg) bombs

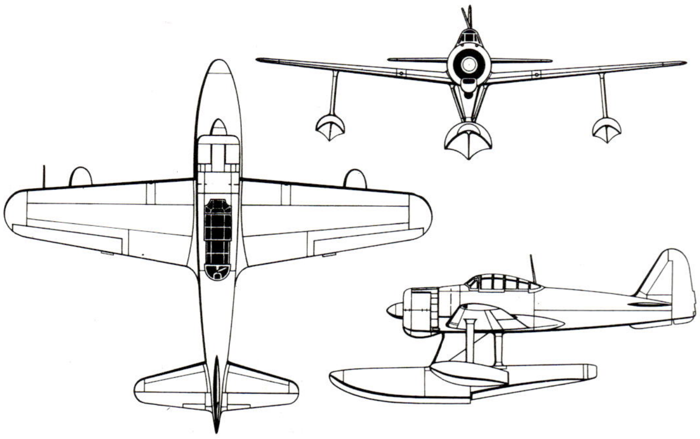

**The A6M-2N 'Rufe' was a floatplane fighter derived from the Mitsubishi A6M 'Zeke'. After disappointing service in the role, the 'Rufe' was used as a coastal patrol aircraft by the French in Indochina.**

## Nakajima Ki-43 'Oscar'

Pending arrival of its Spitfires, the Armée de l'Air tried with little success to put back in operation a dozen Japanese Ki-43-IIs and Ki-43-IIIs. Taken on charge in December 1945 by G.C. I/7 'Provence', these aircraft were not used in combat.

**Specification** (Ki-43-IIb)
**Type:** single-seat fighter
**Powerplant:** one 1,150-hp (856-kW) Nakajima Ha-115 radial piston engine
**Performance:** maximum speed 329 mph (530 km/h) at 13,125 ft (4000 m); climb rate 16,405 ft (5000 m) in 5 min 49 sec; service ceiling 36,750 ft (11200 m); combat range 1,095 miles (1760 km)
**Weights:** empty 4,211 lb (1910 kg); loaded 5,710 lb (2590 kg)
**Dimensions:** span 35 ft 6.8 in (10.84 m); length 29 ft 3.2 in (8.92 m); height 10 ft 8.7 in (3.27 m); wing area 230.3 sq ft (21.4 m²)
**Armament:** two fuselage-mounted 0.5-in (12.7-mm) machine-guns, plus two 66 lb (30 kg) bombs

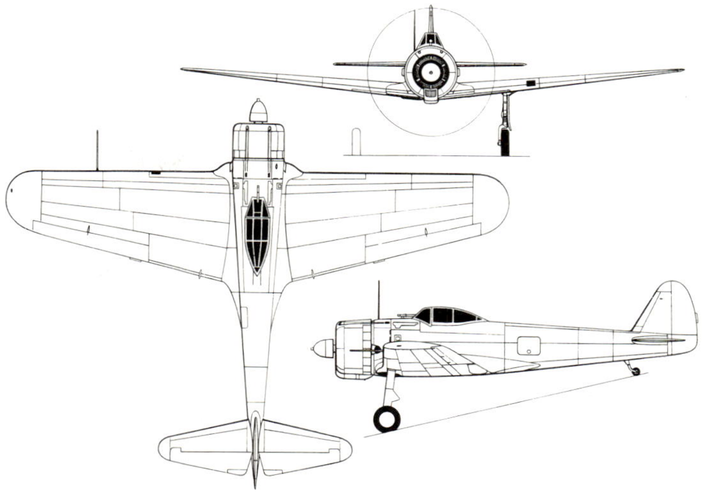

**The Japanese used the Ki-43 widely in the theatre, it proving far superior to Allied aircraft in terms of agility, but greatly lacking in speed, toughness and armament. The French did not use their captured aircraft in actual combat.**

## Nord 1001 and 1002 Pingouin

These four-seat liaison aircraft are other examples of German aircraft (in this instance the Messerschmitt Bf 108) which remained in production after the Liberation for use by the French military. The French versions had their Argus engine replaced by a Renault 6Q-10 (Nord 1001) or 6Q-11 (Nord 1002). A small number of both models were operated in Indochina.

**Specification** (Nord 1002)
**Type:** four-seat liaison aircraft
**Powerplant:** one 240-hp (179-kW) Renault 6Q-11 inline piston engine
**Performance:** maximum speed 190 mph (305 km/h); service ceiling 20,340 ft (6200 m); range 620 miles (1000 km)
**Weights:** empty 1,775 lb (805 kg); loaded 2,976 lb (1350 kg)
**Dimensions:** span 34 ft 5.4 in (10.50 m); length 27 ft 2.8 in (8.30 m); height 7 ft 6.6 in (2.30 m); wing area 172.2 sq ft (16.0 m²)
**Armament:** none

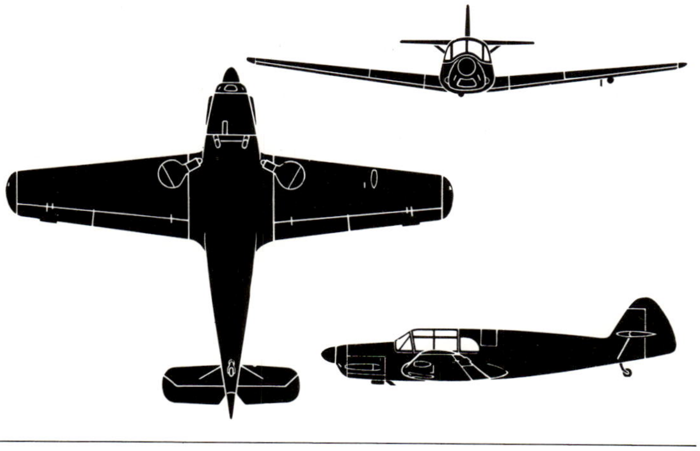

**The Nord 1001 shows its obvious connections with the Messerschmitt Bf 108 Taifun. The type was license-built by Nord, with a French engine installed. These were used for liaison and intra-theatre transport.**

## Nord 2501 Noratlas

Similar in layout to the twin-boom Fairchild C-119, but smaller and lighter than the American aircraft, the Nord 2501 military transport made its appearance in Indochina during the last phase of French air operations. The type was mainly used to relocate non-Communist Vietnamese from the North to the South.

**Specification**
**Type:** tactical personnel (36 paratroops or 45 equipped troops) or cargo (maximum payload of 13,227 lb/6000 kg) transport
**Powerplant:** two 2,090-hp (1559-kW) SNECMA-built Bristol Hercules 738 radial piston engines
**Performance:** maximum speed 252 mph (405 km/h) at 9,845 ft (3000 m); climb rate 1,180 ft/min (360 m/min); service ceiling 23,295 ft (7100 m); range 1,710 miles (2750 km) with payload of 14,991 lb (6800 kg)
**Weights:** empty 29,321 lb (13300 kg); loaded 48,502 lb (22000 kg)
**Dimensions:** span 106 ft 7.5 in (32.50 m); length 72 ft 0.2 in (21.95 m); height 19 ft 8.2 in (6.00 m); wing area 1,087.2 sq ft (101.0 m²)
**Armament:** none

**Joining the airlift late in the war, the Noratlas represented the resurgent French transport industry following World War II. This GT 2/64 machine is seen at Haiphong in April 1955.**

## Nord Centre N.C. 701 Martinet

The Martinets were French-built versions of the Siebel Si 204A (N.C. 702) with a conventional stepped nose and the Si 204D (N.C. 701) with unstepped glazed nose. Both were powered by French engines instead of the original Argus As 410 of the German aircraft.

**Specification**
**Type:** eight-passenger liaison aircraft
**Powerplant:** two 590-hp (440-kW) Renault 12S-00 inline piston engines
**Performance:** maximum speed 226 mph (364 km/h) at 9,845 ft (3000 m); climb rate 3,280 ft (1000 m) in 3.3 min; service ceiling 24,605 ft (7500 m); range 1,120 miles (1800 km)
**Weights:** empty 8,708 lb (3950 kg); loaded 12,346 lb (5600 kg)
**Dimensions:** span 69 ft 11.8 in (21.33 m); length 39 ft 2.5 in (11.95 m); height 13 ft 11.3 in (4.25 m); wing area 495 sq ft (46.0 m²)
**Armament:** none

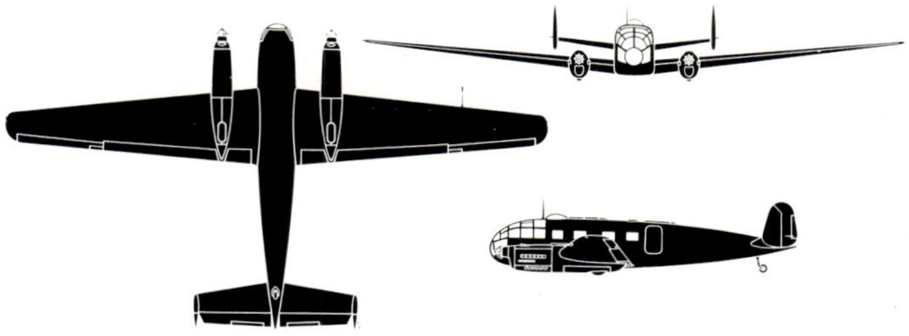

**Another German type built under license in France was the Siebel Si 204, built as the N.C.701 Martinet. As with other German aircraft, these had French engines in place of the original. The Martinet saw service on liaison and light transport tasks.**

## North American RA-5C Vigilante

Along with the RF-8s of VFP-63 and occasional detachments of RA-3Bs from VAP-61, RA-5Cs from RVAH squadrons provided reconnaissance for CTF-77 throughout the duration of US involvement in South East Asia.

**Specification**
**Type:** two-seat carrier-based reconnaissance aircraft
**Powerplant:** two 11,870-lb (5384-kg) dry thrust and 17,860-lb (8101-kg) afterburning thrust General Electric J79-GE-10 turbojets
**Performance:** maximum speed 1,385 mph (2230 km/h) at 40,000 ft (12190 m); service ceiling 64,000 ft (19505 m); combat range 2,650 miles (4265 km)
**Weight:** loaded 66,818 lb (30308 kg)
**Dimensions:** span 53 ft (16.15 m); length 75 ft 10 in (23.11 m); height 19 ft 5 in (5.92 m); wing area 769 sq ft (71.44 $m^2$)
**Armament:** none

**This RVAH-11 RA-5C is seen on the catapult of USS *Constellation*. Vigilantes were one of the fastest and heaviest aircraft to see carrier service.**

## North American F-100 Super Sabre

On 9 June 1964, Super Sabres became the first jets to drop ordnance in South East Asia. The type grew in importance until by 1967 the F-100Ds were the most numerous fighters in South Vietnam. In addition to their all-important role in the in-country war, both single-seat F-100Ds and two-seat F-100Fs were also active in Laos and, to a lesser extent, in Cambodia and over the North Vietnamese panhandle. Detachment 1 of the Tactical Warfare Center made the initial use of *Wild Weasels* when it deployed its specially configured F-100Fs to Korat in November 1965. The last Super Sabres in South East Asia were those of the 35th TFW which ceased operations at Phan Rang AB in June 1971.

**Specification** (F-100D)
**Type:** single-seat tactical fighter
**Powerplant:** one 11,700-lb (5307-kg) dry thrust and 16,950-lb (7688-kg) afterburning thrust Pratt & Whitney J57-P-21A turbojet
**Performance:** maximum speed 864 mph (1390 km/h) at 35,000 ft (10670 m); climb rate 16,000 ft/min (4875 m/min); service ceiling 45,000 ft (13720 m); combat range 1,500 miles (2415 km)
**Weights:** empty 21,000 lb (9525 kg); loaded 29,762 lb (13500 kg)
**Dimensions:** span 38 ft 9 in (11.81 m); length 49 ft 6 in (15.09 m); height 16 ft 2.9 in (4.95 m); wing area 385.2 sq ft (35.79 $m^2$)
**Armament:** four 20-mm M-39 cannon and up to 7,500 lb (3402 kg) of external stores

**Bearing the brunt of the in-country war, the F-100 was employed almost solely as a 'mud-mover', using unguided rockets and conventional bombs as its primary weapons. This example unleashes Mk 82 'slicks' over VC positions.**

## North American OV-10 Bronco

Developed to meet Tri-Service requirements for counter-insurgency aircraft (with secondary light transport/aeromedical evacuation capabilities), the Bronco was flown in South East Asia by Air Force, Navy and Marine units. The Broncos' main mission was FAC but the OV-10As of VAL-4 were used by the Navy as light attack aircraft in support of riverine operations.

**Specification** (OV-10A)
**Type:** two-seat counter-insurgency aircraft
**Powerplant:** two 715-eshp (533-ekW) AiResearch T76-G-10 turboprops
**Performance:** maximum speed 281 mph (452 km/h) at 10,000 ft (3050 m); climb rate 2,800 ft/min (853 m/min); service ceiling 29,000 ft (8840 m); combat range 380 miles (610 km)
**Weights:** empty 7,190 lb (3261 kg); loaded 12,500 lb (5670 kg)
**Dimensions:** span 40 ft (12.19 m); length 39 ft 9 in (12.12 m); height 15 ft 1 in (4.60 m); wing area 291 sq ft (27.03 $m^2$)
**Armament:** four 0.30-in (7.62-mm) machine-guns and 3,600 lb (1633 kg) of external stores

**Both the Marines and the Air Force used the Bronco for FAC duties. The large cockpit gave excellent visibility for both crew, while the low aspect ratio and powerful engines gave the type phenomenal manoeuvrability at low level.**

## North American T-6G Texan

Fifty-five T-6Gs were delivered to the VNAF when the United States took over responsibility for the training of Vietnamese aircrews in 1955. Their usefulness was limited as most Vietnamese pilots soon received their advanced training at American facilities in CONUS.

**Specification**
**Type:** two-seat basic trainer
**Powerplant:** one 550-hp (410-kW) Pratt & Whitney R-1340-AN-1 radial piston engine
**Performance:** maximum speed 212 mph (341 km/h) at 5,000 ft (1525 m); climb rate 1,640 ft/min (500 m/min); service ceiling 24,750 ft (7540 m); range 870 miles (1400 km)
**Weights:** empty 4,271 lb (1937 kg); loaded 5,617 lb (2548 kg)
**Dimensions:** span 42 ft (12.80 m); length 29 ft 6 in (8.99 m); height 11 ft 8.25 in (3.56 m); wing area 253.7 sq ft (23.57 $m^2$)
**Armament:** none

**The classic trainer of World War II soldiered on with many air forces after the war, also being used for attack duties. The VNAF and Royal Thai Air Force employed the T-6 as a trainer.**

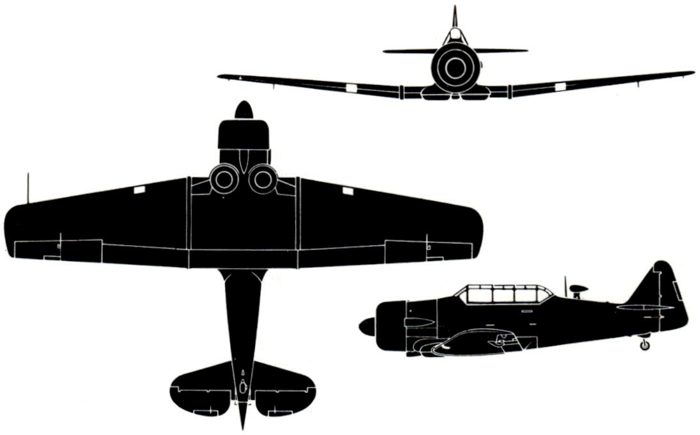

## North American T-28 Trojan

Displaced by jet trainers in the USAF training scheme, the Trojan proved easily adaptable to the counter-insurgency role. Both ex-USAF T-28As and ex-Navy T-28Bs were used in this capacity by the VNAF (including some RT-28Bs for reconnaissance), the Royal Khmer Aviation, and the *Farm Gate* detachment. After these early versions were grounded due to structural failures, T-28Ds, with more powerful engines, heavier armament and beefed-up structure, were also operated by the Khmer Air Force and the Royal Lao Air Force.

**Specification** (T-28D)
**Type:** two-seat counter-insurgency aircraft
**Powerplant:** one 1,300-hp (969-kW) Wright R-1820-56S radial piston engine
**Performance:** maximum speed 352 mph (566 km/h) at 18,000 ft (5485 m); climb rate 5,130 ft/min (1564 m/min); service ceiling 37,000 ft (11280 m); combat range 1,200 miles (1930 km)
**Weights:** empty 6,512 lb (2954 kg); loaded 8,118 lb (3682 kg)
**Dimensions:** span 40 ft 7 in (12.37 m); length 32 ft 10 in (10.00 m); height 12 ft 8 in (3.86 m); wing area 271.2 sq ft (25.19 m$^2$)
**Armament:** up to 4,000 lb (1814 kg) of external stores, including gun pods

**North American's big trainer proved adept at counter-insurgency operations, carrying its ordnance on six underwing pylons. Part of the original *Farm Gate* detachment, the T-28s saw much action during the early years of US involvement.**

## Northrop F-5 Freedom Fighter and Tiger II

Procured for MAP delivery to allied air forces in developing countries, the single-seat F-5A and two-seat F-5B fighters were intended to see only limited USAF service in training foreign pilots. Prior to proceeding with a plan to procure additional aircraft (the projected F-5C and F-5D versions) for Air Force use in South East Asia, F-5As and F-5Bs were sent to South Vietnam to undergo the *Skoshi Tiger* combat evaluation. This six-month project in 1965-66 was followed by 15 months of regular operations. Even though the type proved quite effective, it was considered to lack sufficient range and offensive load-carrying capability for continued Air Force use. It was nevertheless selected as the first fighter aircraft for the VNAF. Obtaining its first 17 F-5As and F-5Bs in June 1967, the VNAF received 126 Freedom Fighters (including the RF-5A reconnaissance version) during *Enhance Plus*. Beginning in May 1974, more capable F-5E and F-5F Tiger IIs replaced some of the earlier models.

**Specification** (F-5A)
**Type:** single-seat tactical fighter
**Powerplant:** two 2,720-lb (1233-kg) dry thrust and 4,080-lb (1850-kg) afterburning thrust General Electric J85-GE-13 turbojets
**Performance:** maximum speed 977 mph (1572 km/h); at 36,000 ft (10975 m); climb rate 33,000 ft/min (10060 m/min); service ceiling 50,300 ft (15330 m); combat range 1150 miles (1850 km)
**Weights:** empty 10,380 lb (4708 kg); loaded 14,150 lb (6418 kg)
**Dimensions:** span 25 ft 3 in (7.70 m); length 47 ft 2 in (14.38 m); height 13 ft 2 in (4.01 m); wing area 170 sq ft (15.79 m$^2$)
**Armament:** two 20-mm M-39 cannon and 6,200-lb (2812 kg) of external stores

**Seen Stateside, this F-5A is one of the aircraft of the *Skoshi Tiger* operational evaluation. Although fast and agile, the F-5 did not have the range or weapon load to be truly effective in the theatre.**

## Piasecki CH-21 Workhorse

The obsolescent twin-rotor Workhorse was operated in Vietnam by Army Transportation Companies for two years commencing in December 1961.

**Specification** (CH-21C)
**Type:** military transport (14 troops) helicopter
**Powerplant:** one 1,425-hp (1063-kW) Wright R-1820-103 radial piston engine
**Performance:** maximum speed 131 mph (211 km/h) at sea level; climb rate 1,080 ft/min (329 m/min); service ceiling 9,450 ft (2880 m)
**Weights:** empty 8,665 lb (3926 kg); loaded 15,000 lb (6804 kg)
**Dimensions:** rotor diameter (each) 44 ft (13.41 m); fuselage length 52 ft 6 in (16.00 m); height 15 ft 5 in (4.70 m)
**Armament:** none

**Among the first US aircraft in South Vietnam were the Piasecki CH-21s of the US Army. This example is seen (with door gunner) shortly after receiving an all-over olive drab paint scheme.**

## Piper L-4B Grasshopper

A small number of L-4Bs were used in 1945-46 for artillery spotting and observation by the French Army's 9ème Division d'Infanterie Coloniale.

**Specification**
**Type:** two-seat artillery spotting and observation aircraft
**Powerplant:** one 65-hp (48-kW) Continental O-170-3 air-cooled piston engine
**Performance:** maximum speed 83 mph (134 km/h) at sea level; climb rate 5,000 ft (1525 m) in 14.4 min; service ceiling 9,300 ft (2835 m); range 190 miles (305 km)
**Weights:** empty 730 lb (331 kg); loaded 1,220 lb (553 kg)
**Dimensions:** span 35 ft 3 in (10.74 m); length 22 ft 5 in (6.83 m); height 6 ft 8 in (2.03 m); wing area 179 sq ft (16.63 m$^2$)
**Armament:** none

**The Piper L-4 Grasshopper (military version of the J-3 Cub) had been used for artillery spotting and observation throughout World War II by US forces. The French continued using the Grasshopper in this role throughout the early days of the war in Indochina, but their place was quickly taken by more capable types such as the M.S.500 Criquet.**

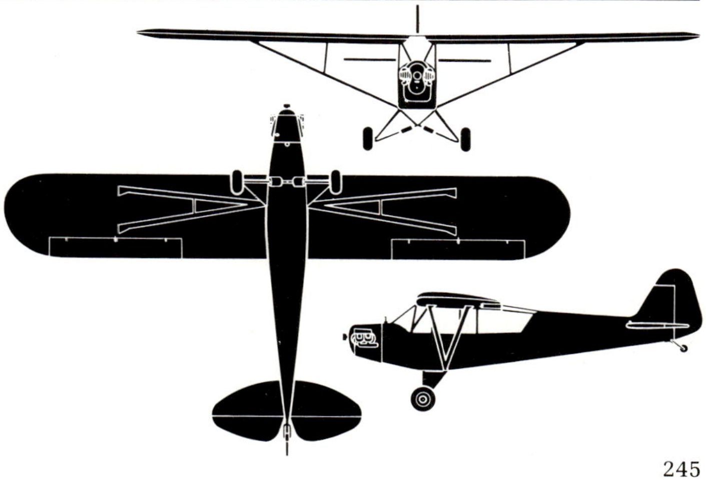

## Republic F-105 Thunderchief

Designed as a nuclear strike fighter with internal stowage for a special store, the Thunderchief lacked multi-mission capability. Accordingly the Kennedy Administration terminated its production in favour of the more flexible F-4. Nevertheless, single-seat F-105Ds and two-seat F-105Fs, which had been modified for external carriage of large loads of conventional stores, became the primary strike aircraft flown by the USAF against the North from 1965 until 1970. In addition to their conventional missions, F-105D/Fs were used extensively for *Iron Hand* defense suppression missions. *Wild Weasel* operations were undertaken initially by F-105Fs, with specially-configured F-105Gs continuing in this role until the US withdrawal. Blind bombing sorties were flown by 30 T-Stick IIs (F-105Ds with additional electronic equipment in a bulged dorsal spine). Between 1965 and 1967, F-105s accounted for more America combat losses than any other type. All told, 397 Thunderchiefs were lost to combat and operational causes in South East Asia (18.3 percent of USAF fixed-wing losses, or 10.1 percent of total US fixed-wing aircraft losses).

**Together with the F-4 Phantom, the F-105 took the war to North Vietnam. Flying from Thai bases, the 'Thuds' were used mainly on medium- and low-level bombing missions, although they had their fair share of MiGs. This F-105D carries bombs with fuze extenders.**

**Specification** (F-105D)
**Type:** single-seat tactical fighter
**Powerplant:** one 17,200-lb (7802-kg) dry thrust and 24,500-lb (11113-kg) afterburning thrust Pratt & Whitney J75-P-19W turbojet
**Performance:** maximum speed 1,390 mph (2237 km/h) at 36,000 ft (10975 m); climb rate 34,500 ft/min (10515 m/min); service ceiling 52,000 ft (15850 m); combat range 1,850 miles (2975 km)
**Weights:** empty 27,500 lb (12474 kg); loaded 38,034 lb (17252 kg)
**Dimensions:** span 34 ft 11.25 in (10.65 m); length 64 ft 3 in (19.58 m); height 19 ft 8 in (5.99 m); wing area 385 sq ft (35.76 $m^2$)
**Armament:** one 20-mm M-61 cannon and up to 14,000 lb (6350 kg) of external and internal stores

## Sikorsky CH-3, HH-3 Jolly Green, and SH-3 Sea King

Serving in far fewer number than the UH-1s, OH-6s, CH-46s and CH-47s the military versions of the Sikorsky S-61 and S-61R provided a useful adjunct to the American helicopter inventory in South East Asia. The principal Air Force versions were the CH-3A and CH-3E with a rear vehicle-loading ramp, which were used for logistic support and recovery drones, and the HH-3E with armour, armament and retractable flight refuelling probe, which was operated for combat rescue and recovery. The main Navy versions were the SH-3A, SH-3D, and SH-3G, which were deployed aboard carriers for 'plane guard' and anti-submarine operations, and the HH-3A which was used for combat rescue and recovery.

**Specification** (HH-3E)
**Type:** search and rescue helicopter
**Powerplant:** two 1,400-shp (1044-kW) General Electric T58-GE-10 turboshafts
**Performance:** maximum speed 162 mph (261 km/h) at sea level; climb rate 1,310 ft/min (399 m/min); service ceiling 12,000 ft (3660 m); combat range 625 miles (1005 km)
**Weights:** empty 13,255 lb (6012 kg); loaded 18,000 lb (8165 kg)
**Dimensions:** rotor diameter 62 ft (18.90 m); fuselage length 57 ft 3 in (17.45 m); height 18 ft 1 in (5.51 m)
**Armament:** two 0.30-in (7.62-mm) M-60 flexible machine-guns

**Of the many versions of H-3 which served in South East Asia, none were more important than the CH/HH-3 rescue machines. These were used to retrieve downed airmen from hostile territory.**

## Sikorsky UH-19 Chickasaw

First obtaining S-55s from the British licensee (Westland), the Armée de l'Air subsequently received military Sikorsky H-19s from the United States. The French-purchased S-55s were retained by the Armée de l'Air, but 10 of the US-supplied H-19s were transferred to the VNAF in 1955.

**Specification** (H-19B)
**Type:** military transport (10 troops) helicopter
**Powerplant:** one 800-hp (597-kW) Wright R-1300-3 radial piston engine
**Performance:** maximum speed 112 mph (180 km/h) at sea level; climb rate 1,020 ft/min (311 m/min); service ceiling 10,500 ft (3200 m); range 360 miles (580 km)
**Weights:** empty 5,250 lb (2381 kg); loaded 7,900 lb (3583 kg)
**Dimensions:** rotor diameter 53 ft (16.15 m); fuselage length 42 ft 3 in (12.88 m); height 13 ft 4 in (4.06 m)
**Armament:** none

**Sikorsky S-55s were flown by the French on transport and assault duties. This helicopter was among the first really successful designs.**

## Sikorsky UH-34 Choctaw

Used in greater number than any other type of piston-powered helicopter, Choctaws were the main assault transport helicopters of the USMC and VNAF until fully replaced by UH-1s. Prior to the 1968 phase-out of their Choctaws, the Marines lost more UH-34s than UH-1s.

**Specification** (UH-34D)
**Type:** military transport (18 troops) helicopter
**Powerplant:** one 1,525-hp (1137-kW) Wright R-1820-84 radial piston engine
**Performance:** maximum speed 123 mph (198 km/h) at sea level; climb rate 1,100 ft/min (335 m/min); service ceiling 9,500 ft (2895 m); range 185 miles (300 km)
**Weights:** empty 7,900 lb (3583 kg); loaded 14,000 lb (6350 kg)
**Dimensions:** rotor diameter 56 ft (17.07 m); fuselage length 46 ft 9 in (14.25 m); height 14 ft 3.5 in (4.36 m)
**Armament:** TK-1 kit consisting of two 0.30-in (7.62-mm) M-60 forward-firing machine-guns and two pods with 18 2.75-in (70-mm) rockets

**Principal US Marine Corps assault helicopter during the early years of the war, the UH-34 was replaced by the ubiquitous UH-1.**

## Sikorsky CH-37 Mojave

Until the advent of twin turboshaft helicopters, the CH-37 was the only type of helicopter in service with the US military capable of airlifting damaged aircraft. However, the Mojave was not very reliable and saw only limited use with the USA and the USMC.

**Specification** (CH-37C)
**Type:** heavy transport (20 troops or up to 6,675 lb/3028 kg of cargo) helicopter
**Powerplant:** two 2,100-hp (1566-kW) Pratt & Whitney R-2800-54 radial piston engines
**Performance:** maximum speed 121 mph (195 km/h) at sea level; climb rate 1,280 ft/min (390 m/min); service ceiling 13,800 ft (4205 m); range 335 miles (540 km)
**Weights:** empty 21,502 lb (9753 kg); loaded 31,000 lb (14061 kg)
**Dimensions:** rotor diameter 72 ft (21.95 m); fuselage length 58 ft 5 in (17.81 m); height 16 ft 8 in (5.08 m)
**Armament:** none

**Only small numbers of CH-37s were employed on combat duties in South East Asia, mostly providing heavy airlift capability. These were quickly supplanted by Sikorsky CH-53s and Boeing Vertol CH-47s.**

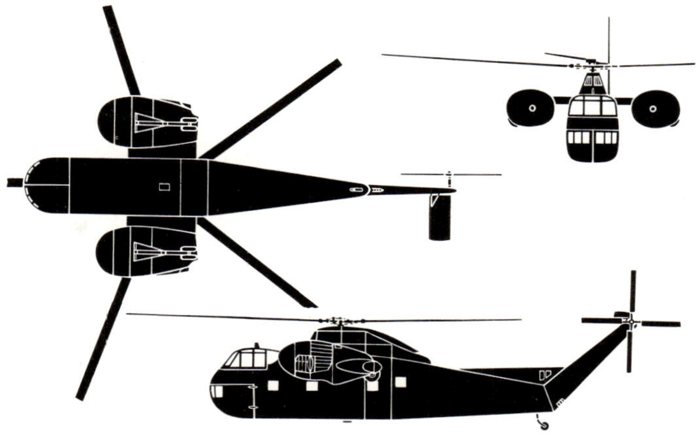

## Sikorsky CH-53 Sea Stallion and HH-53 Super Jolly Green

The CH-53A was a large assault helicopter specially developed for the Marine Corps and was first deployed to Vietnam in January 1967. With the USMC, this initial version was followed by the more powerful CH-53D version. Combat rescue and recovery versions operated by the USAF were the HH-53B and HH-53C, while the Navy used the RH-53A version for mine sweeping and countermeasures.

**Specification** (CH-53D)
**Type:** heavy assault (38 troops) helicopter
**Powerplant:** two 3,925-shp (2927-kW) General Electric T64-GE-13 turboshafts
**Performance:** maximum speed 172 mph (277 km/h); at sea level; climb rate 2,180 ft/min (664 m/min); service ceiling 17,500 ft (5335 m); range 885 miles (1425 km)
**Weights:** empty 23,628 lb (10717 kg); loaded 36,695 lb (16645 kg)
**Dimensions:** rotor diameter 72 ft 2.7 in (22.01 m); fuselage length 67 ft 2 in (20.47 m); height 24 ft 11 in (7.60 m)
**Armament:** none

**Rescue capability in South East Asia was greatly enhanced by the introduction into service of the Sikorsky HH-53. Greater range, better armour and armament and increased lifting ability made the HH-53 the complete rescue helicopter.**

## Sikorsky CH-54 Tarhe

The CH-54 flying cranes were the most powerful rotary-wing aircraft deployed to South East Asia (the gearbox could absorb 7,900 hp/5891 kW from the two 4,800-shp/3579-kW T37-P-700 turboshafts powering the CH-54B version). Tarhes were used to transport underslung construction and combat vehicles and to recover downed aircraft (CH-54s were credited with saving more than 380 aircraft valued at over $210 million).

**Specification** (CH-54B)
**Type:** heavy flying-crane helicopter
**Powerplant:** two 4,800-shp (3579-kW) Pratt & Whitney T37-P-700 turboshafts
**Performance:** maximum speed 127 mph (204 km/h) at sea level; climb rate 1,700 ft/min (518 m/min); range 255 miles (410 km)
**Weights:** empty 19,234 lb (8724 kg); loaded 42,000 lb (19050 kg)
**Dimensions:** rotor diameter 72 ft (21.95 m); fuselage length 70 ft 3 in (21.41 m); height 25 ft 5 in (7.75 m)
**Armament:** none

**Seen refuelling from a portable bladder, this CH-54 Tarhe demonstrates the straddling landing gear which allowed the carriage of portable buildings and trucks without slinging the load on strops.**

## Supermarine Seafire and Spitfire

Unable at first to send its American-fighters (e.g., the Republic P-47Ds which would have been well-suited to the task), the Armée de l'Air elected to equip its Groupes de Chasse in Indochina with British-made Spitfire Mk. IXs and Mk. XVIs. In 1945-46, pending arrival of these aircraft from France, G.C. II/7 operated a number of Mk. VIIIs on loan from the RAF. The Mk. IXs and Mk. XVIs remained in Indochina until November 1950. Two Griffon-powered carrier-based Seafire XVs saw limited use aboard the *Arromanches* in 1948-49.

**Specification** (Spitfire L.F. IXE)
**Type:** single-seat fighter
**Powerplant:** one 1,720-hp (1283-kW) Rolls-Royce Merlin 66 liquid-cooled piston engine
**Performance:** maximum speed 404 mph (650 km/h) at 21,000 ft (6400 m); climb rate 20,000 ft (6096 m) in 6.4 min; service ceiling 42,500 ft (12955 m); combat range 430 miles (690 km)
**Weights:** empty 5,610 lb (2545 kg); loaded 7,500 lb (3,402 kg)
**Dimensions:** span 32 ft 7 in (9.93 m); length 31 ft 4.5 in (9.56 m); height 12 ft 7.75 in (3.85 m); wing area 230 sq ft (21.37 $m^2$)
**Armament:** two 0.50-in (12.7-mm) machine-guns and two 20-mm cannon, plus two 250-lb (113-kg) bombs

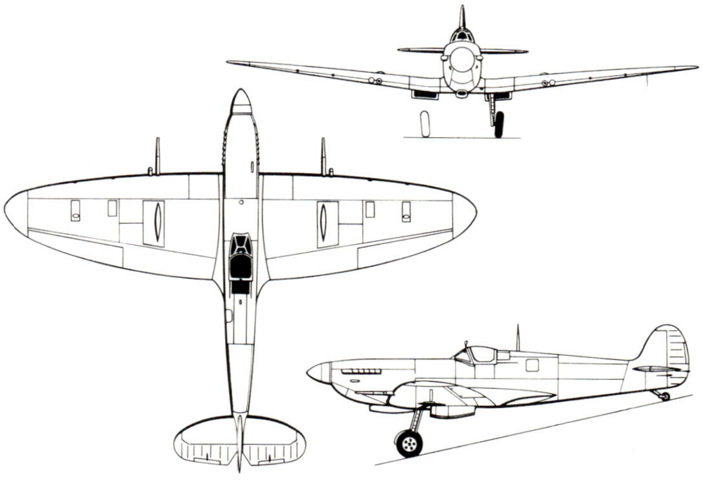

**Supermarine's famous Spitfire was used widely by the French during the early years of the Indochina war, mainly as a fighter-bomber. The principal version was the Mk IX (illustrated).**

## Supermarine Sea Otter

Sea Otter single-engined flying-boats, including six originally acquired by the Customs Administration, were operated in Indochina from 1947 until 1952 by Escadrilles 8S and 9S of the French Navy.

### Specification

**Type:** four-seat utility flying-boat
**Powerplant:** one 965-hp (720-kW) Bristol Mercury XXX radial piston engine
**Performance:** maximum speed 163 mph (262 km/h) at 4,500 ft (1370 m); climb rate 870 ft/min (265 m/min); service ceiling 17,000 ft (5180 m); range 690 miles (1110 km)
**Weights:** empty 6,805 lb (3087 kg); loaded 10,000 lb (4536 kg)
**Dimensions:** span 46 ft (14.02 m); length 39 ft 10.75 in (12.16 m); height 15 ft 1.5 in (4.61 m); wing area 610 sq ft (56.67 m²)
**Armament:** none normally fitted to French aircraft

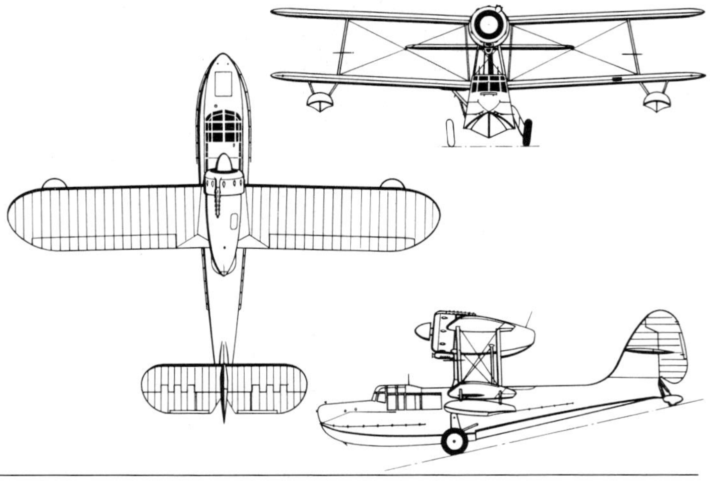

**The Sea Otter was derived from the Walrus, which had been used extensively on air-sea rescue duties by British forces. The Sea Otter featured a tractor engine as opposed to a pusher. The French made use of its amphibious capabilities for coastal patrol.**

## Vought A-7 Corsair II

The intended successor of the Skyhawk light attack aircraft was first deployed to the Gulf of Tonkin by VA-147 in December 1967. Thereafter rapidly increasing numbers of VA squadrons converted from A-4s, first to TF30-powered A-7As, A-7Bs, and A-7Cs, and then to TF41-powered A-7Es, so that by 1972 only three VA Squadrons aboard the *Hancock* still flew A-4Fs with CTF-77. With the Air Force, which had adopted the Corsair II as a tactical fighter with limited all-weather capability, A-7Ds were first deployed to Thailand by the 354th TFW in October 1972. In the spring of 1975, Air Force A-7Ds and Navy A-7Es were among the last US aircraft to fly combat sorties in South East Asia when they supported the *Mayaguez* rescue and the *Eagle Pull* and *Frequent Wind* evacuations.

### Specification (A-7D)

**Type:** tactical fighter
**Powerplant:** one 14,250-lb (6464-kg) thrust Allison TF41-A-1 turbofan
**Performance:** maximum speed 698 mph (1123 km/h) at sea level; climb rate 8,000 ft/min (2438 m/min); service ceiling 37,000 ft (11,280 m); combat range 1,430 miles (2300 km)
**Weights:** empty 19,490 lb (8841 kg); loaded 42,000 lb (19051 kg)
**Dimensions:** span 38 ft 8.25 in (11.79 m); length 46 ft 1.25 in (14.05 m); height 16 ft (4.88 m); wing area 375 sq ft (34.84 m²)
**Armament:** one 20-mm M-61 cannon and up to 15,000 lb (6804 kg) of external stores

**Rapidly taking over the position of the Navy's premier light attack platform, the A-7 mirrored its A-4 and A-1 predecessors by having a massive weapon load allied to good manoeuvrability.**

## Vought F-8 Crusader

When the Navy went to war in South East Asia, the gun-and-missile Crusader had already been replaced in the VF squadrons operating from the larger carriers by the missile-armed Phantom II. Nevertheless, being single-seaters and carrying a built-in cannon armament, F-8s were still well liked by fighter pilots. Moreover, the inability of the smaller carriers to accommodate the heavier Phantom IIs ensured a continued role for the F-8s. To meet the needs of the VF squadrons aboard the smaller carriers, the Crusader was withdrawn from use in the land-based Marine squadrons and its F-8C, F-8D and F-8E versions were rebuilt and updated respectively to F-8K, F-8H, and F-8J standards. Similarly, the RF-8As operated by detachments of VFP-63 aboard many of the CTF-77 carriers were brought up to the RF-8G standards. In Marine service, Crusader fighters were operated in 1965-67 from Da Nang by three VMF(AW) squadrons, and between April and December 1965 by VMF(AW)-212 aboard the *Oriskany*. VMCJ-1 sent RF-8A detachments to carriers in 1964 and then took its aircraft to Da Nang until October 1966.

**Although overshadowed by the F-4 Phantom, the Crusader was a much-loved fighter which served the US Navy and Marine Corps well. The variable incidence wing was a novel feature.**

### Specification (F-8J)

**Type:** single-seat carrier-based fighter
**Powerplant:** one 10,700-lb (4853-kg) dry thrust and 18,000-lb (8165-kg) afterburning thrust Pratt & Whitney J57-P-20A turbojet
**Performance:** maximum speed 1,120 mph (1802 km/h) at 40,000 ft (12190 m); climb rate 57,000 ft (17375 m) in 6.5 min; service ceiling 58,000 ft (17680 m); combat range 1,200 miles (1930 km)
**Weight:** loaded 27,500 lb (12474 kg)
**Dimensions:** span 35 ft 8 in (10.87 m); length 54 ft 6 in (16.61 m); height 15 ft 9 in (4.80 m); wing area 375 sq ft (34.84 m²)
**Armament:** four 20-mm MK-12 cannon and four AIM-9 Sidewinder infrared-guided air-to-air missiles

## Westland S-51

Four Sikorsky S-51s, licence-built in the United Kingdom by Westland, were the first helicopters ordered in 1952 by the Armée de l'Air for operations in Indochina. An additional batch was procured later for use by the 65ème Escadre d'hélicoptères alongside Westland-built S-55s and Sikorsky H-19s.

### Specification (S-51 Mk. IA)

**Type:** four-seat utility helicopter
**Powerplant:** one 540-hp (403-kW) Alvis Leonides 521/I radial piston engine
**Performance:** maximum speed 95 mph (153 km/h) at sea level; climb rate 1,000 ft/min (305 m/min); service ceiling 13,200 ft (4025 m); range 300 miles (485 km)
**Weights:** empty 4,366 lb (1980 kg); loaded 5,700 lb (2585 kg)
**Dimensions:** rotor diameter 49 ft (14.94 m); fuselage length 41 ft 1.75 in (12.54 m); height 12 ft 11.5 in (3.95 m)
**Armament:** none

**The S-51 was licence-built in England by Westland, and these aircraft were supplied to the French for Indochina service. These undertook many duties alongside the other helicopter types operated by the French.**

VF-111 'Sundowner' F-4B 'buddy-bombs' with a Phantom from its VF-51 sister squadron. This method of bombing, using navigation fixes was not accurate and was only used as a last resort. AIM-9 Sidewinders were carried for self-defence.

# BIBLIOGRAPHY


Anderton, David A., **Republic F-105 Thunderchief**
London, England: Osprey Publishing Limited, 1983.

Anderton, David A., **Strategic Air Command, Two-thirds of the Triad**
New York, NY: Charles Scribner's Sons, 1975.

Anderton, David A., **The History of the U.S. Air Force**
London, England: The Hamlyn Publishing Group Limited, 1981.

Bail, René., **Les Pingouins d'Indochine, L'Aéronavale de 1945 à 1954**
Paris, France: Editions Maritimes & d'Outre-Mer, 1979.

Ballard, Jack S., **Development and Employment of Fixed-Wing Gunships, 1962-1972**
Washington, D.C.: Office of Air Force History, 1982.

Basel, G. I., **Pak Six**
La Mesa, California: Associated Creative Writers, 1982.

Bowers, Ray L., **Tactical Airlift**
Washington, D.C.: Office of Air Force History, 1982.

Buckingham, William A. Jr., **Operation Ranch Hand – The Air Force and Herbicides in Southeast Asia, 1961-1971**
Washington, D.C.: Office of Air Force History, 1982.

Chassin, Général L. M., **Aviation Indochine**
Paris, France: Amiot/Dumont, 1954.

Dabney, Joseph Earl., **Herk: Hero of the Skies**
Lakemont, Georgia: Copple House Books, 1979.

Doubek, Thomas J., editor for the 100th Strategic Reconnaissance Wing., **Strategic Reconnaissance 1956-1976: A History of the 4080th/100th SRW**
Dallas, TX: Taylor Publishing Company, 1976.

Drendel, Lou., **Air War over Southeast Asia – A Pictorial Record, Volumes 1, 2 and 3**
Carrollton, Texas: Squadron/Signal Publications, Inc., 1982 (vol. 1), 1983 (vol. 2), 1984 (vol. 3).

Drendel, Lou., **. . . and Kill MiGs**
Warren, Michigan: Squadron/Signal Publications, Inc. 1974.

Drendel, Lou., **Huey**
Carrollton, Texas: Squadron/Signal Publications, Inc., 1983.

Drury, Richard S., **My Secret War**
Fallbrook, California: Aero Publishers, Inc., 1975.

Fails, Lt. Colonel William R., USMC., **Marines and Helicopters, 1962-1973**
Washington, D.C.: History and Museums Division, Headquarters US Marine Corps, 1978.

Futrell, Robert F. et al., **Aces & Aerial Victories**
Washington, D.C.: Officer of Air Force History, 1976.

Futrell, Robert F., **The United States Air Force in Southeast Asia – The Advisory Years to 1965**
Washington, D.C.: Office of Air Force History, 1981.

Gordon, Thomas F. et al., **Historical Highlight of the First Twenty-Five Years of PACAF, Pacific Air Forces, 1957-1981**
Hickam AFB, Hawaii: Headquarters Pacific Air Forces, 1982.

Gunston, William., **F-4 Phantom**
New York, NY: Charles Scribner's Sons, 1977.

Gunston, William., **F-111**
New York, NY: Charles Scribner's Sons, 1977.

Gropman, Lt. Colonel Alan L., USAF., **USAF Southeast Asia Monograph Series, Vol 5, Airpower and the Airlift Evacuation of Kham Duc**
Washington, D.C.: Office of Air Force History, 1979.

Harvey, Frank., **Air War – Vietnam**
New York, NY: Bantam Books, 1967.

Hopkins, Charles K., **SAC Tanker Operations in the Southeast Asia War**
Offut AFB, Nebraska: Office of the Historian, Headquarters Strategic Air Command, 1979.

Jackson, Berkely R., **Douglas Skyraider**
Fallbrook, California: Aero Publishers, Inc., 1969.

Jones, First Lieutenant Brett A., USMC., **A History of Marine Attack Squadron 223**
Washington, D.C.: History and Museums Division, Headquarters US Marine Corps, 1978.

Jones, Major Oakah L. Jr., **Organization, Mission and Growth of the Vietnamese Air Force, 1949-1968**
Hickam AFB, Hawaii: Headquarters Pacific Air Forces, 1968.

Kilduff, Peter., **Douglas A-4 Skyhawk**
London, England: Osprey Publishing Limited, 1983.

Ky, Nguyen Cao., **Twenty Years and Twenty Days**
New York, NY: Stein and Day Publishers, 1976.

Lavalle, Major A. J. C., USAF., **USAF Southeast Asia Monograph Series, Vol. 1, The Tale of Two Bridges, and The Battle for the Skies over North Vietnam**
Washington, D.C.: Office of Air Force History, 1976.

Lavalle, Major A. J. C., USAF., **USAF Southeast Asia Monograph Series, Vol. 2, Airpower and the 1972 Spring Invasion**
Washington, D.C.: Office of Air Force History, 1976.

Lavalle, Major A. J. C., USAF., **USAF Southeast Asia Monograph Series, Vol. 3, The Vietnamese Air Force, 1951-1975, an Analysis of its Role in Combat, and Fourteen Hours at Koh Tang**
Washington, D.C.: Office of Air Force History, 1977.

Lavalle, Lt. Colonel A. J. C., USAF., **USAF Southeast Asia Monograph Series, Vol. 4, Last Flight from Saigon**
Washington, D.C.: Office of Air Force History, 1978.

Leary, William M., **Perilous Missions: Civil Air Transport and CIA Covert Operations in Asia**
Tuscaloosa, Alabama: University of Alabama Press, 1984.

Le Gro, William E., **Vietnam from Cease-Fire to Capitulation**
Washington, D.C.: US Army Center of Military History, 1981.

Littauer, Raphael, and Norman Uphoff, editors., **The Air War in Indochina**
Boston, Massachusetts: Beacon Press, 1971.

McCarthy, Brig. General James R., USAF, and Lt. Colonel George B. Allison, USAF., **USAF Southeast Asia Monograph Series, Vol. 6, Linebacker II: a View from the Rock**
Washington, D.C.: Office of Air Force History, 1979.

Mersky, Peter B., **U.S. Marine Corps Aviation, 1912 to the Present**
Annapolis, Maryland: The Nautical and Aviation Publishing Company of America, 1983.

Mersky, Peter B., and Norman Polmar., **The Naval Air War in Vietnam**
Annapolis, Maryland: The Nautical and Aviation Publishing Company of America, 1981.

Mikesh, Robert C., **B-57 Canberra at War, 1964-1972**
New York, NY: Charles Scribner's Sons, 1980.

Miller, Jay., **Lockheed U-2**
Austin, Texas: Aerofax, Incorporated, 1983.

Momyer, General William W., USAF., **Air Power in Three Wars (WWII, Korea, Vietnam)**
Washington, D.C.: Department of the Air Force, 1978.

Nalty, Bernard C., **Air Power and the Fight for Khe Sanh**
Washington, D.C.: Office of Air Force History, 1973.

Nalty, Bernard C., George M. Watson, and Jacob Neufeld., **An Illustrated Guide to the Air War over Vietnam – Aircraft of the Southeast Asia Conflict**
New York, NY: Arco Publishing, Inc., 1981.

New York Times Staff., **The Pentagon Papers**
New York, NY: Bantam Books, Inc., 1971.

Parker, Lt. Colonel Gary W., USMC., **A History of Medium Helicopter Squadron 161**
Washington, D.C.: History and Museums Division, Headquarters US Marine Corps, 1978.

Pierson, James E., **A Special Historical Study of Electronic Warfare in SEA, 1964-1968**
San Antonio, Texas: Headquarters, United States Air Force Security Service, 1973.

Rausa, Rosario., **Skyraider – The Douglas A-1 "Flying Dump Truck"**
Annapolis, Maryland: The Nautical and Aviation Publishing Company of America, 1982.

Sambito, Major William J., USMC., **A History of Marine Fighter Attack Squadron 232**
Washington, D.C.: History and Museums Division, Headquarters US Marine Corps, 1978.

Sambito, Major William J., USMC., **A History of Marine Attack Squadron 311**
Washington, D.C.: History and Museums Division, Headquarters US Marine Corps, 1978.

Sambito, Major William J., USMC., **A History of Marine Fighter Attack Squadron 312**
Washington, D.C.: History and Museums Division, Headquarters US Marine Corps, 1978.

Shulimson, Jack., **U.S. Marines in Vietnam – An Expanding War, 1966**
Washington, D.C.: History and Museums Division, Headquarters US Marine Corps, 1982.

Shulimson, Jack, and Charles M. Johnson, Major, USMC., **U.S. Marines in Vietnam – The Landing and the Buildup, 1965**
Washington, D.C.: History and Museums Division, Headquarters US Marine Corps, 1978.

Stanton, Shelby L., **U.S. Army and Allied Ground Forces in Vietnam – Order of Battle**
Washington, D.C.: US News Books, 1981.

Stockholm International Peace Research Institute., **Arms Trade Registers, The Arms Trade with the Third World**
Cambridge, Massachusetts: The MIT Press, 1975.

Swanborough, Gordon, and Peter M. Bowers., **United States Military Aircraft since 1908**
London, England: Putnam & Company Limited, 1971.

Swanborough, Gordon, and Bowers, Peter M., **United States Naval Aircraft since 1911**
London, England: Putnam & Company Limited, 1968.

Teulières, André., **La Guerre du Vietnam, 1945-1975**
Paris, France: Editions Lavauzelle, 1978.

Thompson, James Clay., **Rolling Thunder – Understanding Policy and Program Failure**
Chapel Hill, North Carolina: The University of North Carolina Press, 1980.

Tilford, Earl H., Jr., **Search and Rescue in Southeast Asia, 1961-1975**
Washington, D.C.: Office of Air Force History, 1980.

Tillman, Barrett., **MiG Master: the Story of the F-8 Crusader**
Annapolis, Maryland: The Nautical and Aviation Publishing Company of America, 1980.

Van Haute, André., **French Air Force – Volume 2: 1941-1974**
Shepperton, England: Ian Allan Ltd., 1975.

Wagner, William., **Lightning Bugs and other Reconnaissance Drones**
Fallbrook, CA: Aero Publishers, Inc., 1982.

Whitlow, Captain Robert H., USMCR., **U.S. Marines in Vietnam – The Advisory & Combat Assistance Era, 1954-64**
Washington, D.C.: History and Museums Division, Headquarters US Marine Corps, 1977.

Wragg, David W., **Helicopters at War: A Pictorial History**
London, England: Robert Hale Limited, 1983.


## PICTURE ACKNOWLEDGMENTS


The publishers would like to thank the following agencies, organizations and individuals for their assistance in providing photographic material for this book.

**2, 3:** US Air Force. **6:** US Navy via Robert L. Lawson. **12:** USIS: **13:** Imperial War Museum. **14:** ECPA. **15:** ECPA (two). **16:** ECPA (three). **17:** Marc Rostaing via René J. Francillon/ECPA/Bruce Robertson. **18:** ECPA (three). **19:** ECPA/via René J. Francillon. **20:** ECPA (two). **21:** via René J. Francillon (two). **24:** ECPA (three). **25:** ECPA (three). **26:** ECPA (three). **27:** ECPA (three). **28:** ECPA (four). **29:** ECPA (three). **30:** ECPA (two). **31:** ECPA (two). **32:** ECPA (two). **33:** ECPA (two). **34:** ECPA (four). **35:** ECPA. **36:** ECPA. **37:** US Air Force (two). **38:** US Air Force (two). **39:** US Air Force. **40:** US Air Force (two). **41:** US Air Force (two). **42:** US Air Force (three). **43:** US Air Force (three). **44:** US Air Force (two). **45:** US Air Force (two). **46:** US Air Force. **47:** US Air Force (two). **50:** US Air Force (three). **51:** US Air Force (two). **52:** US Air Force (three). **53:** US Air Force (two). **54:** US Air Force (three). **55:** US Air Force (three). **58:** US Air Force (two). **59:** US Air Force (two). **60:** US Air Force (two). **61:** US Air Force. **62:** US Air Force (two). **63:** US Air Force (three). **66:** US Air Force (three). **67:** US Air Force (three). **68:** US Air Force. **69:** US Air Force. **70:** US Air Force (three). **71:** US Air Force (three). **72:** US Air Force (three). **73:** US Air Force (three). **76:** US Air Force (three). **77:** US Air Force. **78:** US Air Force (two). **79:** US Air Force (three). **82:** US Air Force. **83:** US Air Force. **84:** US Air Force (three). **85:** US Air Force (four). **86:** US Air Force (two). **87:** US Air Force (three). **88:** US Air Force (three). **89:** Associated Press/US Air Force. **90:** US Air Force (three). **91:** US Air Force (three). **92:** Robert F. Dorr/US Air Force. **93:** US Air Force (two). **94:** US Air Force/Lockheed/Bruce M. Bailey/100th SRW via David Donald. **95:** Bruce M. Bailey/US Air Force. **96:** Bruce M. Bailey (three). **97:** Bruce M. Bailey/US Air Force. **98:** 100th SRW via David Donald/Bruce M. Bailey/Lockheed/Bruce M. Bailey. **99:** US Air Force (four). **100:** US Air Force (three). **101:** US Air Force. **102:** US Air Force/Bruce M. Bailey (three). **103:** US Air Force (three). **104:** US Air Force (two). **105:** US Air Force/Robert F. Dorr/McDonnell Douglas. **106:** US Air Force (three). **107:** US Air Force (two). **110:** US Air Force (five). **111:** US Air Force. **112:** US Air Force (two). **113:** US Air Force (two). **114:** Associated Press/US Air Force. **115:** US Navy via Robert L. Lawson/Associated Press. **116:** Robert L. Lawson. **117:** US Navy (three). **118:** Jerry Edwards via René J. Francillon/US Navy (two). **119:** US Navy (two). **120:** US Navy via Robert L. Lawson/US Navy (two). **123:** US Navy. **124:** René J. Francillon/US Navy (two). **125:** US Navy/US Navy via Robert L. Lawson. **128:** US Navy/US Navy via Robert L. Lawson/US Navy. **129:** US Navy (three). **132:** US Navy/courtesy Cdr. Richard W. Schran, US Navy. **133:** US Navy (two). 134: US Navy via Robert L. Lawson/US Navy. **135:** US Navy. **136:** Peter B. Lewis via René J. Francillon/US Navy/Cdr. David P. Erickson. **137:** US Navy (two)/Cdr. David P. Erickson. **140:** US Navy (two)/Lt. Clark Van Nostrom. **141:** Capt. Stephen T. Millikin, US Navy. **142:** US Navy (two)/US Navy via Robert L. Lawson. **143:** Jerry Edwards via René J. Francillon/US Navy. **144:** Douglas D. Olson/US Navy (two). **145:** US Navy (two). **146:** US Navy (three). **147:** US Navy. **148:** Peter B. Lewis via René Francillon/US Marine Corps. **149:** US Marine Corps (three). **150:** US Marine Corps/Associated Press/Peter B. Lewis via René J. Francillon/US Marine Corps. **151:** US Marine Corps (two). **152:** US Marine Corps (three). **153:** US Marine Corps (two). **154:** US Marine Corps (two). **155:** US Marine Corps (two). **156:** US Marine Corps (two). **157:** US Marine Corps (two). **160:** US Marine Corps (three). **161:** US Marine Corps (three). **162:** US Marine Corps (three). **163:** US Marine Corps/René J. Francillon. **165:** US Army/Bell. **166:** Associated Press/US Army (two). **167:** US Army. **168:** US Army (three). **169:** US Army (two). **170:** US Army (two). **171:** Bell/US Army (three). **174:** US Army (four). **175:** Grumman/US Army (two). **176:** ECPA via René J. Francillon. **177:** via J. Lebourg via René J. Francillon/Lt. N'Guyen Than Tong via Marc Rostaing via René J. Francillon. **178:** Lt. N'Guyen Than Tong via Marc Rostaing via René J. Francillon (two). **179:** US Air Force, via René J. Francillon. **180:** US Air Force (two). **181:** US Air Force (two). **182:** US Air Force (two). **183:** US Air Force (two). **184:** via René J. Francillon, US Air Force (two). **185:** US Air Force (two). **186:** US Air Force (two). **187:** US Air Force (two). **188:** MacClancy Collection/Associated Press. **189:** MacClancy Collection. **190:** US Navy (two). **191:** US Navy (two). **192:** US Army/US Air Force. **193:** US Air Force/US Army. **194:** US Army/US Air Force. **195:** Associated Press/Jean Cuny via René J. Francillon. **196:** US Air Force. **197:** ECPA/René J. Francillon collection. **198:** René J. Francillon collection/US Air Force (two). **199:** US Air Force (three). **200:** Vietnamese Embassy. **201:** Vietnamese Embassy/US Air Force/MacClancy Collection. **202:** Vietnamese Embassy (two)/MacClancy Collection. **203:** US Air Force/MacClancy Collection. **204:** Vietnamese Embassy/MacClancy Collection/Vietnamese Embassy. **205:** Vietnamese Embassy (two). **206, 207:** US Air Force. **217:** US Air Force. **218:** ECPA. **219:** Beechcraft/René J. Francillon/Bell. **220.** Bell/coll. Jacques Sirougnet via René J. Francillon. **221:** US Air Force (two)/Boeing. **222:** US Air Force/US Marine Corps/US Army/US Air Force. **223:** US Air Force/Cessna. **224:** US Air Force (two)/Bruce Robertson. **225:** ECPA (two)/Dassault-Breguet. **227:** US Navy/McDonnell Douglas/US Navy. **228:** US Navy/Jean Cuny via René J. Francillon/US Air Force. **229:** US Air Force/ECPA. **230:** US Air Force (two). 231: US Air Force (two). **232:** US Air Force/US Navy (two). **233:** US Navy via Robert L. Lawson/ECPA (two). **234:** US Navy/US Air Force. **235:** US Air Force/ECPA. **236:** US Air Force. **237:** US Air Force (two). **238:** US Air Force (two)/Lockheed (two). **239:** Bruce M. Bailey/100th SRW via David Donald. **240:** US Air Force/US Navy (two). **241:** US Air Force. **242:** US Air Force/ECPA. **243:** ECPA. **244:** US Navy/US Air Force/North American Rockwell. **245:** US Air Force (two)/US Army. **246:** US Air Force(two)/ECPA/MacClancy Collection. **247:** US Air Force/US Army. **248:** US Navy (two). **249:** US Navy via Robert L. Lawson.

# INDEX

Page numbers in **bold** indicate an illustration.

An asterisk following a page number indicates an entry in Appendix B, giving brief historic and specification details of the aircraft concerned.

# Index

# V



# W



# X



# Y



# Z